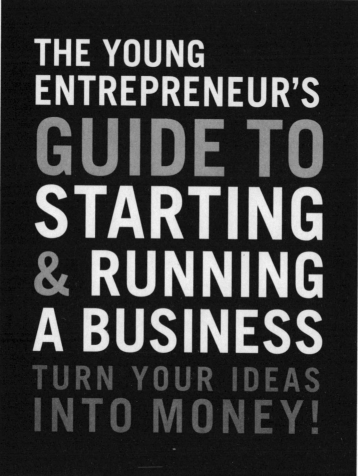

THE YOUNG ENTREPRENEUR'S GUIDE TO STARTING & RUNNING A BUSINESS

TURN YOUR IDEAS INTO MONEY!

THE YOUNG ENTREPRENEUR'S GUIDE TO STARTING & RUNNING A BUSINESS

TURN YOUR IDEAS INTO MONEY!

STEVE MARIOTTI WITH DEBRA DESALVO

CURRENCY
NEW YORK

Published in the United States by Currency, an imprint of the Crown Publishing Group,
a division of Penguin Random House LLC, New York.
currencybooks.com

CURRENCY and its colophon are trademarks of Penguin Random House LLC.

Originally published in hardcover and in different form in the United States by
Crown Business, an imprint of the Crown Publishing Group, a division of
Penguin Random House LLC, New York, in 1996. Subsequently published in trade
paperback in different form by Three Rivers Press, an imprint of the Crown Publishing
Group, a division of Penguin Random House LLC, New York, in 2000. Subsequently
published in trade paperback by Crown Business, an imprint of the Crown Publishing
Group, a division of Penguin Random House LLC, New York, in 2014.

Currency books are available at special discounts for bulk purchases for sales
promotions or corporate use. Special editions, including personalized covers, excerpts of
existing books, or books with corporate logos, can be created in large quantities for special
needs. For more information, contact Premium Sales at (212) 572-2232 or
e-mail specialmarkets@penguinrandomhouse.com.

Library of Congress Cataloging-in-Publication Data
Mariotti, Steve
The young entrepreneur's guide to starting and running a business:
turn your ideas into money!/Steve Mariotti with Debra DeSalvo.—3rd Edition.
pages   cm
1. New business enterprises. 2. Small business—Management.
3. Young adults—Employment. I. DeSalvo, Debra. II. Title.
HD62.5.M357   2014
658.1'141—dc23   201304882

ISBN 978-0-385-34854-6
Ebook ISBN 978-0-307-81551-4

Printed in the United States of America

Book and cover design by Maria Elias
*Cover photography: Benjamin Franklin on $100 bill and
Ulysses S. Grant on $50 bill © Randall Fung/Corbis*

13   15   17   19   20   18   16   14   12

To Karen Pritzker, John Whitehead, and Diana Davis Spencer of the Shelby Cullom Davis Foundation

CONTENTS

PART 2 CONNECT WITH CUSTOMERS

PART 3 MANAGE YOUR MONEY

PART 4 PROTECT YOUR BUSINESS

PART 5 GROW YOUR BUSINESS

PART 6   HARVEST YOUR BUSINESS

PART 7   WRITE A WINNING BUSINESS PLAN

"INVICTUS"

I encourage you to memorize the poem "Invictus" by William Ernest Henley. It expresses, better than I ever could, my belief that learning to create and operate a small business will make you master of your own fate.

Invictus

Out of the night that covers me,
Black as the pit from pole to pole,
I thank whatever gods may be
For my unconquerable soul.

In the fell clutch of circumstance
I have not winced nor cried aloud
Under the bludgeonings of chance
My head is bloody, but unbowed.

Beyond this place of wrath and tears
Looms but the Horror of the shade,
And yet the menace of the years
Finds and shall find me unafraid.

It matters not how strait the gate,
How charged with punishments the scroll,
I am the master of my fate:
I am the captain of my soul.

PREFACE

The Young Entrepreneur's Guide to Starting and Running a Business is for the young entrepreneur looking for a field-tested guide to starting and running a successful small business. The Young Entrepreneur's Guide will teach you how to become an entrepreneur and will walk you step-by-step through writing a detailed business plan that you can use to raise money to launch your own small business.

You will learn how to negotiate with a wholesale dealer, open a bank account, register your business, create a marketing campaign, develop social media profiles and use them effectively, and sell your product or service for a profit.

The book you're currently reading is a significantly updated new edition of the original Young Entrepreneur's Guide to Starting and Running a Business, a top seller in the field first published in 1996. With so many people struggling to find work since the global recession that began in 2008, this significantly updated edition of The Young Entrepreneur's Guide is more relevant and necessary than ever. Whether you are still in high school or are graduating from college and looking for your first professional job, this is a challenging time to be young and starting a career.

The Young Entrepreneur's Guide includes fascinating profiles of young entrepreneurs who started businesses whose products you probably use, such as Craig Newmark (Craigslist), Mark Zuckerberg (Facebook), and Stewart Butterfield and Caterina Fake (Flickr). Amazon, Apple, eBay, and Facebook all began as tiny entrepreneurial companies. You'll read their stories in The Young Entrepreneur's Guide to Starting and Running a Business.

In addition, The Young Entrepreneur's Guide profiles young people who studied entrepreneurship through my nonprofit organization, the Network for Teaching Entrepreneurship, and are now running their own successful businesses, such as Jimmy McNeal of Bulldog Bikes and Robert Reffkin of Urban Compass.

The Young Entrepreneur's Guide also lets you in on the latest in business technology and communication, explaining tools and concepts from cloud computing to project management software. The new edition features significantly beefed-up chapters on Internet marketing and social networking, and shares the most current methods for using social media and blogging to brand and market a small business.

The book also explores socially responsible business and green business. We'll look into the growing field of social enterprise, including new business legal structures such as the benefit corporation and the flexible purpose corporation, which give companies more flexibility to pursue social and environmental goals. The book's glossary has been updated to include new terms relevant to entrepreneurship today, such as "greenwashing" and "cause-related marketing."

I began my entrepreneurship career as a public high school teacher in some of New York City's most disadvantaged neighborhoods. At first, I didn't know how to get control of my classes. They were pure chaos! But I quickly discovered that whenever I talked about business, my students were riveted. They wanted to learn how to make money; they were eager to understand our economic system and participate in it.

Even my most difficult students—the ones instigating fights and yelling insults at me in class—were excited by the prospect of owning a small business. I taught them to buy low, sell high, and keep good records. My students started a wide variety of simple enterprises, such as selling candy or other items they bought wholesale, painting nails, or silk-screening T-shirts. Once they caught on to entrepreneurship, they found a concrete reason to improve their math, reading, and writing skills, and to stay in school, so they could run their businesses successfully.

Discovering entrepreneurship gave these young people the feeling that they could take charge of their future. Owning a business gave them pride and self-esteem, and they began to achieve goals they had never imagined possible before—such as going to college, getting great jobs, and giving back to their communities.

They discovered that ownership is power. Once you understand that, your life will never be the same. You will never feel powerless over your circumstances because you will know how to create better circumstances for yourself.

When I saw how much learning entrepreneurship increased my students' self-esteem, confidence, math and reading skills, and prospects for the future, I wanted every young person to have the same experience. So, in 1987, I founded the Network for Teaching Entrepreneurship. Today, NFTE teaches entrepreneurship to hundreds of thousands of students in the United States, Europe, Africa, China, India, and the Middle East. Visit our website at www.nfte.com to find a NFTE program near you.

There are many NFTE success stories, but we've had terrible losses, too. Fourteen of our students have been murdered, and I've attended too many funerals. This has only strengthened my commitment to teaching entrepreneurship as a path out of poverty.

The idea that teaching people about ownership and entrepreneurship is key to eradicating poverty, crime, and violence is gaining momentum. In October 2009, finalists from NFTE's national business plan competition were invited to meet President Obama at the White House. On January 24, 2010, *New York Times* op-ed columnist Tom Friedman wrote: "The president should vow to bring the Network for Teaching Entrepreneurship to every low-income neighborhood in America."

I'm optimistic that if you learn about entrepreneurship, you can achieve all your dreams. I've taught entrepreneurship for thirty years to at-risk inner-city youth who are surrounded by poverty and violence. I've personally witnessed thousands of young people with bleak prospects come alive with hope for their futures once they learned to start and operate a small business—no matter how the economy was doing.

Having experience as an entrepreneur gives you an edge in this tough economy. It gives you confidence in your ideas and in your ability to turn those ideas into reality . . . and money! It makes you business literate, and that, in turn, makes you far more employable than another young person who doesn't know how to read an income statement or make a sales call.

Entrepreneurship is about freedom, too—the freedom to work how and when you want, and the freedom to make your career truly enjoyable and rewarding. As an entrepreneur you can work when you are the most productive (designing web pages at three A.M., for example!). You create your own opportunities. You create a work environment that reflects *your* values, not someone else's. And, in a world where corporations no longer provide the lifelong job security they used to, you take control of your financial future by creating your own job.

My students learned to start and operate successful small businesses, and so can you—whether you live in a city, a rural area, or the suburbs. If you follow the tried-and-true methods in this book, you will be able to create your own business and become master of your fate. I say this with confidence because so many of my students have used entrepreneurship education to move out of poverty and desperation into rich, fulfilling lives. They have helped revitalize their communities, too, by creating new businesses, mentoring other young people, and sharing the power of entrepreneurship to transform lives.

The Young Entrepreneur's Guide to Starting and Running a Business includes not only the core material that made the initial *Young Entrepreneur's Guide* a success, but also the breakthroughs in teaching entrepreneurship that earned NFTE's high school textbook the Golden Lamp Award for excellence in educational publishing in 2009 and the Association of Educational Publishers award for best math curriculum in 2010.

With help from experts, we have developed a clear method for teaching accounting and financial statements designed specifically for young entrepreneurs. You can use the charts in this book to easily set up record keeping for your own business. You'll learn how to use your records to do your taxes properly, too.

As you read this book, think about this: You have *unique knowledge* that can be turned into a money-producing business. What is this unique knowledge? It is how well you know your schoolmates, colleagues, friends, and neighbors. What problem might they have that your business could solve? What product can't they find that you could sell to them? Start thinking like an entrepreneur!

Entrepreneurship is an act of creation. It is an art, not a science—the art of creating products and services that your friends and neighbors will want to buy. And, like any art, it needs to be practiced and enjoyed.

So, please, don't just read this book—use it to create some fun and excitement in your life. Your business could have a powerful impact on your life, your community, and perhaps even on the world.

Please feel free to write to me—I'd love to hear from you.

STEVE MARIOTTI
National Foundation for Teaching Entrepreneurship, Inc.
120 Wall Street, 18th Floor
New York, New York 10005
SteveM@nfte.com

PART 1
CREATE YOUR BUSINESS

CHAPTER 1

OWNERSHIP IS POWERFUL

THINK LIKE AN ENTREPRENEUR TO CHANGE YOUR LIFE

People who own property feel a sense of
ownership in their future and their society.
They study, save, work, strive, and vote.
People trapped in a culture of tenancy do not.

—Henry Louis Gates, Jr.

Julia Morgan, twenty-two, loves organic smoothies, but they were difficult to find in her neighborhood. Julia had a lot of friends in her neighborhood who also liked organic food, so she decided to invest her savings and a lot of time and energy into creating and opening Julia's Super Smoothies. Now Julia is an **entrepreneur**—someone who creates and runs a business.

Her business quickly attracted so many customers that Julia was able to hire her friend Mary to work part-time. Mary created a new smoothie that Julia put on the menu. Julia risked some of her money on ingredients, and she risked a drop in sales if customers didn't like the smoothie. But it was a hit. Sales increased. Mary received a raise as a reward, but Julia benefited the most because she owns the business.

Soon, Julia was able to hire two more friends to work at Julia's Super Smoothies. She noticed that there were often overflowing garbage cans on the street where her shop was located, so she got involved with her community board and led an effort to add more garbage pickups. This brought even more customers into Julia's Super Smoothies.

Learn the Lingo

Most people earn money through **business,** which is the buying and selling of **products** and **services** in order to make money.

Products (also called "goods") are *tangible,* meaning they can be seen and touched. A smoothie is a product.

Services are *intangible;* they can't be touched. Web design is a service.

Over time, Julia was able to save enough money from her business to open a second shop. Her successful business attracted an **investor.** In terms of entrepreneurship, an investor is someone who puts money into a business in exchange for a share of the business's profits. When people invest in the stock market, they are doing the same thing—they are buying stock shares, which give them ownership of a share of a business.

With the investor's money, Julia was able to open a small chain of smoothie shops. Because she always kept good financial records, she was able to show that her business was profitable, and, as a result, eventually Julia sold the business for several million dollars. Her investor received some of the money and Julia used the rest to travel, buy a home, and help her nephew go to college. She also began investing in real estate.

Green Tip

Julia made her business more successful by buying fruits and vegetables from local farmers markets—and advertising that fact to her customers.

A **locavore** is someone who eats food grown locally and patronizes businesses that source locally, because:

1. Local fruits and veggies are fresher, taste better, and retain more nutrition than produce shipped from far away.

2. Buying locally keeps money in the community and strengthens the local economy.
3. Buying locally saves gas that would have been used to ship produce, and reduces carbon emissions from delivery trucks and planes.

Check out www.locavores.com to learn more.

WE'RE ALL ENTREPRENEURS

Julia's story of success through entrepreneurship has been repeated by many people, and it can be your story, too. Starting even a very small business gives you something that *you* own. Ownership has a powerful psychological effect; it improves your self-esteem and makes you feel connected to the world.

Even if you're a waitress or a bookstore clerk, you should still think like a business owner because you are selling your time, which you own. At the end of the day, we are all entrepreneurs. We sell our time, energy, and expertise in order to earn a living. You are the owner of the business of you!

In the business of you, are you selling the most valuable service or product that you can offer? Or are you earning minimum wage at a boring dead-end job?

Even if you do not choose to become a full-time entrepreneur like Julia, learning how to create and operate a business will make you financially literate, and it will teach you to turn what you have to offer into more money and more fun. This book will show you how to read financial statements, do basic accounting, write a marketing plan, make a sales call, and much more. All these skills make you more employable, and you will be able to put them on your résumé after you finish this book. Business owners prefer to hire people who understand how business works.

Thinking like an entrepreneur can also help you make smarter decisions about managing the money you earn. This includes keeping good personal records, making wise purchases, investing personal funds to earn more money, and planning for retirement.

Learning about entrepreneurship often inspires people to develop a **vision** for their life. A vision is a picture of what you want the future to be. What kind of life do you want? What things are most important to you? Once you've formed a vision, the principles of entrepreneurship can also help you create a **mission**. A mission is a plan that outlines how to achieve your vision. In other words, a mission answers the question "How do I get where I want to be?"

Learn the Lingo

Increasingly, businesses today are encouraging **intrapreneurship**. They are encouraging employees to function as in-house entrepreneurs who set aside a portion of their workdays in order to experiment with new products and services.

YOU HAVE UNIQUE KNOWLEDGE OF YOUR MARKET

The beauty of business is that you already have the most important knowledge that you need to succeed. You know your **market**—the people your business serves—better than anyone else. Your market, for example, might be your friends, neighbors, classmates at school, or colleagues at your current job. What might these people want to buy? No one knows the answer better than you do.

Some successful entrepreneurs did not do well in school; some—born into poverty—never even had a chance to go to school. But they all used their unique market knowledge to create successful businesses.

Julia knew her neighborhood well. She knew there was no place to get organic smoothies. She also knew that her neighborhood friends would flock to a place that sold organic smoothies. With that unique knowledge of her market, she was able to start a successful business.

Like Julia, you can develop your own unique market knowledge by applying your creativity and intelligence to your market. What do people in your market need? Want? Enjoy? You know your neighborhood better than someone from another neighborhood ever could. You have had life experiences that no one else has had.

These experiences make up your knowledge of the world, and you can use that knowledge to become a successful entrepreneur. Entrepreneurship is about connecting your business ideas to the needs of your market.

The great thing about entrepreneurship is that your success is not limited by your abilities or education. You should never feel that you are not good enough, creative enough, or smart enough to succeed. Your creativity and intelligence are limitless—just as long as you use them.

Tech U

Pay-as-you-go cloud computing platforms such as Amazon Web Services (AWS) make it much easier to create an e-commerce platform for your new business and begin making online sales right away. You pay for only as much bandwidth as you need to start your business, and you can increase it whenever you need to do so.

Before pay-as-you-go services came about, you'd have to guess how much bandwidth you were going to need, buy it, and hope it was enough. If you didn't buy enough, you could lose customers if your website got too much traffic and crashed. But if you bought too much and customers didn't flock to your website, you were wasting money.

SERIAL ENTREPRENEURSHIP

Most people who find something they love want to keep doing it. It's no different with entrepreneurs. Serial entrepreneurs are business owners who start a series of businesses. They learn from their first businesses and apply those lessons to their next businesses. Julia, for example, could have taken the knowledge, contacts, and customer base she gained with her smoothie shop and used this information to open a knitting store, for example.

Serial entrepreneurship is more common today than it was in the past. It's easier than ever to start a business. You can even sell your products online without having to rent a store. With customers only a click away, many new businesses can become wildly profitable in just a few years. In particular, technology companies can develop and mature quickly, meaning their founders can sell the companies while they're still young and use the money to start new businesses.

Websites such as Entrepreneurs.com and ForEntrepreneurs.com are great for serial entrepreneurs who are interested in connecting with one another. Check them out!

HOW ENTREPRENEURS AND EMPLOYEES DIFFER

An **entrepreneur** is someone who creates and owns a business. An **employee** is someone who works for a business. Many entrepreneurs are both owners and employees—like Julia, they work for the businesses that they create. Julia's business became successful enough for her to hire Mary. This is how entrepreneurs create jobs, and why entrepreneurship is considered the "engine" of the American economy.

As business owners, entrepreneurs are in control of the money made by their businesses. They also have final say in all business decisions. Entrepreneurs are responsible for the success or failure of their businesses.

When an entrepreneur starts a new business, he or she takes on significant **risk**. Risk is the chance of losing something. An entrepreneur invests money, time, and energy hoping to be rewarded with money, satisfying work, a good relationship with the community, and other things that he or she values. The risk is that the business will fail and the entrepreneur will lose the money put into the business, and will have wasted time and energy.

THE RELATIONSHIP BETWEEN RISK AND REWARD

The relationship between risk and reward is very straightforward: the riskier the **investment,** the higher its potential reward. Conversely, the higher the reward an investment promises, the riskier it is.

Take Julia's employee Mary, for example. She took a small risk by developing a new smoothie recipe. The risk was that her boss, Julia, might not like it. But Mary didn't risk much else—she didn't spend money on the ingredients needed to make the smoothie in the shop for customers. Julia wasn't going to fire her if the smoothie wasn't popular. Because Mary's risk was low, her potential reward was as well: She got a small raise.

In contrast, Julia risked all her savings and lots of her time and energy on her smoothie shop. She did so because she was hoping to earn a lot of money from her business. Julia's risk was higher than Mary's, therefore Julia's potential reward was higher as well. If the smoothie shop had failed, Julia would have lost all the time, energy, and money she had put into her business.

As you can see from this example, entrepreneurs have to be risk takers. If you have endured a rough childhood or experienced other life challenges, take heart. Many of the world's most successful entrepreneurs had challenging childhoods that equipped them well to handle the risk and uncertainty that come with entrepreneurship.

Learning to handle risk, financial uncertainty, and a lack of resources are skills that can be taught. Sometimes we learn these skills from our childhoods. We can also learn them from trying entrepreneurship. The more you learn about business, the better you will cope with the inevitable stresses that come with earning and managing money.

Super Success Story

When eBay founder Pierre Omidyar was thirty-one he became a billionaire in one afternoon. It was 1998, and as the online auction site he created went public, he became "ridiculously rich," as he called it.

The French-born Iranian had moved to the United States with his family at age six. He wrote code for his site, Auction Web, at twenty-eight and renamed it eBay after learning that his first choice, Echo Bay, was already taken. The first item he ever sold on the site was his broken laser pointer, for $14.83.

Since then, his focus has been on giving most of his money away in his lifetime. In fact, Omidyar signed the Giving Pledge in 2010, which is a pledge signed by some of the world's wealthiest individuals to dedicate the majority of their wealth to philanthropy. Omidyar gives eBay shares to the Omidyar Network, which gives grants to worthy causes. Recent recipients of grants include tech incubators in Nigeria and Kenya. He's also been investing closer to home, teaming up with a cattle ranch in his home state of Hawaii to test new forms of grass-fed beef farming to help increase local food production.

Omidyar also works with Humanity United to help stop human trafficking and sex slavery, and with HopeLab, an innovative organization that uses technology to help improve the health of young people with chronic illness.

VOLUNTARY EXCHANGE

All business is made up of **voluntary exchange**. Voluntary exchange is a trade between two people who agree to trade money for a product or service. When you buy new software for your computer, no one is forcing you to trade. You and the seller of the software agree to the exchange because you both benefit from the trade.

The opposite of voluntary exchange is **involuntary exchange**. A mugging is an involuntary exchange. One person forces the other person to give up something and get nothing of value in return. Involuntary exchange requires force. Only one person benefits from an involuntary exchange. To start a successful business, you will need to sell a product or service for which someone will *want* to exchange money.

WHAT IS A "SMALL BUSINESS"?

When you think of a "business," does your mind go to large companies such as Apple or Nike? In reality, businesses much smaller than these make up the backbone of the American economy. According to the U.S. Small Business Administration (SBA), a government agency that provides loans and advice to small businesses, small firms with fewer than 500 employees accounted for 64 percent of the net new jobs created between 1993 and 2011 (11.8 million of the 18.5 million net new jobs). Since the latest recession, from mid-2009 to 2011, small firms, led by the larger ones in the category (20 to 499 employees), accounted for 67 percent of the net new jobs.

This is why, during the global financial crisis that began in 2008 and caused American unemployment to rise to over 8 percent, President Obama often referred to entrepreneurship as "the engine of our economy." He cut taxes for small businesses eighteen times during the recession to boost their job-creating power.

Jeffry A. Timmons, professor of entrepreneurial studies at Babson College, calls this explosion in entrepreneurship, in America and around the world, "the silent revolution." He notes that today more than one in seven Americans chooses to be self-employed. Meanwhile, the big corporations that used to employ so many Americans have been steadily shedding jobs.

Presently, almost half of all new products are created by small, entrepreneurial companies. According to the U.S. Census Bureau, roughly half of the workforce in the United States is employed by small businesses.

Whole Foods Goes From Small to Large

Even though most businesses begin small, they obviously don't all stay that way. Sometimes a business may become so successful that it grows beyond the wildest expectations of its owners. That is exactly what happened to Whole Foods Market. It started in 1980 as one small store in Austin, Texas. Four businesspeople decided the natural food industry was ready for a supermarket format. And they were right!

Beginning with a staff of nineteen, Whole Foods Market was an immediate hit with **consumers** and expanded rapidly to Houston, Dallas, and New Orleans when it purchased Whole Food Company in 1988. In 1989, Whole Foods Market opened a store in Palo Alto, California. While continuing to open new stores from the ground up, Whole Foods fueled its rapid growth by acquiring other natural foods chains throughout the 1990s, including chains in North Carolina, Rhode Island, Florida, and the Midwest.

Today, Whole Foods Market is the world's leader in natural and organic foods, with more than 270 stores in North America and the United Kingdom and more than fifty-four thousand employees worldwide.

Get the Stats

According to the SBA, more than six hundred thousand new businesses are started in the United States every year—and about five hundred thousand close. Entrepreneurship can be very rewarding, but clearly it is also risky.

WOMEN AND MINORITIES ROCK ENTREPRENEURSHIP

Because starting a business does not necessarily require large amounts of time, money, or experience, entrepreneurship has proven to be an effective way for minorities and women to enter the business world.

The SBA reports that 70 percent of all African American–owned start-ups, or new ventures, are funded from personal savings or by family and friends. Most are started with less than $5,000 in up-front costs.

Census data shows that the growth of minority-owned businesses nationwide has outpaced business formation rates among nonminority owners by almost two to one. From 2002 to 2007, the number of minority-owned businesses grew by 46 percent, to 5.8 million, or more than twice the rate of businesses as a whole.

Women and people from minority groups are becoming entrepreneurs in droves. As of 2012, women own about 40 percent of all private businesses in the United States, according to the Center for Women's Business Research.

There are more than 8.3 million women-owned businesses in the United States, generating nearly $1.3 trillion in revenues and employing 7,697,000 people.

Between 1997 and 2012, when the number of businesses in the United States increased by 37 percent, the number of women-owned firms increased by 54 percent—a rate one and a half times the national average.

YOUR GOAL: ADD VALUE TO SCARCE RESOURCES

Entrepreneurs have a powerful impact on society. A successful entrepreneur can create jobs, products, services, and wealth. These creations appear when the entrepreneur makes good choices about how to use **scarce resources**. Resources are things such as oil, wood, cotton, **capital** (money), labor, or land that businesspeople use to create products and services.

Most resources are scarce, meaning that the available supply is limited. As an entrepreneur, *your goal is to add value to scarce resources.*

Let's say you are selling homemade cookies. You buy butter, eggs, flour, sugar, and other ingredients to make your cookies. These ingredients are your resources. You hope that people will like your cookies so much that they will be willing to buy them for a price that covers the cost of the ingredients *and* provides you with a profit.

If customers buy your cookies, you have added value to your resources. The cookies are worth more than the resources you used to make them. If your cookies taste bad, however, and customers don't want to buy them, you have to throw the cookies away. You have wasted your scarce resources.

Profit Proves You've Added Value to Scarce Resources

Profit is determined directly by the choices entrepreneurs make about how to use scarce resources.

Let's say your homemade cookies were a hit last week. To make more profit, you might decide to buy margarine instead of butter this week because margarine is cheaper. Here's the catch: Your cookies might not taste as good. Will your customers notice?

This type of choice is called a **trade-off**. You are giving up one thing (taste) for another (money). If your customers don't notice the change and continue to buy your cookies, you have made a good choice. You have conserved a scarce resource (money) and increased your profit by lowering your costs. The increase in profit confirms that you have made the right choice.

Loss Proves You've Subtracted Value from Scarce Resources

But what if your customers notice the change and buy fewer of your cookies? Your profit will decrease. The decrease in profit signals that you have made a bad choice. The trade-off wasn't worth it.

As you can see from the cookie example, a loss in profit also gives an entrepreneur valuable information. If butter is too expensive, you could keep looking for a tastier butter alternative, or a cheaper supplier of butter. This is how entrepreneurs allow their profits and losses to guide them toward success.

Don't be ashamed of your losses—they are all part of being an entrepreneur. Every great entrepreneur has had losses. The goal is to learn from them!

FAILURE IS A CHANCE TO BEGIN AGAIN

Failure is an inevitable part of entrepreneurship—and that's OK. Some famous entrepreneurs have even gone bankrupt, only to succeed later. Henry Ford went bankrupt twice before founding the Ford Motor Company. As he famously said, "Failure is a chance to begin again more intelligently."

A new business usually takes time to turn a profit. If a new business continues to lose money, however, and the entrepreneur can't pay the bills, the best decision may be to close the business. A business that is losing so much money that it can't cover its bills is **insolvent**. Closing a business is nothing to be ashamed of; it may be the best decision that can be made.

Some entrepreneurs will try very hard to keep a business open, even when it is losing money. If money from sales continues to be too low to cover the bills, however, the business will eventually go **bankrupt**.

A business goes bankrupt when it is declared legally unable to pay its bills. A court can force the owner to sell items of value owned by the business, or assets, to raise money to pay off the business's debts. Sometimes, even the personal possessions of the owner are sold, and the proceeds are given to creditors—the people to whom the business owes money.

IS ENTREPRENEURSHIP FOR YOU? PROS AND CONS OF BEING AN ENTREPRENEUR

I recommend that everyone learn how to create and run a small business. It's an important skill to have—after all, you never know when you might lose your job. It's empowering to know how to create your own job.

Not everyone is suited to becoming a career entrepreneur, though. Running a business is not like working a nine-to-five job. It's more like a twenty-four-hour-a-day obsession. Being your own boss can be exhilarating one minute and terrifying the next. It can be stressful to be financially responsible for the success or failure of your enterprise—and the jobs of any employees you may have. If you value financial security and the support of colleagues, you may do better as an employee rather than as an entrepreneur.

Being able to buy low and sell high is never guaranteed. A product can lose value before it can be sold, or it may be stolen, or it can sit in a warehouse because demand is low. A desirable product may never take off because the right consumers never hear about it. Timing can be everything. Both the risks and the potential rewards are high.

As you read the pros and cons listed below, think about what you want out of life. What are your priorities? If being independent, working hard, and building your own fortune are goals of yours, and you aren't afraid of taking risks and possibly failing, entrepreneurship may be for you.

Pros of Entrepreneurship

Independence: Business owners do not have to follow orders or observe working hours set by someone else. Entrepreneurship gives you an opportunity to prove what you can accomplish. In the 1960s, Thomas Burrell came to believe that, because he was African American, no matter how good he was at his advertising job, he wasn't going to be promoted any further by the ad agency that employed him. He quit and started his own company, Burrell Communications Group. Today, with annual sales of more than $60 million, it is the largest African American–owned ad agency in the United States.

Satisfaction: Turning a skill, hobby, or other interest into your own business can be very satisfying. In 1948, an amateur photographer named Edwin Land created a camera that developed and printed photos in under sixty seconds. He founded Polaroid Corporation and turned his love of photography into a multimillion-dollar business.

Super Success Story

Polaroid inventor Edwin Land was your classic obsessive entrepreneur. When Land came up with a new idea, he would experiment and brainstorm until the problem was solved. He needed to have food brought to him and be reminded to eat. Land once wore the same clothes for eighteen straight days while working on a new product. At Polaroid, he had teams of assistants working in shifts at his side. As one team wore out, the next team was brought in to continue his work.

His friend and colleague Elkan Blout said Land was "a true visionary; he saw things differently from other people, which is what led him to the idea of instant photography. He was a brilliant, driven man who did not spare himself and who enjoyed working with equally driven people."

Financial Reward: Most of the great fortunes in this country were built by entrepreneurs. Countless small businesses have grown into large companies that produced fortunes for their owners. Entrepreneurs have also created fortunes by selling their businesses when they become profitable. Seventeen-year-old Nick D'Aloisio of Britain, for example, sold his top-selling content-shortening app, Summly, to search giant Yahoo! for an estimated $30 million in 2013.

Self-Esteem: Knowing you created something valuable can give you a strong sense of accomplishment. African American oil tycoon Jake Simmons, Jr.'s, first job was as a porter on a train. When a white passenger told him, "Boy, come here and get my bags!" Simmons told the man that he resented being called "Boy." The man's response was, "Young man, if you don't want to be called a boy, then don't do a boy's work, because boys carry bags for men." Simmons was so shaken that he left the job as soon as he could, determined to be his own boss. He went on to create the world's most successful minority-owned oil conglomerate, Simmons Royalty Company.

Cons of Entrepreneurship

Risk of Failure: You risk losing not only your own money but also money invested in your business by others. But failure provides an entrepreneur with the opportunity to start fresh, with all the knowledge and experience learned from the previous venture.

Obstacles: You will run into problems that you will have to solve by yourself. You may even face discouragement from family and friends. Liz Claiborne's family was against her becoming a fashion designer and starting her own business. Her father was afraid the business world would be too rough on her. Claiborne proved him wrong by building Liz Claiborne, Inc. into a billion-dollar clothing company.

Loneliness: It can be lonely and even a little scary to be completely responsible for the success or failure of your business. In the early 1900s, Madame C. J. Walker traveled all over the United States by herself for two years, promoting her hair-care products—a brave move, in those days, for a widowed African American woman with little education. She became the first female self-made millionaire in the United States.

Financial Insecurity: As a business owner, you are not guaranteed a **salary** or any benefits. You may not always have enough money to pay yourself. King C. Gillette invented the disposable razor and started the Gillette Company, which is a billion-dollar business today. In 1901, though, Gillette's fledgling company was $12,500 in debt, which was a lot of money back then. As Gillette recalled, "We were backed up to the wall with our creditors lined up in front waiting for the signal to fire." Gillette managed to secure financing from a Boston millionaire and save the company. An entrepreneur may face such intense financial challenges many times.

Long Hours: You will probably work long hours to get your business off the ground. Some entrepreneurs work six or seven days a week. During the early years of establishing McDonald's restaurants around the country, Ray Kroc worked about eighty hours a week. His simple motto was "Press on."

As you may realize while reading these pros and cons of entrepreneurship, they often represent two sides of the same coin. The hard work of establishing and running your own business can reap great financial rewards and build your self-esteem. Although you may face loneliness, financial insecurity, and other setbacks, as you overcome these obstacles you will become a much stronger person. Even if your business fails, you will gain valuable business experience. Your next business will be more likely to succeed.

When I was self-employed in the import-export business, for example, I worried more about money than I did when I was working for Ford. But I felt happier. I truly enjoyed not being dependent on anyone but myself for my job security. And I was having a lot more fun!

Do you think you have what it takes to give entrepreneurship a try?

Learn the Lingo

Why not get some experience in the business world with an **internship**? An internship is a program at a business that provides on-the-job training in a business setting, sometimes in exchange for college credit. There are both paid and unpaid internships.

Let's say you would love to start a film company and make independent films. An internship at a film production company would provide you with invaluable experience and contacts.

An **apprenticeship** is a type of internship that provides training in a trade skill such as carpentry or plumbing. Internships and apprenticeships can last from a few weeks to a year or more.

ANYONE, ANYWHERE CAN START A SMALL BUSINESS

You may worry that you don't have enough money, time, or experience to create and operate your own small business. But Michelle Araujo, who runs a clothing resale company called A La Mode, insists that there is always time to start your own business, even if you're a single mother *and* a full-time college student.

Michelle should know; at age nineteen, she started her company while attending college and caring for her two young daughters and newborn son. Before she started her company, Michelle knew nothing about running a business and had very little money. She was living a difficult life as a single mother of three children. But today, she's a successful entrepreneur.

THE GOLDEN RULE OF ENTREPRENEURSHIP: BUY LOW, SELL HIGH!

Michelle loved fashionable clothes, but she lived in New Bedford, Massachusetts, where the stores didn't always sell the latest fashions.

During an NFTE entrepreneurship class, Michelle took a field trip to Manhattan's wholesale clothing district. Michelle was surprised that wholesale prices were *much* lower than department store prices.

During her visit to the wholesale district, Michelle learned that all she needed to buy from a wholesaler was a sales tax identification number. Anyone can apply for a sales tax number by calling the state sales tax office and requesting an application.

Learn the Lingo

A **wholesaler** is a business that purchases products in bulk from the manufacturer and sells smaller quantities to **retailers**. Retailers buy small quantities from wholesalers and sell single items to customers. At each step along the road from the manufacturer to the customer, the price of the product increases.

Michelle knew there were many young women in New Bedford who would love to buy the latest fashions at reasonable prices. Michelle decided to buy clothes wholesale in New York City and sell them to her neighbors. She invited a dozen friends to her house for a clothes-buying party. If she sold the clothes out of her home, Michelle reasoned, she could offer the latest styles at lower prices than the stores in her town were charging.

Michelle had stumbled on the key to business success: Buy (or make) something for less than someone else is willing to pay for it. Before she visited the wholesale district again, she collected size information and special requests from her twelve friends. Michelle's customers are happy to pay the difference between the wholesale cost and the prices she charges because they are getting a great value.

Michelle was afraid she would have to buy large quantities in order to get the wholesalers to sell to her, but she found that most are comfortable selling her as few as two or three items. They like dealing with Michelle because she doesn't ask for credit. She pays in full when she makes her purchases.

Michelle resells the clothes for twice the wholesale price she paid. Sales are made from her home or on visits to customers' houses. Michelle's friends and neighbors are delighted to have a less expensive alternative to the local mall. Her customers also enjoy shopping in a fun, intimate setting.

By following the simple rule "Buy low and sell high," Michelle created a successful small business. As Michelle says, "Who would ever think a teenage mother with three children could own her own business and graduate from college?" After she finishes college, Michelle plans to open her own clothing boutique. She hopes her success will spark a revival of small businesses in her community.

CHARACTERISTICS OF SUCCESSFUL ENTREPRENEURS

I've worked with young entrepreneurs for more than thirty years, and I've noticed that no one is born with all the characteristics needed to be a successful entrepreneur. But if you keep a positive attitude and believe in yourself, you can develop the necessary qualities to succeed.

In the following list, notice the personality traits you already possess. How could you strengthen the traits you need to develop?

- **Courage:** A willingness to take risks in spite of possible losses.
- **Creativity:** Inventing new ways of doing things; thinking outside the box.
- **Curiosity:** The desire to learn and ask questions.

- **Determination:** Refusing to quit in spite of obstacles.
- **Discipline:** The ability to stay focused and follow a schedule to meet deadlines.
- **Empathy:** Being sensitive to the thoughts and feelings of others.
- **Enthusiasm:** Being passionate and excited about something.
- **Flexibility:** The ability to adapt to new situations; a willingness to change.
- **Honesty:** A commitment to being truthful and sincere with others.
- **Patience:** Recognizing that most goals are not reached overnight.
- **Responsibility:** Being accountable for your decisions and actions; not passing the buck.

Try It!

Interview a small business owner in your community. Ask this entrepreneur to share stories of successes and failures. Ask which personal characteristics or skills have contributed most to his or her success. Ask what the owner would do differently if he or she were starting the business today.

Stay Positive

I've noticed that successful entrepreneurs deliberately cultivate a positive attitude. Instead of seeing a situation as a problem, they look at it as an opportunity. This helps them find solutions more easily than people who think negatively.

Think about your own experience. Positive thinking and talking tend to make you feel happier and have more energy. You feel motivated to take steps toward accomplishing your goals. In contrast, negative thinking and talking probably make you feel less happy and energetic. Try consciously cultivating a positive attitude—it really makes a difference!

Watch your thoughts; they become words.

Watch your words; they become actions.

Watch your actions; they become habits.

Watch your habits; they become character.

Watch your character; it becomes your destiny.

—*Chinese proverb*

Read a Classic

To develop a positive attitude, check out Napoleon Hill's inspiring classic *Think and Grow Rich: Your Key to Financial Wealth and Power*.

Game Changer

Thomas Edison was born in 1847. He was a lousy student and was practically deaf by age twelve, but by then he was already an entrepreneur. Edison sold newspapers, candy, and snacks on the Grand Trunk Railroad to Detroit. With his earnings, he bought a printing press and started a newspaper, the *Weekly Herald,* which he sold on the train. He convinced more than three hundred commuters to subscribe to his paper.

Edison became one of the most prolific inventors in history. He invented the record player, and created practical and economical systems for distributing electric light, heat, and power that changed the world forever.

"I never quit until I get what I'm after," Edison said. "Negative results are just what I'm after. They are just as valuable to me as positive results."

An Entrepreneur Like You

Robert Reffkin

URBAN COMPASS

www.urbancompass.com

When Robert Reffkin was eleven, he realized his mother was struggling financially as a single parent running their small household in Berkeley, California. "I knew that I wanted to earn money to help her out. For the next three years I thought about how to do that," Robert recalls. When he saw a DJ at work at a party, Robert thought DJing might be a good way for him to earn money to help his mother. "The DJ was making good money and having fun, and had a lot of independence," says Robert. "I love music so I decided to become a DJ."

Becoming a DJ

For the next three years, Robert saved up every dollar he could. When he had enough money, he bought some DJ equipment and started his business. "I created professional contracts, a music list, a request list, and some business cards. I started to advertise, and got my first job that summer. It was a small house party that paid only fifty dollars, but people liked my work and referred me to their friends. I was on my way!"

Robert worked at school dances, homecomings, Bar Mitzvahs, weddings, NAACP parties, and Black Student Union dances. He also organized his own events.

Learning How to Run a Business

In high school, Robert took an entrepreneurship course and learned some critical business and professional skills. He wrote a business plan, which won him a $500 grant to invest in his business. Robert's success in business gave him the confidence to pursue bigger dreams, even though many people in his life discouraged him. When his high school counselor said he would never be admitted to Columbia University, for example, Robert decided to apply anyway.

Using Business Skills to Change His Life

When applying to Columbia, Robert used everything he had learned in his entrepreneurship course and from running his own business. He interacted with the university's admissions officers with the same level of professionalism he employed with his clients. He gave them his business card, sent them his résumé, wrote them thank-you letters, and kept them apprised of major developments in his life. Robert believes that this led to his acceptance at Columbia. He received a partial scholarship and paid the rest of his college tuition with money he earned DJing.

Robert says his early experience as an entrepreneur gave him "extraordinary confidence and the entrepreneurial belief that anything is possible." He graduated from Columbia in two and a half years and became a business analyst. Next, he earned his MBA, and became a White House fellow and then a Wall Street investment banker. Reffkin has also started a nonprofit called New York Needs You (www .newyorkneedsyou.org).

Urban Compass

In 2012, Robert cofounded a new "hyperlocal" service called Urban Compass with engineer Ori Allon. They quickly attracted $8 million in **seed money,** or initial financing, for their start-up.

Existing location services such as Google and Foursquare know where you have been, but don't know who you are as a person and don't make quality recommendations for where you should eat or where you can find a particular good or service. That's a problem Urban Compass plans to solve by developing a "human network" of people employed by the company to go to urban areas to collect data. With $8 million in start-up capital, it can afford to hire the best minds around to help!

Think Like an Entrepreneur

1. Robert picked a business that appealed to his love of music. What hobbies or passions do you have that you could turn into a business?
2. Robert's career took off when he took an entrepreneurship class. Is there somewhere you could take an entrepreneurship class? What skills do you think you need to learn to start and run a successful business?
3. How confident are you? How could you improve your confidence and open more doors in your life?

CHAPTER 2

RECOGNIZING BUSINESS OPPORTUNITIES

TURN PROBLEMS INTO PROFITS!

A pessimist sees the difficulty in
every opportunity; an optimist sees
the opportunity in every difficulty.

—Winston Churchill

Tom Szaky was a nineteen-year-old college student when he visited some gardening-crazy friends who were using red worms to compost waste into plant fertilizer. The idea captured his imagination, and he wrote a **business plan** for TerraCycle, an environmentally friendly company that would convert trash into fertilizer.

Today, TerraCycle provides free waste collection programs, and then turns the waste into affordable green products such as fertilizer, recycled plastic bins and planters, backpacks, and even bicycle chain picture frames.

TerraCycle products are carried in the world's largest retailers, including

Walmart, Target, and Home Depot. The company runs programs that involve entire communities in recycling. Sales exceed $20 million per year, and the company has recycled billions of pieces of waste.

Tom Szaky turned trash into treasure and created an **sustainable** business. A sustainable business is one that strives to have no negative impact on the global or local environment. TerraCycle plant food has twice been named the most eco-friendly product carried by Home Depot.

Learn the Lingo

A **green company** is one that adopts business practices aimed at protecting or improving the environment.

Excellent Packaging & Supply, for example, distributes "biomass" packaging made from sustainable, recyclable resources. One of these products is SpudWare, utensils made from corn and potato starch that can withstand boiling water, but will break down easily once thrown away. Sure beats Styrofoam or plastic!

WHAT IS A BUSINESS OPPORTUNITY?

What does the word "opportunity" mean to you? Is it a chance to get something for nothing? A job? An education?

You may have never thought of a problem as an opportunity, but it is. Many amazing businesses have been created by entrepreneurs who noticed problems and developed businesses to solve them.

Tom Szaky saw a **business opportunity** in the world's overwhelming piles of trash. A business opportunity is a consumer need or want that can potentially be met by a new business. A **need** is defined as something that people require in order to survive, such as water, food, clothing, or shelter. A **want** is a product or service that people strongly desire.

Anita Roddick was tired of paying for perfume and fancy packaging when she bought makeup, so she founded the Body Shop, a store that sells natural, ethically produced skin-care products. Roddick created simple, inexpensive packages and encouraged customers to recycle their containers once they were empty. She kept her prices low and her advertising down-to-earth. Today, you can find a Body Shop store in nearly any mall.

Bill Gates turned a problem into a business that made him one of the richest people in the world. Before Gates started Microsoft, most software was so hard to use that it was downright terrifying to the average person. Gates saw a need for software that was easy to use, and turned it into a multibillion-dollar business.

To train your brain to recognize business opportunities, Anita Roddick suggests you ask yourself the following questions:

- What product or service would make my life easier or more enjoyable?
- What makes me annoyed or angry?
- What product or service would take away my aggravation?

WHERE OTHERS SEE PROBLEMS, ENTREPRENEURS RECOGNIZE OPPORTUNITIES

An entrepreneur recognizes opportunities where other people see only problems.

When Hayley Hoverter was six, her single working mom brought her along to her job at Starbucks, early in the morning before school. Even at that young age, Hayley was distressed by the volume of discarded sugar wrappers that she saw in the trash cans.

"I couldn't figure out," says Hayley, now a high school junior, "with all of the innovations in the business world—why a person must waste so much to do something as trivial as sweeten a favorite beverage."

Hayley saw this problem as an opportunity. She created Sweet (dis)SOLVE, a sweetener made from organic sugar wrapped in a soluble organic starch that melts into your drink without adding calories, odor, or taste.

She targeted local cafés with reputations for selling "green" products, but her biggest challenge was getting up the courage to approach them.

"I was afraid that they would tell me that it was a terrible idea, and that it would never work, or that their customers would hate it," Hayley admits. "I felt like I was playing an adult's game in an adult's world. I thought I would fail or that they wouldn't take me seriously because I was too young."

Hayley forced herself to pitch to potential clients, and was pleasantly surprised. "The feedback from the café owners has been one hundred percent positive," she reports. "They are very excited about the product, and are eager to help me develop my business."

Hayley hopes to license her product to sugar companies, adding, "I learned that if you can dream up something great, it is your responsibility to follow through with it. When you look at it that way, you can do no wrong."

DREAMING UP OPPORTUNITIES

Business opportunities are created when entrepreneurs daydream about products or services they would love to have in their own lives. Prime your imagination by asking yourself (and your friends) questions such as:

- What is the one product you'd love to have more than anything else?
- What does it look like?
- What does it do?

Try It!

Train your mind to recognize opportunities and you will be a successful entrepreneur. Write down three problems that annoy you. Brainstorm some business solutions for each problem.

WIDEN YOUR WORLD

The best way to train your mind to recognize opportunities is to broaden it with new experiences. Keep an eye out for opportunities, no matter what you are doing. Some great (and fun!) ways to broaden your mind include:

- Traveling
- Meeting new people
- Learning a language
- Reading books you might not normally read
- Attending lectures, poetry readings, and concerts
- Trying new hobbies
- Watching the news; reading newspapers and magazines
- Discussing news events with friends and mentors
- Internships

AN IDEA IS NOT NECESSARILY AN OPPORTUNITY

An opportunity is an idea that meets a consumer need or want.

There's a catch, however. Not every wild business idea you have is an opportunity. Many a small business has failed because the entrepreneur's product didn't address a large enough need.

How do you recognize when an idea is a true opportunity? Professor Jeffry A. Timmons, co-author of *New Venture Creation: Entrepreneurship for the 21st Century,* suggests that you look for four characteristics:

1. It is attractive to customers.
2. It will work in your business environment.
3. It can be executed within the **window of opportunity** that you have.
4. You have the resources and skills to create the business, *or* you know someone who does.

Learn the Lingo

The window of opportunity is the amount of time you have to get your business idea to market before someone else acts on the same idea. If competitors have already had the same idea and gotten their product to the market first, that window of opportunity has slammed shut.

THE SIX ROOTS OF ENTREPRENEURIAL OPPORTUNITY

Train your mind to recognize business opportunities by memorizing these six roots of opportunity:

1. **Problems:** Make a list of problems that are bugging you or your friends, or even your relatives. Could you start a business to solve one of them?
2. **Change:** Watch the news and read the newspaper to stay on top of our ever-changing world. Look for changing laws, situations, or trends. Many new business opportunities have arisen because people are becoming more aware of climate change, for example.

3. **Unique Knowledge:** No one knows your friends better than you do. What would they want to buy? What does your community need? Use your unique knowledge of the people close to you to brainstorm some business opportunities.

4. **Inventions and Technological Advancements:** Got a problem? What could you invent to solve it? Even if you don't invent something, you might find a creative way to sell or market an existing product. Maybe you could be the one to bring a new invention to your community first! Technology is developing at lightning speed. Read magazines that cover technologies that you find interesting.

Tech U

Sometimes the best technology is low-tech. The HurriQuake is a construction nail designed to resist pulling out of wood during hurricanes and earthquakes. It was invented by Ed Sutt for Stanley Works.

Sutt was inspired to invent the HurriQuake when he traveled to some Caribbean islands after a hurricane. A civil engineer, Sutt inspected the wreckage of the island's homes and business that had been destroyed, and he discovered that wood failure was not what made them fall apart. The nails holding the wood together had failed to hold during the high winds, causing the buildings to collapse.

Because building a house with HurriQuake nails costs only about $30 more than building a house without them, yet offers a lot of protection from natural disasters, a lot of builders are purchasing HurriQuake nails instead of regular nails.

5. **Competition:** If you can find a way to beat the competition, you can create a very successful business with an existing product or service. Look at the businesses in your community. Could you do a better job than they do? Could you be faster? More reliable? Cheaper? If so, you may have found a business opportunity.

Game Changer

Ingvar Kamprad discovered as a child how to make money by buying low and selling higher. He would buy boxes of matches at a low price and sell them in smaller quantities at a higher price. He invested the money he made in this and other small business ventures.

When Kamprad was seventeen, he founded IKEA, a furniture business that kept its prices lower than the competition's by creating sleek, modern designs, and packaging furniture in flat boxes and requiring customers to assemble it. Many customers were happy to do so if it saved them money on furniture. Today, IKEA has expanded from its origins in Sweden to more than three hundred stores in more than thirty-five countries—and Ingvar Kamprad is now one of the top ten wealthiest people in the world.

6. **Existing Products and Services:** You can get ideas for opportunities from businesses that already exist. This is *not* the same thing as copying a product or service and then calling it by another name (which is illegal). Instead, it means looking for ways to significantly improve a product, perhaps in a way that allows you to sell it at a lower price. It could also involve improving the quality and manner in which customers are served—including such features as better locations, longer hours, or quicker service.

Game Changer

One Laptop Per Child (OLPC) is a nonprofit organization that provides laptops for children worldwide. OLPC saw an opportunity in the need for children in impoverished communities to have access to computers. OLPC developed a low-cost laptop called the XO. OLPC also reduced the laptop's energy use by 90 percent by inventing a new kind of screen display, making it cheaper to run.

INTERNAL AND EXTERNAL OPPORTUNITIES

Opportunities fall into two categories: internal and external.

1. **Internal opportunity** comes from inside you—from a hobby or passion that you have. Passion won't ignite a successful business, though, unless you can inspire others to share your passion—or find people who already do.

     No matter what business you start, it has to meet a consumer need. Many successful entrepreneurs, however, have started businesses that *initially* did not appear to meet much of a need, but that found a customer base in due course. Many entrepreneurs have gotten started on passion alone.

2. **External opportunity** comes from something you see outside of yourself. Maybe you notice that people in your neighborhood are complaining about the lack of available day care, so you start a day care center. The business might succeed, but you could burn out quickly if you aren't the type of person who loves to be around screaming toddlers all day long. That's the problem with external opportunities—your business idea may fill a need for the market, but you may not have the interest, skills, or passion to enjoy putting in the time and energy needed to make it a success.

The best business opportunities are both internal and external. Ideally, a business that you are passionate about also meets a huge external need in the marketplace.

Super Success Story

My goal has been to present urban culture in its most true form to the people who love it and the people who live it.
—Russell Simmons

As of 2011, Russell Simmons had a net worth estimated at $340 million—all built on his love of hip-hop. Simmons grew up in a mostly African American middle-class section of Queens, New York. He fell in love with rap as a teen and began promoting rap parties in Harlem and Queens with his friend Kurt Walker. Walker became a rapper, changing his name to Kurtis Blow, and he and Simmons cowrote a minor hit called "Christmas Rappin'."

For Simmons, rap was an internal opportunity to start a business. After getting his first taste of success with Blow, Simmons formed Rush Communications in 1979 and began managing other local rap acts. Simmons paired younger brother Joseph Ward Simmons, who went by the name of Run, with MC Darryl Matthew McDaniels and DJ Jason Mizell and named the group Run-DMC. The group's first two records were instant hits.

In 1984, Simmons met Rick Rubin, a white NYU student who was a talented producer. Simmons and Rubin each kicked in $5,000 to found Def Jam Recordings. The two had complementary skills—Rubin was a production genius who loved loud, rebellious music, and Simmons was a relentlessly enthusiastic, shrewd businessman.

Just two years into Simmons and Rubin's bare-bones operation, Columbia Records approached Def Jam with an offer to promote, market, and distribute Def Jam's new rap recordings for a share in their profits. At the time, Def Jam and Run-DMC were primarily marketing hip-hop to African Americans. The label's next two moves, however, would change that.

First, Def Jam teamed Run-DMC with Aerosmith to record a rap version of the rock band's hit "Walk This Way." The song was a smash hit with both rock and hip-hop fans and landed Run-DMC on MTV, which until then had played rap only reluctantly. Run-DMC and Simmons found themselves with a number four *Billboard* hit—the first rap song to break the top five. The single also helped the band's third album, *Raising Hell,* sell four million copies.

Next Def Jam signed the first all-white rap act, the Beastie Boys. The group's bratty lyrics and rock 'n' roll guitar riffs brought in an even wider audience, and the band's first album, *License to Ill,* sold eight million copies.

As it turned out, there was an external opportunity for rap, too. Lots of music fans were bored with rock and craved a fresh new sound. Rap met that need.

Simmons eventually bought out Rubin and created the multimillion-dollar Def Jam empire, which included the record label, a series of Def Jam comedy television shows, and a clothing line. He sold Def Jam to Universal Music in 1999 to focus on other hip-hop-related businesses, including Rush Artist Management, which had built the careers of the Beastie Boys, LL Cool J, Public Enemy, and Run-DMC.

Thanks to Simmons, hip-hop is no longer only black culture or urban culture—it's American culture. And no one thinks it's a fad anymore. "With my first act in seventy-nine, people said hip-hop was dead," Simmons has said. "Now hip-hop culture is so strong we're doing underwear."

THE TEAM APPROACH TO OPPORTUNITY

Simmons and Rubin turned Def Jam into a huge success because they made a good team. Alone, neither of them had enough money to launch a record label, but together they were able to do it. Plus, they each knew different artists and had different contacts in the record industry.

Every person you know is a potential business-formation opportunity. Your friends or family members may have skills, equipment, or contacts that would make them valuable business partners.

Let's say you're a sneakerhead—you would love to start a custom sneaker business, but you're not an artist. If you have a friend who is an artist, the two of you can start a business together.

Or maybe you'd like to form a DJ business, but you have only one turntable. If you form the business with a friend, you can pool equipment and records.

When forming a business team, organize the business so that everyone involved shares in the ownership and profits. People work much harder when they are working for themselves.

No matter how enthusiastic you and another person get about a business idea, however, remember that not every business idea is an opportunity. For an idea to be an opportunity, it must lead to the development of a product or service that is of value to customers.

EVALUATING AN OPPORTUNITY

Even though entrepreneurs take risks, successful ones take **calculated risks**. They carefully evaluate the potential costs and benefits of pursuing a business opportunity before committing time, energy, money, and other scarce resources to its creation.

Once you've brainstormed some business opportunities, it's time to evaluate their **feasibility**. An idea is feasible if it makes sense to pursue it. Let's look at three easy methods for evaluating the feasibility of your business ideas:

1. Cost-Benefit Analysis

Cost-benefit analysis adds up all the expected benefits of an opportunity and then subtracts all the expected costs. If the benefits outweigh the costs, the opportunity may be feasible.

Costs can be onetime payments, such as the purchase of a car, or ongoing, such as rent. Benefits are most often received over a period of time. Let's say you want to buy a computer but you currently don't have the money to pay for it. The purchase price could be a onetime cost if you save up and pay **cash** for it in six months. Or you could use a credit card to buy the computer today, and then pay it back over time.

How much interest will you pay if you use your card to get the computer today? If buying the computer now enables you to earn more money than the credit card interest that you will pay, the benefit may outweigh the cost. If you are not going to earn enough with the computer to pay off the interest, don't use the card.

2. Opportunity Cost Analysis

An **opportunity cost** is the potential benefit that you forfeit when you choose one course of action over another. This is vital to look at when you are considering where to spend your money, time, and energy.

Suppose you are offered a one-year internship at a company where you will gain valuable work experience, but you won't be paid. To make the best decision, you should compare the benefits the internship offers with opportunities you will be losing or postponing, such as the opportunity to earn money at a different job, go to college, or start a business.

One challenge of cost-benefit analysis is assigning a monetary value to **intangible** things—such as your time. What is the value of your time? Only you can decide.

3. SWOT Analysis

Another way to determine an idea's feasibility is to perform a **SWOT analysis**. SWOT stands for four categories:

Strengths: What skills do you have that will help you execute this opportunity? What resources do you have available? Do you have any unique knowledge or experiences that give you an edge?

Weaknesses: What resources, skills, or knowledge are you lacking? What might potential customers see as a weakness in your product or service?

Opportunities: Is this business idea a valid opportunity? Does it fill an unmet need or want? Are there any trends or changes happening in your community that you could use as an advantage? What could you do better than other companies that already are in the same type of business? Does the proposed business location give you any advantages?

Threats: What obstacles stand in the way of pursuing this opportunity? What current trends could potentially harm your business? How fierce is the competition in this business area? Does this business idea have a short window of opportunity?

Here's a simple SWOT analysis for starting a DJ business. Use SWOT charts to quickly see if you currently have the strengths you need to take advantage of existing opportunities. Ask yourself, "What can I do to build my strengths so I can make the most of my opportunities?"

SWOT Analysis: Starting a DJ Business

STRENGTHS	OPPORTUNITIES
I have experience working in a music store and know what type of music is bought most often. Together, my potential partner and I have the necessary equipment and music resources. I have an older brother who was a DJ when he was younger. He can answer questions and provide helpful tips.	Some friends have already asked me to DJ at upcoming parties. My potential partner knows another DJ who says we can sub for him. People in our area really like salsa music. Maybe we could add that to our playlist.
WEAKNESSES	THREATS
I'm not sure how dependable my potential partner will be. He is often late. We need money to continue building our music library and keep it current. We need a way to transport our equipment from place to place.	There are several good DJs already in the neighborhood. People planning parties don't know us and already know the established DJs. If times are hard economically, people won't pay for expensive parties with DJs.

Weaknesses and threats are placed side by side in a SWOT analysis. This allows you to evaluate whether your weaknesses make existing threats more serious. Ask yourself, "What can I do to address my weaknesses so I can minimize potential threats?"

Keep in mind that you can also use a SWOT analysis to evaluate a business after it is up and running. Many companies perform a SWOT analysis periodically to keep abreast of changes that could help or harm their businesses.

Try It!

Imagine that you've been asked to help plan a strip mall to be built near your school. Get together with some friends and brainstorm ideas for businesses for the mall.

Based on what you know about the community, what types of businesses would do well in this location? Then, let each person pick a potential business and do a SWOT analysis of it.

Share your results. Which ideas have the most business potential? Which ideas have the least?

THE TRIPLE BOTTOM LINE: PEOPLE, PLANET, PROFIT

You may have heard the term "bottom line." Traditionally, businesses focused on the "bottom line," which is the last line of an **income statement,** a financial report that shows whether a business made a profit or lost money.

Today, many businesses seek to have a positive **triple bottom line**. Not only do they want to make a profit; they also want to show that they are environmentally friendly and are good for society, too. They want to succeed in three categories: people, planet, and profit.

Thinking about business in this way can lead to new opportunities. Growing concern for the environment, for example, is creating lots of opportunities for entrepreneurs.

Maria Coler used her degree in physics and her interest in improving the environment to start Hydrotechnology Consultants, a company that brings New Jersey building sites into compliance with environmental laws. When a contractor wants to build an apartment building on some land that was previously used by a factory, for instance, the land and water must first be tested to make sure they're not too polluted for residences.

That's where Maria comes in. She tests the ground and water, and then tells the contractor what needs to be done, if anything, to clean the site. If cleaning has to be done, she hires and supervises crews to do the work, and then retests the site to certify that it complies with all environmental cleanup standards.

Now that her business is so successful, Maria is looking at giving back to her favorite city—Newark, New Jersey. She plans to develop a beautiful abandoned Victorian factory into a center for small, artisanal manufacturers from Newark to develop their businesses and sell their products. This, in turn, will help to revitalize Newark's economy.

One of the most moral acts an entrepreneur can do is to use resources—land, air, water, and so on—frugally and economically so that future generations can enjoy them, too. Not so coincidentally, using resources as efficiently as possible also keeps your business competitive. Reduce, reuse, and recycle!

Green Tip: Watch Your Carbon Footprint

Your **carbon footprint** is the impact your daily activities have on the environment. If you drive to school, for example, the emissions from your car pollute the air. Here are three free apps you can use to track and reduce your carbon footprint.

1. **Carbon Track (iOS):** This app shows businesses how they can become greener and save money. It tracks CO_2 emissions caused by daily business activities such as travel, electricity usage, and waste creation. Discover ways of lessening your impact by switching your mode of travel or type of office equipment, for instance.

2. **ecoFootprint (Android):** This app measures your personal ecological footprint, based on information and statistics provided by the World Wildlife Fund. It provides tips on how to reduce your footprint.

3. **My Planet (Android):** This lighthearted app measures your carbon footprint while letting you personalize your interface, earn badges, get tips, and share achievements on Facebook.

Tech U

Not sure how or when to recycle where you live? Check out the iRecycle app: http://earth911.com/irecycle.

ENTREPRENEURS ARE CREATIVE THINKERS

Entrepreneurship is a wonderfully creative act! Here a few techniques to get your creative juices flowing.

Challenge the Usual. Ask "Why?" and "What if?" Challenge what you believe about how products should work or how things are done.

Think Backward. Sometimes solving a problem is easier when you start by imagining the end result you want. Then mentally trace imaginary steps backward to see how you could get there.

Be Flexible. Go with the flow! Take Post-it Notes, for example. Dr. Spencer Silver, a chemist at 3M, was attempting to develop a super-strong adhesive, but instead he accidentally created some glue that was not very strong. A colleague of his, Art Fry, came up with the idea of using the mildly tacky adhesive to anchor his bookmark in his hymnbook—and Post-it Notes became a hugely successful product for 3M.

Don't Judge. Don't worry about being practical while you are brainstorming. Don't judge your ideas—let your imagination run wild! Not all ideas have to make sense in the beginning. You'll have time later to decide which ones are feasible. Sometimes ideas that seem silly at first inspire other, more useful, solutions later.

Draw Idea Maps. Use whiteboards, chalkboards, and poster boards to sketch out ideas. Drawing ideas often helps you to see a bigger picture, with new possibilities that you might have otherwise missed. You might also try using sticky notes on a wall or poster board. This method allows you to move ideas around.

Brainstorm in a Group. Ask friends, family, colleagues, and classmates to help you generate ideas. The old saying "Two heads are better than one" is often true. All these thinking techniques work great with groups.

Daydream. With your eyes closed, practice visualizing what your new product or service would be. What would it look like, smell like, taste like, feel like, sound like?

As former first lady Eleanor Roosevelt wrote: "The future belongs to those who believe in the beauty of their dreams."

Read a Classic

Want to learn to think more creatively? Read *Six Thinking Hats* by creative thinking expert Edward de Bono.

An Entrepreneur Like You

Shomari Patterson

SHAMAZZLE'S DAZZLES

http://shamazzlesdazzles.tumblr.com

Shamazzle's Dazzles is a handmade jewelry company founded by Shomari Patterson that is helping to rescue girls from the sex trade in Thailand.

Shomari always knew she wanted her jewelry-making business to incorporate an element of social responsibility. Many worthy causes called to her, but the one that commanded her immediate attention was the plight of girls sold into sexual slavery. For each piece of jewelry that her company sells, she makes a donation to a program that rehabilitates and empowers girls rescued from the sex trade by giving them "jewelry compassion kits."

Each compassion kit is sent overseas with all the materials and instructions needed to make matching bracelets or necklaces. Once the kits reach the girls, they are able to learn how to make jewelry and sell it at their local market. They keep all of the profit from their sales.

Shamazzle's Dazzles is a **social enterprise**—a business with a mission to help improve society, in this case by raising awareness of human trafficking and helping its victims learn new skills and become self-sufficient. Shomari plans to help women in the United States, as well, by hiring women from local shelters to help with production and marketing as her business grows.

Shomari counts on **viral marketing** to spread the word about her cause and business. She promotes her business and educates people about human trafficking through her Facebook page, Twitter feed, and Tumblr mini-blog.

But as much as Shamazzle's Dazzles has helped others, nobody has benefited more than Shomari herself.

"Before I took a NFTE course, I had lost all hope in myself and my future. I was unsure about what I wanted to do in life. I also didn't think that college was for me," says Shomari.

"Now I'm a completely different person. I have hope again, I'm able to set a goal and go through with it, I'm more optimistic, and I'm a lot happier. I can honestly say that becoming an entrepreneur has changed my life for the better.

"You have to be daring and willing to take risks," Shomari adds, "because sometimes the risks you take will be the best choices you have made for your business."

Think Like an Entrepreneur

1. Visit the Tumblr and Facebook pages of some businesses you like. What would you do to improve them? What did they do right?
2. Do you think a business also needs a website? Or is it enough to have a social media presence? Why or why not?
3. What are some other businesses you are aware of that would qualify as "social enterprises"?

CHAPTER 3

ENTREPRENEURSHIP AND THE ECONOMY

SUPPLY AND DEMAND, COMPETITION, AND HOW PRICES COMMUNICATE INFORMATION

> Small businesses are the engine of
> economic growth in this country.
>
> —Barack Obama

E ver since the financial crisis of 2008 and the long recession and severe unemployment that followed, the state of the economy has been a huge topic on the news and in political races. But what exactly is "the economy"? And how does entrepreneurship fit into it?

WHAT IS "THE ECONOMY"?

An **economic system** or **economy** is the system used by a society to allocate goods and services among its people. When you buy bread at the store, you are participating in the economy. Political, moral, and cultural factors affect what kinds of economic systems develop and thrive in different societies.

The two main types of economic systems are the **market economy** and the

command economy. Every economic system answers four basic questions, called the Fundamental Questions of Economics:

1. What goods and services are produced?
2. What quantity of goods and services are produced?
3. How are goods and services produced?
4. For whom are goods and services produced?

The Market, or "Free Enterprise," Economy

In a market economy, suppliers produce whatever goods and services they wish and set prices based on what consumers are willing to pay. The United States, Canada, Australia, Hong Kong, Singapore, and many western European nations have market economies.

Another name for the market economy is the **free enterprise system**. People are free to become entrepreneurs and own and operate **enterprises** (businesses). Individuals can freely invest money into their own businesses, or into businesses owned by other people.

Money invested into a business is called capital. That's why the market economy or free enterprise system is also called **capitalism**.

The market economy is characterized by individual freedom of choice and voluntary exchange. Voluntary exchange is a transaction in which both suppliers and consumers believe they benefit.

If you walk into a store to buy some bread and you don't like the price, you are free to go look for bread at other stores until you find the price you want to pay. In order to stay competitive, the store that has the high-priced bread will probably lower its price once it realizes customers are buying bread elsewhere.

The democratic political system is strongly associated with the market economy. Democracies typically favor personal choice, voluntary exchange, and the right of individuals to own property, businesses, and capital. The U.S. government does exert some economic control. It regulates businesses, enforces labor and product safety laws, imposes taxes, and takes other actions that affect economic activity. There is an ongoing debate in American politics over how large a role government should play in the economy.

The Command Economy

In a command economy, the government controls the production, allocation, and prices of goods and services. Examples of command economies include North Korea, Cuba, and China.

In a command economy, the government owns or manages the nation's resources and businesses. The government sets prices and tells businesses what to produce.

North Korea, for example, is currently run by a dictator whose government closely controls the economy. Sadly, many people in North Korea live without heat and don't have enough food. Command economies have historically been associated with shortages because dictatorships can choose, for example, to command businesses to produce weapons instead of food.

In a command economy, central government planners make economic decisions and long-term plans for the nation. The government owns most resources and businesses. Entrepreneurship may be allowed to a small degree, so long as it does not interfere with the overall government control of the economy.

Socialism and communism are two political systems strongly associated with command economies. The former Soviet Union was a communist country with a command economy. Fidel Castro became the socialist leader of Cuba after he ousted dictator Fulgencio Batista in the Cuban Revolution in 1959. Although Castro expanded education and health care for the Cuban people, his repressive regime has suppressed freedom of the press and religion, and imprisoned many Cubans who spoke out against his government.

China has had a command economy since the communist revolution in 1948, but in 1978 the government began slowly introducing economic reforms that added some freedom and competition to the marketplace. This has helped China's economy grow to become the second largest in the world.

Read a Classic

For a reader-friendly explanation of the principles of economics, try *The Economic Way of Thinking* by Paul Heyne.

Capitalism and Freedom by Milton Friedman is another classic book on economics.

SUPPLY AND DEMAND

In a market economy, businesses are motivated to provide products and services because consumers will pay money for them.

Supply Curve

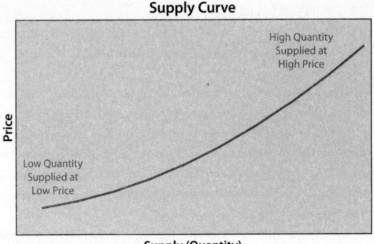

Businesses typically want to get the most money possible for the goods (products) and services they offer. Consumers typically want to pay the least amount of money possible for what they buy. These two opposing forces work together to make the market economy operate efficiently.

Supply is the quantity of goods and services a business is willing to sell at a specific price and a specific time.

Demand is the quantity of goods and services consumers are willing to buy at a specific price and a specific time.

Suppliers decide what quantity of a good or service they are willing to sell at a particular price. Consumers decide how much they are willing to pay for a given good or service.

In a market economy, the price of a particular good or service is determined by this friction between supply and demand.

Law of Demand

According to the law of demand, as the price of a product or service goes up, the quantity demanded by consumers goes down. As the price falls, the quantity demanded by consumers rises.

Let's say you get permission to sell soda at a Little League baseball game. During the early innings of the game, you charge $2.00 per can of soda and sell two dozen cans. During the later innings, you try lowering your price to $1.00 per can. You sell five dozen cans.

The people attending the game have "obeyed" the **law of demand**: If everything else remains the same, people will demand more of something at a *lower* price than they will at a *higher* price.

Law of Supply

On the other side of every market is a supplier. The supplier also reacts to price changes.

If you have a small baking business, for example, how many cookies would you be willing to make if you thought that the cookies would sell for $0.25 each? What if people were willing to pay $1.00 each? You would probably work harder and try to supply more cookies at that price.

The entrepreneur who acts this way is obeying the **law of supply**: If everything else remains the same, businesses will supply more of a product or service at a *higher* price than they will at a *lower* price.

Setting the Price

Together, these laws of supply and demand determine how much will be bought and sold and what the price will be. Businesses would like to charge high prices for their products and services. Consumers seek low prices. The market price is a compromise between what the buyer wants to pay and what the entrepreneur wants to charge.

There is a price that both buyers and sellers will accept. It is the point where the supply curve and the demand curve cross. This "equilibrium point" is the **market clearing price**. It is the spot where the supply and demand curves cross.

Demand Curve
A demand curve shows the quantity and price relationship acceptable to consumers.
Comparing/Contrasting. *Why is the demand curve sloping in a different direction from the supply curve?*

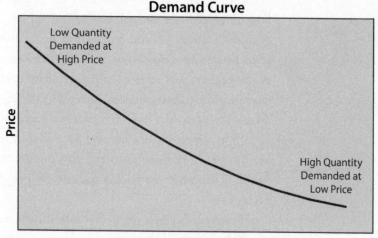

Demand Curve

Low Quantity Demanded at High Price

Price

High Quantity Demanded at Low Price

Demand (Quantity)

Supply and Demand Curve

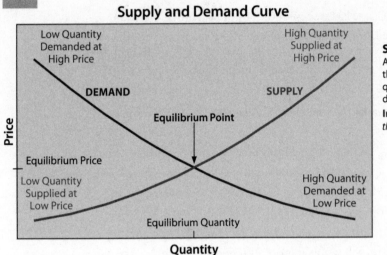

Supply and Demand Curve
A supply and demand curve shows the price relationship between the quantity supplied and the quantity demanded.

Interpreting graphs. *Where is the market clearing price?*

Using the Laws of Supply and Demand to Make Good Decisions

Understanding the laws of supply and demand helps you make good business decisions.

If you believe the demand for a product is going to rise, for instance, it would be wise to start selling that product, because if demand rises, the price that people are willing to pay for it will rise, too.

What will happen to the demand for air conditioners in the summer? What is likely to happen, therefore, to the price of air conditioners in the summer?

The demand for air conditioners rises in the summer because more people will want air conditioners to cool their homes and offices. At first, therefore, the price of air conditioners will rise. Suppliers of air conditioners will be able to raise their prices because more people will be demanding air conditioners. The higher prices of air conditioners will, in turn, encourage more suppliers to sell air conditioners. As more suppliers enter the market, attracted by the high price, the competition among them will start to drive down the price of air conditioners.

If you suspect that the demand for a product is going to drop, it would make sense to get out of that market and start producing something else. What do you think will happen to the price of gasoline, for example, if more people begin using electric cars?

If everyone begins using electric cars, the demand for gasoline will fall. Suppliers will be forced to sell gasoline at a lower price to try to attract consumers away from electric cars. Many suppliers will probably stop selling gasoline and move into another market.

Each time you make any choice regarding your business, you quickly get feedback from your market: The demand for your product or service rises or falls. If the demand for your product or service falls, the market is telling you to lower the price. If you still can't sell it at a lower price, the market is telling you to move on to a different product or service.

So, don't be ashamed if your business fails. The market is just telling you to move on to a new enterprise.

Tech U

Get organized with Evernote, a free app that has an amazing ability to search any scanned file or document. Snap a photo, record some audio, and save it. You can tag and note anything you want to remember. Check it out on http://evernote.com.

COMPETITION KEEPS PRICES DOWN

The laws of supply and demand work best in competitive markets. When businesses are free to compete with one another, they try to attract consumers by lowering prices, improving quality, and developing new products and services. Consumers benefit!

Anything that keeps entrepreneurs from entering a market will make a market less competitive. Less competition leads to higher prices, poorer quality, and fewer new products and services. This is a situation that often develops in command economies.

Prices Communicate Information

In a market economy, price relays information between the consumer and the entrepreneur. The entrepreneur knows quickly when the price of a product is too high, because consumers refuse to buy the product. The entrepreneur knows when the price is too low because the product sells out very quickly and consumers want more.

Nobel Prize–winning economist Friedrich Hayek was the first to describe price as a mechanism for rapidly communicating information, in his famous 1945 essay "The Use of Knowledge in Society." Hayek argued for keeping the market as unregulated as possible, so that information could flow without interference from the government.

Monopoly

When a market has only one supplier of a product or service, that supplier has a **monopoly**. The word "monopoly" comes from two Greek words—*monos,* which means "single," and *polein,* which means "to sell."

A monopoly is the opposite of competition and has the opposite effect. If there is only one grocery store in your neighborhood, there is less incentive for that store to lower its bread price to attract customers.

In a monopoly, the supplier has no incentive to lower prices or improve quality to attract the consumer. The consumer has no choice but to go to that supplier. Monopolies keep prices high and quality low.

In free markets, monopolies seldom last long. Other entrepreneurs will enter the market with the same or similar products, and will compete for the same customers. Someone will come into your neighborhood and open a grocery store with lower prices to compete with the grocery store with the high prices—destroying its monopoly.

The best ways to prevent monopolies are to keep markets free, make it easy for people to start businesses, and encourage as many people as possible to learn the basics of entrepreneurship.

Competition Encourages Innovation

Competition has another benefit. It encourages innovation and variety. Entrepreneurs introduce new and different goods and services to avoid (or at least delay) direct competition from similar businesses. This results in a wide variety of goods and services being offered for sale. After Amazon introduced the Kindle e-reader, for example, Barnes & Noble responded with its Nook e-reader.

Competition between suppliers is good for consumers because it leads to low prices and many choices.

Competition between suppliers makes it tougher for businesses to succeed, but it forces them to work smarter and harder, just as competition in sports pushes athletes to perform better.

Entrepreneurs use their cleverness and skills to outperform their competitors. Smart entrepreneurs look for ways to avoid competing solely based on price. They either offer new and different products or they ensure that their products have an advantage over similar products sold by other businesses.

Competition Between Consumers

In a market economy, there is not only competition between suppliers but also competition between consumers. When consumers compete against one another to buy a product, they push prices upward.

For example, parents rush to stores in December to buy a popular toy as a holiday gift for their children. Consumers compete against one another to buy the limited supply of that toy. Suppliers can charge more for that toy in December than at other times of the year because demand is higher than usual.

WHEN THE BUBBLE BURSTS: THE 2008 FINANCIAL CRISIS

Sometimes, competition pushes the price of a product very high, and people start to forget that the price could fall again someday. In 2008, a financial crisis caused an economic meltdown in the American economy that left most people asking one question: What happened?

The short answer is that the housing **bubble** burst. Housing prices, which had been rising for so long that many people began to assume they would always rise, began to fall.

A bubble develops when people get so excited about buying or investing in something that its price rises, which, in turn, gets even more people excited about it. This happened in the 1990s with dot-com companies.

Those early exciting "can't fail" Internet companies were growing so fast and looked like such great investments that many people bought their stock. Unfortunately, many of the companies did not succeed, and their stock prices fell. Thousands of dot-com companies failed, including Pets.com, fashion retailer boo.com (which spent $135 million of investors' money in eighteen months), and BroadbandSports .com. When this bubble burst, it really hurt investors who had invested lots of their money in these companies, hoping to become wealthy.

A similar situation developed with housing in the early 2000s. Housing prices were only going up, so people began to think they could get rich by buying a house or an apartment, holding it for a few years, and then selling it for a big profit. As real estate prices kept rising, more people wanted in on the game, and a housing bubble began to develop.

Enter the Flippers

"Flippers"—people who would buy a new condo on opening day, for example, and "flip" it a few weeks or months later for a much higher price—were pocketing thousands of dollars from each sale. The increase in demand from flippers created truly dramatic real-estate price increases.

Most people need a loan called a **mortgage** in order to buy real estate. The banks, assuming that housing prices were only going to rise, began to give mortgages to people who couldn't really afford to be speculating in the housing market.

Unfortunately, housing prices peaked in 2006 and began to decline. Many people were left owing mortgage loans that cost more than the real estate they had bought was worth. They couldn't "flip" the real estate for a profit anymore.

People began defaulting on their mortgage loans, resulting in great losses for the banks who had issued the loans. This made it harder for banks to make loans to businesses that, as a result, didn't have enough money to hire employees or expand. The American economy stopped growing, and many people lost their jobs.

Read a Classic

Devil Take the Hindmost by Edward Chancellor is a fascinating narrative of financial bubbles dating back to the Middle Ages.

Remember our discussion of risk and reward from chapter 2? During bubbles, participants only want to talk about how much money they are making. There is no discussion of risk—just reward.

Never buy something without first assessing not only the money you could make, but also what you could lose. Beware of these expressions: "It's going up like a rocket," "It's like shooting fish in a barrel," or "You can always sell it at a higher price." That's greed talking, or, to quote former Federal Reserve chairman Alan Greenspan, "irrational exuberance." These kinds of statements are bubble markers.

Anytime there is the potential for high reward, risk is high as well. There is no exception to this rule.

FIVE WAYS TO SATISFY A CONSUMER NEED

For your business to be successful, it must satisfy a need for enough consumers to generate **revenue,** which is money from sales. There are five basic ways an entrepreneur can satisfy a **consumer** need:

1. Develop a new product or service.
2. Uncover new resources or technologies.
3. Apply existing resources or technologies in new ways.
4. Find new markets for an existing product or service.
5. Improve an existing business.

PROFIT MOTIVE

In very simple terms, a business makes a profit when the amount of money coming in from sales (revenue) is greater than the business's expenses. This **profit motive** is an incentive that encourages entrepreneurs to take business risks in the hope of making a profit.

In a market economy, entrepreneurs may choose how to use their profits. They can save, spend, invest, or donate them. Entrepreneurs can use profits to grow existing businesses, start new ones, or invest in businesses started by other people. In addition, an entrepreneur can save profit for use when the business is not doing well financially.

Math Moment

You buy glow sticks for $0.50 each and sell them for $1.00 each at concerts. What is your profit on every sale? If you sell 100 glow sticks at a concert, what's your revenue?*

---

*   Answers: $0.50, $50.00.

SOCIAL ENTERPRISES

Although profit is a strong incentive, it is not the only goal that motivates entrepreneurs.

As you learned in chapter 2, green companies adopt business practices aimed at protecting or improving the environment and seek to meet a triple bottom line—the "people, planet, profit" style of business. Some businesses donate part or all of their profits to worthy causes. These businesses are called social enterprises, because they are enterprises that help benefit society. Social entrepreneurs seek to be economically successful by making a profit, while also seeking to have positive impacts on society and the environment.

In 1982, actor Paul Newman established Newman's Own to produce and sell grocery items, such as salad dressing, orange juice, and popcorn. All profits from this business go to charities. As of 2012, the donations from Newman's Own add up to more than $330 million. This money has been used to help people all around the world.

Green Tip: Bag the Habit

Bag the Habit (www.bagthehabit.com) is a small business that makes reusable shopping bags from eco-friendly textiles. If you shop for groceries once a week and use plastic bags every time, in five years you'll have added anywhere from 250 to 1,000 plastic bags to landfills.

By carrying your own cloth shopping bags, you can save thousands of plastic bags from ending up in landfills, or—even worse—in ecosystems where they can harm living creatures.

Bag the Habit anticipated a consumer need and is satisfying it—while meeting the triple bottom line.

NONPROFIT BUSINESSES

Some people prefer to use their entrepreneurial skills to start a nonprofit rather than a for-profit business. A **nonprofit** organization operates solely to serve the good of society. Nonprofit entrepreneurs sacrifice the chance to build personal wealth and financial independence for the personal satisfaction they obtain through nonprofit work.

Nonprofits operate much like for-profit businesses. Money comes into the nonprofit from donations, government grants, or the sale of goods and services to consumers.

Nonprofit companies also have costs. If the money coming in is greater than the money going out, a nonprofit company will have a surplus (profit).

Nonprofits differ from social enterprises in one important way. By law, *all* profit a nonprofit earns must be used to support the organization's social mission. None of the profit may be used for the financial gain of the people running the nonprofit.

The owner of a social enterprise, in contrast, gets to choose how much or how little of the business's profit is used to help society.

An Entrepreneur Like You

Nadia Campbell-Mitchell
THE VICTORIAN HANDS FOUNDATION

www.tvhf.org

Nadia Campbell-Mitchell became an entrepreneur when she was eleven. In 1994, she started the Victorian Hands Foundation, a nonprofit that arranges for young volunteers to visit senior citizens to provide assistance and companionship.

Nadia was motivated to start her nonprofit after watching a documentary on elders who were abused and neglected. Her company's stated mission is "To enhance awareness and respect among younger generations for our elderly."

"It's extremely gratifying," says Nadia. "Even volunteers who were skeptical in the beginning were able to see the difference their time was making."

Running her nonprofit business gave Nadia more than eighteen years of experience in managing teams, record keeping, controlling costs, administration, and promoting volunteerism. She has been featured in the *New York Times,* the *New York Daily News,* and *Essence* magazine and has been interviewed on Fox Business Network and XM Satellite Radio.

Starting a For-Profit Company

At age twenty-four, Nadia started her first for-profit company, when she saw a need for a day spa in her neighborhood of Crown Heights in Brooklyn. Nadia had been to spas for facials and massages, but she didn't have any experience running one. Still, she had learned the basics of business from running her foundation and from an online entrepreneurial course.

"I did a lot of research on the community as well as on the spa industry and how it's improved," says Nadia. For her Brooklyn spa, called Jewel in the Crown, she rented two floors of a building. Then she put together a staff of experienced professionals. "We have a great team. We have the top people in each field to make sure our clients are happy."

Making Mistakes

Like any businessperson, Nadia made some mistakes. Against the advice of her family, she hired a receptionist for the spa who didn't work out. "It was a waste of money," said Nadia, "money I should have been saving." Her solution was to contact a local college and find student interns willing to staff her reception desk without pay, in exchange for mentoring and business experience.

Managing interns is a skill Nadia had learned from her earlier experience in the nonprofit. There, she had had no problem finding volunteers to help with everything from Web design to visiting seniors. But in the for-profit world, Nadia discovered that she couldn't count on volunteers or unpaid interns. "You have to pay people to do work, even to pass out a brochure," Nadia notes.

Learning on the Job

For Nadia, running a spa has given her the opportunity to learn about herself. "I didn't realize I knew how to do things like coming up with creative marketing techniques," she said. "I've been able to explore my creative side in ways I didn't get to, running my not-for-profit foundation."

She is marketing her spa online, as well as advertising on the radio and in newspapers. "We've sponsored events. We've given out flyers. We're open to a lot of types of marketing," she says.

Think Like an Entrepreneur

1. Nadia researched her community to determine how to price the services in her spa. What other reasons are there to research a community?
2. Why didn't people want to volunteer their services to help Nadia with her spa? Would you have been surprised at this?
3. What are some creative marketing ideas you would use to try to promote Nadia's spa? What about to promote her nonprofit's mission?

CHAPTER 4

CHOOSING THE RIGHT LEGAL STRUCTURE FOR YOUR BUSINESS

UNDERSTANDING SOLE PROPRIETORSHIPS, PARTNERSHIPS, AND CORPORATIONS

> When two men in a business always agree,
> one of them is unnecessary.
>
> —William Wrigley, Jr.

BUSINESS TYPES

A business usually falls into one of four types:

1. Manufacturing: A business that makes tangible products (ones you can touch).
2. Wholesale: A business that buys products from manufacturers and sells them to retailers.

3.   Retail: A business that sells directly to the final consumer.

4.   Service: A business that sells intangibles (things you can't touch) such as time, skills, or expertise.

It's important to know what type of business you are starting, because each type needs different advertising, accounting, and management.

The Distribution Chain: A Real-World Example

My first small business was a service business. I represented manufacturers from West Africa, Pakistan, and Bangladesh who made wooden sculptures, jewelry, instruments, and other goods. I took samples of their products around to wholesalers in New York City. The manufacturers overseas were my clients. I was selling them my time, my contacts, and my familiarity with New York.

If the wholesalers liked the products, they would place large orders with me and I would give them a **volume discount**. The more products they ordered, the lower price per unit I would charge. Bulk, or "volume," orders are usually grouped in lots of a dozen or a hundred, depending on the product.

I would then send the orders to the manufacturers, who, in turn, shipped the products to the wholesalers. The wholesalers, in turn, sold my clients' products to retail stores. The retail stores sold them to customers.

At each step along the way, the price of each product was raised, or "marked up," to give each business along this **distribution chain** a profit.

Manufacturers typically give wholesalers a volume discount because wholesalers buy a large quantity at once. A guitar manufacturer, for example, may value a single guitar at a retail price of $600 but sell a hundred guitars to a wholesaler for $300 per guitar—giving the wholesaler a volume discount for taking so many guitars.

A guitar store owner, in turn, might buy a dozen guitars from the wholesaler for $400 each. The store owner, then, will sell the guitar in the store at the "suggested retail price" of $600—earning a $200 profit on each sale.

At each step along the way, the price of each product is raised or "marked up" to give each business along this distribution chain a profit.

Let's take a closer look at the four basic types of business.

Manufacturing

A **manufacturing** business makes a tangible product. A manufacturer rarely sells its products directly to consumers. It typically sells large quantities of its product to wholesalers, or it may hire a manufacturer's representative to sell its products to wholesalers.

Sometimes small manufacturing businesses also sell directly to the public. An entrepreneur making birdhouses at home could sell them directly to friends and other customers. He doesn't necessarily have to go through a wholesaler to reach customers.

If the demand for his birdhouses grew, though, he might want to start selling them through a wholesaler in order to get them placed in retail stores far beyond his neighborhood.

Large manufacturing businesses, in contrast, usually do not sell directly to consumers. You wouldn't go to a car factory to buy a car, for example. Car factories sell cars in large quantities to wholesalers who, in turn, sell the cars in smaller quantities to car dealerships.

MANUFACTURING BUSINESS EXAMPLE

Kohler manufactures plumbing fixtures. You've probably seen faucets imprinted with the Kohler name. But you can't buy a new water faucet for your sink directly from Kohler. Kohler sells its faucets to wholesalers, who then sell them to retail stores and online dealers such as Home Depot or Build.com.

Green Tip

The easiest way to cut your energy bill is to switch to compact fluorescent lightbulbs (CFLs). Compared to regular bulbs, CFLs use a quarter of the energy and last ten times longer. For a warmer light, go for CFLs with a lower Kelvin rating (2,700K–3,000K).

Wholesale

A **wholesale** business rarely sells directly to the public, and it doesn't manufacture anything. It buys products from manufacturers in bulk at a volume discount.

Next, the wholesaler sells smaller quantities to retailers from its warehouses. Some wholesalers also have store outlets, but they will not sell to consumers. If you see a store with a sign that reads "To the Trade Only," it is a wholesaler.

Wholesale and retail businesses together are referred to as **trade businesses**. If you become a business owner, you will be able to apply for a permit to buy from a wholesaler as a member of "the trade." Once you have that, you will be able to buy products directly from a wholesaler.

You will have to buy in bulk—most wholesalers require a minimum of one dozen products for every sale. In return, you will get a good price! You can then increase the price on each product and sell it to your customers for a profit.

Learn the Lingo

Wholesalers are also known as middlemen, go-betweens, distributors, or intermediaries because they provide a link between manufacturers, who make products, and retailers, who sell products to consumers.

WHOLESALE BUSINESS EXAMPLE

The Hudson Heating Wholesaler is a family-owned business that buys heating and air-conditioning equipment from manufacturers. The family owns a thirty-thousand-square-foot warehouse where it stores the equipment, which it then sells to contractors who are building houses and apartments.

Retail

Retail businesses buy products from a wholesaler and sell them directly to consumers. Retailers run stores or other selling units that are open to the public. Your favorite clothing or video game store is a retail business.

Retail businesses include stores people visit in person, and online stores. Some retailers also sell to consumers through catalogs.

In most states, a retail business can obtain a special permit called a **reseller's permit** enabling it to purchase goods tax-free from wholesalers. The retail business, in turn, collects sales tax whenever it makes a sale to a customer. The retailer typically must pay that collected sales tax to the state government.

Wholesale and retail businesses together are referred to as trade businesses.

RETAIL BUSINESS EXAMPLE

Old Navy runs retail stores where you can choose from a variety of clothing it has sourced from various wholesalers.

Service

A **service** business provides intangibles such as time, skills, or expertise in exchange for a fee. Babysitting is a service business; so is a law firm, your doctor's office, and a dry cleaner.

Most states and some local governments impose licensing requirements for people who provide particular services. This applies to professionals (doctors, dentists, engineers, lawyers, and so on) as well as other types of service providers, such as hairstylists, automobile mechanics, and day-care providers.

In addition, some states require service businesses selling taxable services to have a permit to collect sales tax from their customers.

SERVICE BUSINESS EXAMPLE

H&R Block is the largest preparer of federal income tax returns for individuals. H&R Block provides tax preparation service to more than ten million customers every year. H&R Block is a *retail* service business because it sells its service directly to the end consumer. There are also service businesses that serve wholesale or manufacturing customers.

Special Types of Businesses

Some businesses don't slot easily into the four categories we've just discussed. Farming is a good example—sometimes it is like manufacturing, if, for example, a farm produces wheat that is bought by wholesalers who, in turn, sell it to bakeries to make bread. Sometimes, farms sell their fruits or vegetables directly to the consumer, behaving like retail businesses.

Mining is another special type of business. It is called an "extraction business," because miners extract resources from the earth such as copper and oil. These resources are then sold to manufacturers.

The Decline of U.S. Manufacturing . . .

Prior to the 1950s, manufacturing was the dominant business type in the American economy. Wholesale and retail businesses were also important, and service businesses played a relatively minor role in the economy.

After 1950, manufacturing gradually became less important in the U.S. economy. By 1970, service, wholesale, and retail businesses began to account for the majority of America's economic production.

The vast majority of businesses started in the 2000s have been service and trade businesses. Private companies in the service industry created nearly two-thirds of America's economic production in 2006.

Get the Stats

Many Americans believe we are losing jobs because American companies are **outsourcing** them to other countries. Surprisingly, the U.S. Bureau of Labor Statistics has found that the effect of outsourcing has been minimal.

. . . and Back Again!

Since 2010, American manufacturing has grown steadily, countering the long-standing trend. During the 2008 recession, the three big American car manufacturers—General Motors, Ford, and Chrysler—would have gone bankrupt if it weren't for a significant bailout from the federal government. The government made loans to American auto manufacturers in exchange for promises from them to develop more energy-efficient vehicles.

The federal government also assisted American manufacturing by funding projects such as a high-tech manufacturing hub in Youngstown, Ohio, called the National Additive Manufacturing Innovation Institute. The institute won a $30 million grant from the federal government for its vision. It proposed connecting more than sixty universities with manufacturing advocacy groups, business incubators, and manufacturing companies from the Tech Belt, which encompasses northeast Ohio, West Virginia, and southwest Pennsylvania, to combine forces. The partners contributed $40 million, for $70 million total.

The institute is focused on 3-D printing, or "additive manufacturing," which speeds up production time while reducing costs. Plans are in the works to create fifteen of these hubs to further boost American manufacturing.

Small-scale, local manufacturing has become more popular, as well, as fans of the locavore movement seek out local suppliers of food and drink. In Brooklyn, New York, for example, young entrepreneurs have started **artisanal** businesses ranging from microbreweries such as Brooklyn Brewery to rooftop beekeepers and honey producers, such as Brooklyn Honey.

Learn the Lingo

An **artisan** is someone skilled at a manual craft, such as furniture making, sewing, or brewing beer. Artisanal businesses focus on quality, rather than quantity, and often use traditional methods to create their products.

In the third quarter of 2012, when more than one hundred thousand workers were laid off, less than 1 percent of these workers lost their jobs because their jobs had been moved to another country.

Markups and Markdowns

As you've learned, manufacturing, wholesale, service, and retail businesses make up the distribution chain (or **distribution channel**). This is the series of steps through which products flow into or out of a business.

In order for each business in the chain to make a profit, the price of a product increases as it travels along the distribution chain. This price increase is called a **markup,** and the new price is the **markup price**. Manufacturers set a price based on their costs and desired profit. Wholesalers pay that price and then set a higher price to cover their costs and earn a profit. Retailers then add a markup to cover *their* costs and earn a profit.

Here's an example for a pair of jeans:

Manufacturer Price: $12/pair of jeans

↓

Wholesaler Price: $20/pair of jeans

↓

Retailer Price: $40/pair of jeans

Typically, a percentage is used to calculate the markup. A retailer may decide to always mark up its goods 30 percent, for example. If it buys a product from the wholesaler for $100, it will sell it in the retail store for $130.

Sometimes retailers mark down a product's price in order to sell it faster. A retailer will use a **markdown price** when it has too much of a product on hand. A clothing store will mark down its summer clothing at the end of the summer to get rid of warm-weather clothing and make room for fall and winter clothes. A store selling sandals for $100, for example, might advertise a 50 percent markdown. The sandals would be priced to sell at $50.

Math Moment

A manufacturing company produces brushes and sells 500 for $300 to a wholesaler. The wholesaler sells a quantity of 20 for $15 to a retailer who sells each brush for $1.50. Calculate the percentage by which the price per brush increases at each step.*

---

* Answers: 25 percent; 50 percent.

Super Success Story

Craig Newmark was not planning to start a business when he began sending out emails with lists of upcoming San Francisco–area events to his friends. In 1995, Newmark was a software engineer at Charles Schwab and sent the emails for fun. His friends started calling them Craig's List, and the name stuck.

The number of people who asked to be included on his emails kept growing until Newmark realized he had a business opportunity on his hands. In 1999, he left his job to begin operating Craigslist full-time, carrying not only event listings but also items for sale, apartment rental listings, and more.

Craigslist's annual revenue rose from $7 million in 2003 to $81 million in 2012, and is at $115 million as of 2012. It generates in excess of twenty billion page views and has approximately fifty million unique visitors monthly, with more than seven hundred local sites in seventy countries.

Craigslist charges fees only for brokered apartment listings in New York City, job advertisements in some cities, and ads in its adult services category. The company relies upon word of mouth for advertising and trust for content.

Newmark himself continues to serve as the company's customer service representative and founder, with a team of about thirty that handles everything else. The company has steadfastly refused to budge from its simple website design, making only minor tweaks to it for more than a decade.

If it ain't broke, don't fix it!

CHOOSING THE BEST LEGAL STRUCTURE FOR YOUR BUSINESS

After you determine the type of business you want to be in, you will need to choose a legal structure for it. There are five basic legal business structures:

1. Sole proprietorship
2. Partnership
3. Corporation
4. Limited liability company (LLC)
5. Cooperative

Some of these legal structures "limit" how much **liability** a business owner has, and some do not. Liability is the legal obligation of a business owner to use his or her personal money and possessions to pay any debts the business incurs.

Unlimited liability means that a business owner can be legally forced to use personal money and sell his or her possessions to pay the debts of the business. **Limited liability** means that a business owner cannot be legally forced to use personal money and possessions to pay business debt.

SOLE PROPRIETORSHIP

A sole proprietorship is the simplest, least expensive legal structure for a business, but it does expose the business owner to unlimited liability.

A **sole proprietorship** is owned by one person, who may also be the only employee. The owner receives all the business profits.

The sole proprietor is personally liable, or responsible, for any lawsuits that arise from accidents, faulty merchandise, unpaid bills, or other business problems. Let's say someone trips on a display in your store and falls and breaks his leg. He could sue you for his medical costs, plus pain and suffering.

If he wins, he could collect money not only from your business but also ask a court to force you to sell some of your personal possessions to pay him. You could lose your house or car, for example.

There is liability insurance that you can buy to protect yourself from these kinds of lawsuits, but your best bet is to try to avoid them. Stick with selling products or services that are highly unlikely to hurt anyone. Avoid selling skateboards or offering rock-climbing lessons, for example!

Stat Fact

The vast majority of businesses in the United States are sole proprietorships.

Advantages of Sole Proprietorship

1. Easy and inexpensive to start.
2. Because the owner and the business are one and the same, just one tax return is required.
3. The sole proprietor is the decision maker, with complete control over the management of the business.

Disadvantages of Sole Proprietorship

1. One individual is responsible for all the work.
2. Unlimited liability for business debts and lawsuits.
3. Can be hard to borrow money or attract investors.

Registering Your Sole Proprietorship

To sell a product or service legally, you need to register your business. In most areas, it is easy and inexpensive to register a sole proprietorship. Once you do, you will have a real business! Contact the county courthouse or local chamber of commerce to find out which licenses and permits are necessary in your area.

Registration usually takes the following steps:

1. Choose a name for your business. Do an online search to make sure the name you've chosen isn't already in use.
2. Fill out a "Doing Business As" (DBA) form, indicating the name of your business and your name. The state will then have a record of the name of the person doing business.
3. Fill out a registration form and pay the fee required in your area.
4. Find out whether a **notary** must witness your signature on the DBA. A notary is a person authorized to witness the signing of documents and to certify them as valid. Most banks have a notary or can refer you to one. There may be one at the registration office. You will have to show the notary your photo ID.

Sales Tax Identification Number

In most towns, you must also obtain a sales tax identification number and collect sales tax on the products you sell. This tax is paid to the state government, not the federal government.

To find out what sales taxes are required in your area, call your state's sales tax office. The office can send you an application for a sales tax number.

Business Cards

After you have registered your business, you should have business cards made. A business card bears your name, title, and business name, and your phone, fax, and Web information. The card should fit into the credit card section of your wallet. Always carry business cards with you. Give them to business contacts and prospective customers.

PARTNERSHIP

A **partnership** is a legal business structure consisting of two or more owners. They make decisions for the business together and share profits, losses, and unlimited liability. Partners can bring different strengths, skills, and resources to the business.

Herbert had a business plan for a T-shirt screening business, but he had no room in his apartment to set up a business. He formed a partnership with Koung because Koung had a garage. Before Herbert and Koung went into business together, I warned them that their partnership could ruin their friendship. I counseled them to write down all their agreements. They did, and their business (and friendship) has lasted seven years so far.

Partnership disagreements can destroy a business. If you form a partnership, be sure to write out a formal agreement with your partner. State each partner's financial and work obligations to the business. It's a good idea to see a lawyer and draw up a **partnership agreement** that carefully defines the responsibilities of each partner and how profits and investments will be shared.

Learn the Lingo

A **partnership agreement** is a legal document that clearly defines how the work, responsibilities, rewards, and liabilities of a partnership will be shared by the partners. It also specifies what will happen if a partner dies or decides to leave the business. A well-written partnership agreement can help partners avoid conflicts and concentrate on managing and growing the business.

Before you sign a partnership agreement, have a lawyer go over it for you first!

Types of Partnerships

There are three types of partnership arrangements:

1. **General partnerships** divide profits, liability, and management duties equally among partners.
2. **Limited partnerships** are more complex than general partnerships. Limited partnerships specify different degrees of liability for each partner, and different degrees of involvement with managing the business. These limits are tied to the amount of money each partner has invested. Limited partners generally just want to invest money in a business; they do not wish to be involved in its day-to-day operation, and they want to limit their liability. The business is usually managed by one partner who is designated as the "general partner."
3. **Joint ventures** are general partnerships that are set up only for a limited period of time, or for a single project.

Advantages of Partnership

1. Simple to set up.
2. Brings the skills, time, energy, and capital of at least two individuals to the business.
3. Can be easier for a partnership to borrow money or obtain outside investors.
4. Employees can be motivated by promises that they can become partners if they work hard.

Disadvantages of Partnership

1. Any profit is split between the partners.
2. Each partner is responsible (and liable!) for the business-related actions of all the others. In a general partnership, they each have unlimited liability.
3. Disagreements between partners can cause problems.

Read a Classic

Learn how to develop great business relationships with Dale Carnegie's famous book *How to Win Friends and Influence People.* Many successful people have credited this book with teaching them how to overcome shyness, build self-confidence, and, well, get people to do what they want!

CORPORATION

As soon as you can afford to spend $500 to incorporate, you should consider doing so to shield your personal assets. A small business with fewer than seventy-five employees can incorporate as a Subchapter S corporation.

Any type of **corporation** is an independent legal entity owned by shareholders. This means that the corporation itself, not the shareholders who own it, is held legally liable for the actions and debts the business incurs. The business itself is considered a type of "person" (often referred to as an "entity") under the law, and limited liability is granted to the business owner(s).

If a corporation is sued, only the business's assets can be sold to settle the suit or pay debts. The courts are not allowed to go after the personal assets of the business owners.

Learn the Lingo

The word "corporation" is derived from *corpus,* Latin for "body."

Although a corporation may have only one owner, most have multiple owners. A **share of stock** is a unit of ownership in a corporation. Anyone who owns a share of a company, whether it is incorporated or not, is a **shareholder**. Shares of corporations are called **stock** and stock owners are called **stockholders**.

Corporations sell shares to raise money. They may limit share ownership (to family members, for example) or sell to the general public through the **stock market**. The stock market is not one single place; rather, it is a collection of different stock exchanges, such as the New York Stock Exchange and NASDAQ, where shares of stock may be listed, bought, and sold. "Going public" by selling stock to the public in an **initial public offering (IPO)** enables corporations to raise financing.

Shareholders receive **equity** (financial ownership) in the corporation. In other words, anyone who owns at least one share is an owner. Each share may earn its owner a **dividend,** which is a portion of the corporation's profit.

Most states require a corporation to have a board of directors. This is a group of shareholders who are elected by the other shareholders to manage the company. The board of directors has the power to hire and fire and to spend or not spend the company's money. Some entrepreneurs, in fact, have been fired from their own companies by their boards of directors!

Apple Computer founder Steve Jobs, for example, was fired by John Sculley, the executive from Pepsi whom Apple brought on as CEO to run the company and oversee Jobs. Jobs clashed with Sculley, and Sculley canned him. In 1997, a foundering Apple rehired Jobs as CEO.

"My sense is that it probably would never have broken down between Steve and me if we had figured out different roles," Sculley told the *Daily Beast* in 2010. "Maybe he should have been the CEO and I should have been the president. It should have been worked out ahead of time, and that's one of those things you look to a really good board [of directors] to do."

Advantages of a Corporation

1. The life span of a corporation is not tied to the life span of its owners. Many of America's largest corporations have been in business for hundreds of years. Management of a corporation is delegated to the board of directors, who hire the corporation's managers. All of this means corporations can raise and borrow money more easily than sole proprietorships and partnerships can.
2. A corporation may issue stock to raise money. Essentially, the company sells pieces of itself to stockholders, who then become co-owners of the company. Some corporations also issue stock to their employees, using employee stock ownership plans, or ESOPs.
3. A corporation provides limited liability. Unlike sole proprietorships and partnerships, the owners of a corporation cannot have their personal assets taken and sold to pay business lawsuit settlements or debts. Only the assets of the corporation can be used to pay corporate debts. When Jerry started his DJ business at age sixteen, he was

spinning records for local parties. Today, his Nu X-Perience Sound and Lighting Company provides sound and lights for parties and parades. Now that he's dealing with heavy lighting equipment that could conceivably hurt someone in an accident, Jerry has incorporated to protect his personal assets.

Disadvantages of a Corporation

1. They are more difficult and expensive to set up and maintain than simpler business legal structures. Corporations are regulated under state laws, so a corporation must remain in accordance with the laws of the state where the business is located. States require corporations to follow very specific procedures for keeping records and selling shares.

2. Corporate profit is taxed twice. Corporations are not taxed in the same way as sole proprietorships and partnerships are. First, the corporation must file its own tax return and pay corporate income tax on its earnings. Later, when the corporation distributes its earnings as dividends to stockholders, the stockholders must include the dividends as personal income on their tax returns.

Types of Corporations

Incorporation is beneficial because it enables a business owner to raise money by selling equity and provides liability protection.

Most corporations are **C corporations,** or "C corps." There are other types of corporations, however, that are appropriate for different types of businesses.

1. NONPROFIT CORPORATION

A nonprofit corporation must have a specific mission to improve society. Churches, museums, charitable foundations, and trade associations are examples of nonprofit corporations.

Nonprofit corporations are **tax-exempt**. They do not pay taxes on their income because the income is being used to help society. On the other hand, nonprofits may not sell stock or pay dividends. No one owns a nonprofit corporation.

2. SUBCHAPTER S CORPORATION

A **Subchapter S corporation** limits the number of stockholders to seventy-five. It offers most of the limited liability protection of the corporation, but Subchapter S corporate income is taxed only once—as the personal income of the owners.

Many small companies are Subchapter S corporations because this legal structure allows a small company to avoid the double taxation of corporations.

3. BENEFIT CORPORATION (B CORP)

A **benefit corporation,** or "B corp," is required by law to benefit society as well as create profit for shareholders. B corps must undergo annual audits to prove that they have a positive impact on the environment, the community, their employees, and society.

Super Success Story

In 2012, Ben & Jerry's became the first subsidiary of a publicly traded company to become a certified B corporation. Founded in 1978, Ben & Jerry's is considered a pioneer in the socially responsible businesses movement in the United States. But in 2000, when Unilever acquired the business, some had concerns that Ben & Jerry's might struggle to maintain its values.

Unilever, however, agreed to help Ben & Jerry's achieve B corp status. Ben and Jerry's changed its charter to say that founders or the board can consider the community, employees, and social impact as well as shareholder profit when making a business decision.

4. FLEXIBLE PURPOSE CORPORATION (FLEX C)

A **flexible purpose corporation,** or "Flex C," is a class of corporation in California that is free from the corporate requirement to maximize profit as long as it is fulfilling at least one "special purpose" defined in its charter. This "special purpose" must create a benefit for society.

Unlike a benefit corporation, a flexible purpose corporation does not have to undergo yearly audits to prove that it is benefiting society. It is up to the shareholders to make sure the corporation stays on course with its stated "special purpose."

5. EMPLOYEE-OWNED CORPORATION

An **employee-owned corporation** is created when a company provides its workforce with ownership in the company through an **employee stock ownership plan (ESOP)**. Shares are given to employees as part of their compensation. Typically, the shares are held in an ESOP trust by the corporation until the employee retires or leaves the company. At that point the employee may sell the shares.

Notable U.S. employee-owned corporations include the 150,000-employee supermarket chain Publix Super Markets, McCarthy Building Companies, and photography studio company Lifetouch.

LIMITED LIABILITY COMPANY (LLC)

A **limited liability company** combines the best features of partnerships and corporations, making it an excellent choice for many small businesses. The LLC offers a more flexible structure and more flexible cost- and profit-sharing arrangements, making it a popular business structure for entrepreneurs.

With an LLC, income is taxed only once, as the personal income of the partners. The partners receive the same protection of their personal assets from creditors and lawsuits, however, that they would receive within a corporate business structure.

In addition, many of the restrictions that apply to Subchapter S corporations—such as the number and type of shareholders—do not apply to LLCs, making them even more attractive.

COOPERATIVE

A **cooperative** is a business that is owned, controlled, and operated by its members. They pool their money to buy resources, market their products, and sell them. Farmers form cooperatives, for example, to buy farming equipment that they share, and to sell their crops.

In the United States, cooperatives are often organized as corporations under state-specific laws. Cooperatives typically share their earnings with members as dividends, which are divided among the members according to their participation in the enterprise.

TYPES OF BUSINESS OWNERSHIP

Ownership Issues	Sole Proprietorship	General or Limited Partnership	C Corporation	Subchapter S Corporation	Nonprofit Corporation	Limited Liability Company
Who owns?	Proprietor	Partners	Stockholders	Stockholders	No one	Members
What is liability?	Unlimited	Limited in most cases	Limited	Limited	Limited	Limited
How is it taxed?	Individual rate (lowest rate)	Individual rate (lowest rate)	Corporate rate ("double taxation")	Individual (lowest rate)	None	Individual (lowest rate)
How are profits distributed?	Proprietor receives all	Partners receive profits according to partnership agreement	Earnings paid to stockholders as dividends in proportion to the number of shares owned	Earnings paid to stockholders as dividends in proportion to the number of shares owned	Surplus cannot be distributed	Members receive profits per agreed-on operating procedure
Who votes on policy?	Not necessary	Partners	Common voting stockholders	Common voting stockholders	Board of directors/trustees agreement	Members per agreed-on operating procedure
How long can company exist?	Terminates on death of owner	Terminates on death of partner	Unlimited	Unlimited	Unlimited through trustees	Variable
How easy is it to capitalize?	Difficult	Easier than sole proprietorship	Very easy (ownership is sold as shares of stock)	Same as partnership	Difficult (there is no ownership to sell as stock)	Same as partnership

EVERY ENTREPRENEUR NEEDS A BOARD OF ADVISORS

A **board of advisors** is a group of people who agree to help you make decisions about your business. If you are not going to incorporate, you don't need a board of directors, but nothing says you can't build a board of advisors.

If you want to start designing your own line of clothing for snowboarding, for example, your board of advisors might include:

- A friend who is a competitive snowboarder and can test your clothing and connect you with snowboarding competitions and potential customers.
- An uncle who has worked in the fashion industry and can connect you with pattern makers and suppliers.
- A friend with a degree in fashion design who's working for a major designer.
- A sibling who owns and operates his or her own business.

Choose people who can help your business because they have some knowledge that you don't have and contacts they are willing to share with you. Look for those who can make key introductions that can help your business grow.

Ask your board to meet personally with you for a brainstorming session at least once a month. Keep them up to date on any press you receive and make sure you give them samples of your product or service to enjoy and share with their friends and family.

An Entrepreneur Like You

Zoe Damacela

ZOE DAMACELA APPAREL

http://zoedamacela.com

Zoe Damacela grew up in a single-parent home, with a mother who was struggling to make ends meet. The two lived on food stamps and moved constantly, spending many nights sleeping in relatives' guest rooms, on floors, and in basements. "I didn't know that things could be better," Zoe says.

Her greatest life lesson came at the age of eight. Zoe desperately wanted a scooter, but her mother couldn't afford the $60 price tag. She told her daughter that if Zoe could raise half the cost of the scooter, she would come up with the rest.

"I pulled out my construction paper, my markers, and my stickers and started to make dozens of greeting cards," Zoe recalls. She spent the next day selling her greeting cards for $2 each. By nightfall she had the $30 she needed. "That's what sparked my interest in business," she explains.

Over the next five years, the young entrepreneur sold jewelry and artwork. But when Zoe got her first sewing machine as a gift, she found her true calling. She took a sewing class and began making clothes for herself and her friends.

At fourteen, Zoe starting selling custom-made clothes. "I felt a great sense of pride because I made the money myself," she says. At the time, however, Zoe was underpricing her clothing. "I was charging $40 for dresses that should have cost $250," she notes.

So, during her junior year, Zoe enrolled in an entrepreneurship course at Whitney M. Young Magnet High School. "It totally changed my outlook on business," she says, "and taught me to be more responsible and focused."

She wrote a business plan for Zoe Damacela Apparel that took top honors at the NFTE Chicago Citywide Business Plan Competition, and placed second in the

NFTE National Youth Entrepreneurship Challenge. She used the prize money to expand her business.

Today, Zoe pays herself $20 an hour and reinvests most of her profits in state-of-the art sewing machines and other equipment. Zoe has worked with Chicago designers Nicole Valeri and Tennille White, and she has gained valuable experience in fashion show production.

The young entrepreneur has her own website and style blog, and she has been featured on the Oprah Winfrey Network and *The Tyra Banks Show*. She even spoke at the Clinton Global Initiative about how entrepreneurship changed her life.

Zoe is attending Northwestern University on a full scholarship. Eventually, she plans to open her own store. Her advice to other aspiring young entrepreneurs: "Find something that you're good at and enjoy, and figure out a way to turn it into a business."

Think Like an Entrepreneur

1. Do you have any hobbies or interests that you could develop into a business?
2. How much are you thinking of charging for your product or service? Do you think you are under- or overcharging? How could you find out?
3. Are there any classes you could take that would help you improve your skills or run your business? Some good places to look include community colleges and community centers such as Boys & Girls Clubs.

CHAPTER 5

RAISING THE MONEY TO START IT UP!

FINANCING STRATEGIES THAT WORK FOR THE YOUNG ENTREPRENEUR

A bank is a place that will lend you money
if you can prove that you don't need it.

—Bob Hope

As mentioned in chapter 2, the Body Shop was started by young British mother Anita Roddick, who just wanted to support her two daughters. Today, there are more than 2,400 Body Shop stores in sixty-one countries around the world.

Back in the 1970s, however, banks refused to lend Roddick money for her business because she was a woman. Since borrowing was not an option, Roddick sold half of her would-be company to her friend Ian McGlinn. In exchange, he invested £4,000 (around $7,000) in her company. In return for his investment in Roddick's business, McGlinn was entitled to a share of the Body Shop's profits.

McGlinn's investment grew to be worth more than $240 million, yet Roddick always said she had no regrets about their deal. Without McGlinn's financing, she would not have been able to start her business!

FINANCING

Raising money to start or expand a business is called **financing**. Sometimes entrepreneurs can raise all the money they need to start and operate their businesses by themselves, through their earnings and savings. If they cannot, they need to either borrow money or sell some of the company.

How much money will you need to get your business going? A **start-up investment** is the amount of money you will need to get your business started.

Learn the Lingo

The start-up investment is also called seed money or **start-up capital**.

The start-up investment for a new company has two components:
1. Start-up costs
2. Cash reserves (for emergency fund and reserve for fixed expenses)

Start-Up Costs

The start-up costs for opening a restaurant would include purchasing stoves, food processors, tables, chairs, dishes, silverware, and other items that won't be replaced frequently. The start-up costs might also include purchasing land on which to have the restaurant built, or paying for the renovations needed for an existing space.

Terry wants to start a new business called The Total Taco. He plans on selling his specialty tacos from a food cart. The start-up costs for The Total Taco are:

The Total Taco Start-Up Costs

Food cart (plug-in, with refrigeration bins)	$3,000
License from the city	$500
Starting supplies of tortillas, fillings, condiments, etc.	$700
Business cards and flyers (advertising)	$400
Commercial refrigerator, cabinets (to store food)	$800
Total start-up costs	$5,400

Cash Reserves

In addition to start-up costs, you should have adequate cash reserves for:

EMERGENCY FUND

This is money kept on hand for the emergencies and unforeseen costs that often arise when a company is getting off the ground. A good rule of thumb is to have an emergency fund equal to half of the start-up investment. After the initial start-up period is over and things have settled down, an entrepreneur can decide how much money to keep in the emergency fund.

FIXED COSTS

This is enough money to cover your bills (rent, utilities, insurance, and so forth) for at least three months. These costs are called **fixed costs,** because they do not change depending on how many units you sell. Your rent stays the same every month no matter what you sell. The reserve for fixed costs is maintained for the life of the business. It is there to cover the business's fixed costs if the company experiences a downturn in sales.

Include the costs of your emergency fund and the reserve for fixed costs as part of your start-up investment.

> **Start-Up Costs + Emergency Fund (equal to ½ Start-Up Costs)**
> **+ Reserve for Fixed Costs (3 Months of Fixed Costs)**
> **= Start-Up Investment**

The start-up costs for The Total Taco are $5,400. Terry should save up an emergency fund for half of that amount, or $2,700. The monthly fixed costs for The Total Taco are $1,300, so Terry also saves up a three-month reserve for fixed costs, or $3,900.

The total start-up investment for The Total Taco would be:

Start-Up Costs	$5,400
Emergency Fund (½ Start-Up Costs)	$2,700
Reserve for Fixed Costs (Three Months of Fixed Costs)	$3,900
Start-Up Investment	$12,000

To be honest, many small entrepreneurs aren't able to afford to set aside an emergency fund or a reserve for fixed costs. They start their businesses anyway and take their chances. Nevertheless, it is important to address both in your business plan.

Payback

So when will your start-up investment begin to earn you a profit? That's the **payback,** which is the amount of time, measured in months, that it takes a business to earn enough profit to cover its start-up investment.

To calculate payback, you will need to "guesstimate" or "project" how much money your business will earn after expenses each month. This is called **net income**.

**Start-Up Investment ÷ Net Income per Month
= Payback (in Months)**

Let's say that Terry obtains $6,000 in financing from his uncle and is able to contribute an additional $4,000 of his own money. His start-up investment is $10,000. This wasn't the $12,000 he had hoped for, but he decides it's enough to open the business. He thinks he will earn around $2,000 per month after expenses.

$10,000 ÷ $2,000 = 5 Months

It will take Terry approximately five months to pay back the start-up investment.

Math Moment

The start-up investment for your business is $36,000. Your net income per month is $6,000. What is the payback period for your investment?*

---

*   Answer: 6 months.

Return on Investment (ROI)

Just as you want to know when you will earn back your start-up investment, your investors want to know their **return on investment (ROI)**. They want to know what they will get back for investing in your business.

ROI is a percentage that expresses the profitability of your business. Here's how to calculate it.

1. Start with the amount of money you possess at the close of a business period. Call this your end-of-period wealth (A).
2. Subtract the amount of your original investment in the business. Call this investment your beginning-of-period wealth (B).
3. Divide the resulting number by your beginning-of-period wealth.
4. Multiply by 100 to express your return as a percentage.

$$\frac{A - B}{B} \times 100$$

Let's say you invest $10,000 in your business and at the end of the first year your net profit is $15,000.

$$\frac{\$15,000 - \$10,000}{\$10,000} = \frac{\$5,000}{\$10,000} = 0.5 \times 100 = 50\%$$

Your ROI is 50%. Not bad! Most investors want you to prove to them that they will earn an ROI of 45% or more.

WHERE TO GET THE MONEY

There are two places to get the money to start your business—from yourself and from other people. Here are the pros and cons of some common financing strategies used by entrepreneurs to start up their businesses.

Bootstrapping

Have you ever heard the phrase "pulling yourself up by your bootstraps"? It means to do something completely on your own, without any outside help.

Many successful entrepreneurs began their businesses by bootstrapping, using strategies such as:

1. Hiring as few employees as possible; using temporary service agencies for staffing needs to avoid expenses such as health insurance and payroll tax.
2. Leasing rather than buying equipment.

3. Getting suppliers to extend credit terms so the business can take longer to pay its bills.
4. Working from home, or borrowing office space, to save on fixed costs such as rent and utilities.
5. Putting profits back into the business to keep it going.

Using Personal Savings

If you have enough money in your **savings account** for your start-up investment, you can be the sole owner of your business. All the profits will belong to you. But if your business fails, you will have lost all your savings.

In addition, you will have lost the interest the money would have earned in a savings account or another investment. You also have to consider the opportunity cost of using your savings. Is there something else you could have done with the money that would have benefited you more in the long run, such as paying for college?

Using your personal savings to start a business is a very serious undertaking. Make sure to weigh the advantages and disadvantages carefully.

Using Credit Cards

Certainly, some businesses have been financed on credit cards, but this strategy has some *very* significant disadvantages.

The major disadvantage is the interest rate charged by the credit card companies, which is often 20 percent or more. Unless your business is able to make enough profit to pay the total amount you owe each month, the interest payments will add up very quickly.

Some entrepreneurs try to use credit cards with 0 percent introductory rates and 0 percent transfer fees to finance their businesses. This strategy requires vigilance in locating and transferring balances to new low-rate credit cards as soon as the introductory rate expires on the old ones.

Keeping high balances on your credit cards can also damage your credit rating. With a low credit rating, you may not be able to purchase merchandise from your suppliers on account.

Other than in unusual circumstances, where you will very quickly earn back the money you borrow, using credit cards for your start-up investment is *not* a good idea. It's always good to keep a credit card on hand for emergencies, but don't get into the habit of using credit cards to keep your business afloat. It's too expensive.

Other People's Money (OPM)

If you cannot personally supply the start-up investment for a business, consider tapping into **other people's money (OPM)**. There are two ways to raise OPM. Each affects a business differently:

1. **Debt.** The business borrows money and pays it back over a set period of time at a set rate of interest. You could borrow money from family and friends, or ask a bank to finance your business. Corporations sell debt in the form of **bonds**.

2. **Equity.** The business trades a percentage of ownership for money. Like Anita Roddick's friend Ian McGlinn, the equity investor receives a percentage of future profits from the business. Corporations sell equity in the form of **stock**. You cannot sell stock unless your business is incorporated, but you *can* sell equity. You can offer shares of your future profits in exchange for financing.

DEBT FINANCING

To finance through debt, an entrepreneur borrows money from a person or an institution, such as a bank. The entrepreneur signs a promise to repay the sum and also pay **interest**. That promise is called a **promissory note**.

Interest is figured by multiplying the **principal** by the interest rate. The principal is the amount of the loan not including interest payments.

If an entrepreneur borrows $1,200 from his parents and agrees to pay them back in a year, with 10 percent interest, the interest on the loan is:

$$\$1,200 \times .10 = \$120 \text{ interest}$$

The parents would earn $120 in interest for having lent the entrepreneur $1,200.

Advantages of Debt Financing

1. The lender has no say in the future or direction of the business as long as the loan payments are made.
2. Loan payments and interest are predictable.

Disadvantages of Debt Financing

1. If loan payments are not made, the lender can force the business into **bankruptcy** to get the loan back. Bankruptcy is a legal procedure that involves selling off the property of a business that cannot pay its debts, in order to raise money that will be used to pay back creditors.

2. If the business is not incorporated, the lender can go to court and force the business owner to sell personal items such as a home or car in order to pay back the lender.

The beginning entrepreneur should consider taking on debt very carefully. It often takes a long time for a new business to show a profit. The risk of debt is that failure to make loan payments can destroy the business before it gets the chance to prove itself.

Borrowing from Banks

Banks are very careful with their loans: They want to get their money back, with interest.

One of the things a bank looks at when considering loaning money to an entrepreneur is the entrepreneur's credit score. It's hard to get approved without a credit score in the high six hundreds. The credit score sums up your credit history, which is the record of any money you've ever borrowed (college loans, store charge cards, credit cards, car loans, and so forth) and whether you made the required payments on time and in full. This history is what lenders consider when they decide whether to make a loan.

The bank will also look for a track record of success, and it will also want to see a solid business plan.

Learn the Lingo

A **credit score** is a number between 300 and 850 that reflects a person's history of using credit. The higher the number, the more likely the person is deemed to use credit responsibly. If you are turned down for a credit card, you have the right to ask to see your credit score and credit report. You can also investigate your credit score on websites such as www.freecreditscore.com.

To determine how much it might be willing to loan you, the bank will calculate your **bank debt ratio**. This number shows your monthly income compared to your debts.

(Monthly Debt Payments ÷ Monthly Income) × 100
= Bank Debt Ratio (percentage)

A good bank debt ratio is typically 40 percent or less. Banks have found that customers with debt ratios over 40 percent are often unable to repay their loans.

Here's an example: Suppose Artie's Web design business brings in a monthly income of $5,000 and has debt payments of $2,500.

($2,500 ÷ $5,000) × 100 = 50 percent

Wow, half the money the business brings in is going right back out the door to pay off debt. A bank would probably not give Artie another loan.

Banks also use the bank debt ratio to determine how much they will loan you. Let's say Artie has a monthly income of $5,000 and debts of only $1,500. How much might a bank loan Artie then?

($1,500 ÷ $5,000) × 100 = 30 percent

Because Artie is already using 30 percent of his business income to pay its existing debt, the bank might be willing to loan him about 10 percent of his monthly income (40 percent – 30 percent = 10 percent).

Ten percent of his monthly income is $500 ($5,000 × 0.1 = $500). So, Artie could probably borrow an amount that would be repaid at $500 per month. This would allow him to spend 40 percent of his monthly income for debt payments, a percentage that is more acceptable to the bank.

($2,000 ÷ $5,000) × 100 = 40 percent

The actual dollar amount of the loan would vary based on the length of time and the interest rate. But the bank would make sure that Artie's monthly payment would not exceed $500.

The bank will also ask Artie for collateral against a loan. **Collateral** is property or assets that you pledge to a bank to secure a loan. If you fail to repay the loan, the bank will own your collateral and will resell it to get all or some of its money back.

For example, if Artie owns his car, the bank might ask him to use the car as collateral. If he failed to repay the loan, the bank would take possession of the car and sell it.

The bank may also ask Artie to provide a cosigner for a loan. A **cosigner** is an individual who will sign a loan agreement to guarantee the loan payments in case Artie, the first signer, is unable to make them. If Artie asks relatives or friends to cosign his loan and then isn't able to make the payments, they—the cosigners—will have to make them.

The biggest disadvantage of a bank loan for Artie is what happens if he fails to repay it. The bank will probably bring a lawsuit against him. He is likely to lose his business, and his credit rating could be ruined.

You need to be careful when using debt financing. Make sure you can make the payments before you grab the cash.

Math Moment

Calculate a business's bank debt ratio, based on the following data:

Monthly Income: $20,000

Monthly Debt Payments: $4,000

Would this company be a likely prospect for a loan?*

---

* Answers: 20 percent; yes.

Credit Unions

A **credit union** is a nonprofit cooperative organization that offers low-interest loans to members. Many entrepreneurs have financed their businesses through credit union loans.

Credit unions, like banks, will loan you money for growing your business. Credit unions may offer you lower interest rates than banks, however. Because most credit unions will make loans only to members, you must first join the credit union. If you do not meet the membership requirements, you cannot get the loan.

A credit union, just like a bank, may ask for collateral or ask you to provide a cosigner. And, like a bank, if you fail to repay a loan, a credit union can bring a lawsuit against you.

Borrowing from Relatives and Friends

The start-up capital for many businesses has come as a loan from the entrepreneur's relatives or friends. But what happens if your business does not generate sufficient sales to make a profit, or if it fails entirely? How would you feel if you had to tell your friends or relatives that you were unable to repay them?

The advantage of borrowing from relatives or friends is that you have a willing and supportive source of capital for your new business. The pride and confidence they would have in you and your business venture is often worth the risk. You are offering them an opportunity to receive a return on their investment—if your business is successful.

If you are planning to borrow money from friends or relatives for start-up capital, you must thoroughly and honestly explain the risks and the opportunities of the business. Be very clear about the interest rate you will pay, and on what date repayment will be made. Put it all in writing. With proper communication among all parties involved, this financing strategy can be very effective.

Microloans

In the past, small business owners had to go to a bank for a loan. Today, there is another option: the **microloan**. "Micro" means "small," and that's just what a microloan is: a small loan.

A microloan is a relatively small amount of money—typically under $10,000—and generally carries a higher rate of interest than a bank would charge.

Microloans are usually extended to small business owners by nonprofit organizations through the U.S. Small Business Administration. There is also a new movement linking borrowers around the world directly to private lenders through websites such as Kiva (www.kiva.org).

A microloan is ideal for a small start-up company that doesn't need much capital and has a limited credit history.

Game Changer

Kiva is a not-for-profit that connects businesses in need of small amounts of credit with individuals who want to support them. Kiva's mission is "to connect people through lending for the sake of alleviating poverty."

What makes Kiva noteworthy is that its lenders do not receive any interest. Using this person-to-person lending model, the delinquency (late payment) rate has been only 3.82 percent, and the default (failure to pay) rate has been just 1.39 percent. Visit www.kiva .org to follow online journals kept by many Kiva borrowers—in countries from Nicaragua to Nepal—and learn about the exciting small businesses Kiva borrowers have started.

How Overreliance on Debt Financing Almost Took Down Donald Trump

Companies that rely heavily on debt financing are described as "highly **leveraged**." "Leveraged" means financed with debt. This financial strategy works well only when business is very good. When business is slow, debt payments are more difficult to meet.

It is very dangerous for a company to rely solely on debt. Creditors can force the company into bankruptcy or take over company property.

Donald Trump, real estate tycoon and host of the TV show *The Apprentice*, made exactly this mistake in the 1980s. Trump invested millions of dollars in revitalizing Atlantic City's gambling strip. He also bought New York's landmark Plaza hotel and built Trump Tower, a skyscraper of ultraluxurious apartments that were purchased by oil sheikhs and movie stars. Trump owned some very valuable properties—but he was deeply in debt. Soon, Trump couldn't make his loan payments.

Trump was forced by his lenders to sell off his airline, Trump Shuttle, and some of his casinos. By pruning his real estate holdings and paying off some of his debt, Trump was able to make a comeback in the 1990s.

EQUITY FINANCING

In equity financing, shares of ownership of a business are traded for money. Let's say you need to raise $10,000 to start your business. You have $6,000 saved up, and you have borrowed $2,000 from your mom. To raise the last $2,000, you could sell a share of the company to a friend or relative. That person is now a part owner of your company, entitled to a share of its profits.

Only you can decide what percentage of your company you are willing to offer for $2,000. If you give your investor a 10 percent share in exchange for $2,000, that investor is now entitled to 10 percent of the business's profits. The investor is hoping that, over time, 10 percent of your profits will be more than the initial investment of $2,000.

The equity investor assumes greater risk than the debt lender. If the business doesn't make profits, neither does the investor. An equity investor cannot force a business into bankruptcy to get back the original investment. If a business is forced into bankruptcy by its creditors, they get paid off first from the sale of the business's assets. Equity investors have a claim on whatever is left over after debt investors have been paid.

Although the equity investor's risk is higher than that of the debt lender, so is the potential for return. The equity investor could make the investment back many times over if the business prospers. For that reason, he or she accepts a higher level of risk than the debt lender. The debt lender's risk of losing his or her investment is lower, but so is the debt lender's return.

With equity financing, the money doesn't have to be paid back unless the business is successful. However, through giving up ownership, the entrepreneur can lose control of the business to the equity holders.

Read a Classic

Guerrilla Financing: Alternative Techniques to Finance Any Small Business by Bruce Blechman and Jay Conrad Levinson is loaded with great ideas you can use to raise capital.

Advantages of Equity Financing

1. If the business doesn't make a profit, the investor does not get paid. The equity investor cannot force the business into bankruptcy in order to get paid.
2. The equity investor has an interest in seeing the business succeed, and is likely, therefore, to provide helpful advice and valuable contacts.

Disadvantages of Equity Financing

1. Through giving up ownership, the entrepreneur can lose control of the business to the equity holders.

2. Equity financing is riskier for the investor, so the investor frequently wants both a say in how the company is run and a higher rate of return than a lender.

Giving Equity Shares to Relatives and Friends

Getting equity financing from relatives and friends is similar to borrowing money from relatives and friends—with the same advantages and disadvantages—but with one big difference. Your friends and relatives now own part of the business. If they feel you are running it badly, or if they want to question a business decision, they have a right to tell you. Make sure you want to deal with that before you accept equity financing.

Angel Investors

Angels are wealthy private individuals who are interested in investing in entrepreneurial ventures for a variety of reasons, from friendship to a desire to support entrepreneurship in a given field. Like any investor, an angel wants to make a profit but may have additional reasons for investing. Bill Gates, for example, has invested in several biotechnology start-ups because of his interest in that field.

If your business has good management in place and a solid business plan, you might be able to raise angel financing. This type of investment is typically in the $100,000 to $500,000 range. Angels tend to seek a return of ten times their investment at the end of five years, but their requirements vary widely.

Angels can be hard to find, but there are a number of national and regional venture capital networks, which often connect entrepreneurs and angels. Regional networks can be helpful because angels tend to invest in businesses they can visit frequently. New websites, such as Angel List (https://angel.co), are tapping into social media to help entrepreneurs reach beyond their own regions as well.

If you search for angel investors, look for people who are interested in or familiar with your markets and field. Angels prefer manufacturing, energy, technology, and some service businesses. They tend to avoid retail ventures.

Sometimes an angel takes an interest in an individual entrepreneur or might just want to be involved in something interesting. Because of a particular interest, an angel will often accept a lower return on an investment than other sources of equity capital.

Typically, angel investors invest only on an equity basis; they don't make loans. Ideally, you'll want to get one angel in place and then ask that person to help you find more investors.

Tech U

Search for angel investors on the following websites:

Accion USA	www.accionusa.org
Angel Capital Association	angelcapitalassociation.org
Association for Enterprise Opportunity	www.microenterpriseworks.org
Angel List	https://angel.co
Opportunity Finance Network	www.opportunityfinance.net

Be wary of any service that requires up-front payment, will not provide complete references, or in any other way raises a red flag. If a financing source seems to be too good to be true, it often is.

That does not mean you should ignore or reject all online options. Explore them, but use good judgment.

There are also investors and investment companies who specialize in financing high-potential entrepreneurial companies. Because they often provide the initial equity investment, or venture capital, to start a business venture, they are called **venture capitalists**.

Venture capitalists seek high rates of return. They typically expect to earn six times their money back over a five-year period, or a 45 percent return on investment.

Professional venture capitalists will not usually invest in a company unless its business plan shows it is likely to generate sales of at least $25 million within five years. The ideal candidates for venture capital are businesses with financial projections that support revenue expectations of more than $50 million within five years, growing at 30 to 50 percent per year, with pretax profit margins over 20 percent.

If your business plan supports those kinds of numbers, you may be able to interest venture capitalists in your idea. Venture capitalists want equity in return for their capital. They are willing to take the higher risk for higher returns.

Venture capitalists sometimes seek a majority interest in a business so that they will have the final word in management decisions. They can structure deals in a variety of ways.

Venture capitalists typically reap the return on their equity investments by selling their percentage share of the business to another investor through a private transaction, or waiting until the company goes public (starts selling stock on the open market) and selling their shares for cash.

Steve Jobs: Losing—and Regaining—Control of Apple

Relying too heavily on equity can be the downfall of a business owner, because if you sell more than 50 percent of your company, you can be outvoted and lose control of it. To finance Ford Motor Company, Henry Ford gave up 75 percent of his business for $28,000 in capital that he desperately needed. It took Ford many years to regain control of his company.

Still, many small business owners turn to venture capital when they want to grow the business and banks are not willing to lend them money. When Steve Jobs and Stephen Wozniak started Apple Computer, they were young men with very little money, and debt financing was out of their reach. To raise money, they sold off chunks of the company.

By the late 1980s, Apple was very successful—so successful that Jobs was able to hire a prominent PepsiCo executive, John Sculley, to take over as Apple's chief executive.

As mentioned earlier, Sculley and Jobs clashed, and Sculley set out to persuade Apple's board of directors that Jobs was a disruptive influence on the company. Eventually, the shareholders had to settle the matter. The number of votes each shareholder had was related to the number of shares he or she owned. Jobs didn't own enough of Apple's equity to fight off Sculley's effort to fire him. He was outvoted and thrown out of the company he had started.

After leaving Apple, Jobs founded NeXT Computer in 1985, with $7 million. A year later, Jobs was running out of money, and, with no product on the horizon, he appealed for venture capital. He attracted the attention of billionaire Ross Perot, who invested heavily in the company.

In 1996, Apple bought NeXT for $427 million, in order to bring Jobs back to Apple as CEO. Under Jobs's guidance, the company increased sales significantly with popular new products such as the iPod and iPhone.

Jobs earned only $1 a year as CEO of Apple, but he held 5.426 million Apple shares that, all told, were worth $2.1 billion. Jobs liked to joke that he was paid 50 cents for attending one meeting and 50 cents for his performance.

Super Success Story

When Debbi Fields was nineteen, she married an older man who was a brilliant economist. Fields wanted to accomplish something, too. She had baked her popular chocolate chip cookies for friends and families since she was thirteen, so she decided to start a business selling her cookies to the public.

No one—not her family, not her friends, not even her husband—thought this was a good idea. Her cookies were soft and chewy, not crisp like store brands. They needed to be eaten fresh to taste their best.

Fields refused to abandon her idea, so her husband decided to give her his full support, even though he thought it would never work. The banker who had given her and her husband the mortgage on their house arranged a loan. He, too, told her that her business would never work, but he trusted the couple to pay back the loan.

Fields opened a small store in Palo Alto, California, in August 1977. On her first day of business, she hadn't sold a single cookie by noon. Trying not to panic, Fields loaded up a tray with cookies and walked around the shopping arcade offering them to shoppers for free.

Her strategy worked. Within an hour, customers were at her store buying cookies. She sold $50 worth that day and $75 worth the next. She was in business, and she had discovered a strategy. To this day, Mrs. Fields stores give customers free samples to encourage them to buy cookies.

The business grew rapidly, but most of the profits were earmarked to pay off bank loans used to open new stores. Despite her success, Fields constantly had to fight for financing from the banks. Again and again she was told that selling cookies was not a "real" business like selling steel or cars.

In 1986, her husband joined her business. Although the company was now profitable, bank loans were still needed to open new stores. The Fieldses were tired of dealing with bankers who doubted their business plan, so they set out to replace their debt financing with equity financing. They decided to sell shares in the company to the public and use the cash to pay off the banks and finance further expansion.

The Fieldses sold stock on the London Stock Exchange's unlisted securities market first, because this approach was easier and cheaper than selling stock on the American market. The stock was offered in London in the spring of 1986. It did not do well at first because the company was not that well known in Britain, but eventually the stock price improved.

When the stock was offered in the United States the following year, it did very well. Today, Mrs. Fields Cookies is a $450 million company financed with a blend of debt and equity.

OTHER FINANCING SOURCES

Here are some more sources of financing for entrepreneurs:

SMALL BUSINESS INVESTMENT COMPANIES

Small business investment companies (SBICs) provide equity financing, as well as loans, for small businesses. SBICs are partially financed through guaranteed loans from the government. SBICs charge lower interest rates than other sources of debt financing such as banks and credit unions. There are hundreds of SBICs that specialize in equity investments and loans for small businesses.

MINORITY ENTERPRISE SMALL BUSINESS INVESTMENT COMPANIES

African Americans, Hispanics, Asians, and other minority groups—as well as women—can apply to **minority enterprise small business investment companies (MESBICs)** for start-up capital. MESBICs are private investment firms, chartered by the SBA, that provide both debt and equity financing for new small businesses. Just as with SBICs, MESBICs often accept lower interest rates than other sources of debt financing.

CUSTOMER FINANCING

As your customers get to know and appreciate your products or services, some of them may become willing to provide either debt or equity financing for your business.

BARTER FINANCING

Your hardware store may sell lawn mowers, while a local landscaping business provides a lawn-mowing service. As the owner of the hardware store, you need to have your property properly landscaped, so you make a deal with the owner of the landscaping business. You trade two of your lawn mowers to the landscaper for three months of landscaping services. The advantage of a barter system is that both parties get what they want without spending any money.

CROWDFUNDING

Increasingly, young entrepreneurs are turning to **crowdfunding**—raising money from fans of their products or services—to finance their businesses. Although a crowdfunding website like Kickstarter (www.kickstarter.com) bans start-up businesses and allows money to be raised only for creative projects, others, like Indiegogo (www.indiegogo.com), are great for raising money to start a business. You have to build a following through social media first for crowdfunding to work, though.

Success Stories

Some fun crowdfunding success stories include:

FORM 1: Researchers from the MIT Media Lab created an affordable, professional 3-D printer for the masses, and the masses responded with more than two thousand backers and nearly $3 million pledged (far beyond the project's $100,000 goal).

TikTok: Chicago designer Scott Wilson made history as one of the biggest successes to ever hit Kickstarter at the time. His TikTok and LunaTik wristbands, which converted the Apple iPod Nano into a watch, attracted 13,500-plus backers, and almost $1 million in funding. He'd originally asked for $15,000. TikTok and LunaTik are now sold by Amazon, Walmart, and Apple.

Amanda Palmer: Singer Amanda Palmer's record deal is the highest-funded Kickstarter music project ever, breaking the million-dollar mark for her record, art book, and tour with Grand Theft Orchestra. Her original goal of $100,000 was reached within a day.

Diaspora: Diaspora is an open source social network created by four young programmers from NYU. The students blew through their original $10,000 goal to raise more than $200,000 from 6,479 backers—including Facebook founder Mark Zuckerberg.

BUSINESS INCUBATORS

A **business incubator** is a place that affordably provides entrepreneurs with everything from office space to access to equipment such as photocopiers, computers, and fax machines, plus access to advisors and potential investors.

The Business Development Incubator, sponsored by the Temple University Small Business Development Center, works with entrepreneurs between ages fifteen and twenty-two. Entrepreneurs who qualify pay a small fee per month for a desk and file space, a computer, a phone, and a fax. They also receive counseling and can attend entrepreneurship workshops and seminars.

How do you know if an incubator is right for you?

- Know your needs and work habits. Some facilities are open 24/7, while others allow entrepreneurs to work only during fixed business hours. If you are a night owl, be sure you can access your office when you want.
- Read the fine print. Be cautious about giving away an equity stake in a start-up business to an incubator organization. Read all agreements carefully for any language that might give shares or rights to the incubator.
- Question incubator fund-raising promises. Ask for references and proof that the incubator has connections that will be useful to you in raising financing for your start-up.
- Compare pricing. Be wary of incubators that try to sell you business support services such as legal assistance, accounting, Web design and hosting, advertising, and so forth, or that contractually require you to use their preferred service **vendors**.

To look for an incubator near you, start with your local universities and colleges. This could be a great option for you!

Learn the Lingo

Vendors (also called suppliers) are businesses that sell products or services to other businesses.

USING A BUSINESS PLAN TO RAISE CAPITAL

To approach a bank for a loan or an investor for capital, you'll need a business plan. This document explains exactly what your business idea is, how you intend to market your product or service, and your plan for operating the business. You may have a brilliant business idea, but if it is not set forth in a well-written plan that includes **sales forecasts**, projected financial statements, and a marketing plan, no potential investor will be interested.

Investors crave information. The more information you offer investors about exactly how their money will be used to develop, market, distribute, and sell your product or service, the more willing they will be to invest in your business. Your plan should be so thoughtful and thorough that the only question it raises in an investor's mind is "How much can I invest in this exciting new business?"

At the end of this book is a business plan workbook you can use to create your own business plan. The business plan includes:

- **Executive summary:** One- or two-page summary of the business plan's highlights and the key selling points of the investment opportunity
- **Mission statement:** One- or two-sentence summary of the aims and values of your company
- Your qualifications
- Analysis of your competition
- Your competitive advantages: What do you do better than the competition?
- Short- and long-term growth goals
- Challenges to your business
- Marketing plan
- Sales methods and estimates
- Financial information and operations
- Projected financial statements (**income statement, balance sheet, cash flow statement**)
- Start-up investment
- Financial ratio analysis
- Exit strategy

Nearly all the young entrepreneurs profiled in this book succeeded, in part, because they wrote a business plan before they made a single sale. A well-written plan not only helps you raise money; it also guides you as you develop your business.

As you write your plan, problems you might not have thought of before will be uncovered. Working them out on paper will save you time and money down the road.

The Lean Start-Up

Although writing a business plan is a very valuable exercise, not to mention a great tool to raise capital, you might want to explore the **lean start-up** concept developed by Eric Ries in 2008. A lean start-up is a business started with minimal capital and planning, and the flexibility to evolve in response to feedback from customers. Ries argued that entrepreneurs should launch their business first, and plan second. In other words, leap in and adjust as you go!

Zappos, the world's largest online shoe store, did just that. When starting the store, founder Nick Swinmurn simply took pictures of shoes from stores and posted them online. Rather than investing in warehouses and thousaands of pairs of shoes, Swinmurn plunged right in—essentially conducting his market research while already in business. He could quickly see which types of shoes customers wanted, what sizes were most popular, and so forth, without pouring a lot of money into the business.

Swinmurn created what Ries calls a "façade"—anything that gets your business up and running in front of customers, like a website, for example. He started Zappos with what Ries labels **minimum viable product (MVP),** the smallest amount of product needed to begin selling to potential customers.

The deal-of-the-day website Groupon is another fascinating example of a business that got up and running using lean start-up ideas. Groupon founder Andrew Mason started by rapidly assembling a set of deals without a lot of focus on the presentation. He incentivized customers to give rapid feedback so he could quickly find out which deals were the most popular—and then he'd go out and get more of those deals to sell.

In short, the lean start-up favors getting the business up and running as soon as possible, instead of doing a lot of pre-planning, and using customer feedback to tweak the business. Ries believes that relying on customer feedback during **product development** ensures that the business does not invest time designing features or services that consumers do not want.

Ries says, "Lean has nothing to do with how much money a company raises"; instead, being lean is about listening to the specific demands of consumers and responding to them rapidly, using the least amount of resources possible.

Read a Classic

In his bestseller *The Lean Start-Up: How Today's Entrepreneurs Use Continuous Innovation to Create Radically Successful Businesses,* Eric Ries explains his innovative business philosophy in detail.

Michael Simmons and Sheena Lindahl
EMPACT

http://iempact.com

Michael Simmons caught the entrepreneurship bug early. Simmons ran a Web development shop in high school. "My friend and I made forty thousand dollars our senior year of high school, working ten hours per week," Simmons told *Inc.* "It completely changed my paradigm of what was possible as a young person." In college he wrote a book called *The Student Success Manifesto.* He also taught inner-city high school students about entrepreneurship.

At NYU, Michael met his girlfriend Sheena Lindahl, who shared his entrepreneurial mindset. At seventeen, Sheena became financially independent from her parents. She paid her way through college by working at GreenHills Ventures, a venture capital firm, and teaching at Project READ, a nonprofit organization that seeks to raise the reading skills of inner-city children.

Together, Michael and Sheena founded Empact, which is dedicated to helping college students realize their dreams through entrepreneurship, by providing networking opportunities, mentorship, and education. Michael and Sheena also got married and started a family.

Making a Strategic Shift

At first, Michael and Sheena had intended to be publishers of entrepreneurial books, articles, and guides. After publishing *The Student Success Manifesto,* they believed they were moving in the right direction. The book was profitable, but it wasn't earning enough to support them full-time.

To sell more books, Michael and Sheena began seeking bulk purchases from schools and other youth organizations. One marketing strategy included traveling to talk to groups of students when their schools purchased books. This tactic helped Michael and Sheena realize that people would pay them to speak, whether books were purchased or not. So, they started charging for their speaking services.

Next, they launched the Extreme Entrepreneurship Tour (EET). Each tour event includes a successful young entrepreneur as the keynote speaker, exhibits, a workshop, speed networking, and a panel discussion with local entrepreneurs.

Event organizers can visit the EET website at www.extremetour.org. The schools are responsible for the promotion, event venue, refreshments, and the like. EET develops and prints an event program/workbook with speaker biographies.

Michael and Sheena have found sponsorship financing to be very effective for EET. Each tour event is financed by local companies and economic/workforce development organizations. In turn, student body participation and media coverage benefit the event sponsors by allowing them to connect with hundreds or even thousands of students in a positive way.

Empact has held more than four hundred events exposing young people to entrepreneurship through its Extreme Entrepreneurship Tour, supporting early stage entrepreneurs through its Virtual Speaker Series and JourneyPage Virtual Business Incubator, and celebrating the role of young entrepreneurs through its annual Empact100 List, which showcases top entrepreneurs under thirty.

Think Like an Entrepreneur

1. How did Michael and Sheena build their entrepreneurial knowledge/skills?
2. How do Michael and Sheena finance their EET tours?
3. How do they keep their business on track?

PART 2
CONNECT WITH CUSTOMERS

CHAPTER 6

MARKET RESEARCH

AFFORDABLE WAYS TO FIND OUT WHO YOUR CUSTOMERS ARE, WHAT THEY WANT, AND HOW TO REACH THEM

The aim of marketing is to know and
understand the customer so well the product
or service fits him and sells itself.

—Peter F. Drucker

Once you have created a product or service that you want to sell, how do you get people to buy it? First, you have to conduct some **market research,** which will help you figure out who your potential customers are, what they want, and how to reach them and get them excited about your business. In this chapter we'll explore affordable tactics you can use to survey your potential customers . . . and the competition!

WHO IS IN YOUR TARGET MARKET?

A **market** is a group of potential customers—people or businesses—who are willing and able to purchase a particular product or service. You reach them through **marketing**. Marketing is any type of communication you use—from email blasts to a sign on the corner pointing toward your store—to reach the people in your market and convince them to buy from your business. Market research tells you what kind of marketing will work.

The goal of market research is to identify your unique **target market**—the group of customers most likely to want to buy your product or service—and learn about them. Once you understand who the people in your target market are, you will be better able to come up with innovative ways to reach them with your marketing.

It's tempting to try to sell your product or service to everyone in the world. This is called a **mass market** approach. For most small businesses, this approach isn't the best strategy. Why spend time and money trying to sell your graffiti-artist-designed sneakers to your grandmother? Selling to a mass market takes a great deal of resources. Instead, use market research to pinpoint your target market.

MARKET THE BENEFITS, NOT THE FEATURES

Why does a customer go to a hardware store to buy a drill? Because he needs to make a hole. The *hole* is what the customer needs, not the drill. If the hole could be bought at the hardware store, the customer wouldn't bother to buy the drill. If you are marketing a drill, therefore, your marketing should explain to the customer what good holes your drill makes. That is the benefit of your product.

The **features** of a product are what it does and how it appears to the senses (sight, sound, taste, smell, and touch). The **benefits** of a product are the reasons customers choose to buy it. Examples of benefits include saving time, increasing social status, protecting the family, getting rid of a problem, improving a relationship, reducing worry, providing entertainment, and saving money.

Nike sells sneakers. It distributes sneakers to stores where customers can buy them. But Nike also *markets* sneakers. Its marketing department has done market research that determined that what Nike's target market wants most from sneakers is to feel inspired to exercise. So Nike's marketing department creates advertisements and promotions designed to persuade customers that Nike sneakers will inspire them to "Just Do It." The inspiration is the benefit Nike provides.

Marketing is an art. It requires creative thinking and boldness. To market a product successfully, ask yourself: What does the customer need this product to do? Answering that question will help you identify a benefit of your product or service. All you have to do next is show your customer that your product provides that benefit.

Try It!

A business school professor drove a van onto the stage of his lecture hall and challenged his students to spend the rest of the class coming up with one thousand uses for it. Students brainstormed everything from using the van as a garden planter to turning it into a small mobile apartment.

List twenty benefits that your product or service could provide for a customer. Think outside the box—get creative!

WHAT'S YOUR COMPETITIVE ADVANTAGE?

Once you've brainstormed the benefits your product or service can deliver, it's time to figure out your **competitive advantage**. Your competitive advantage is the one benefit you can deliver better than the competition. It's also sometimes called a business's "core competence."

Can you hit a lower price? Can you deliver better quality? What is special about your business? If you can answer that question with confidence, you have hit upon your competitive advantage.

If you are clear about your competitive advantage, your marketing decisions will start to fall into place. Every ad, graphic, and promotion should be designed to get customers in your target market excited about your competitive advantage.

One Competitive Advantage Can Create a Business

Many great businesses have been based on marketing a simple competitive advantage.

The original McDonald's restaurant was a small hamburger stand in San Bernardino, California. Two brothers, Maurice and Richard McDonald, ran the stand. Ray Kroc was a fifty-two-year-old salesman of Multimixers, the mixers the McDonald brothers used to make their shakes. When Kroc received an order for eight Multimixers—enough to make forty milkshakes at once—from this hamburger stand on the edge of the desert, he flew out to see the business for himself.

With sales of more than $350,000 a year, McDonald's was one of the most successful little restaurants in America. Customers loved the simple, cheap food and the fast service. Kroc realized that customers cared more about fast service, consistent product, and a low price than they did about the ultimate hamburger. These were the benefits that brought them to the product.

The McDonald brothers knew they had a hot little business that they could expand around the country, but there was just one problem—both brothers hated to fly. When Kroc offered to form a partnership with them and expand their business to other locations, they signed on the dotted line.

Kroc became the president of McDonald's, and got to work marketing the company's competitive advantage—a consistent product delivered fast at a low price. This marketing insight by Ray Kroc turned McDonald's into the huge success it is today.

Domino's Pizza decided its competitive advantage was going to be delivering pizzas in less than thirty minutes. Marketing that competitive advantage has also created a hugely successful company.

Read a Classic

Check out the worldwide bestseller *The Zen of Social Media Marketing: An Easier Way to Build Credibility, Generate Buzz, and Increase Revenue* by Shama Kabani to learn the smartest ways to use social media to drive traffic to your website and get customers to buy from you.

Gather Competitive Intelligence

Not sure yet what your competitive advantage is? Investigate the competition, and it will come to you. Get out there and gather some **competitive intelligence**—information that will help you compare your competitors' strengths and weaknesses with your own.

Of course you'll want to check out the competitions' websites, but another great way to gather valuable competitive intelligence is to pose as a customer and visit a competitor's store. Go at different times of the day and on different days of the week, and note which times were busiest and what kinds of customers were there. As you walk through, ask yourself these questions:

- What products do they carry? How are the products displayed? How much do they cost?
- What is their customer service like? Did the staff offer to assist me? Were they friendly and helpful?
- How many other potential customers are in the store? How old are they? Are they male or female? Are they rich or poor? How much do they spend, on average?

- Does the competitor offer any special purchasing terms, such as credit with no interest? Do they provide any other special services, such as free delivery? What is their policy for returning purchases?

Use a Competitive Matrix to Analyze the Competition

A **competitive matrix** is a useful chart you can use to compare your business with your competitors'.

First, determine your chief **direct competitors**. Next, plug the competitive intelligence you have been collecting into the matrix. Use it to pinpoint your potential competitive advantages.

Here's a simple example. You can vary the factors you wish to compare depending on the business opportunity you are exploring.

Competitive Matrix

FACTORS	YOUR BUSINESS	COMPETITOR A	COMPETITOR B	COMPETITOR C
Price				
Quality of Product/Service				
Location				
Reputation/ Brands				
Delivery Method				
Customer Service				
Website				
Unique Factors				

What Makes Your Business Different?

Creating a competitive matrix will help you spot holes in your market research. It can also enable you to see patterns in the data. Most important, it can show where your business fits in the marketplace.

Your competitive advantage could consist of one or more **differentiators**. These are unique characteristics that distinguish your business from others. Ask yourself these four questions to help identify potential differentiators for your business:

- What product or service can my business provide that my competitors don't?
- What *mix* of products or services can my business provide that my competitors don't?
- What specialized selling or delivery method can give my business a competitive edge?
- In what unique ways can my business meet customers' wants or needs?

Green Tip

Do your competitors practice green business? If not, maybe that's an area in which you could shine. As you survey your potential customers, ask them whether it's important to them that a business is "green." Do they want to know if a business recycles or watches its carbon footprint, for example? Do they prefer organic products?

If so, see if there's an aspect of your business that could go green. That could become a valuable differentiator.

Answering these questions can help you differentiate your business, setting it apart from your competitors. When thinking about your business, resist the temptation to copy exactly what other successful companies have done. The approach that works well for one business may not work for another.

Here are some examples of successful companies that used differentiators to create a competitive advantage that set them apart:

- FedEx Office combines photocopying and other business services with FedEx's fast delivery options. It developed this competitive advantage by realizing that its target market—customers who need to ship important documents overnight—often also need copies of those documents.
- Amazon.com used an unusual mix of selling and delivery methods to set itself apart from competitors. It was one of the first businesses to use only the Internet to sell and market. This enabled Amazon to sell books at lower prices than bookstores.

- When the cable channel Black Entertainment Television (BET) was launched, it tapped into a target market that hadn't yet been served in the cable television market: African Americans who wanted programming geared toward them.

MARKET RESEARCH HELPS YOU GET TO KNOW YOUR CUSTOMERS

These businesses succeeded because they researched their potential customers and discovered what they wanted. Through market research, business owners ask consumers questions and listen to their answers. Market research can vary from a simple survey of friends and neighbors, which can be completed in one day, to detailed statistical studies of a large population over a long period of time.

Let's say you've invented a new type of Frisbee and you think it could sell really well to people at your college, which has 20,000 students. One way to research your market would be to survey a random sample of 200 students, showing them the product and asking these questions:

- Do you play Frisbee? How often?
- Would you be interested in purchasing this Frisbee, if it were available? What colors would you like to see the most?
- Where do you currently purchase your Frisbees? What do you like or dislike about the current seller? What do you think about the price?

If 50 of the 200 students surveyed seem interested in your Frisbee, you can multiply those numbers by 100 to estimate that roughly 5,000 of the 20,000 students on your campus are in your target market.

Explore Market Segments to Define Your Target Market

Market segments are small groups of consumers or businesses that have one or more things in common. By exploring various market segments, you can begin to form a clear picture of your target market. A target market often includes more than one market segment.

Here are some methods you can use to group customers into market segments.

- **Demographics:** Demographics are social and economic facts about customers such as age, gender, marital status, family size (number of children), education, occupation, annual income, and whether they own a home or rent. People under twenty-five who are in college could be a demographically defined market segment for your Frisbee, for example.

- **Geographics:** Basing market segments on where consumers live or where businesses are located is called **geographics**. Groupings could include geographical regions (such as the Northeast), individual states or provinces, counties, cities, or neighborhoods. Your geographic market segment for your Frisbee could be people who live on campus.

- **Psychographics:** Psychological characteristics of customers, such as their attitudes, opinions, beliefs, interests, personalities, lifestyles, political affiliations, and personal preferences, are called **psychographics**. You might want to sell your Frisbee to people who enjoy sports, or college students who like certain types of bands.

Buying patterns are often influenced by a combination of market segment characteristics. For example, you can objectively measure how many times a year people buy airplane tickets, but they may be most likely to travel around holidays to spend time with family members.

Tech U

There are some cool apps available to help you collect market research as you talk to potential customers. Check out iSurvey (www.isurveysoft.com) and SurveyMonkey (www.surveymonkey.com)

With iSurvey, you don't need an Internet connection while you are out conducting marketing surveys in the field. Your offline results will be stored on the portable device and can be uploaded later.

Survey Your Potential Customers

Surveys are a great way to get information about your target market. You can collect market research data with surveys by interviewing your friends, neighbors, and relatives. Here are some useful questions:

- Would you buy this product/service?
- How much would you be willing to pay for it?
- Where would you buy it?
- How would you improve on it?

Game Changer

Prior to the late 1960s, major corporations had pretty much ignored African American consumers. Companies eventually became more conscious of the potential buying power of black consumers, but were unsure how to reach them.

Thomas Burrell noticed this problem and recognized it as an opportunity. In 1971, Burrell opened one of the first black-owned advertising agencies in the United States.

The success of the African-American "Marlboro Man" Burrell created for Philip Morris, convinced McDonald's to hire Burrell Advertising in 1972 to help it market to the African American community. Burrell Communications became the largest black-owned advertising agency in the United States by creating TV commercials featuring black actors that established McDonald's in the urban market.

Soon, Burrell's corporate clients included household names such as Coca-Cola, Ford Motor Company, American Airlines, and Procter & Gamble.

Burrell describes his marketing philosophy as "positive realism." He also develops marketing campaigns for nonminority target markets. Among these groups are the youth market, the "mature" (or older) market, and the urban market.

Burrell himself best describes why being African American encouraged him to try entrepreneurship: "I felt that no matter how successful I might have been at that time [the late 1960s], there was a ceiling that would certainly prevent me from going all the way in someone else's company. And even if I could go all the way it would still not be my company. I felt I had something special to say. I had a special approach to running an advertising business that I could do best in my own establishment. And I figured I had nothing to lose."

Despite the original orientation of his firm toward the African American market, Burrell feels his agency has proven that it can handle advertising to any market. "It's an unfortunate thing," he says, "that being a black-owned company means, for some people, that you should be limited to addressing blacks only. I've got to believe that who owns an ad agency will at some point become irrelevant. What will matter will be the kind of advertising the agency does, how capable the agency is."

Smiling, he adds, "I've been a black person all my life and I will be for the rest of my life. The only thing I know how to do is stay positive. You stay positive and something good will happen."

Test Your Product or Service in Focus Groups

Before launching your business, try using a **focus group** to test your product or service. A focus group is a small group of people from a target market who give feedback about products so changes can be made before the products are launched.

Test audiences for feature films are a type of focus group. Nielsen National Research Group is the company many Hollywood producers turn to for focus group testing. Nielsen selects people who are in the target market for each film. The focus group is invited to a free private screening of the film, long before it is actually released.

After the film, the focus group members fill out comment cards or take part in a discussion about the movie. Based on the reactions of the focus group to the film, a movie studio can tweak the film before releasing it to make it more appealing to the target market.

Math Moment

Suppose you are interested in opening a dry cleaning business in your town of 40,000 adults. Currently, there are two dry cleaners in town. You think there's room for another dry cleaner—in fact, you've decided you will be the "green" dry cleaner in town. That is your competitive advantage.

You decide to approach ABC Bank for a business loan. The bank officer says that before he can give you a loan, you must prove that your business will attract a minimum of 7,500 potential adult customers.

Assuming that every adult in town is a potential customer, what would the average number of potential customers be per dry cleaning business if you started your company? Does this figure fall within the bank's requirement?*

---

* Answers: 13,333; yes.

Analyze the Buying Process

How do you identify the target market for *your* business? First, ask yourself what need your product serves. Arm & Hammer makes baking soda. The company has turned it into a gold mine by convincing consumers of baking soda's deodorizing properties and then creating new products such as baking soda toothpaste, air and carpet fresheners, and deodorants.

Next, think about who might actually buy your product. Remember that the people who use it are not always the buyers. Parents buy children's clothes, for example, so if you are making kids' playsuits, they have to be easy to clean.

Let's analyze the "buying process" that will lead consumers to your product. As you read this list, think about how you could reach your target market at each step:

1. **Awareness:** The consumer realizes a need for something. Advertising is designed to make consumers aware of potential needs for everything from dandruff shampoo to new cars.

2. **Information Search:** The consumer seeks information about what product could fulfill the need. A consumer looking for a multivitamin might take a brochure from a stack on the counter of the local health food store.

3. **Evaluation of Alternatives:** The consumer looking for a multivitamin might check out the vitamins available in the local health food store and compare them, for price and content, with the more commercial brands sold in the supermarket.

4. **Decision to Purchase:** The first purchase is really a test; the consumer is trying the product to see how well it performs.

5. **Evaluation of Purchase:** If the product performs well, the consumer may buy again and begin to develop loyalty to that brand.

After you have figured out *what* need the product/service fulfills, *who* will buy it, and *how* they will buy it, you will have a much better idea of how to market it.

Use your market research to write a **customer profile**. This is a detailed description of your target market's characteristics.

Learn the Lingo

Companies that sell to individuals are called **business-to-consumer (B2C) companies**. The customer profile of a B2C company might include characteristics such as age, gender, occupation, and the neighborhoods where consumers live.

Companies who sell to other companies are called **business-to-business (B2B) companies**. In this case, the customer profile might include details such as the company size, the type of industry, and the geographical location. Automobile manufacturing involves a lot of B2B companies. Auto parts like tires, batteries, hoses, and door locks may be manufactured by different companies, and the auto manufacturer must purchase these parts from each company.

Anticipate Future Competition

As you conduct market research, keep this in mind: Just because you have a competitive advantage in your target market today doesn't mean it will last. Once you start a business, your competitors could copy you, cut their prices to meet yours, or come up with a million other ways to eliminate your differentiating characteristics. And new competitors could enter the market at any time.

Market research is an ongoing process. You need to continuously watch trends in your industry and in the general economy as well. Stay alert to any customer needs and wants that may start to change. Continue to monitor what your current competition is doing. In particular, keep an eye out for any new direct competitors that begin selling to your target market.

ESTABLISHING A BRAND IN THE CUSTOMER'S MIND

More valuable to McDonald's than all the Big Macs it sells every year is the perception, in the minds of McDonald's customers, that every time they visit a McDonald's, they will receive food that tastes exactly the same as it does at every other McDonald's franchise around the world.

When Kroc bought out the McDonald brothers for $2.7 million in 1961, he rigidly followed their original recipes for their hamburgers, fries, and shakes. Kroc wanted every McDonald's customer, from Anchorage to Miami, to get an identical product. According to Bill Bryson's fascinating book *Made in America*, Kroc "dictated that McDonald's burgers must be exactly 3.875 inches across, weigh 1.6 ounces, and contain precisely 19 percent fat. Big Mac buns should have an average of 178 sesame seeds."

Consistency is how a business establishes its **brand**. A brand is a name that represents, in the customer's mind, an image associated with the business's product. By keeping its food and service so consistent, McDonald's has established a brand. Whenever you see those golden arches, you know exactly what kind of food, service, and price to expect.

You don't have to be first to be successful; you just have to choose your competitive advantage and get it into the customer's mind. To figure out how, use your market research.

Ray Grandoit
RAY GRAND APPAREL
www.raygrand.com

"I've always been an entrepreneur at heart," says Ray Grandoit. "As a kid, I took out trash for the elderly and got paid weekly." Ray dreamed of playing in the NBA and being the CEO of his own company. However, at age fourteen he contracted spinal meningitis, which left him in a coma for weeks, paralyzed from the waist down.

Amazingly, Ray looked at being paralyzed as a blessing. He was grateful to be alive and decided he would still do everything he wanted to do—including playing basketball from his wheelchair and owning his own business.

When he spent close to a year in the hospital with medical complications, Ray turned his hospital room into an office. "If you're not succeeding the way you want to succeed," Ray explains, "you just have to keep fighting and fighting. But in that fight, you still grow. Even though you're actually down, it's the best because you're learning so much. I never stop fighting."

At sixteen, Ray starting designing and selling basketball shirts for his high school intramural leagues. The shirts were a hit with his friends, and pretty soon students throughout the school began requesting and purchasing his shirts as well. Ray's Gear, his first company, was born. Ray believed that with hard work, persistence, and dedication he could get the rest of the world to buy and wear his clothes.

The Grand Approach

In high school, Ray had a target market that was easy for him to reach—after all, he went to school with his target market every day.

After he graduated and started going to community college, Ray discovered that he needed to do some market research. "As I learned about business, I realized you have to have a niche," he notes. "I made a lot of money, but Ray's Gear wasn't anything that stood out."

The first thing he did was change his company's name to Ray Grand Apparel. "Everything we market is going to be Grand. Everything has to be done to my best capability, in a grand way." Ray also used the words "Ray Grand" to define his motto: "Royalty As You Gain Respect And Numerous Dollars."

To showcase his clothes, Ray put on fashion shows and gave out flyers. "You can spend a lot of money for marketing, but if you're not pulling in the money, as far as the product goes, you're basically losing it. You've got to remember that the point of business is to make a profit," he points out.

Expansion and Growth

The company sells its clothing through local stores and on its website. "I approach the business as an entrepreneur and a fashion designer," says Ray. "Now I'm in the process of doing business overseas, with different fashion cuts and stitches, all types of stuff."

Ray Grand Apparel has successfully furnished many campus organizations and various companies, teams, and clubs with custom graphic design and T-shirts.

Think Like an Entrepreneur

1. Ray changed the name of his company to reflect the competitive advantage he wants customers to understand. Can you think of any other companies that have changed their names to better market themselves?
2. Ray developed a motto for his company. Write a motto for your business.
3. What did Ray mean when he said, "Even though you're actually down, it's the best because you're learning so much"?

CHAPTER 7

MARKETING (ONLINE AND OFF!)

STRATEGIES THAT GET YOUR CUSTOMERS TO COME TO YOU

In my factory we make cosmetics, but in my
stores we sell hope.

—Charles Revson

E very decision you make about your business should reinforce your competitive
advantage. In the previous chapter, you learned how to use market research to
find out who your customers are and what they want. You have also thought about
your competitive advantage and the benefits it provides to your customers.

Once you have figured these things out, you will want to convey them in every
type of marketing you do—from a sign in your store window to a **banner ad** on a
website.

Learn the Lingo

A banner ad is an advertisement that appears at the top or bottom of a website or in the
website's sidebar. The banner links to the advertiser's website.

WRITE A MARKETING PLAN THAT WILL REACH YOUR CUSTOMERS

To do this successfully, you will write a **marketing plan**. A marketing plan has two parts:

1. Marketing goals
2. Strategies for reaching your goals—also called the **marketing mix**

Marketing Goals

First, decide what you want to accomplish with your marketing. These are your marketing goals. Make them specific and action oriented. You should be able to measure your marketing goals in practical ways.

"I want to increase the number of customers that come to my store" is too general. "I want to increase the number of customers that come into my store by twenty-five percent," in contrast, is a goal you can measure.

Marketing goals are typically broken into three time frames:

1. Short-range goals: What do you want to accomplish in the next year? You may find it helpful to break one-year goals into smaller periods, such as quarters (three months).
2. Mid-range goals: What do you want to achieve in the next two to five years?
3. Long-range goals: Where do you see your business ten or twenty years from now?

MARKET SHARE

Market share is the percentage of your target market that is buying a particular product or service from your business. Market share is another way to measure your marketing goals.

$$\text{(Total Sales} \div \text{Total Market Size)} \times 100$$
$$= \text{Market Share (percentage)}$$

Let's say your goal is to sell $100,000 worth of your organic homemade bath soap in the first year. Based on research, you know that your target market spends about $2 million per year on organic bath soap from your competitors. Use the following formula to determine your estimated market share:

($100,000 ÷ $2 million) × 100 = 5 Percent Market Share

Your marketing goal, therefore, is to gain a 5 percent market share of the organic bath soap market.

Math Moment

Suppose you are calculating financial estimates for a new business. Based on research available to you, assume that the total sales your target market spends for your type of product is $500,000 per year.

What annual sales amount will your company earn if it gains a 15 percent market share in its first year of business?*

_____

* Answer: $75,000

POSITIONING: ESTABLISHING YOUR COMPETITIVE ADVANTAGE IN THE CUSTOMER'S MIND

The goal of marketing is to position your brand in a prospective customer's mind, so that whenever the customer sees anything about your company, your company's competitive advantage immediately springs to mind.

What is the competitive advantage of FedEx? Overnight delivery—I bet that came to you right away. How about Nike, Apple, or Starbucks? See if you can think of some other companies and quickly rattle off the competitive advantage that has enabled them to earn a position in your mind.

Read a Classic

Positioning: The Battle for Your Mind by advertising gurus Al Ries and Jack Trout is a must-read for any entrepreneur looking to market a business. Learn how to build a strategy around your competitor's weaknesses, choose the best name for your products, and more.

We are bombarded with advertising all day long—online, on television, driving, or walking down the street. So how do you make *your* business stick in someone's mind? You've got to choose a simple, clearly communicated message and stick with it.

The easiest way to get into a consumer's mind is to be first to introduce a unique product to them. The iPhone will always be the first touch screen phone, even though so many other phones with touch screens have followed.

By being the first to claim a unique position in a customer's mind, a business can cut through the noise of other businesses' advertising. Miller Lite, for example, was not the first light beer, but it was the first to include "lite" in its name and really go after the position.

On the other hand, Avis Car Rental struggled for years, while number one car rental company Hertz dominated the market. Avis finally gained traction and began to do very well once its marketing team came up with this clever line that told customers about its competitive advantage: "Avis Is Number Two. We try harder."

What unique position could your product or service establish in a customer's mind?

Get the Stats

According to *Positioning* by Al Ries and Jack Trout, the top three brands in a product category typically occupy market share in a ratio of 4:2:1. That is, the number one brand has twice the market share of number two, which has twice the market share of number three.

Your Marketing Mix: The Five Ps of Marketing

Now that you are clear on who your customers are and how you plan to position your product or service, you can write your marketing plan. You will use this plan to let your target market know about your business and its competitive advantage. If you've done your market research, the strategies contained within your plan will get consumers excited about buying your product or service.

You communicate your competitive advantage with your customer in many ways. Even the price of your product or service communicates it! If your competitive advantage is that you are cheaper than the competition, you had better communicate that through a lower price. On the other hand, if your competitive advantage is that you offer higher quality than the competition, you do not want to offer the lowest price—because you want to be perceived as high quality.

Price is one of the five Ps of marketing. These are the five elements of your marketing mix. You communicate constantly with your customers through the five Ps of marketing. As you go through the five Ps, you will see that most of them emerge from your market research.

1. **People:** Who are your target customers? Where do they live? Where do they shop? What do they want?

2. **Product:** What product or service are you selling? How does it meet or create a consumer need?

3. **Place:** How and where will customers be able to buy or receive your product or service? Location is extremely important. Ideally, you'll want your store or business to be in a place your target market frequents.

4. **Price:** What price will your target market feel is reasonable, or perhaps even a good deal, for your product or service? The product (or service) must be priced low enough for the public to buy it, yet high enough for the business to make a profit.

5. **Promotion:** How do you intend to advertise and publicize your business? All your promotion should constantly remind potential customers of your competitive advantage.

Let's explore the 5 Ps in more detail.

Green Tip

Greenwashing is fraudulent marketing designed to make a company seem more environmentally friendly than it really is. To help prevent deceptive claims, the federal government released tougher standards in 2012 for marketing products as green, warning companies not to use broad terms such as "eco-friendly" without providing specifics and proof.

The Federal Trade Commission's Green Guides say marketers need to substantiate product claims. You can't claim your product is biodegradable, for example, unless you can prove that it will entirely break down and return to nature within a year of disposal.

PEOPLE: MARKETING MIX ELEMENT NUMBER ONE

You've already explored this marketing mix element in detail by conducting market research and learning who the people in your market are. Use what you've learned from your market research to visualize the people who make up your target market. Try writing a profile of your ultimate customers.

How old are they? What kind of income do they earn? What do they eat for breakfast? What benefit of your product or service would attract your ideal customer? Make that benefit the center of your marketing.

If you are advertising a rap concert, for example, it would be a waste of money to take out an ad in a magazine for senior citizens. By visualizing your customer, you avoid wasting money on advertising to customers who aren't interested in your product or service.

PRODUCT: MARKETING MIX ELEMENT NUMBER TWO

To attract people in your target market, choose a product that matches well with your customers' needs or wants. When given a choice, customers buy the product with the features and benefits that best meet their requirements.

Product Packaging

Packaging is a great opportunity to attract customers and emphasize your competitive advantage.

Packaging must appeal to your target market. It must promote the image of the brand and be distinguishable from competitors' products. Packaging for certain types of products must meet legal requirements (for example, think about childproof medicine bottles).

If you choose to sell more than one product, you need to consider how the products relate to one another. Does the packaging have some common design element that instantly tells customers they are all from your company, for example? The combination of products a business sells is called its **product mix**. The mix you choose will largely depend on the product image you want to communicate.

Bliss Spa, for example, sells skin care and other types of spa beauty products, and owns and runs spas in upscale hotels and other locations that cater to its target market of young, affluent women. The company motto is "Achieve a higher state of happy," and all its packaging uses the same bright happy colors: royal blue, yellow, and white.

Product Branding

To brand a product is to establish a connection in the minds of customers between something that identifies the product, and its competitive advantage. Coca-Cola's

old-fashioned green bottles and the Nike "Swoosh" logo are examples of ways companies have branded their products.

Names, logos, product packaging—these are all elements in branding a product. Sometimes a brand becomes so popular that it enters the English language.

Today, everyone immediately knows that to Google something means to use the **Web search engine** to find information online. Microsoft tries to compete with its own search engine, Bing. But by turning the company name into a verb, Google created a very strong brand, which it has only strengthened further with the creative daily logos Google's marketing team creates for the home page.

Super Success Story

Google founders Larry Page and Sergey Brin met at Stanford University in the mid-1990s, where they were both working on doctorates in computer science. Initially, they didn't hit it off, but they became good friends while working on a research project about search engines.

At the time, search engines ranked results by counting how many times the search terms appeared on a page. This encouraged people to repeat **keywords** on their pages many times to "game" the system. Page and Brin came up with a better system they named PageRank that analyzed relationships between websites, instead of just counting keywords.

In early 1999, Page and Brin decided the search engine project, although a potentially good business, was taking up too much of their time at grad school. They tried to sell it to Excite CEO George Bell for $1 million. Lucky for them, he rejected the offer. On June 7, 1999, their company raised $25 million from venture capital firms.

Brin and Page named the company Google, from the word "googol," which is the number "1" followed by one hundred zeroes. They left school to focus on the business. Google grew rapidly and went public in 2004. The stock sale was a huge success, and the company used the $1.2 billion it raised to acquire other useful companies. In 2004, for example, Google bought Keyhole, the start-up that developed Earth Viewer, and renamed it Google Earth. In 2004, Google acquired YouTube for $1.65 billion in Google stock.

After the initial stock sale, Brin, Page, and CEO Eric Schmidt requested that their salaries be cut to $1 per year. Their stock holdings in Google have already made them extremely rich. Page and Brin are estimated to be worth about $20.3 billion each. Together, they own about 16 percent of Google.

The founders continue to nurture Google's unique company culture by offering perks at Google such as games, snacks, and lack of an office dress code. Its philosophy includes statements such as: "You can make money without doing evil," "You can be serious without a suit," and "Work should be challenging and the challenge should be fun."

Google software engineers are encouraged to spend 20 percent of their work time on projects that interest them—a policy called Innovation Time Off. Some of Google's most profitable products, such as Gmail, Google News, Orkut, and AdSense, came from these employee innovations.

PLACE: MARKETING MIX ELEMENT NUMBER THREE

Location is critical. A store can be selling terrific stuff, but if it's located far from where its target customers like to shop, staying in business is going to be tough. So are setting the best hours during which customers can buy the product.

Good place marketing strategies include:

- Choosing the best possible location for a physical store.
- Staying open during the days and hours when *your* customers like to shop.
- Providing a responsive website that looks great and works well on any device, from a laptop to a cell phone.
- Taking orders via a toll-free telephone number.

PRICE: MARKETING MIX ELEMENT NUMBER FOUR

Base the price of your product on two things: your target market and the potential profits for your company. Who are the people in your target market? What can they afford? Do they want value? Or are they seeking prestige and might prefer a more expensive product?

Choose a Price Objective

What do you want the price to "say" about your product? Here are some price objectives:

- **Build or Maintain an Image:** Price affects the image of a product in consumers' minds. People may think a lower-priced product is of lower quality than similar items sold at a higher price, for instance. Test your prices with some target customers before launching your business. Ask them what they would be willing to pay for your product or service, and what pricing conveys to them.

- **Increase Sales Volume (Quantity):** Prices lower than the competition's should increase your sales. You can charge a slightly higher price than the competition, though, if your product has more features or benefits.

- **Obtain or Expand a Market Share:** Sometimes an initial lower price can help a new business attract customers from competitors. After you obtain your target market share, you can try increasing your prices slightly to improve profits.

- **Maximize Profits:** If you are introducing a new product into a market, you could charge a high price to maximize profits. Later on, if competitors imitate your product or find some other way to reduce its attraction, you could drop the price.

Select a Pricing Strategy

The next step is to pick a strategy for determining exactly how to price your product or service. There are three basic pricing strategies. Your decision about which one to use will depend on your product mix, your price objectives, and the market you are targeting.

1. **Demand-Based Pricing:** This pricing method charges the highest price that an actual customer would be willing to pay. A demand-based pricing strategy is most useful when customers perceive your product as unique or having greater value than similar products. Demand-based pricing would work for a painting or an antique, for example. You can determine a maximum price by surveying potential target customers.

2. **Competition-Based Pricing:** This pricing method focuses on what the competition charges. After you find out your competitors' prices, you can decide to charge the same price, slightly more, or slightly less. Because the focus of this strategy is on staying competitive, you will need to regularly review what your competitors are doing and make price adjustments if needed. Walmart has used this strategy by promising to beat any competitors' advertised price with its "Ad Match Guarantee."

3. **Cost-Based Pricing:** This pricing method sets a product's price based on what it costs your business to provide it. **Keystoning**—doubling the wholesale cost to get the retail price—is a common form of cost-based pricing. Cost-plus (or "markup") pricing is widely used in retailing. An advantage of this approach is that the business will know that its costs are being covered. The main disadvantage is that cost-plus pricing may lead you to price your products uncompetitively.

Price Factors for Services

Time is the primary factor used to determine price for a service. Some services are charged simply by the hour. Vendors such as car mechanics or electricians commonly add a separate fee for materials in addition to their hourly charge. A brake job may require replacing expensive parts, inexpensive parts, or perhaps none at all, for example.

Another way that businesses charge for services is by a flat fee. Both material costs and time are built into one price for a particular service. Consider a business that performs oil changes in cars. The amount of time it takes to complete an oil change, as well as the new oil and oil filter that are put into the car, are factored into one price.

BUNDLING

Bundling is the practice of combining the price of several services (and/or physical products) into one price. The travel industry uses bundling to create vacation packages that include airline tickets, hotel accommodations, and a rental car—all for one price.

Bundling can be convenient for customers who are willing to pay a premium in order to save time and effort they would have spent researching the different pieces of the bundled product or service. Sometimes it also allows the business to sell services at a slightly lower price because customers are buying a greater quantity of goods or services.

PROMOTION: MARKETING MIX ELEMENT NUMBER FIVE

Did you know a customer needs to see an ad as many as nine times before he or she will respond to it and make a purchase?

Promotion must be an ongoing process. **AIDA** is a popular communication model used by companies to plan, create, and manage promotion. The letters in AIDA stand for the following steps that are necessary for any promotion to be successful:

1. **Get Attention:** How will you grab the attention of your target market? Using a celebrity to endorse a product is an extreme example (and usually an expensive one!) of a promotion that may cause people to take notice of it. How could you affordably get attention? Get creative!

2. **Keep Interest:** Once your potential customers notice your product, focus your message on the product's benefits and features. Clearly communicate to potential customers how these features and benefits specifically relate to them.

3. **Raise Desire:** Now that your customers have noticed and have some interest in the product, how can you make your product desirable? A discount for first-time buyers might encourage them to make a purchase, for example.

4. **Call to Action:** Finally, ask consumers to take action—to buy your product or service. This is your **call to action**. Give them a reason to act right away, such as a discount offered for a limited time.

Keeping Customers

Retain customers by rewarding them for purchasing your product or service with discounts, frequent-buyer programs, or special price offers.

Stay aware of how your competitors are promoting their products. Ask your customers what's important to them, and listen to them closely. When they buy your product, offer them immediate ways to provide feedback. Offer a coupon if they fill out a short email survey, for example.

Choosing a Promotional Mix

The combination of promotional elements that a business chooses is called a **promotional mix**.

The six elements of a promotional mix are:

1. **Advertising:** A public promotional message paid for by an identified sponsor or company.

2. **Visual Merchandising:** Displays of merchandise to attract customers.

How attractive are the displays in your storefront windows? Is there an eye-catching sign outside?

Companies that provide services should also consider the visual impact they make. A place of business that looks clean and well-organized sends a more positive message than one with dirty floors and windows.

3. **Public Relations (PR):** Activities aimed at creating goodwill toward a product or company, such as supplying free drinks at a softball game, for example.

4. **Publicity:** Any form of media exposure for which a company does not pay, such as reviews of your product or service or articles that include interviews with you.

5. **Personal Selling:** Direct (one-to-one) efforts made by a company's sales representatives to get sales and build customer relationships.

6. **Sales Promotion:** A short-term activity or buying incentive, such as conducting product demonstrations or providing coupons or free samples. Think of sales promotions as temporary "specials" used to motivate potential customers.

As you think about how to balance the various elements in your mix, try to visualize how each relates to the others. Look for ways that one type of promotion can be used to back up or support another. This will help make the most of your promotional efforts.

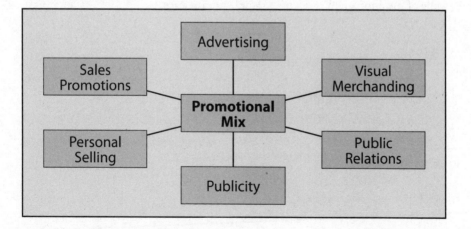

Learn the Lingo

Advertising uses various **media,** or communication channels, to send promotional messages to potential customers. Media outlets include radio, television, newspapers, magazines, and blogs.

Public Relations and Publicity

Many companies have a PR department to help build and maintain a positive public image. You can also **retain**—or temporarily hire—a PR firm to help you obtain mentions of your company in the media.

As a new entrepreneur, you can save money by handling PR and publicity yourself. If you can learn to pitch your story well to journalists and influential bloggers, you will gain invaluable exposure for your business. Journalists love to hear from young entrepreneurs, as long as your approach is professional.

Use these tools to get publicity:

Press Release: A short (one page or less) factual note sent to journalists to inform them about a story—such as the opening of your business! Every press release should answer these questions: who, what, when, where, and why.

Include a clear, concise subject line that will inspire the journalist to open the email. In the sample press release below, the headline "Local High School Students to Teach Marketing Workshop for Community Teens" also makes a good email subject line. Attach one or two clearly titled, high-resolution (300 dpi) photos. If you save the reporter the hassle of contacting you and asking you for a photo, you increase your chances of getting a photo into the publication. Make sure to include the name of the photographer. Here's a sample press release.

FOR IMMEDIATE RELEASE

May 15, 20—

Contact: Maria Gonzales, mariagonzales@gmail.com,
(555) 123-4567

**Local High School Students to Teach Marketing Workshop
for Community Teens**

Anytown, NY — Wayne High School students Amy Chang,
Tom O'Connor, and Brian Jones will be conducting a 5-day
workshop for Anytown teenagers who want to learn how to
market their own business.

The workshop will be held at the town hall June 16 to 20,
from 7:00 to 9:00 PM. The workshop fee of $25 per person
will include educational handouts. Participants will practice
newly learned information in small-group activities.

According to Mrs. Anita Andretti, a teacher at Wayne High
School, "These students want the opportunity to share
some of what they learned in the Entrepreneurship course
last semester. They feel it's important to contribute to the
community."

For more information, please contact Maria Gonzales at the
above contact information.

Learn the Lingo

A **retainer agreement** is a work-for-hire contract. When you retain someone, you pay
him or her for work that will be done in the future. You might pay a publicist $2,000, for
example, to execute a promotional campaign for your business.

A **contract** is an agreement signed by two parties with the expectations that its
terms would be enforceable in a court of law.

Pitch Letter: A short cover letter sent with a press release to introduce yourself and
suggest one or more possible stories that could be written about your event.

Sponsorships: Helping to pay for an event that promotes a good cause can create favorable publicity. You could plan a dinner, entertainment, or sports event in which all the money from ticket sales goes to a local charity group. Or you could sign on as a sponsor for an event someone else is giving. Sponsors' names are usually included on the signage or programs for sponsored events—great publicity for your business. You can also donate samples of your product or gift certificates. If you sponsor an event, that's a great excuse to send out a press release!

Contests: Contests help create excitement about your product or business. They also provide opportunities to learn more about customers or to get their feedback. Ask customers who visit your store to drop a business card into a box for a contest drawing. Or, enter people into a contest after they complete a short survey. Like community events, a contest is also a great opportunity to send out a press release.

Tech U

To increase the odds of your press release photos being published as part of an article, format your photos as JPEGs and make sure they meet these standard specs: 3,000 pixels longest side, 300 dpi resolution, standard JPEG compression.

MORE PUBLICITY TIPS

Here are some more ways to build your media contacts and gain publicity for your business. Remember, publicity means customers!

1. **Write articles** for newspapers, magazines, trade publications, and newsletters. Always ask to include your business website in a short bio beneath anything you publish.

2. **Meet reporters.** Introduce yourself as someone they can call as a source for quotes on your industry, city, youth entrepreneurship, and so forth.

3. **Give talks.** Talk to various groups about being a young entrepreneur. This is a wonderful way to create buzz about your business. Try community groups, libraries, and schools.

4. **Send out photos.** Local newspapers, TV stations, weekly shoppers, trade publications, and other media are always looking for interesting photos. If you can get a funny or weird photo of someone using your product—send it in!

5. **Give free classes and demonstrations** at schools and colleges, or at your own business. Invite the media to attend.

6. **Participate in online forums and discussion groups**. Do not sell yourself or your business; instead, offer helpful advice. You will gain customers and may get noticed by journalists looking for story sources and business owners to interview.

7. **Encourage your customers to review your business** on Yelp!, Angie's List, and other sites that collect customer reviews.

Tech U

A newsgroup is an online message board where people post information about a particular topic. These messages form an ongoing discussion. Although newsgroups are not used for advertising, they help you "meet" new people, gain insights from potential customers, and build trust and your reputation.

ONLINE MARKETING

These days, to be successful, you need to market your business online. People are spending hours a day online, and you need to reach them there, too. If you love being online, use social media to promote your business.

Online Marketing Tips

1. **Your website must be mobile friendly.** Forget a fancy website with an animated home page. Most people will be checking out your site with their phones. Make sure it opens quickly and offers an incentive for them to join your email list from the get-go. If you're running a record label, for example, offer a free song download in exchange for an email address.

Get the Stat

The time your customers are spending reading the newspaper, listening to the radio, and watching TV is declining, and time spent online is increasing. A recent Nielsen survey found that American consumers spend on average 40 percent or more of their days online.

2. **Use keywords on every page of your website.** Your customers are online, trying to find your business. Even if you don't sell online, your business *must* be discoverable when your customers try to search for you online. **SEO** stands for **search engine optimization,** and refers to all the techniques used to help your website and web pages rank well in search engine results.

Tech U

Here's what you need to know about keywords:

- A keyword is a word or multiple-word phrase that represents a web page's content. If you're running a wedding photography business, for example, you might choose the keyword "wedding photography."

- Google provides a keyword tool called Keyword Planner that you can use to help find the best keywords for your website: To access Keyword Planner, sign in to your AdWords account at https://adwords.google.com. Click the Tools and Analysis drop-down menu and select "Keyword Planner."

- Your product name is typically not your keyword. Your keyword is the more generic term for what your product/service is. Ask yourself, "What do people call products like mine?"

- Add keywords to the page's title tag, URL page header (H1 tag), and throughout the body of the page, especially near the top.

- Do not, however, stuff the page with keywords that don't make sense. This is a very old technique that is likely to turn customers off of your website. Instead, vary your keyword on your web page in natural ways: using singular and plural forms, different word orders for keyword phrases, close synonyms, and natural keyword modifiers.

- Use your keywords as links on other pages in your website.

Let's say you sell custom cowboy hats. Your keyword phrase is "custom cowboy hats"; in other words, you want to show up when someone is searching online for a really cool cowboy hat. To reach more people, consider changing up the adjective "custom" to reach more searchers. You could try "specialty" or "custom-designed," for example. By using this tactic, you give yourself a chance to rank for those similar keywords, plus you let the search engines know more about your page and what it's about. The more a search engine knows about your page, the higher your page will rank!

3. **Use social media to reach customers.** Your customers want to "like" you on Facebook and "follow" you on Twitter, especially if you provide incentives for them to do so. Offer a discount that's exclusive to your Facebook friends, for example, or a special deal code for your followers on Twitter. Set up a YouTube channel for videos of your product or service in action, and testimonials from your customers.

    You might also consider keeping profiles on Google+ and LinkedIn. You want to be wherever your customers might be spending time.

    Look on LinkedIn for groups relevant to your business and post interesting information. Do not just spam about your business; instead, contribute to the discussions that are already taking place. If you have a business teaching guitar lessons via Skype, for example, join groups that cater to guitarists and share practice tips or unusual scales. As you become known as an expert, people will become interested in and open to hearing about your lessons.

4. **Resist the urge to sell to your online followers. Socialize and chat with them instead.** It's tempting to constantly try to sell your business on Facebook, Twitter, and so on, but resist the urge. Pretend, instead, that these followers have just wandered into your store. Would you rush up to them and start pushing them to buy something? No way! You'd give them some space to look around, and then perhaps say hello and chat about the weather or a recent event.

    Don't be afraid to get personal. Share fun photos of you and your employees goofing off. Let your personality shine. Ask questions—get people talking on your Facebook page.

    Let your customers get to know you via social media, and they'll want to buy from you.

5. **Become a thought leader online.** A **thought leader** is someone other people recognize as having innovative, forward-thinking ideas that work. You can develop a reputation as a thought leader in your fields of business by sharing your insights and opinions in newsgroups and forums and on your website blog.

Being a thought leader has been described as "having the answers to the biggest questions in the mind of your customers." Think about what your customers need and want to know, and seek to answer their questions online.

360° MARKETING MIX

360° marketing communicates with your prospects and customers from all directions. A 360° marketing mix might include a company website, emails to existing customers, faxes, direct mail postcards and catalogs, instant messaging, and telephone calls to customers alerting them to new promotions. It might mean becoming involved with the local community to meet new customers. It could involve face-to-face meetings with prospects and customers in nonbusiness settings.

Entrepreneurs who practice 360° marketing take **networking** seriously. They join clubs, organizations, and online social networks. They offer free consultations and demonstrations.

An entrepreneur using 360° marketing might publish an online newsletter, write a blog, or host an online conference related to the company's product. In the future, more and more entrepreneurs will use the Internet and participate in the rich variety of channels and opportunities it offers to surround their prospects and customers with messages about their products.

Learn the Lingo

Networking is the act of meeting new people though current friends and business contacts. Everyone you meet is a potential sales prospect for your business—so put some effort every week into meeting new people. People you know refer you to people they know. In turn, these new people introduce you to more people, widening your circle of contacts.

You can also meet new contacts at networking events. These are gatherings at which businesspeople meet and socialize with other entrepreneurs in their locality.

MEASURING THE EFFECTIVENESS OF YOUR PROMOTIONS

Conversion is the sale of your product or service to a customer whose interest was sparked by your promotion. The question you want to answer is: Does my promotion cause conversion?

Online ads typically offer data such as "clicks" and "views," but these days marketing researchers show a stronger correlation between ad "hover time" and conversion. In other words, it doesn't matter how many potential customers view your online ad; what matters is whether they actually hovered over it long enough to read it.

In fact, this research indicates that ads may not be as effective in converting lookers into buyers as "sticky" content such as blog posts. And if you do use online advertising, make sure you are only paying when viewers "click through."

The **click-through rate** (**CTR**) tells you how many customers who saw a Web ad actually clicked on it. The click-through rate is the number of times a click is made on the advertisement divided by the total impressions (the times an advertisement was served):

Click-Throughs ÷ Impressions = Click-Through Rate (percentage)

In most cases, a CTR of 2 percent or higher is considered pretty successful.

GUERRILLA MARKETING: LOW-BUDGET PROMOTION STRATEGIES

Here are some great ways to keep your promotion costs down:

Swap Services: Trade your company's products or services for airtime on a radio station. This is called a **trade-out**.

Cooperative Advertising: When two companies who have an interest in selling the same product share the cost of advertising, it is called **cooperative advertising** ("co-op" for short). A wholesaler who distributes snack food and a convenience store retailer might work out an agreement to split advertising costs, for example. Ask your suppliers if they offer any co-op programs.

Testimonials and endorsements: If customers, news sources, or organizations praise your products or services, ask if you can quote them in brochures or catalogs or on your website. If you join a trade organization or your local Better Business Bureau, mention it in your promotional materials. You can also use their membership logos on your website.

Join a Co-op: Cooperative, nonprofit business groups can promote their businesses together with events, publications, and pooled marketing resources. Examples include Madison Originals in Wisconsin (www.madisonoriginals.org) and San Francisco's Locally Owned Merchants Alliance in California (www.sfloma.org). These groups educate consumers on the advantages and pleasures of patronizing local businesses. Instead of thinking of other small business owners as the competition, see them as friends with similar goals.

Read a Classic

Guerrilla Marketing: Easy and Inexpensive Strategies for Making Big Profits from Your Small Business by Jay Conrad Levinson. Levinson has revolutionized marketing for the small business owner with his creative, low-budget strategies.

An Entrepreneur Like You

Rahfeal Gordon

RAHGOR MOTIVATIONS

hwww.rahgor.com

Growing up, Rahfeal Gordon faced many hardships—from crack-addicted parents to homelessness. But Rahfeal knew he could make it if he stayed focused.

At fifteen, Rahfeal started his first company, Infinite Productions, which put on events and parties. "I was a social butterfly, and music kept me going during the hard times." His younger brother was murdered after turning to the streets and selling drugs. It was then that Rahfeal decided to tell people about his own life and struggles.

How Hip-Hop Saved His Life

Today, Rahfeal is a motivational speaker. He helps people follow their dreams. He talks about how hip-hop saved his life. "I grew up in the hip-hop generation," says Rahfeal. "Not all of the music is great or positive, but there are always little jewels of wisdom in the music. And that's what I took out."

Rahfeal also studied the hip-hop artists who became successful entrepreneurs, and ran multimillion-dollar companies. "They taught me lessons on how to survive," he explains.

Rahfeal's company, RahGor Motivations, serves as a platform for his speaking engagements and provides products, such as shirts and posters that inspire and motivate. Rahfeal hopes to expand RahGor Motivations so other individuals can present their stories through the company.

Rahfeal has written a book, *You Won't Make It,* which you can find on Amazon. It includes a short autobiography, plus thirty lessons on life, faith, and how to follow your dream.

The Bigger Things Come at the End

RahGor Motivations is small, but thriving. "I don't really need too much help in regard to certain things, but I have a booking manager, a publicist, and an administrative assistant. Everybody else is either a freelance consultant or interns who deal with the promotion aspect," Rahfeal explains.

When Rahfeal is booked for an appearance, everyone involved gets a percentage of what he makes. "If I'm not getting booked, then there's no need for staff. Everything is very organized, so I can juggle multiple things to keep expenses down." He believes in a team approach and gives credit to everyone who contributes. "I'm promoting myself, but I'm also promoting others," he says.

Rahfeal thinks that the most important thing in life is knowing what you love to do, even if you're not getting paid for it yet. He also believes that discipline and dedication can pay off in a big way. "You've got to make sacrifices, but you sacrifice now for greatness later—the bigger things come at the end," Rahfeal explains, adding, "The things I dreamed when I was younger are now happening."

Think Like an Entrepreneur

1. Does adversity make it more difficult to succeed?
2. What are the advantages of having everyone work for a percentage? When would such an approach work? When wouldn't it?
3. Do you believe in sacrificing today for better things in the future? Explain your answer.

CHAPTER 8

DOING GOOD IS GOOD BUSINESS

WHY BEING SOCIALLY RESPONSIBLE
MAKES YOUR BUSINESS MORE PROFITABLE

Men who leave vast sums may fairly be
thought men who would not have left it at
all had they been able to take it with them.
The man who dies thus rich dies disgraced.

—Andrew Carnegie

When you feel that a business has overcharged you or treated you badly, do you go back? Probably not.

Business success is not built by enticing a customer and taking as much of his or her money as possible. Success comes from **repeat business**—customers who come back again and again, and tell their friends how wonderful your business is.

It's more profitable to run your business honestly and ethically than it is to cheat and exploit customers, employees, your community, or the environment. So, if you've ever had doubts about going into business because you think you'll be forced to make unethical decisions, don't worry—doing good is good for business!

We tend to think that only companies involved with social or environmental causes are "doing good." But, in fact, the primary way entrepreneurs improve society is by finding creative, efficient ways to use scarce resources.

ENTREPRENEURS AND PHILANTHROPY— A RICH TRADITION

Philanthropy is concern for other beings, expressed through giving money to charities or foundations. There is a long, proud tradition of philanthropy among entrepreneurs who donate time, energy, and money to help improve their communities, as well as society at large.

Foundations are organizations that manage donated money and use it to finance programs that help people.

Ironically, some of the most aggressive entrepreneurs in American history—like Andrew Carnegie—have also been the most generous. Andrew Carnegie grew up in a poor Scottish immigrant family and began working in a factory as a boy. He made his great fortune by building the United States steel industry in the late 1800s and early 1900s, and earned a reputation as a very competitive—even ruthless—businessman.

In 1901, Carnegie sold his steel company to J. P. Morgan for $420 million. Overnight, Carnegie became one of the richest men in the world. Carnegie spent most of his time giving away his wealth to libraries, colleges, museums, and other institutions that still benefit people today. By the time he died in 1919 at age eighty-four, Carnegie had given away $350 million to libraries, universities, schools, and cultural centers—such as Carnegie Hall, the famous concert hall in New York City.

Many of our great museums, libraries, universities, and other valuable institutions have been financed by entrepreneurs. The Rockefeller Foundation, the Coleman Foundation, the Charles G. Koch Foundation, the Ford Foundation, and the Carnegie Corporation are among the famous foundations created by entrepreneurs.

ENTREPRENEURS AND PHILANTHROPY TODAY—IN THE BILLIONS

Today's wealthy entrepreneurs carry on this tradition. The Bill & Melinda Gates Foundation received $26 billion from Microsoft's Bill Gates and his wife, Melinda, between 1994 and 2006. The couple plans to give away more than $60 billion in their lifetimes. Their foundation tackles problems in health and education around the world.

Get the Stats

Since 2007, Bill Gates has given away $28 billion—or 48 percent of his net worth—to charity.

WEALTHIEST CHARITABLE NONPROFIT FOUNDATIONS

Rank	Organization	Location	Endowment
1	Bill & Melinda Gates Foundation	Seattle, Washington	$35.1 billion
2	Wellcome Trust	London	$26.4 billion
3	Howard Hughes Medical Institute	Chevy Chase, Maryland	$18.6 billion
4	Ford Foundation	New York, New York	$13.7 billion
5	The Church Commissioners for England	London	$10.5 billion
6	J. Paul Getty Trust	Los Angeles, California	$10.1 billion
6	Li Ka Shing Foundation	Hong Kong	$10.1 billion
7	Robert Wood Johnson Foundation	Princeton, New Jersey	$10.0 billion
7	Mohammed bin Rashid Al Maktoum Foundation	Dubai	$10.0 billion
8	William and Flora Hewlett Foundation	Menlo Park, California	$8.5 billion
9	W. K. Kellogg Foundation	Battle Creek, Michigan	$8.4 billion
10	Lilly Endowment	Indianapolis, Indiana	$7.6 billion

BUSINESS ETHICS

If you follow the news, however, you may have heard more about illegal deals involving large corporations than you've heard about business philanthropy. The American energy company Enron, for example, lied to employees about its financial health, and encouraged its workers to invest their money in the company's stock. The business then declared bankruptcy, wiping out the savings the workers had counted on for retirement. Mattel was forced to recall millions of toys containing lead-based paint, which was banned years ago as a health hazard to children.

Stories like these have tarnished the image of business. They've also brought attention to the topic of **business ethics,** which are moral principles applied to business. **Ethics** are rules you can use to guide your behavior. The Golden Rule,

"Do unto others as you would have others do unto you," is a famous ethic. It is an example of an ethic that can help you with any decision you face.

As an entrepreneur, you set the tone for your business. You have considerable influence on your company's ethics. Like operating a business itself, this is both an opportunity and a responsibility.

Successful entrepreneurs apply the Golden Rule to everything they do. They run their businesses honestly and treat their customers with respect—not only because it's the right thing to do but because it builds repeat business. Customers who are treated well come back to make more purchases—and tell their friends!

Game Changer

PeaceWorks (www.peaceworks.com) is a business that seeks to foster peace and understanding in the Middle East through entrepreneurship. This global business has Arabs and Israelis working as partners to create a line of food products using local olives, vegetables, and olive oil. By making entrepreneurs out of enemies, PeaceWorks is using entrepreneurship to foster peace.

DO THE RIGHT THING

In Spike Lee's classic 1989 film *Do the Right Thing*, a black Brooklyn neighborhood explodes when the Italian owner of a pizzeria refuses to allow a customer to post any pictures of African American celebrities on the restaurant's "Wall of Fame." The entrepreneur's racism ignites a fight, during which an African American teenager is killed by police and the business is trashed by an angry mob. Sobered, the owner and his African American employees and neighbors reconcile and the pizzeria reopens.

As Spike Lee observes, the smartest thing for an entrepreneur to do is to "do the right thing." Here are three reasons why an ethical business is a *profitable* business:

1. Customers are more confident buying goods and services from an ethical company. People don't trust a company to offer high-quality goods and services if it has a reputation for cheating its employees or lying to customers.

2. An ethical workplace motivates employees. Have you ever seen other students copy a paper or cheat on a test and not get caught? You may have wondered why you should play by the rules when people who break them seem to succeed just as well. Employees feel discouraged

and frustrated when their workplace is not ethical. They are more likely to steal from the company, lie, and cheat. In contrast, people are proud to work for a company that maintains high ethical standards. They feel better about their jobs and are likely to be more loyal.

3. Ethical behavior helps prevent legal problems. Defending yourself in court can be expensive. Lawsuits cost money for lawyers' fees, judgments, and penalties. They also damage a business's reputation, which cause you to lose customers for years to come.

WHISTLE-BLOWING

A **whistle-blower** is someone who decides to report illegal or unethical conduct to superiors or to the public—sometimes at great personal risk. If you've seen the film *Erin Brockovich,* starring Julia Roberts, you learned the story of one of the most famous whistle-blowers of our time.

As a law clerk without any real legal training, Brockovich uncovered a rash of mysterious illnesses in Hinkley, California. While conducting research, she became convinced these health issues were linked to the presence of hexavalent chromium in wastewater from a nearby Pacific Gas and Electric plant. PG&E denied the chemical was toxic, but Brockovich's research showed that it was linked to the many cases of cancer in the community.

In 1996, PG&E settled for $333 million, the largest settlement in U.S. history at the time. In 2006, PG&E paid another $295 million to people affected by the toxic chemical.

Sometimes whistle-blowers are forced by their consciences to speak up about their own employer. As vice president for internal audits at WorldCom, the nation's second largest phone company, Cynthia Cooper uncovered one of the biggest financial frauds in history. She was told to stop her investigation by WorldCom's chief financial officer, but she continued anyway. Cooper discovered $3.8 billion in fraud at WorldCom, and went public with her story. In 2002 she was named one of *Time* magazine's "People of the Year."

Whistle-blowers can face threats, and sometimes even violence, but the law is on their side. The Sarbanes-Oxley Act of 2002 made it illegal to fire or punish employees who help authorities investigate stock market fraud. Other laws protect individuals who report workplace safety and environmental violations.

Management's response to whistle-blowing, beyond these legal requirements, sends a message about its commitment to business ethics. Does a company encourage employees to speak up when a job or situation troubles them? Does it discourage employees who pressure whistle-blowers to keep silent? It's smart to take whistle-blowers seriously and act fast to correct unethical practices.

CONFLICT OF INTEREST

A **conflict of interest** arises when personal considerations, loyalties, or professional obligations interfere with each other. A lawyer may not represent both the victim of a crime and the person accused of committing it, for example.

Although hiring friends or family members is often a logical first step for a growing business, it's important to be aware that hiring friends or family members can create potential conflicts of interest. As you begin to hire people who are not friends or family members, you must be very careful to treat all your employees with equal fairness.

Dan's cousin was a lawyer with a successful practice. Dan felt confident about hiring her as his company's legal advisor, but the appearance of conflict of interest raised doubts among his employees and clients. They wondered if she was the best lawyer for the job, or if Dan had hired her only because she was his cousin. As it happened, Dan's cousin wasn't able to give the company her full attention.

When Dan had to fire her, it seemed that his employees and customers had been right. Besides hurting his relationship with his family, Dan hurt his reputation as a businessman. He was perceived as engaging in **nepotism,** which is the unfair practice of favoring relatives or friends by giving them jobs or preferential treatment on the job.

Of course, many businesses are run successfully by families and by friends. What's important is that you never treat a family member or a friend better than you do any other employee. You must treat all your employees fairly to avoid charges of nepotism and to avoid any conflict of interest.

CONFIDENTIALITY

As an entrepreneur, you will be gathering a good deal of sensitive information. You may run a background check to learn whether a job applicant has a criminal record, or a credit check on a potential investor or partner. You'll pick up ideas from former employers and hear stories about other businesspeople from clients.

How you and others in your company use this information can be an ethical matter, and the decision isn't always clear-cut. On one hand, you have a duty to respect the confidentiality (privacy) of others. On the other hand, keeping silent when you learn about criminal or unethical behavior could expose some people to harm.

Some businesses require their employees to sign a **nondisclosure agreement (NDA)**. An employee who signs an NDA is legally barred from sharing some types of information with others, even after leaving the company.

TRADE SECRETS

A **trade secret** is any information that a business or individual keeps confidential to gain advantage over competitors. NDAs also help prevent your employees from stealing trade secrets.

Let's say you've built a successful restaurant on your grandmother's special recipe for fried chicken. Your recipe is your **trade secret**—protect it by having anyone who works at your restaurant sign an NDA agreeing to never reveal the recipe. If any employee does, you can sue him or her for damages to your business.

As an accountant with a large company, Angela knew the financial details of many clients' businesses. When she left to start working for herself, she could have tried to take her clients with her. Instead, she chose to build up her own clientele through her talent and hard work and not "steal" her old company's customers.

If she had attempted to take her clients with her, Angela could have been sued by her former employer, especially if she had signed a nondisclosure agreement.

CREATE TRANSPARENCY

Transparency is a big buzzword in business these days. It refers to openness and accountability in business decisions and actions.

The idea behind transparency is this: What if a business stops trying to present a perfect image in public and instead lets customers see its operations? Letting people see what a company is doing, and why, is a strong deterrent to unethical behavior. It also builds trust with consumers, even when the company makes a mistake.

In the past, companies communicated with the public and even employees only through carefully crafted and polished memos, press releases, and press conferences. Today, companies are realizing that this can make them seem dishonest and untrustworthy. Increasingly, companies are embracing transparency as a way to do business more honestly and prove that they behave ethically.

In the age of social media, when news travels like lightning through Twitter feeds and on blogs and Facebook pages, transparency is becoming more important. It's harder to hide a corporate goof.

When Facebook revised their user terms of service, for example, the company did not openly communicate the changes to Facebook users. As soon as users figured out that their privacy settings had been changed without notification, many became angry at the company, and for good reason. News traveled quickly through the blogosphere, damaging Facebook's reputation. These bungled privacy concerns did not help the company's IPO of its stock—which failed to reach the price it was expected to fetch.

Photo-sharing app Instagram stumbled into a similar mess when it attempted to slide this language into its privacy policy, without openly and transparently informing Instagram users:

> **To help us deliver interesting paid or sponsored content or promotions, you agree that a business or other entity may pay us to display your username, likeness, photos (along with any associated metadata), and/or actions you take, in connection with paid or sponsored content or promotions, without any compensation to you.**

A public backlash followed, forcing Instagram to issue public apologies. Co-founder Kevin Systrom quickly pledged to remove the new language and added, "I want to be really clear: Instagram has no intention of selling your photos, and we never did. We don't own your photos—you do." He promised to be more transparent in the future.

In contrast, when Whole Foods CEO John Mackey published an article about health-care reform that some Whole Foods customers did not like, the company wisely encouraged their customers to post comments both positive and negative on the Whole Foods Facebook page and other social media sites. That kind of openness earns respect.

Every business has setbacks and challenges. Companies make mistakes. Being honest about your mistakes may be a better idea than trying to hide them.

Transparency can help you:

- **Build Trust:** Letting your customers see your mistakes and your efforts to correct them can create long, loyal relationships.
- **Improve Customer Service:** If something goes wrong, get out in front of it and be honest about it. Keep customers apprised of your efforts to fix the problem. Let them know you want them to tell you if there's a problem.
- **Control the Message:** Wrong information can spread quickly, so get the truth out there as fast as you can.
- **Improve Employee Relations:** Being open about salaries and bonuses teaches employees what to expect and inspires them to work harder. Being open to criticism from your employees also encourages a more transparent workplace and may bring you valuable information.

CORPORATE SOCIAL RESPONSIBILITY

Corporate social responsibility (CSR) is the concept that the relationship between business and society ought to go deeper than profit.

Barny Haughton is owner and executive chef at the upscale Bordeaux Quay Restaurant in Bristol, England. Katie VandenBerg owns Eli's Coffee Shop in the small town of Morton, Illinois. What do these two people, in very different circumstances and half a world apart, have in common? They both demonstrate corporate social responsibility by running their businesses in ways that achieve profit and growth and also benefit society and the environment.

Barny designed Bordeaux Quay as a model of resource conservation, from its recycling program to its low-flush toilets (which are refilled by captured rainwater).

At Eli's Coffee Shop, Katie serves only ethically sourced coffee. **Ethical sourcing** means buying from suppliers who provide safe working conditions and respect workers' rights. Both businesses benefit from CSR by publicizing their efforts, which attracts and inspires customers.

Corporate social responsibility makes good business sense. It leads to positive publicity and makes customers feel good about buying.

CUSTOMER ETHICS

Business owners are bound by law to treat customers fairly. A wise entrepreneur, however, understands that the ethical obligation goes beyond these legal minimums.

It costs more to attract a new customer than it does to maintain an existing one.

Cultivate these four qualities, which cost nothing to put into practice, and you will develop great relationships with your customers:

1. **Honesty:** Be honest and transparent in all areas. Inform customers about both the advantages and drawbacks of your product. If you offer a service, describe your qualifications and abilities accurately. Honestly estimate the time and cost of completing a project. Admit mistakes without making excuses.

2. **Respect:** Take customer complaints seriously. These are opportunities to improve your business. Research shows that only one of every fifty unsatisfied customers complains to the merchant. When you fix a situation that made one customer unhappy, you may be saving forty-nine other customers from the same frustration—and retaining them as customers.

3. **Accessibility:** Keep to the business hours you advertise. Be available when you promise to be. Honor your appointments with clients and don't be late. Give customers contact information where they can reach you with questions.

4. **Attention:** Focus your attention on the customer with whom you are working at the moment. Be present for that customer whether the sale is big or small. Don't be distracted by your cell phone!

ENVIRONMENTALLY FRIENDLY ENTERPRISE

Going green is ethical—and profitable! Surveys show that consumers look favorably on businesses that show a commitment to protecting the environment.

Concern for the environment is creating new industries and expanding older ones. What entrepreneurial ventures can you imagine creating in the following four fields?

1. **Sustainable Design:** Design that is **sustainable** meets people's current needs while preserving resources for future generations. Sustainable design ranges from planned, "walkable" cities that reduce the need for automobiles to fashions made from natural fabrics and dyes that don't pollute the water supply.

2. **Alternative Energy:** Heavy reliance on oil and coal for energy has seriously damaged the environment. Researchers are working to make

alternatives such as solar, wind, and hydrogen power more efficient. They're testing biofuels extracted from corn, sugar cane, and even vegetable oil left over from frying foods.

3. **Organics:** Organic products are made from crops and animals raised without potentially toxic chemicals. Organic produce, grains, and meats make up a small but steadily growing segment of the food market. Organic personal care items are also gaining popularity.

4. **Fair Trade: Fair trade** is business conducted fairly with small farmers and skilled crafters in developing countries. These micro-entrepreneurs form cooperatives to set prices and product standards, helping to ensure a fair wage and a specific level of quality for their work. Most fair trade items are then sold through a network of independent wholesalers and retailers. Sales of fair trade goods have risen worldwide by double digits in the last decade as consumers grow more aware of the impact of their spending decisions.

Math Moment

How much money in water costs would a restaurant owner save annually by replacing three conventional dishwashers with three Energy Star models?*

Commercial Dishwasher: Annual Costs

ANNUAL OPERATING COSTS	ENERGY STAR UNIT	CONVENTIONAL UNIT
Electricity	$890	$1,556
Water	$112	$222
Total	$1,002	$1,778

---

*   Answer: $330.

THE ENERGY-EFFICIENT WORKPLACE

An energy-efficient workplace saves money and can attract customers.

Here are five ways a business can lower its expenses, while also helping the environment:

1. **Recycle.** Most communities have paper and plastic recycling programs. Your community also might have businesses that recondition older computers and other office electronics. Use recycled and recyclable products when available.

2. **Go paperless.** Pay bills and place orders with vendors online or by phone. If you send newsletters to regular customers, encourage them to subscribe to an email version instead of paper.

3. **Buy supplies in bulk.** Items sold in large quantities usually cost less per piece and may use less packaging.

4. **Replace incandescent lightbulbs with fluorescent ones.** Compact fluorescent lightbulbs last much longer and save money.

5. **Use environmentally friendly transportation.** Adjust employee schedules or business hours to take advantage of carpooling or public transportation. Offer employees low-cost incentives, such as a gift card from a bicycle shop for those who ride to work. Encourage the use of hybrids or other energy-efficient cars.

Green Tip

Read product packaging, being alert for any indication that it is recyclable. Tell suppliers that you prefer to order items packed with recyclable containers and padding.

In response to Amazon customers who complained about the environmental effects of Styrofoam packing, for example, the company replaced Styrofoam peanuts with bags filled with air,

SHRINK YOUR CARBON FOOTPRINT

Your business can help the environment by purchasing **carbon offsets**. A carbon offset is a unit of carbon dioxide. By "buying" it from a nonprofit group, you give the group money to invest in renewable energy producers or resource-conservation projects, to counter the amount of carbon dioxide your business activity (such as taking a plane trip) has put into the atmosphere.

If your company leaves a heavy carbon footprint, you might want to look at carbon offsets as an option. Look closely, however. Regulation of carbon offset trading is uneven, and benefits can be hard to verify.

Tech U

Here are some free apps to help you figure out your business's carbon footprint and offset it:

Carbon Track	https://itunes.apple.com/us/app/carbon-track/id476736021?mt=8
Carbon Footprint Calculator	http://www.futuresme.eu/strategic-apps/carbon-footprint-calculator
Ride Remedy	http://www.appolicious.com/shine/apps/212259-rideremedy-corgar-llc

THE GIVING PLEDGE

Billionaire investor Warren Buffett, with Melinda and Bill Gates, developed the Giving Pledge (http://givingpledge.org), a public promise for wealthy people to make to give most of their wealth away during their lifetimes. As of September 2012, they had persuaded eleven of their billionaire peers to pledge to give away half of their wealth, including tech billionaires Gordon Moore and Reed Hastings.

The Giving Pledge is expected to kick-start a new era of American philanthropy in which wealthy business owners start making donations earlier in their lives, while they can still be involved in choosing how to spend it.

How will you use *your* fortune to leave behind a better world?

HOW TO START DOING GOOD—AND DOING GOOD BUSINESS!—TODAY

You may not have a million dollars (yet!) to give to your favorite charity, but there are still many ways that, as a business owner, you can do good in your community by running your business ethically.

Obey the Rule of 250. Joe Girard, one of the world's top salesmen, came up with this rule. He observed that every person knows around 250 other people who would attend his or her funeral. This means if you treat just one customer badly, 250 people could hear about it! So obey the rule of 250: Treat customers like gold, and you can bet that at least some of their friends will hear good things about your business and come check it out themselves.

Treat your employees like family. In Japan, employees are considered members of the business owner's family. The owner does everything possible to ensure that employees keep their jobs, and treats them very well. In turn, the employees are very motivated and do great work.

You can motivate your employees in many ways:

1. **Treat them fairly and considerately.**
2. **Make them owners of the company, too.** You work long hours because you own and love your business. Now, what if you could inspire that feeling in your employees?

   Bill Gates used this strategy early in Microsoft's history because he knew he would be asking computer programmers to work long hours on very difficult tasks. As a result, many Microsoft employees became millionaires—and they still want to work at Microsoft!
3. **Support lifelong learning.** Employees are happier if they're growing, personally and professionally, at their job. The best companies pay for their employees to go to seminars and conferences, and even to school. You may not be in a position to do that, but you can make an extra effort to teach your employees as many skills as possible. One simple way to do this is to create a lending library at your business that any employee can use.
4. **Create an environment that makes your employees want to stay.** When some major corporations realized they were losing brilliant female executives to motherhood because the companies failed to provide adequate maternity leave, day care, and flexible scheduling, for example, they changed their policies to give female employees what they needed to be able to come back to work.

   Encourage your employees to strike a healthy balance between their jobs and their personal lives. Always remember that your employees have personal lives and responsibilities. It will make you a better boss with more loyal, appreciative employees.

CAUSE-RELATED MARKETING

Cause-related marketing is a partnership between a business and a nonprofit group for the benefit of both. The nonprofit is committed to a cause and the for-profit business partners with it to help it achieve its mission.

At its best, cause-related marketing accomplishes two goals: It increases sales for the business and raises money and awareness for the nonprofit group.

A travel agency, for instance, could be a corporate sponsor of a community's Little League baseball team, making participating in the league affordable for more children.

In exchange, the business's name and logo could appear on the ball-field fences and the back of team shirts. The team's website would have a link to the travel agency. The travel agency would contribute to the community's quality of life while advertising to the community. The community and the business would both benefit.

Guess which travel agency the parents would be likely to call when planning their next family vacations?

Other types of cause-related marketing include:

- **Facilitated Giving:** A business makes it easier for customers to contribute to a cause. For example, a store puts canisters at the checkout counter from a local charity to encourage customers to drop in their change.
- **Purchase-Triggered Donation:** For every purchase of a particular item the business contributes a percentage of the purchase price to charity. Restaurant owners used this technique to raise $12 million for victims of Hurricane Katrina. Some seventeen thousand restaurants took part in the one-day campaign, called Dine for America, donating the proceeds to the American Red Cross.

It's a good idea to partner with a nonprofit with which you have a special connection. Wendy's hamburger restaurant chain, for instance, runs a cause-related marketing program that encourages the adoption of foster children. The fact that Wendy's founder Dave Thomas had been an adopted child himself made this partnership a resonant choice for his company.

GIVE BACK BY MENTORING

The word **mentor** comes from a character in the Greek classic *The Odyssey*. When Odysseus leaves home to fight in the Trojan War, he asks Mentor, his "wise and trusted friend," to guard his house and family for him.

A mentor is someone who agrees to share expertise and caring in an ongoing relationship with another person who could use this help. A teacher who takes extra time after class to help you with a science project, or who inspires you to become a writer and helps you apply to colleges with good writing programs, is a mentor.

As you become a more experienced entrepreneur, consider mentoring someone who is just starting his or her own business. Not only will you feel great about being an advisor, but, through sharing your mentor's experience, you will learn even more about business and will meet more contacts.

Visit the National Mentoring Partnership at www.mentoring.org and look for mentor programs in your area.

How to Find a Mentor for Yourself

You may already have a mentor in your life. Is there someone who has shown an interest in your business and has helped you with advice or contacts? Perhaps he or she would be willing to become your mentor. You can also meet potential mentors at events held by any professional organizations in your field.

Jimmy McNeal is a young entrepreneur who took a year off to teach entrepreneurship after closing his first business. While teaching for NFTE, he met Peter Janssen, one of the top young investment bankers in New York City. Peter was putting together the financing for a company called United States Bicycle Corporation.

Because Jimmy is a professional bike racer who hopes to create his own bike brand, Bulldog Bikes, Peter introduced him to the owner of U.S. Bicycle and helped Jimmy negotiate a lucrative deal to develop Bulldog Bikes as a subsidiary of U.S. Bicycle.

This is how mentoring works—the right mentor can provide contacts and hands-on guidance that can take your business forward beyond your wildest dreams.

VOLUNTEER!

You can also help your community by encouraging your employees to volunteer. Volunteers from a local business who help with a community project are making a visible statement that the business is committed to the community's health. In addition, volunteer projects are a fun way to foster unity and teamwork among employees.

Although time is a scarce resource for many entrepreneurs, giving back to your community is a chance to build professional and personal relationships. It also provides market research, giving you on-the-ground information about what people in your area need. Finally, volunteering gives you a nice mental and physical break from the pressure to make a profit.

You couldn't do anything better for your business than to make sure it is socially and environmentally responsible. Not only will this be good for employee morale, help society, and reduce the government's burden, but ethical business practices and philanthropy attract tremendous media attention and will help create a positive image for your business in your community.

Doing good will make you happier, too, and that's the point of entrepreneurship—to create a life that makes you happy!

An Entrepreneur Like You

Terry Hargrove

WE LEND A HAND

When Terrence L. Hargrove was in high school, he started a candle-selling business called Passions. He bought candles wholesale and sold them retail. Several months later, he started Dynasty Cleaners, a cleaning service for schools and businesses.

Both ventures were successful, and Terry made money. He went on to college and also worked as an assistant teacher in a Connecticut high school.

Lending a Hand to Students

After graduating from college, Terry continued teaching in high school. "I saw a lot of kids that had potential," he recalls, "but they were repeat offenders and kept getting in trouble with discipline action—detention, in-school suspension, and out-of-school suspension." Terry met with the principal, trying to figure out what could be done to help these students and keep them from getting into trouble. His next business, We Lend a Hand, was inspired by that meeting.

We Lend a Hand helps students who are at risk of being suspended or expelled by providing mentors and access to community action programs where they can channel their frustrations into productive activity. Students are given their choice of serving detention or in-school suspension or completing a We Lend a Hand project. This could involve, for example, choosing a plot of land on school grounds, transforming it into a mini-garden or walkway, and then writing about the experience.

Raising Money

We Lend a Hand is a not-for-profit company, and everyone working for it, including Terry, is a volunteer. "We raise money through the community," says Terry. "We go to different small businesses and ask them to donate to We Lend a Hand to build up our treasury so that we're able to do different projects."

Although raising money is typically the hardest job in a nonprofit organization, We Lend a Hand has had a different experience. "The community has really jumped on to help out," Terry explains. "I guess they recognize the issue and see the problem and believe that We Lend a Hand has one of the solutions to the problem."

Keeping Books

Terry has found it important to be completely transparent about his nonprofit's financial records, because the money is being donated from outside sources. "We pay close attention to how we do our books," Terry notes, explaining, "Our donors can see where their money is going, and how it's being spent. Our books always have to be correct."

We Lend a Hand reflects Terry's life philosophy: "No matter how successful you can be, you have to remember your community. You can't put yourself always first. You have to use everything that you have to go back and build the next generation, so they can have a better opportunity."

Think Like an Entrepreneur

1. What about the We Lend a Hand program do you think most helps at-risk students?
2. How would you raise money if you had a nonprofit organization like Terry's?
3. What's the difference between using your own money and someone else's to run your organization? Does this explain why Terry pays so much attention to his financial records?

CHAPTER 9

SELL LIKE A PRO

LEARN TO SELL AND YOU'LL NEVER BE BROKE

When there's nothing to lose
and much to gain by trying, try.

—W. Clement Stone

Many of America's greatest entrepreneurs started their careers in sales. All business is based on selling products or services for money. Selling is easy to learn, and if you get good at it, you'll never have to worry about being broke.

Salespeople often become successful entrepreneurs because they hear, on a daily basis, what customers need and want. If the customer is dissatisfied, it is the salesperson who hears the complaint.

If you read this chapter and learn to sell, you will always be able to support yourself.

GET A SELF-SELLER

William C. Durant, the founder of General Motors, began his career as a buggy salesman. He said, "The secret of success is to have a self-seller, and if you don't have one, get one." A self-seller is a product so good that it sells itself.

Durant was from my hometown, Flint, Michigan. I should have remembered his advice when I started selling. One of the first products I tried to sell was a bicycle lock from Taiwan. I was representing the lock exporter. After many phone calls, I finally secured a meeting with an importer who could have ordered thousands of the locks. My commission on the sale would have been $5,000 per month.

During our meeting, the importer picked up one of the locks and yanked it as hard as he could. It broke. Needless to say, I did not make any sales that day.

Read a Classic

How to Sell Anything to Anybody by Joe Girard. In his fifteen-year career as a car salesman, author Joe Girard sold 13,001 cars, a Guinness World Record. As a young boy, he sold newspaper subscriptions door-to-door and learned that the more doorbells he rang, the more money he made. He carried that philosophy forward when he graduated to selling big-ticket items.

CHARACTERISTICS OF SUCCESSFUL SALESPEOPLE

Salespeople have various personalities and styles of selling; however, the most successful salespeople have the following characteristics in common:

Positive Attitude: Successful salespeople focus on the positive, even when times are tough. Their enthusiasm shines through in their conversation and actions. Ron Popeil pioneered the process of selling products such as Mr. Microphone and the Showtime Rotisserie on television by infomercial. "If I create a product, I can market it as well as or better than anyone on the planet," he told *Inc.* magazine. "I have the confidence and the passion. People see that, and they know it is real."

Good Listener: Successful salespeople ask their customers good questions and then listen closely without interrupting. The salesperson can then offer a solution tailored to the customer's specific situation. David Ogilvy, the legendary advertising executive, began his career as a door-to-door salesman of cooking stoves. Ogilvy advises, "The worst fault a salesman can commit is to be a bore. Foster any attempt to talk about other things; the longer you stay the better you get to know the prospect, and the more you will be trusted."

Persistence: Selling is not as easy as some people make it look. Salespeople often make many contacts and have many conversations before making a sale. Cultivate patience and persistence to become skilled at making a sale. The good news is that the more you practice, the easier selling becomes.

Tech U

Nothing beats face-to-face communication for effective selling. If you can't meet a potential customer in person, use Skype, FaceTime, or other forms of videoconferencing to connect personally with them.

Many people appreciate the opportunity to provide feedback as well as receive information. Let them tell you both what they love and what they hate about your product—you will learn valuable information!

Hardworking: Salespeople who take responsibility for their own success make goals for themselves and then form strategies to reach them. They work hard to produce positive results, instead of blaming their company, the economy, or the competition when they fail to make a sale.

Truthful: Some salespeople tell customers only what they think they want to hear, but this approach can lead to misunderstandings and deception. It can be difficult to reestablish trust with a customer once it has been broken. In addition, customers who feel betrayed may tell others about their negative experiences. This can cause an even greater loss of sales and a bad reputation. Always tell the truth about your product or service. It's OK to admit to any flaws or problems—that will only make a customer trust you more.

Reliable: To become successful, you need to be dependable. That means you don't promise something you cannot deliver within a reasonable time frame. If you are unreliable, the customer may get annoyed and decide to buy from one of your competitors. Another form of consistency is keeping in touch with your customers. This could include sending thank-you notes, birthday cards, newsletters, and the like. Consistency builds trust, which leads to better customer relationships. It encourages customer loyalty to your brand or business.

Lifetime Learners: Sales expert Zig Ziglar encourages salespeople to commit to a lifetime of learning and training, and to maintain motivation by constantly visualizing success. The more you learn, the more interesting you are to others—and the more they will enjoy talking to you, which will lead to buying from you!

Super Success Story

From 1878 to 1886, Will Durant tried to start a variety of small businesses. None of them really took off. He had yet to find his "self-seller." When he was twenty-five, however, Durant hitched a ride to work with a friend. He noticed that his friend's new horse-drawn buggy rode smoother than any he had been in. His friend explained that the smooth ride was due to a new kind of buggy spring. Durant was so impressed that he became determined to buy the company that made this new kind of carriage.

Durant learned that the Coldwater Road Cart Company made the buggies with the improved springs. The very next day, Durant went to Coldwater, Michigan. The owner of the cart company was willing to sell it for $1,500. Durant insisted that the deal include the patent for the springs. In two days, the deal was closed. This transaction demonstrated Durant's business philosophy: "Decide quickly, make your pitch, nail down the details, and don't worry about the money."

When Durant made the deal, he didn't have $1,500, but he didn't let that stop him. Durant borrowed $2,000 from the Citizens National Bank of Flint and made two sample buggy carts. He transported one of them to a county fair in Madison, Wisconsin. His entrepreneurial hunch was correct. The cart sold itself; within a week he had orders for six hundred buggy carts.

The business was a great success. By 1893, Durant's original $2,000 investment had grown to $150,000 (or almost $4 million in 2013 dollars). By 1901, his company was the biggest buggy manufacturer in the country.

In 1902, David Dunbar Buick, a Scottish immigrant who ran a plumbing supply business in Detroit, formed the Buick Manufacturing Company. He was not having much success, however, and needed money to save the business. In 1904, he got a meeting with Durant.

Durant took a ride in the still experimental "Buick." He became immediately enthusiastic about the car, which he believed was one of those natural "self-sellers" he was always seeking. He agreed to invest only if he could have absolute managerial control of the company. Durant took over the Buick Company on November 1, 1904.

At the 1905 auto show in New York, Durant "sold" 1,108 cars when the company, until that point, had actually manufactured only 37. By 1906, the Buick Company was worth $3 million. This is the company that became General Motors, one of the world's largest automakers, which is worth around $38 billion, employs more than 200,000 people, and does business in more than 150 countries

FEATURES BECOME BENEFITS

The essence of selling is teaching *how* and *why* the outstanding features of your product or service will benefit your customers. When Will Durant took his buggy cart to the county fair, he showed potential customers how the cart's unique feature—its extra-springy seat—could benefit them by making them more comfortable during a buggy ride.

Let's say you sell hats that last long, are washable, fold without wrinkling, and come in many great colors. These features create the product's benefits: A durable hat will not have to be replaced soon; an easy-to-clean hat will save money; a hat that fits into a pocket or bag will be used often. The benefits sell the hat, not the features.

The features of a product are facts about the product. The creative art of selling is teaching customers how the features will benefit them.

Green Tip

Although consumers are increasingly looking for green products, according to Method cofounder Eric Ryan, a product won't sell better only because it's green.

Even though Method markets environmentally friendly cleaners, "I fundamentally believe that if you build something and ask people to buy it for the sole reason it's green, you'll ultimately fail," Ryan told *GreenBiz,* adding, "That's my best piece of advice."

LISTENING BUILDS TRUST

The most important thing a salesperson/entrepreneur can do is listen. Sales expert Brian Tracy believes most of your time should be spent on getting to know your customers and building their trust by listening to what they have to say, before you even try to make a sale.

Tracy describes the sales process in three steps, which, he notes, are similar to those followed by physicians:

1. Establish rapport (the doctor's exam)
2. Identify a problem (diagnosis)
3. Present a solution (prescription)

"The prospect," Tracy writes in *Advanced Selling Strategies,* "cannot even seriously consider your offer until he or she is convinced that you are his friend and acting in his best interests. Therefore, you must take sufficient time to build a bridge of personal warmth and rapport between yourself and the prospect."

Tracy adds that, with this approach, price should not be discussed until the "solution" phase of the sales process.

KNOW YOUR COMPETITION

Here's a great tip: Experience a sales call from one of your competitor's salespeople. Let the person sell to you. You'll get a gold mine of information. Study the strengths and weaknesses of your competitor's product or service, because your prospects will probably bring them up during your sales calls.

If, during this stage of preparation, you begin to feel that your product or service doesn't measure up, don't try to sell it. Your business will fail if it's not built on a product or service that you believe is the best available in the marketplace for the price.

Remember William C. Durant's advice about having a self-seller, "and if you don't have one, get one." Always be on the lookout for ways to improve your product or to get a better one.

THE SELLING PROCESS

Now let's explore the selling process. It has four steps:

1. Find a Sales Lead
2. Qualify the Sales Lead
3. Make the Sales Call
4. Close the Sale and Follow Up

STEP ONE: FINDING A SALES LEAD

The selling process starts by finding sales leads. Sales leads are obtained in several ways:

- **Promotional Responses:** Some sales leads come directly from people who respond to your promotions. You get sales leads when potential customers fill out surveys or website forms.

- **Referrals:** When a person provides contact information for someone else who may be interested in your product or service, this is called a **referral**. Referrals may be freely offered to a salesperson by a satisfied customer. They also may be obtained at networking events. You could always offer a commission or special discount to customers who bring you referrals.

- **Cold Calls:** When a salesperson contacts someone he or she does not know, and without prior notice, it is called a **cold call**. Another name for cold calling is "canvassing." Email and telephone lists are available for purchase from companies that have made a business out of gathering information, organizing it, and selling it to others. Salespeople use these lists for cold calls.

If a sales lead has many of the characteristics of your target market, the sales lead becomes a **prospect,** or potential customer. A key characteristic might be whether the customer has purchased a product similar to yours in the past. Age and hobbies are other valuable characteristics to uncover.

Learn the Lingo

A **sales lead** is a person or company from your target market that you think might want to buy your product or service.

STEP TWO: QUALIFYING THE SALES LEAD

Keep in mind that not every sales lead turns into a prospect. To avoid wasting time pursuing leads that have little chance of becoming prospects, you need to evaluate each lead and decide whether you should pursue it. This process is called "qualifying the lead."

Sales leads can lose their potential for becoming sales prospects for many reasons. The person or business may no longer need your product or service because they've already purchased something similar. Or, the sales lead may not be able to afford to buy at the current time. A sales lead may also lose its potential if the person you contacted has moved to a different locality or has left a company.

Before making an appointment for a sales call, find out the answer to these questions first:

- Is this person in my market?
- Does this person need my product?
- Can this person afford it?

If the answer to any of these questions is no, it may be a waste of time to make a sales call.

STEP THREE: MAKING THE SALES CALL

Once you have determined which sales leads make good prospects, it's time to go on some sales calls. Before going to a sales call:

Set up an appointment. This ensures that the person you want to see will be available when you visit. It also allows you to make sure you will be talking to the right person. When making an appointment, be sure to ask if any other people need to be involved in the buying decision. You don't want to waste your time making a great pitch, only to learn that the buyer was not in the room.

Learn about the prospect. If you are visiting a company, go through its website and read everything from the "about" section. If the prospect was referred to you, talk to the person who provided the contact and ask for advice on how best to sell to this prospective buyer.

Know your product or service. The more knowledgeable you are about what you are selling, the more confident and relaxed you will likely be during sales calls. Memorize key facts.

Develop an overall selling strategy. Consider the aspects of your product or service that will appeal most to the prospect. Try to anticipate what questions or objections the prospect may have, and come up with answers.

Practice your presentation. Plan what you want to say and what marketing materials you want to show. If you are planning to demonstrate a product, practice those steps as well. If you are going to be selling to a group of people, consider preparing a brief PowerPoint presentation. Practice on your friends or a mentor.

Tech U

Here are some great ways to use technology to sell:

- Videotape a demonstration or presentation of your product and post it on YouTube, Facebook, Twitter, your website, or Tumblr.

- Skype with customers to present new products or answer questions.

- Use software like Plaxo (www.plaxo.com) to keep prospect lists organized and log sales calls. Plaxo sends you alerts whenever a contact's info has changed and automatically updates your address book.

- Boost the visual impact of your PowerPoint presentations with Serious Magic (http://seriousmagic.net) software, which lets you easily add animation, graphic backgrounds, and other features. It even has a countdown clock for each slide to help you keep your remarks short and wrap up your presentation on time.

- Add GPS to your phone so you never get lost trying to get to a meeting with a sales prospect.

- Get a credit card reader that plugs into your mobile phone or tablet, so you can make sales on the go. Square (www.squareup.com) and PayPal Here (www.paypal .com/here) both provide free credit card reading apps and will send you free plug-in readers. Check out the fees for processing payments before choosing a credit card reader.

The Seven-Step Sales Call

Now for the big moment—your first sales call! Follow these seven steps and you will do great:

1. **Preparation.** Prepare yourself mentally. Make sure you are early to the meeting and dressed for success. Prepare all your presentation materials far in advance so that you have them ready to go the day of the sales call. Think about how your product or service will benefit this customer. Have the price, discounts, all technical information, and any other details "on the tip of your tongue." Be willing to obtain further information should your customer request it.

2. **Greeting.** Greet the customer graciously. Do not plunge immediately into business talk. The first few words you say can be the most important. Keep a two-way conversation going. Maintain eye contact, *listen,* and keep the customer's attention.

3. **Show the product or service.** Try to "personalize" it. Point out the benefits for this particular customer. Use props and models (or the real thing) where appropriate.

4. **Deal with objections.** Always acknowledge objections and deal with them. Don't pretend you didn't hear. Don't overreact to objections, and don't be afraid to listen. A famous real estate entrepreneur, William Zeckendorf, said, "I never lost money on a sales pitch when I listened to the customer."

5. **Close the sale.** Review the benefits of your product or service. Narrow the choices the customer has to make. Don't overstay your welcome. There is a rule of thumb that if a customer says no three times, you still have a chance. If he or she says it the fourth time, it's really no. If the answer is no, take it gracefully. Make friends and you may make a sale to this customer in the future.

6. **Follow up.** Make regular follow-up calls to find out how your customer likes the product or service. Ask if you can be of any further help. If the customer has a complaint, don't ignore it. Remember, *a successful business is built on repeat customers.*

7. **Ask for references.** If you did a good job for customers who needed your product or service, ask them to refer you to other potential customers.

Try It!

When you make a sales call, you should always leave your business card, but try giving your prospects something else to help them remember and like your company. A **premium** is a giveaway item or free gift with the company's name, address, and telephone number printed on it. T-shirts, pens, notepads, coffee cups, and calendars are all examples of premiums.

The One-Minute Sales Call

Believe it or not, it's a challenge for most people to pay attention to someone for more than a minute. Unless you are selling a complex product with lots of features you must demonstrate, keep your sales call pitches under one minute, and you'll be more effective.

Write down your sales pitch and practice delivering it to a friend or relative. Have your listener time you. You'll be shocked at how fast a minute can go by!

Here's an example to get you started. Let's say you make baby food from organic fruits and vegetables. You are trying to convince the manager of a gourmet grocery store near you to buy some of your baby food to feature in its "local products" section.

SALES PITCH

Hello, Mr. Ramirez. Thank you for agreeing to see me today. I'm excited about this product and think you and your customers will be, too.

I brought you a jar of our baby applesauce. It's nicely packaged, don't you think? We hand-decorate each jar. They make nice gifts for new or expecting parents. The eye-catching ribbons will be sure to attract your customers.

We use only organic fruits and vegetables, no sugar, and very little salt. Our label explains that some babies are sensitive to the additives and dyes found in some commercial baby foods. These may give sensitive babies headaches or upset stomachs. Our food is very gentle on the baby—and that makes the parents' life much easier!

I understand your concern that our baby food costs twenty-five cents per jar more on average than the brands you presently stock. I think your customers will pay more for our high quality and for knowing that their babies are protected from harmful additives or high levels of sugar and salt. Because we add very little water to our product, we actually offer more food for the money than some cheaper brands.

I really think you could start a trend by stocking our baby food here, Mr. Ramirez. There's been a shift in the food market toward healthy food for adults—and those adults are looking for healthy baby food. Our products combine an eye-catching look with healthy ingredients that new parents and their friends and relatives won't be able to resist.

How many jars would you like to order?

Step 4: Closing the Sale and Following Up

The sale is considered "closed" once payment is received. But your interaction with the customer should not end there. This is the beginning of your long-term relationship!

Follow up to make sure that the entire selling process met his or her expectations. A happy customer will lead to additional sales and plenty of referrals. Make sure your new customer is inspired to talk up your business.

Following up may also include asking a customer for referrals and for written testimonials for use in promotional materials. Maintaining routine contact with a **sales account** (a customer that buys from you regularly) also helps you stay aware of possible changes in the customer's needs.

THE MECHANICS OF SELLING

You'll want to stay organized while selling so you don't accidentally bug one customer too much—or forget to call another one entirely. Here are some useful tools to help you handle the mechanics of selling:

Sales Call Log. Use this form to record each telephone call you make to a prospect or to an established customer. Besides name and contact information, this form typically includes the date the call was made, the purpose, notes about the conversation (including objections and responses), and follow-up tasks (what and when).

You can create a sales call log with Excel or on Google Docs. One advantage of using Google Docs is that you can share your log with other salespeople in your company, and see theirs.

Contact Name	Contact Information	Date of Call	Purpose	Notes	Follow-Up Tasks
John Simmons	Happy Pet 126 Alexandria Blvd. (415) 555-1236	11/30/--	Have Happy Pet carry our line of natural dog treats.	Was interested but concerned that he hadn't heard of us.	Send him sales kit, with video of Channel 12's feature on us. Check back in a week.

▲ *Sales Call Log*

Order Form: Salespeople may use paper order forms to record orders when they do not have access to the company's computer. Order forms may vary in appearance, but most include the elements in the order form shown below. A physical order form is made up of multiple identical pages, so that when the salesperson fills out the form, a duplicate copy is automatically made. Give or email one copy to the customer and keep the other for your records.

Order Form

Date
Salesperson

Address

Sold To	Ship To
Phone	Ship By

Quantity	Item/Description	Price/Item	Subtotal

Total	
Sales Tax	
Shipping Charge	
Amount Due	

Tech U

There are some great phone apps for salespeople available, such as Salesforce (www.salesforce.com) and Zoho (www.zoho.com), that enable you to create sales calls logs, records, and receipts on your smartphone.

Math Moment

Most order forms include a line for sales tax, which is calculated by multiplying the purchase total by the tax rate.

If the cost of an item is $50 and the tax rate is 5 percent, how much is the sales tax?*

---

* Answer: $2.50.

Sales Receipt: This is a document you give the customer to prove that the sale took place and that you were paid. Most retail and service businesses use electronic cash registers for sales transactions. A cash register totals the items being purchased, calculates sales tax, and produces a paper **receipt** for the customer. In addition to sales figures, this receipt often lists short descriptions of items purchased, the date, and how the items were paid for (cash or credit). Square and PayPal Here are two credit card readers that plug into smartphones. You can use them to accept payments and generate electronic receipts that you can text or email to the customer.

It's a good idea to require customers to present their sales receipts when they want to return or exchange a product. Make sure your policy on this is posted clearly on your website and wherever you conduct your sales. You can even have it printed on your receipts.

Sales Contract: The seller or the buyer may draw up a contract when a sale involves many details or is complex. Contracts are also used when a service or product is being delivered over a long period of time. A sales contract provides legal protection for both the seller and the buyer. In most cases, contracts are reviewed by each party's attorney before they are signed.

Sales Proposal: If you have made a sales call on a business, it may issue a **request for proposal (RFP)**. An RFP is a formal way for one business to ask another to make a **bid** for a sale. A business may send an RFP to three or four companies. Each interested company prepares a sales proposal in response to the RFP. The prospect then compares the bids (prices, delivery information, and so forth) offered by each company and uses that information to decide from which company it is going to buy.

GETTING PEOPLE TO SELL FOR YOU

If you have a great product, the first employees you may be able to add to your business will be friends or relatives interested in helping you sell it. You might not be able to afford to pay them, but you could offer them a **commission**. A commission is typically a percentage of the total amount sold. Because a salesperson on straight commission gets paid only if he or she sells something, this approach is directly tied to work performance and results.

Although commission-only might be a good way for you to begin adding salespeople to your business, more-experienced salespeople tend to avoid these deals.

They prefer to have some stable income. Most often, salespeople are paid with a combination of salary and commission. The challenge is to find the right mix of salary and commission to both motivate your sales staff and make them want to stay and grow the business with you.

In addition to salaries and commissions, some companies offer bonuses for salespeople who sell more than their quotas. A **sales quota** is a target amount of sales per month or quarter that a salesperson is expected to achieve. A sales quota is usually based on the type and size of the **sales territory**. A sales territory is the specific geographical area for which a salesperson is responsible, such as a city, county, state, or region.

Most companies also pay salespeople for travel expenses related to their work. These expenses usually include airfare, rental cars, taxis, road and bridge tolls, hotels, and meals.

Each salesperson must obtain receipts when these items are paid for and create an **expense report** that lists each item. The salesperson turns the expense report plus the receipts in to you for payment.

DIRECT SALES ASSOCIATION

If you think you have a knack for selling, you might enjoy **direct selling** for a company such as Avon or Tupperware. To find more, contact the Direct Selling Association (DSA), which is the national trade association of companies that manufacture and distribute products and services sold directly to consumers. Its membership includes Avon Products, Mary Kay Cosmetics, Artistic Impressions, Amway, Tupperware International, and many other popular direct sellers.

Direct selling companies tap into the entrepreneurial dream by training people who want to start and build their own businesses. A Mary Kay salesperson, for example, purchases skin-care products and makeup from Mary Kay Cosmetics at a 40 to 50 percent discount. The salesperson gives facials and skin-care classes in her home or at a customer's home to attract customers, and sells the products directly to them.

A Mary Kay salesperson can also recruit people to sell Mary Kay products. The recruiter receives a percentage of the sales of her recruits. In this way, direct selling has enabled thousands of people to build very profitable businesses with very little capital investment.

Some disreputable companies focus almost exclusively on the recruiting aspect of direct sales, luring salespeople with promises of instant riches. The DSA has been instrumental in educating the public about the dangers of these so-called pyramid schemes.

The primary purpose of a direct selling company should be to sell products that meet consumer needs. Before getting involved with any direct sales company, call or email the Direct Selling Association to check it out carefully.

An Entrepreneur Like You

Julene Fleurmond
ENVIBRANCE STUDIOS
www.envibrance.com

When Julene Fleurmond was in the tenth grade, she entered a website design contest at her South Miami high school. "I began teaching myself how to use different website-design programs," she said. "I didn't think I would win, but I won first place."

Relationships Lead to Business

Along with being awarded a scholarship, Julene also impressed one of the judges, who asked her to work with his organization, the National Urban League, on other projects. Julene began doing community service projects. She researched how to operate a creative graphic design business, took on internships at other firms, networked with professors and mentors, and made sure her work was on a professional level.

After two years of freelancing, Julene started Envibrance Studios, a media and promotional company that creates websites, multimedia, creative content, and publications. Envibrance's motto is "Envision the possibilities; we'll bring them to life."

Relationships Lead to the Right Pricing

Julene was confident about providing her services, but she didn't feel confident about pricing them. "A lot of my first clients were friends of mine," says Julene, "and I wanted to give them discounts. But when I began working with other designers, I was told I was underpricing myself by hundreds of dollars."

Julene researched how similar businesses priced their services. "I still gave discounts to service organizations," she said, "but I learned that underpricing yourself makes your service less worthy in people's eyes, and people might not take you seriously if you underprice."

Julene discovered something else important about pricing: "Don't sell yourself short. Just because someone's your friend, you don't have to do everything for free for them."

Relationships That Count

In the beginning, Julene tried to do everything herself. Eventually she found that "Asking for help is not something you should be afraid of. Sometimes I would ask other designers I knew to do part of a project. Or we would collaborate if I didn't know how to do something. They would do one part of it and I would do the other."

Julene also learned how to take on projects that she's passionate about. "My genre now is mostly youth-oriented organizations or organizations that cater to youths," she says. "Having a genre or an audience that I'm very passionate about really helps me to be more passionate about my work." Her advice to other entrepreneurs is to make sure they're passionate about whatever they do, even if others say it won't be profitable.

"I think that if you pursue what you're truly passionate about and what you were made to do," Julene explains, "financial benefits and everything else will follow naturally."

Think Like an Entrepreneur

1. How do relationships lead to business?
2. How can you be sure you're not underpricing your services?
3. What are you passionate about? How can you incorporate your passions into your current business model?

CHAPTER 10

NEGOTIATION AND COMMUNICATION

TACTICS AND TOOLS TO GET WHAT YOU WANT

You don't get what you deserve;
you get what you negotiate.

—Chester L. Karrass

In his bestselling book *You Can Negotiate Anything,* Herb Cohen tells the story of a brother and sister squabbling over how to divide the last quarter of a pie. Just as the boy gains control of the knife, their mother arrives on the scene. "Hold it!" she says. "I don't care who cuts the pie, but whoever does cut it has to give the *other* person the right to select the piece he or she wants."

To protect himself, the boy cuts the pie into two pieces of equal size. The moral of the story is that *if two people shift their focus from defeating each other to defeating the problem, everybody benefits.*

NEGOTIATION IS ABOUT COMPROMISE, NOT WINNING

Negotiation is the art of achieving your goals through discussion and bargaining with another person. An example of negotiation is a buyer and a seller discussing the price of an item until an agreement is reached.

Negotiation is about **compromise,** not about winning. Compromise is sacrificing something you want so that an agreement can be reached that is acceptable to you *and* the person with whom you are negotiating. In the example above, the brother and sister were initially more interested in beating each other to a bigger slice of pie than they were in satisfying their appetites.

The siblings forgot the most important principle of negotiation: The other person is not your enemy. The best negotiations are those in which both parties are satisfied—they have reached a "win-win" agreement. Conduct your negotiations as if you will be dealing with that person again very soon. In business, you probably will be, so conduct yourself well.

Negotiation is essential to business—not only to *your* business but also to the economy as a whole. Shelly owns a dog-grooming business. She wants to expand her business to include boarding, but a number of problems stand in her way. She has found a property for the kennels but the rent is too high. She can't find employees for the wages she wants to pay. And some prospective customers are unwilling or unable to pay the rates she planned to charge.

If Shelly can't find a way to negotiate these issues, she won't realize her dream. If she doesn't succeed in starting this business, there will be a "ripple effect," and the local economy could suffer. The landlord will have to maintain an empty, unproductive property. Workers won't have jobs. Dog owners will be without a useful service that they would have been happy to buy.

As a new entrepreneur, you might be surprised at how often people are willing to negotiate. You might expect that independent business owners, who have more control over their companies, would be willing to lower a price or add an extra service. But these days, even large chains often give salespeople and managers leeway in making deals. The trend toward negotiating is expected to grow because of increased competition from Internet-based companies. Negotiating is always more popular in tight economic times.

Read a Classic

The following books are among the best ever written on negotiating. Karrass's book is a classic by the father of negotiation theory, and Jandt's book provides an in-depth look at the win-win philosophy.

- *The Negotiating Game: How to Get What You Want* by Chester L. Karrass
- *Win-Win Negotiating: Turning Conflict into Agreement* by Fred Jandt

PRACTICE NEGOTIATION NOW, SO YOU'LL BE READY WHEN OPPORTUNITY KNOCKS

You may not think it's critical to learn to be a good negotiator while you're still just thinking about starting your own business—but you need to get this skill down so you're prepared when opportunity knocks at your door.

In 1980, when Bill Gates was a twenty-four-year-old geek, he probably never imagined he'd have to become a crack negotiator overnight. But at that age, he conducted one of the most important negotiations of his life.

IBM, one of the world's most powerful companies, wanted Microsoft to work with it on IBM's top-secret effort to develop a personal computer. No doubt "Big Blue," as IBM was known, expected little Microsoft, which was a $7 million company with fewer than forty employees at the time, to be a pushover. After all, IBM's annual revenues were hitting $30 billion.

Before his negotiations with IBM, however, Gates set his goals and organized his thoughts. He knew exactly what he wanted to achieve and what his limits were.

IBM offered to pay Microsoft $175,000 to include Microsoft's MS-DOS operating system on IBM's new personal computers. Gates wasn't willing to sell his company's program code for that price, because he knew IBM would want to use the code on a variety of future machines. Gates held out for royalties and continued ownership of MS-DOS. He also retained the right to license copies of the program's code to other parties.

Later, IBM would look back on that negotiation and regret its failure to purchase MS-DOS outright. The licensing deal ended up costing Big Blue a lot of money, and made Bill Gates extremely wealthy.

THREE PRINCIPLES OF SUCCESSFUL NEGOTIATING

The principles of negotiation that Gates used before entering this important negotiation with IBM are the same ones you should use before any negotiation. They are:

1. **Set your goals and organize your thoughts.** What do you want to achieve in the negotiation? Write down your goals and thoughts on note cards, and keep them with you during the discussion.

2. **Define your limits.** Think about what the best deal *for you* would be. Then think about what the worst deal would be. What is the minimum you would be willing to accept? What is the maximum you

are seeking? Knowing these limits ahead of time will prevent you from getting carried away and giving up too much of one thing in order to get something else.

3. **Put yourself in the other person's shoes.** What does he or she want from the negotiation? What is his or her minimum? Maximum? Things that aren't very important to you could be very important to the other person. You could give up these to get what you want.

FIVE NEGOTIATION TACTICS THAT WORK

During the negotiations with IBM, Gates stuck to his plan. Despite the nervousness he felt about negotiating with a very powerful corporation, Gates gave clear, calm presentations to IBM executives regarding the operating system that Microsoft proposed to supply to IBM.

In the past, Gates had jeopardized deals with customers and suppliers by being too intense and too eager to win. This time, he knew he would have to make a worthwhile offer for the deal with IBM to succeed. It would have to be a win-win deal.

IBM's representative, Sandy Meade, was surprised by Gates's boldness on the royalty issue. In the book *Gates,* Meade recalled to authors Stephen Manes and Paul Andrews that, unlike other software companies with which IBM had negotiated, "I never felt they [Microsoft] needed the money."

Meade's negotiating tactic was to remind Gates that his relationship with IBM was a "long-term relationship with the potential for big business." Gates had guessed correctly that IBM would be willing to pay royalties to use Microsoft's program code in IBM's personal computers.

In return for IBM's agreement to pay royalties, Microsoft committed to a brutal delivery schedule. That was IBM's "win."

Gates always had dinner at his parents' home on Sunday nights. After he signed the deal with IBM, Gates told his mother not to expect him for at least six months.

During negotiations, Gates and his team used all of the tactics listed below. Memorize them and practice using them during your negotiations.

1. **Let the other person name a price first.** When discussing a price, try to let the other person make an offer first. This will reveal his or her position.

2. **Try extremes.** If the person won't reveal his or her position, throw

out an extreme figure—very high or very low. This will force the other person to come forward with some type of response that will guide you.

3. **Demonstrate your willingness to bargain.** As negotiations proceed, respond to each counteroffer by giving up something you already decided in advance that you could afford to give up.

4. **Use silence as a tool.** After you have initially stated your case, don't say anything for a few moments. Your silence can prompt the other person to say something that you can turn to your advantage. Do your best to keep silent until the other person speaks. It'll happen eventually!

5. **Always ask for more than you are offered.** When the other person wants you to pay back a loan in ten days, for instance, ask for fifteen. You may have to settle for twelve, but that's better than the original demand.

Math Moment

You run an auto-detailing shop that specializes in custom paint jobs. You have agreed to repaint a classic Ford Mustang at no charge. In exchange, you will get 15 percent of the car's selling price when the owner auctions it on eBay.

The paint and other supplies you need cost $172. You estimate that the job will take you about fifteen hours. The owner expects the Mustang to sell for about $11,000. What would your share be? How much profit would you make? What hourly rate would you earn?*

---

* Answers: $1,650; $1,478; $98.53.

NEGOTIATION IN ACTION

Here's an example of how the techniques listed above can be used in a simple negotiation. Sarah collects vintage clothing. She wants to launch a business by selling pieces from her collection on the weekends at a local flea market. Eventually, she hopes to save enough money from sales to open a vintage clothing store.

Sarah has looked into the fee to sell at the flea market, and it's $100 per day, more than she can afford. She also wants to be able to get into the space before it opens so that she can set up an attractive display for her clothing.

STEP 1: SET YOUR GOALS AND ORGANIZE YOUR THOUGHTS.
Before the negotiation, Sarah determines her goals:
- To be excused from paying the entrance fee.
- To be allowed to set up early.

STEP 2: DEFINE YOUR LIMITS.
Sarah decides that she might be willing to pay some of the fee, but she definitely doesn't want to pay the full fee.

STEP 3: PUT YOURSELF IN THE OTHER PERSON'S SHOES.
Sarah takes some time to think about the flea market manager's needs. What could she offer in exchange for her requests?

As you read the dialogue below, notice that the entrepreneur is careful to make sure the manager understands how the negotiation can benefit the flea market. See if you can spot the negotiation techniques in action.

ENTREPRENEUR: Hi, I'm Sarah, and I'd like to sell here on Saturday. I was wondering if I could talk to you about it.

MANAGER: Sure, go ahead.

ENTREPRENEUR: I think there are three good reasons for having young people like me get involved with the flea market. It's good for community relations, you can probably get some publicity out of it, and it will attract more young people to the flea market as customers.

MANAGER: Well, that sounds great. Do you want to sign up now?

ENTREPRENEUR: I do, but as a young entrepreneur I don't have the money to cover the fee. As I develop my business here, though, I could begin to pay you.

MANAGER: I don't know if I'm willing to waive the fee.

ENTREPRENEUR: [Doesn't say anything.]

MANAGER: How about fifty dollars instead of a hundred?

ENTREPRENEUR: [Doesn't say anything.]

MANAGER: How about forty dollars?

ENTREPRENEUR: I understand what you do here. I think it has value. But my position is that I would be bringing a lot of value to the flea market, and I need to put my initial capital into building my business, which will benefit you in the long run. I'd also like to help you publicize the flea market by putting up posters for it at my school.

MANAGER: All right, I'll waive the fee.

ENTREPRENEUR: I have something else that would really help me. Could I come in an hour early to set up?

MANAGER: No. No way.

ENTREPRENEUR: I need to do this because I feel I'm at a disadvantage with the more experienced vendors.

MANAGER: [Doesn't say anything.]

ENTREPRENEUR: When do you get here?

MANAGER: This Saturday I won't get here until a half hour before we open.

ENTREPRENEUR: That would be great. Could I meet you here and come in with you? That way I won't inconvenience you.

MANAGER: OK.

More Negotiation in Action

Here's a negotiation between Jack, who's selling his old Mac laptop, and Mike, who wants to buy it. Before the negotiation, Mike determines his goals:

- To be able to return the laptop if it stops working within two months.
- To pay one-third what it would cost in the store.

The essence of negotiation is figuring out how to meet the other person's needs, so Mike thinks about what he has to offer in return. Mike can offer:

- To pay immediately in cash.
- To take the laptop away that day.

Next, he sets his boundaries:

- Not to spend more than $500.
- Not to accept less than one month for return if the laptop stops working.

Mike and Jack arrange to chat via Gmail chat and they have the following exchange:

MIKE: Are you still interested in selling the laptop?

JACK: Yes, I am.

MIKE: What price were you looking for?

JACK: I'd like $900.

MIKE: That's a bit more than I can afford.

JACK: Well, I'm willing to negotiate down to $800 but that's my final offer.

MIKE: I'm willing to pay cash and pick up the laptop today. I feel $400 would be fair.

JACK: $400 is ridiculous. I'm willing to go down to $800.

MIKE: I'm willing to go up to $600 but I want two months to return it if something goes wrong.

JACK: Two months is unreasonable.

MIKE: I'm willing to negotiate on that. What can you offer as a price and money-back guarantee?

JACK: I'll go $700 and give you one month.

MIKE: OK. How about $725 and a month and a half guarantee?

JACK: You've got a deal.

DON'T LET "MAYBE" WASTE YOUR TIME

The most frustrating negotiations are not the ones that end in a firm no but those that end with a maybe.

"Maybe" feels encouraging, but it wastes your time and keep you from pursuing other options. When someone can't seem to give you an answer, say something like, "I know you can't say yes right away, but I think it's fair for me to ask you to give me a no by the end of the week."

If he or she says no at the end of the week, fine; now you can move on to a new person. Don't forget to ask the person who says no, "If you can't do it, can you recommend someone who might?"

INTERNATIONAL NEGOTIATIONS

Today, you can do business with anyone anywhere through the Internet. Increased migration and travel have also opened doors to other countries and cultures. Some business owners even bypass markets at home if the opportunities look better overseas.

Although you could do business in a country without visiting it, understanding the culture is definitely an advantage when trying to conduct international negotiations.

Imagine, for example, that one of your classmates is an exchange student. She tells you about a traditional snack in her culture: termites. These insects, she explains, are high in protein and free for the taking. You might not want to eat termites, but it's not a matter of right or wrong—it's a cultural preference.

What seems perfectly acceptable in one culture might be unthinkable in another. Rules of etiquette—the behavior that is accepted and expected in a situation—can vary greatly between societies, which means their ways of conducting business often are different, too.

If you want to sell your graphic novel in Japan, for example, find a Japanese friend or businessperson to help you market it. If you think your death metal band will go over great in Norway, find a Norwegian death metal fan to guide you and help you figure out how Norwegian death metal fans like to consume their music. Do they still like CDs? Will they pay for downloads or do they only want free music? Will they spend money on band T-shirts instead?

Someone who has lived and worked in a particular country will have insights that no one else can offer.

Social Etiquette Across Cultures

In every culture, business negotiations take place within a broader social setting. Every nation has a unique culture, but cultural differences also exist within nations. For example, culture varies from big city to small city, from north to south, from one street to the next.

General rules for proper behavior apply. For example, a businessperson should know how to dress. Because appearance is the first thing people notice, meeting this expectation is a way to make a good impression in a one-on-one negotiation.

Another important thing you should know is how people address one another. Do they call each other by the first name or as "Mister," "Miss," or another title? In some cultures, business relationships are very formal and coworkers may know one another for years without learning each other's first names.

Topics for polite conversation may have a bearing on a negotiation. Political issues may be too sensitive. Discussions of sports and the arts, if they avoid strong personal opinions, are safer.

Outward signs of friendship and respect have a role in business negotiations as well. When people meet, do they bow, shake hands, or kiss on the cheek? Is gift giving appreciated (or even expected)? If so, what gifts are appropriate?

The importance of family relationships can be a powerful influence on business negotiations. Several generations may be involved in running a business. This may make the business a part of the family identity. Negotiated agreements might have to meet the approval of family elders as well as those directly involved. Family members might also be favored over outside parties, even if the deal offered by the nonrelatives makes more sense financially.

On the other hand, family and work life may be kept completely separate, with work taking priority. To ask about a man's wife and family members or to suggest that you meet in someone's home is considered rude in some cultures and perfectly acceptable in others.

The role of religion in public life can also affect business negotiations. Businesses may be closed on certain days and for religious celebrations. Also, certain actions or attitudes that are offensive to the other party's religion could harm your negotiations. You should not eat or drink in front of someone who is engaged in a religious fast, for example.

Because business is often conducted over meals, you should learn the rules of the other party's dining etiquette. People who handle themselves with appropriate manners during meals are more apt to be taken seriously.

Negotiation Etiquette

Different countries also have different attitudes about time, appointments, and schedules. In some countries, a business contact who arrives fifteen minutes late is not being rude. He might be surprised, and even angry with you, if you act impatient.

Attitudes toward written agreements also vary. In the United States, these agreements tend to be extremely detailed. Other cultures see this insistence on accounting for every possibility as a lack of trust. Instead, they view an agreement as an outline. Specific questions are decided as the need arises.

In these cultures, negotiations may be spread out for several days and include social activities that give each side a chance to know the other personally as well as professionally. If both sides believe that the other bargained in good faith, they trust that the agreement will serve them both well. In this sense, the negotiations never close. They continue for the length of the agreement.

Decision-making authority is another question that varies with culture. In some countries, the person you are negotiating with may not actually have the power to cut the deal. The power rests only at the very top of the company, with a president or board chairperson. This is especially true of cultures with well-defined social classes. Elsewhere, such decisions can be made by lower-level management or a board of directors.

Finally, cultures have different attitudes toward the negotiation process itself. In some countries, a loud, forceful argument earns respect; it shows determination and commitment. In other cultures, lengthy arguments are perceived as stubbornness, and loudness is considered impolite. Both may lead to the end of a negotiation.

If you make a mistake, remember that the purpose of learning etiquette is to show respect. If your words and actions communicate appreciation and respect as you know it, others will be likely to tolerate your lack of specific understanding. Simply apologize for not being as familiar with the other party's culture as you would like. Do your best, and let your respectful attitude generate goodwill.

KEYS TO COMMUNICATION

Everything we've talked about in this chapter, including negotiation, falls under the umbrella of "business communication." To be a successful entrepreneur, you have to be able to communicate clearly and succinctly, without wasting anyone's time.

Calvin Coolidge, the thirtieth president of the United States, was a man of few words. Once, at a dinner party, a guest told him that she had bet she could get him to say more than two words that evening. Coolidge replied, "You lose."

As an entrepreneur, you don't want to be quite *that* succinct. But you do want to follow the KISS rule: Keep It Short and Simple (or Keep It Simple, Stupid!). Even if you are your business's only employee, you'll need to communicate—to share information, thoughts, or opinions—with suppliers, customers, family members, friends, business colleagues, and many others.

Not only do you need to share information, you must also have the right tone when you share it. An informal tone is usually not appropriate, nor is one that is either too aggressive or too unassertive.

Although every type of work has its own special vocabulary, you don't need to learn technical terms to communicate in business. In fact, the less technical your writing is, the better. But you will need to communicate effectively. Here are some rules of thumb:

- **Be brief.** Respect your listener's time and get to the point quickly. Identify yourself and the reason for the contact. Avoid getting sidetracked with personal information or other unrelated subjects.
- **Be organized.** Give information in an easy-to-follow format. Some messages might need numbered steps or an outline. For a letter or speech, you should introduce your subject, add details in a logical order, and close by summarizing your main ideas.
- **Be clear.** Your listener may not know all of the facts like you do. Include necessary details; don't assume you are both on the same page.
- **Be relevant.** Supply the right information to the right audience. Wading through unneeded facts can be confusing and time-consuming. Suppose you ask an employee to order pens to give away at a grand opening. That individual needs to know the color, number, and wording you want on the pens. She doesn't need to know how much you're spending on radio ads.
- **Be upbeat and courteous.** Communicate respect and a positive attitude. Assume that the other party is interested in helping you solve your problem. Even if you have to point out someone else's mistake, avoid personal attacks and criticism.

Have you heard the saying "Word of mouth is the best advertising"? That applies to the value of spoken (verbal) messages in other business situations as well. When you need an immediate reply or just want to know the person or people with whom you are working, your best choice is often to meet in person—or over the phone.

You probably know good speakers when you hear them. To be a good speaker, remember these points:

- **Speak clearly.** Having to repeat information can be disruptive, time-consuming, and frustrating to your audience.
- **Draw in the entire audience.** Look and nod at people individually. Make eye contact. Refer to individuals if possible, especially to give them praise or credit.
- **Encourage participation.** Saying something along the lines of "I've heard this is a better approach, but I've never tried it—

what do you think?" asks listeners to offer their own opinions.

- **Read the mood of the room.** If the audience seems relaxed and sociable, act the same. If they are in a hurry, indicate that you are aware of this and attempt to give them the information in the most efficient way possible.
- **Use gestures selectively.** Avoid distracting gestures such as scratching your nose or tossing your hair. Use gestures only for emphasis.

Active Listening

You know how to talk—but are you a good listener? **Active listening** is listening consciously and responding in ways that improve communication. Active listening is a two-part process, and both parts take work.

Part 1: Focus on the speaker. The words and tone of voice give clues to his or her frame of mind. Does the speaker sound unsure? Concerned? Enthusiastic? Don't be distracted by your surroundings. You need to encourage and support the speaker with useful responses, such as nodding your head or saying "I see"—even if you disagree. This shows that you are listening.

Part 2: Give feedback. This tells the speaker that you understand what is being said. Feedback is typically phrased in a way that encourages the speaker to correct any misunderstandings. For example, a financial advisor might say to a client, "It sounds like saving for retirement is more important to you than a quick return on your investment. Is that right?"

Active listening also improves your speaking skills by making you more aware of how facial expression, tone of voice, and other aspects of verbal communication color your message. You can then better use these elements to communicate exactly what you mean.

Conference Calls

A **conference call** allows three or more parties in different locations to speak to one another over the same phone line. For example, someone at the home office in Chicago might arrange a conference call between a salesperson in Nashville and a writer in a satellite office in New York who is writing a brochure.

Scheduling is absolutely necessary to coordinate a conference call. If the callers are located in different time zones, everyone must be sure of the time. Three o'clock in Portland, Maine, for example, is noon in Portland, Oregon.

A quiet setting is important for focusing on several callers at the same time. Landlines are preferable to cell phones, which tend to pick up background noise. Using the "mute" button to silence the line when you are not speaking can also help speakers hear one another if the lines are noisy. If any charts, contracts, or other written materials will be required in the conference call, send copies to all parties in advance.

Skype and Videoconferencing

You probably already use Skype and a webcam to conduct video calls with friends and family. FaceTime works, too.

You can use these tools to conduct business, too. A **videoconference** is a meeting in which participants in different locations see and hear one another via Skype or any other video call system.

Some businesses have videoconference rooms set up with monitors. The party you're talking to appears on one monitor. You and your party appear on the second one. This helps you communicate effectively. If you hold up a chart, for instance, you can see whether it's legible on the receiving end.

Bright colors and detailed patterns in clothing can be distracting on camera. White garments and glittery jewelry can reflect light and create a glare. Wear neutral colors and subtle patterns, which are easier on the eyes.

You also need to be concerned about the audio aspect of videoconferencing. Microphones magnify any noise you make. Habits such as shuffling papers or tapping a pen on the table can quickly become very irritating.

Tech U

Meetings are a fact of life in business. Entrepreneurs must meet with customers, potential investors, and employees. It isn't always possible, or desirable, to fly across the country or drive to an in-person meeting. Web conferencing is a great solution.

Web conferencing uses webcams and microphones to enable people in different locations to have effective meetings. They can share PowerPoint slide presentations. They can take Web tours of specific sites or conduct polls. Web conferencing can be more productive and cost-effective than in-person meetings.

There are many ways for a small business to enable Web conferencing. Check out a Web-based service such as GoToMeeting.com.

Email

Email is great for business communication. You can read and respond to messages on your own schedule. You can forward them to others without paying postage. Email is even environmentally friendly!

Unfortunately, speed and ease of use also make email hazardous. It's easy to send an email to the wrong person or to respond too quickly, without thinking.

Once you have sent an email, you usually cannot retrieve it. In business, the consequences of a badly written, sloppy, or poorly conceived email can be dramatic.

The following guidelines will not only prevent potential trouble but will also help you slow down and give each email proper consideration:

- Write a short, useful description in the subject line.
- Before sending attachments, ask the recipient if he or she can accept them. Many businesses automatically delete attachments to prevent viruses. Make sure attachments are not too large to be rejected by the recipient's server.
- Program an automatic signature that includes your name, the company name, the company phone number and website, and perhaps a company slogan at the end of every email you write.
- To avoid sending an email before you mean to, compose it offline first or save it as a draft. Fill in the "to" field last, just before sending.
- Always get the sender's permission before forwarding an email.
- If you send an email to many people, hide their addresses by using the "bcc" (blind courtesy copy) feature. This respects their privacy and saves them from scrolling through a long list of names to get to the message.
- Using "reply" automatically creates a **message thread,** which shows every previous message in the correspondence. Over time, these may become unnecessary. Start a fresh thread, summarizing the most recent, relevant messages.

Faxes

"Fax" is short for **facsimile,** which is an exact copy of something. A fax machine uses telephone lines to transmit an exact copy of a document. If you need to send a signed copy of a contract, for instance, you can fax it and the recipient of the fax will be able to see your signature.

Each fax you send should be accompanied by a cover sheet that identifies the sender, the recipient, the subject, the date, a brief description of the items being sent, and the number of pages.

Before you send a fax, make sure the recipient knows it's coming. The recipient's machine must be turned on to receive the material, and many small businesses turn off their fax machines to avoid unwanted advertisements.

Remember, many people may read a fax that you send to a workplace. Prior notice helps ensure some degree of privacy; however, faxes are not the best way to send confidential information, because anyone could pick up your document from the fax machine and read it.

904 West Meadows Place
Peoria, IL 61604
(309) 555-7857

Lady Best Apparel

Fax

To:	Tara Sedgewick	**From:**	K. Anne Smith
Fax:	(203) 555-6658	**Pages:**	5
Phone:	(203) 555-6665	**Date:**	11/10/20--
Re:	New Spring Line	**CC:**	Fran Aldasoki

☐ Urgent ☐ For Review ☐ Please Comment ☐ Please Reply ☐ Please Recycle

● **Comments:**

Please look over the suggestions for the new Spring line and let me know what you think. I'd like to finalize this by Thursday.

Instant Messaging and Texting

Advances in technology are always creating new ways for us to communicate. Facebook messaging, Gmail chats, and texting are popular examples. **These forms of communication can save an entrepreneur time and money—just make sure you use them in a professional manner.**

Suppose a carpenter is looking for a door for a house he is renovating. He spots a door that would be perfect and snaps some pictures with his smartphone. He texts the photos to the client. The client chooses the door he or she likes. An hour later, the carpenter is installing it. Lots of time and hassle saved!

Check with your clients first, though, to make sure they are open to being communicated with this way. Some people feel annoyed when they are contacted on Gmail or Facebook, especially when they are busy. Signaling "busy" or "away" limits some intrusions, but not everyone respects these status messages.

And remember, electronic communications offer no guarantee of privacy, because messages can be saved, printed, or shared with others. *Every message you send lives forever online, so never send a statement or image that would embarrass you if it became public.*

Here are some tips to manage instant messaging and texting in a business context:

- Choose a user name that projects the image you want to convey to clients and colleagues. Keep it classy!
- Start a conversation by asking whether the other person has time to communicate.
- Take care when using **emoticons,** punctuation marks that convey emotions, such as a smiley face :-) or a wink ;-). Don't use abbreviations (such as JAM for "just a minute" or BTW for "by the way")—some businesspeople consider them unprofessional. They can also cause confusion or misunderstandings, especially if people don't know what they mean.

Unlike phone calls, instant messaging doesn't allow for visual or audible cues that let others know you're paying attention. Break the "silence" with short replies such as "Good point" or "Let me think for a second."

Tech U

Here are some great tips for getting more out of Gmail and Gchat:

1. Add bots to your chat contacts for quick and easy language translation. Access Google's translation bots here http://support.google.com/chat/bin/answer.py?hl=en &answer=172257.

2. Move your chat window to the right side of your Gmail screen. That way, more of your folders can appear on the left-hand side, and a longer list of chat contacts will appear on the right. Head to Settings > Labs > Right-Side Chat.

3. Set up Gmail chat to text. You can type a text message in a chat window and send it to a friend's phone. To do this, go to Settings > Labs > SMS (text messaging) in Chat.

> ### Green Tip
>
> If every small business owner in the United States conducted one teleconference in lieu of a domestic business trip, *Ecopreneurist* reports this would save $25.4 billion in travel expenses and 10.5 million tons of CO_2 in just one year.

WRITTEN COMMUNICATION

With advances in electronic developments, some people predicted that writing skills would become less important in the business world. Instead, the opposite has occurred. Businesspeople need to express their ideas in writing even more often.

Writing is also important because some messages are best put in writing for legal reasons. If you have a complaint against a nonpaying client, or an idea for an invention, written communication creates a trail that backs up your claim.

Before you send any written communication (including emails), ask yourself: Are my ideas clearly stated? Is the tone friendly but professional? Are the grammar, spelling, and punctuation correct? Even if you use a word-processing program that checks your spelling, you will need to proofread for errors. The program won't know if you've misspelled the recipient's name, or if you should have used "their" instead of "they're" or "there." Or that you meant to type "baked beans," not "naked beans"!

Ask someone else to proofread an important written communication before you send it. If that isn't possible, take a break before you send it and then reread it to make sure the information is correct and the tone is right.

Business Letters

Business letters are used for formal communications, such as a request to someone to join your **board of advisors**, or a thank-you note to someone who donated to your charity event.

A business letter should be typed in an easy-to-read font, in the following format:

- Put your name, business name, and business address at the top of the page, in the center or flush left.
- Type the date in the upper-left corner.
- Skip a line or two and type the recipient's name and address below the date. Use the same name and address you use on the envelope.
- Skip a line and type the **salutation,** or greeting, starting at the left

margin. "Dear" is the accepted greeting, followed by the person's title (Mr., Ms., or Dr., for example), the last name, and then a colon. Use the first and last name without a title if you're not sure whether the recipient is a man or woman. Use a comma only if you are on a friendly basis with the recipient.

- For the body of the letter, either indent the first line of each paragraph or skip a line between paragraphs.

- Start a new line at the left margin for the closing. Use "Sincerely," or "With best regards," to close. End every closing with a comma.

- Skip four lines and type your name and position.

- Sign your full name in the space you left above your name.

Your Business's Address	Gervitas Bakery 456 Elm Ave. Woodbury, NJ 09876 (309) 555-1432 agervitas@gervitas.net
Date	May 4, 2014
Recipient's Name and Address	Ms. Cathryn Whyte Vice President, Purchasing Brennan's Supermarkets 123 Winterthur Hwy. New Castle, DE 56432
Salutation	Dear Ms. Whyte:
Body	I have been a successful, independent wholesaler of baked goods to central New Jersey for five years. My business, Gervitas Bakery, has been named Gloucester County's Favorite Bakery three years in a row. (Please see the enclosed articles from the Woodbury Times.) I am now interested in reaching more distant markets. The Brennan Supermarkets name is synonymous with quality among consumers all along the eastern seaboard, and I believe that adding my products to your other fine offerings would enhance the sales and reputation of both our businesses. I would like to discuss the possibility of becoming a supplier to Brennan Supermarkets. May I contact you or a member of your department? I can be reached at the address, phone number, and e-mail address above, and I look forward to your reply. Thank you for your time and attention.
Closing	Sincerely, *Alexander Gervitas* — Your Name, Written and Printed Alexander Gervitas Enc: Times articles (2)

- RE: If you want, you can also include a reference line under the date. This would begin with the abbreviation "RE:" (for "regarding") and summarize the subject of the letter, much like the subject line in an email.
- CC: If you're sending a copy of the letter to others, skip a line below your address and type "CC:" (for "courtesy copy") at the left margin. After the colon, type the names of the people to whom you will be sending a courtesy copy of the letter.
- Enc.: If you are enclosing a document, such as an ad to be run in a newspaper, type "Enc.:" (for "enclosed") below your name and address (and below the cc: line, if there is one) at the left margin. Then you would add a description of the document.

Memos

Whenever you communicate, you should strive to be concise—to get your point across with as few words as possible. This shows that you respect the other person's time. The **memo** is the ultimate tool for communicating in a concise manner.

A memo is a brief note that informs your employees about a business-related matter. A letter is written to people outside the business, and a memo is written to people within it.

Memos are typically shorter and less formal than business letters. Ideally, a memo should be one page or less.

Memos are a good way to share relevant news, or information employees need to perform a task. The subject might range from a reminder about an office party to a marketing trend that will affect a company's profits.

A memo has two parts:

1. **Heading:** The heading consists of lines that identify the recipients, the sender, the date, and the subject of the memo. A precisely worded subject line lets recipients know whether the message applies to them and how quickly they should respond.
2. **Body:** The body contains the message. Ideally, memos cover only one subject.

TO: Baxter's Bakery Sales Associates
FROM: Ginny Baxter
DATE: May 15, 20--
SUBJECT: Organic Chocolate Ingredients

As of June 15, Baxter's Bakery will be using only organic, sustainably grown chocolate in its baked goods. This includes baking cocoa, baking chocolate, and semi-sweet chocolate chips.

I've ordered promotional pamphlets. Please place one in every bag with customers' purchases. Also read a pamphlet yourself, so you can promote the cause of sustainable agriculture (and our tasty baked treats!) and help answer customers' questions.

Tech U

Word processing software usually includes memo templates. Often, word processing programs will have "families" of templates. Each family has a common name and a similar look. For example, the software might have a "Professional" family of templates, with a "Professional" letter template and a "Professional" memo template. Another style might be designated "Classic" and would have a "Classic" letter template and a "Classic" memo template.

If your software has template families, use the memo version from the same family as your letter template for a consistent look in communications.

When I was a high school teacher in the South Bronx, I would assign my students memos that were due the next day, on a wide variety of topics. I refused to accept any memo that had more than three hundred words, and I announced that I would give an A or F grade after only one reading. The memo had to be clear. If I didn't understand it, the student got an F. If I understood it, the memo earned an A.

Several years later, three of my students were in the wrong place at the wrong time (near a youth who was shooting off a gun) and were picked up by the police. While being held in a detention cell together, they composed a memo explaining exactly what had happened and why they were not connected to the teen with the gun. Their memo was so clear and convincing that they were released!

I was both proud and horrified. The incident reminded me of the dangers my pupils were exposed to when they weren't in school. I was very happy, though, that our memo drills had proved so useful.

An Entrepreneur Like You

Mike Greenberg

KONSPIRACY STUDIOS

www.konspiracystudios.com

When Mike Greenberg of Damascus, Maryland, was in the eighth grade, he discovered he loved working with images. He became the go-to guy for video and graphic design throughout high school.

During his junior year, Mike took an internship at a postproduction facility. He was told that it would be several years before his manager would allow him to work directly with clients. That convinced Mike to start his own business. Within six months he was working full-time for himself.

Mike's company, Konspiracy Studios, provides print, Web, and video services.

"We create videos that ultimately end up on TV, the Web, or DVDs," said Mike. "We've cut several promos for clients to present to networks for funding. We also create corporate identity packages and marketing materials for several firms."

Funding His Business

Mike bought his initial equipment by saving money he earned as a busboy. His parents helped him by matching 50 percent of what he earned at work. Now he's supporting himself completely through his business.

He's managed to keep his overhead extremely low by negotiating and using **barter financing**. Barter financing is trading goods or services with another person or company for goods or services in return.

Mike pays for all his expenses through his debit card, which allows him to track them on his bank statements. "You can see what categories you're spending in," he said, "and it actually generates ways for you to save."

Spending for Profit

When it comes to spending money, Mike feels that "you have to look at what you're buying and see how that fits into the business." He buys additional equipment only when he needs it—like more professional lighting as he expanded into videos for corporate clients. "I didn't make any frivolous expenditures," he says. "I kept looking at the fundamentals of what worked and what didn't." He constantly reviews his progress in terms of both money and his morale—how he felt and how his customers felt.

At times, Mike has made some purchases that didn't pan out because he hadn't done enough research. He once bought a video converter, for example, that wasn't compatible with his computer. On the other hand, he's also made some investments that have proven to be extremely successful. Using an email marketing service, instead of trying to manage all the email addresses he had collected himself, has enabled him to stay in touch with a large number of clients.

Mike charges an hourly rate, although with established customers he offers a long-term fixed contract that includes a monthly retainer. "I reward people for booking me for long periods of time by giving them lower rates," Mike explains.

His website highlights his services. It shows off his reel, displays his awards, and provides case studies demonstrating how he's solved client requests.

Think Like an Entrepreneur

1. How could you use barter financing in your business?
2. Why is researching your buying decisions important?
3. Why should you look at the emotional as well as the financial results of your work?

PART 3
MANAGE YOUR MONEY

CHAPTER 11

ECONOMICS OF ONE UNIT

AN EASY SYSTEM FOR TRACKING COSTS AND PROFITS

Winners never quit and quitters never win.

—Vince Lombardi

Finding creative ways to cut costs often means the difference between having a struggling business and a thriving one. Anyone can spend unlimited amounts of money and create a great product, but then he or she may use up more scarce resources than the product is worth. The entrepreneur's goal is to add value to scarce resources by creating a product for *less* than the consumer is willing to pay for it.

The classic example of this principle in action is the story of Ford Motor Company. When the automobile was invented in 1885, it was very expensive to produce. It was considered a plaything for rich people.

Henry Ford had a vision, however. He imagined a car parked in front of every house. Only the cost of building a "horseless carriage" stood in his way. Ford was determined to find a way to cut that cost and build an automobile that many consumers could afford.

In those days, cars were manufactured one at a time. It was a slow, expensive process. To cut manufacturing costs, Ford invented the assembly line. The cars were put together as they rolled past the workers on a conveyer belt. The concept of the assembly line was adopted by many companies and helped develop many industries.

Ford's idea cut costs enough that it became possible to sell an affordable automobile to the average American and still make a profit. His Ford Motor Company became one of the biggest car manufacturers in the world. He also revolutionized industry by introducing the concept of mass production on a grand scale.

WHAT IS YOUR UNIT OF SALE?

A **unit of sale** is a way to define what a customer buys from you. For Ford Motor Company, for example, one unit of sale is one car. You'll need to decide what one unit of sale will be for your business before you can examine your costs.

If you are selling just one product, defining your unit of sale is easy. Make the unit of sale one product. If you are selling a variety of products, define your unit as the average sale per customer. McDonald's, for example, defines its unit of sale as the price of one sandwich, fries, and a soda.

If you are selling a service, the economic unit is usually one hour of service. Or you could define your unit as the completion of one job. If you run a hair salon, a unit of sale might be one haircut. If you run a lawn-mowing company, your unit of sale might be mowing one lawn. But, because lawns are different sizes, you might have different rates for different sizes of lawns or you might charge by the hour. In that case, you might decide to make your unit of sale equal to one hour of service.

The unit of sale is the basic building block of your business.

Tech U

If you have a service business, you will need to track the time you spend on each client. Check out http://letsfreckle.com—an easy, affordable time-tracking software.

WHAT ARE YOUR BUSINESS COSTS?

The costs of starting and operating a business are divided into the following categories:

1.   Start-up costs
2.   Cost of goods sold
3.   Operating costs, including fixed costs and variable costs

Start-Up Costs

Start-up costs are the onetime expenses of starting a business. Start-up costs are also called "the original investment" or "seed money." For a restaurant, for example, start-up costs would include stoves, food processors, tables, chairs, silverware, and other items that are not replaced on a regular basis. Also included might be the one-time cost of buying land and constructing a building.

For a small restaurant, start-up costs might look like this:

Stoves and Burners	$7,000
Appliances	$5,000
Furnishings	$3,000
Fixtures	$1,400
Tableware (glasses, dishes, silverware)	$1,250
Signage	$900
Total Start-Up Costs	**$18,550**

Operating Costs

The **operating costs** of a business are those costs that are necessary to operate the business, not including the cost of goods sold. Operating costs can almost always be divided into six categories.

An easy way to remember the six operating costs that most businesses will have is to memorize the acronym "USAIIR." It stands for:

1. Utilities (gas, electric, telephone)
2. Salaries
3. Advertising
4. Insurance
5. Interest
6. Rent

Operating costs are also called **overhead.**

Overhead Is Divided into Fixed Costs and Variable Costs

Operating costs are divided into two categories: fixed costs and variable costs. **Fixed costs** are operating costs that stay the same, regardless of the range of sales the business is making. Rent is an example of a fixed cost. Whether a shoe store sells two hundred or three hundred pairs of shoes in a month, it still pays the same rent on the store, so the rent is considered a fixed cost.

Variable costs are operating costs that change, depending on the volume of sales, but cannot be assigned directly to the unit of sale. If a cost can be assigned directly to a unit of sale, it should be viewed as part of the cost of goods sold. If the shoe store pays a commission to its salespeople, that is a variable cost, because the amount of commission the store pays varies with the number of pairs of shoes that each salesperson sells.

Costs that fluctuate with sales should be viewed as variable costs.

Green Tip

Did you know that your computer, printer, TV, and other electronic devices continue to drain power and raise your electricity bill even when you're not using them? "Vampire electronics" are gadgets that consume standby power when they're not in use. They can be big, like your desktop computer, or small, like your phone charger. Any appliance that uses a remote control or displays a clock draws power when turned off or not in use.

Phone and battery chargers also continue to consume energy if they are plugged into an outlet, even if your phone or device isn't currently attached and charging.

Best bet? Plug your electronics into a "smart" power strip with a surge suppressor. These power strips will shut down the power coming from your wall outlets as soon as they sense that an electronic gadget has gone into standby mode.

Cost of Goods or Services Sold

The **cost of goods sold** can be thought of as the cost of selling *one additional unit* of a product. The **cost of services sold** is the cost of serving one additional customer.

The cost of goods sold in a restaurant, for example, is the cost of the food served to a customer.

Here's an example of the cost of goods sold of a turkey sandwich:

Turkey (4 oz.)	$2.60 per pound ÷ 4	$0.65
Bread (large roll)	$0.32 per roll	$0.32
Mayonnaise (1 oz.)	$1.60 per 32 oz. jar ÷ 32	$0.05
Lettuce (1 oz.)	$0.80 per pound ÷ 16	$0.05
Tomato (2 oz.)	$2.20 per pound ÷ 8	$0.28

Pickle (¼)	$0.20 per pickle ÷ 4	$0.05
Wrapper	$10.00 per 1,000 sheets ÷ 1,000	$0.01

Cost of Goods Sold		$1.25

GROSS PROFIT PER UNIT

Once you know your cost of goods sold and have defined your unit, you can calculate your **gross profit per unit**.

The cost of goods sold of the sandwich, subtracted from the price customers pay for the sandwich, equals the gross profit per unit for the sandwich.

Selling Price per Unit – Cost of Goods Sold per Unit
= Gross Profit per Unit

For the turkey sandwich:

Price of Sandwich	$4.00
Cost of Goods Sold	$1.25

Gross Profit per Sandwich	$2.75

As an entrepreneur, you must keep your cost of goods sold secret. If customers learn your cost of goods sold, they'll use that information to try to negotiate a lower selling price. If someone tries to sell you a sandwich for $4.00 and you know it costs only $2.75 to make it, would you be willing to buy it for $4.00? Or would you try to negotiate the seller down to $3.00? What if you knew it cost only $1.25 to make it?

Never reveal your cost of goods sold. If you do, customers will try to negotiate a lower selling price.

Read a Classic

For a highly entertaining read, pick up *Business Stripped Bare: Adventures of a Global Entrepreneur* by Sir Richard Branson. A terrible student who suffered from dyslexia,

Branson still managed to understand business concepts well enough to start seven distinct billion-dollar organizations, including Virgin Airlines and Virgin Mobile. If you've seen their commercials, you know he has a surreal sense of humor.

Total Gross Profit

Gross profit can be figured per unit, as in the turkey sandwich example. To get an idea of how a business is doing as a whole, however, you'll need to figure total gross profit. This is done by subtracting total cost of goods sold from total revenue, as in the following example.

Total Revenue − Total Cost of Goods Sold = Total Gross Profit

Yolanda is saving up for college with a small business selling cell phone charms. To get the latest styles, she orders the charms from a Japanese wholesaler for $10 each. That is her cost of goods sold. She sells the charms for $20. What is her total gross profit for the month when she sells twenty charms?

Total Revenue = 20 charms x $20 = $400

Total Cost of Goods Sold = 20 charms × $10 = $200

$400 (Total Revenue) − $200 (Total Cost of Goods Sold)
= $200 (Total Gross Profit)

Yolanda's total gross profit this month is $200.

Calculating Net Profit

Total gross profit only subtracts total cost of goods (or services) sold from total revenue. To find out what the actual **profit** (also called **net profit**) is for a business, takes one more step: subtracting the operating costs. In other words, Yolanda does not actually keep $200 from the sale of twenty charms this month. She still has operating costs to cover. Her primary operating cost is shipping. She gets her shipment of charms from Japan once a month and pays the wholesaler a shipping and handling charge of $21.00.

Gross Profit − Operating Costs = Net Profit

$200 (Gross Profit) − $21 (Operating Costs) = $179 (Net Profit)

Yolanda's profit for this month is $179.

Profit per Unit

Sometimes an entrepreneur wants to know how much of the sale of each unit is profit. An easy way to calculate profit per unit is to divide total units sold into profit.

Net Profit ÷ Units Sold = Profit per Unit

If Yolanda wants to know how much profit she makes each time she sells a charm, she can divide the number of charms she sells into the profit.

$179.00 ÷ 10 charms = $17.90 Profit per Unit

For every charm she sells, Yolanda earns a profit of $17.90.

THE ECONOMICS OF ONE UNIT

Here's a good question: How much should your selling price be to ensure you make a profit? A good rule of thumb is to keystone, which means to set your selling price at twice your cost of goods sold.

Yolanda is doing this: Her cost of goods sold is $10 per unit and her unit selling price (the price at which she sells one cell phone charm) is $20. By keystoning, she's made sure she is making a profit.

Entrepreneurs use their profits to pay themselves, to expand their businesses, and to start other businesses. Entrepreneurs want to know how much the business earns on the products it sells. To do this, they study the **economics of one unit (EOU)**. This is a method for analyzing the costs of your business in more detail, in order to assess the profitability of your company.

In the previous section, you learned to figure out your net profit by subtracting your fixed operating costs from your gross profit. Now we're going to look at how variable operating costs affect your profit. We're going to subtract the variable costs for a unit from its selling price. This gives us **contribution margin**—the amount that each unit sold *contributes* toward a company's profitability. This analysis is called the economics of one unit (EOU).

Selling Price – Variable Costs = Contribution Margin

EOU for a Manufacturing Business

Suppose a manufacturing business makes high school class rings and sells them wholesale for $40 each. Let's analyze the economics of one unit based on a single ring. The materials used to produce a ring cost $3. Each requires one hour of labor at $15 per hour. So the cost of goods sold per unit would be $18 ($3 + $15). There are no commissions, and the cost of shipping and handling a single ring is $2.

Economics of One Unit: Manufacturing Business

One Unit of Sale = 1 Ring

Selling Price (per Unit):	**$40**
Variable Costs	
COST OF GOODS	
Materials	$3
Labor ($15 per Hour)	$15
Cost of Goods Sold	$18
OTHER VARIABLE COSTS	
Commissions	$0
Shipping and Handling	$2
Other Variable Costs	$2
Total Variable Costs	**$20**
Contribution Margin (per Unit):	**$20**

In this example, the contribution margin per unit is $40 – $20 = $20.

The manufacturer can use this information to make business decisions. One possibility would be to see if a new, less expensive supplier could be found.

EOU for a Wholesale Business

The method used to calculate the EOU for a wholesaler is similar to that of a manufacturing business. The difference is that the wholesale business buys finished products from a manufacturer, so its cost of goods sold per unit doesn't include labor.

In this example, the wholesaler buys rings from a manufacturer at $40 each. The wholesaler packages the rings in quantities of 12 per shipping carton. Shipping and handling for the carton costs $16. Each carton with 12 rings is sold to a retailer for $1,200.

Economics of One Unit: Wholesale Business

One Unit of Sale = 12 Rings in a Carton

Selling Price (per Unit):	**$1,200**
Variable Costs	
COST OF GOODS	
Rings (12)	$480
Cost of Goods Sold	$480
OTHER VARIABLE COSTS	
Commissions	$0
Shipping and Handling	$16
Other Variable Costs	$16
Total Variable Costs	**$496**
Contribution Margin (per Unit):	**$704**

The contribution margin per unit for the wholesaler is $1,200 – $496 = $704.

This might seem high in comparison with the $20 contribution margin per unit for the manufacturer, but remember that the wholesaler's unit of sale is a *carton of 12 rings,* while the manufacturer's unit of sale is a *single ring.* The wholesaler's contribution margin for a single ring would be $58.66 ($704.00 ÷ 12.00). The wholesaler's contribution margin per ring is still more than twice that of the manufacturer.

EOU for a Retail Business

Using the same ring example, let's look at a retail business. The retailer purchases the rings for $1,200 for a carton of 12 rings and then sells the rings one at a time. The unit of sale, therefore, is one ring.

The retailer's cost of goods sold per unit is $100 ($1,200 ÷ 12 rings). Like the wholesaler, the retailer buys finished products, so there are no labor costs. The retailer pays his salesperson a 15 percent commission on the sale of each ring. The ring is sold to high schools from a catalog and then shipped to each student purchaser. The price of shipping and handling is $7.

The retailer sells each ring for $200.

Economics of One Unit: Retail Business

One Unit of Sale = 1 Ring

Selling Price (per Unit):	**$200**
Variable Costs	
COST OF GOODS	
Ring (1)	$100
Cost of Goods Sold	$100
OTHER VARIABLE COSTS	
Commissions	$30
Shipping and Handling	$7
Other Variable Costs	$37
Total Variable Costs	**$137**
Contribution Margin (per Unit):	**$63**

In this case, the cost of goods sold is $100. Additional variable costs include commissions ($30) + shipping and handling ($7) for $37 in other variable costs. We add cost of goods sold ($100) to other variable costs ($37) for total variable costs of $137. To calculate the contribution margin, subtract total variable costs ($137) from selling price per unit ($200) and you get a contribution margin of $63.

The Economics of One Unit

An entrepreneur buys plain backpacks and decorates them at home with hand-drawn art, stitching, buttons, and stickers before reselling them at the flea market for $25 each.

Because each backpack is different, the entrepreneur uses an average backpack as the unit of sale.

The expenses to the entrepreneur per unit of sale are:

Plain backpack	$11.00
Ink, thread, buttons, etc.	3.00
Labor	6.00
Expenses per unit of sale	**$20.00**

The economics of one unit of sale are:

Selling price per unit of sale	$25.00
Expenses per unit of sale	− 20.00
Profit per unit of sale	**$5.00**

The profit as a percentage of sales is:

$$\frac{\text{Profit per unit of sale}}{\text{Selling price per unit of sale}} \times 100 \qquad \frac{\$5.00}{\$25.00} \times 100 = 20\%$$

The Economics of One Unit
The economics of one unit is a calculation of the profit or loss from a unit of sale.
Analyzing Data. *How could the entrepreneur make a larger profit?*

EOU for a Business Selling More Than One Product

A business selling a variety of products has to create a separate EOU for each product to determine whether it is profitable. When there are many similar products, however, you can develop a "typical EOU."

David sells four brands of candy bars at his booth at the local food market. The cost for each candy bar is similar.

Costs for Candy Bars

NUMBER	BRAND	COST
1	Chocolate Dee-Light	$0.36
2	Almond Happiness	$0.38
3	Fruit 'n' Joy	$0.42
4	Junior Chocolate Roll	$0.44

Rather than calculating EOUs for each of these similar products, David uses the average contribution margin of each transaction as his EOU. First, he adds up the cost of the four candy bars. Then he divides that total by four to get the average cost. The average cost is $0.40.

Chocolate Dee-Light	$0.36
Almond Happiness	$0.38
Fruit 'n' Joy	$0.42
Junior Chocolate Roll	$0.44
Total	$1.60

$1.60 ÷ 4 = $0.40 (Average Cost)

David sells the candy bars for $1.00 each. The economics of one unit of sale (EOU) for David's business is developed by using the average of $0.40 per candy bar. As you can see from the EOU analysis below, David's contribution margin per unit is $0.60.

Economics of One Unit: Business with More Than One Product

One Unit of Sale = 1 Candy Bar (Average Cost)

Selling Price (per Unit):	**$1.00**
Variable Costs	
COST OF GOODS	
Candy Bar (Average Cost)	$0.40
Cost of Goods Sold	$0.40
OTHER VARIABLE COSTS	
Commissions	$0
Shipping and Handling	$0
Other Variable Costs	$0
Total Variable Costs	**$0.40**

Contribution Margin (per Unit):	**$0.60**

EOU for a Service Business

Sometimes it's difficult to figure out what a unit of sale is for a service business. It might be one tutorial lesson, one lawn-mowing job, or one income tax preparation. Or it could be one hour of consulting, or a three-hour block of time.

In addition, you might need to purchase supplies to perform the service. For example, before you can give a haircut, you might need hair gel, shampoo, conditioners, or other products. These are variable operating costs because they are directly related to the services being sold. They vary depending on how many customers you serve.

Joan Oh has her own hairstyling business. She calculates an EOU based on each haircut. She estimates that it takes her one hour to complete a hairstyling job. She values her time at $30 per hour, and estimates that each job requires about $5 worth of supplies (shampoo, conditioner, gel, and so on). She charges $55 to style a customer's hair.

Economics of One Unit: Service Business

One Unit of Sale = 1 Hairstyling Job

Selling Price (per Unit):	**$55**
Variable Costs	
COST OF SERVICES SOLD	
Materials (Shampoo, etc.)	$5
Labor ($30 per Hour)	$30
Cost of Services Sold	$35
OTHER VARIABLE COSTS	
Commissions	$0
Shipping and Handling	$0
Other Variable Costs	$0
Total Variable Costs	**$35**
Contribution Margin (per Unit):	**$20**

In this case, Joan is both the person providing the hairstyling and the owner of the business. She will earn $30 as the hairstylist (labor cost, above) and $20 as the entrepreneur. If she could hire someone else to do the hairstyling for $30 per hour, she would still receive the contribution margin of $20.

Even better, if she could hire a stylist at $20 per hour, she would then have a contribution margin of $30 per styling job. Her cost of services sold per unit would be $25 and her contribution margin would be $30 ($55 − $25 = $30). By hiring additional stylists she would be able to increase the business's volume and also increase her profits. This is how you grow a business!

Math Moment

Dana Wright operates an airport limousine service. He owns the limo and does his own driving. He values his driving time at $25 per hour. He pays a commission fee of $10 to the person who brings him the business. A trip to the airport takes three hours and uses $25 worth of gasoline.

If Dana charges each customer $200, what is his contribution margin per unit of sale? How much does Dana make on each trip as a driver? As the owner of the business?*

---

*   Answers: $75; $40, $90.

Dave Pantoja

DAVE'S PENS

https://www.facebook.com/Woodtech4139

When Dave Pantoja took an entrepreneurship course in high school and began thinking about what kind of business he should start, his woodshop teacher suggested that he make pens. "It was something I knew how to do and it would give me some money right away," Dave explains, adding, "And I could use the money I gained from this business to launch other ventures in the future."

Starting Dave's Pens

Dave started Dave's Pens at the beginning of his junior year in high school. He made pens out of wood, plastic, and more exotic materials such as onyx, deer antler, buffalo horn, and snakeskin. Dave figured that each pen cost him approximately $12 to make, and he sold them for $15 to $25, depending on the material. "But as time went on, my own clients were telling me to raise my prices to match my competition," he says. "They felt I was ripping myself off with the prices. So I started studying my market and my competition a lot more to see where I stood with everything, and that's how my prices slowly increased."

Underpricing His Labor

One area where Dave underpriced his pens was his own labor. At the beginning, he was paying himself only minimum wage. Now he's increased his prices to account for the time and effort he spends. It can take Dave between ten and fifteen minutes to make a wooden pen, and up to an hour and a half for a specialty pen requiring detailed work.

Dave keeps careful records for his business, explaining that "when someone orders materials or places an order with me, I keep records of the date they did it, what they ordered, how much it cost me to make it, the time it took me to make it, and what they paid."

Learning the Hard Way

And he has learned some lessons that are even more important. "Before I started this business," he admits, "I was huge on procrastinating. I learned the hard way—but I definitely learned not to procrastinate. The entire experience has been a huge maturing process of how to prioritize and set my priorities straight."

When he goes to college, Dave plans to continue operating his pen business on the side. "I appreciate entrepreneurship," Dave says, "because it's such a general area to enter into. No matter what you want to do in the future, you can start a business."

Think Like an Entrepreneur

1. How would you calculate a price for your labor?
2. Dave waited for his customers to tell him he was undercharging. How would you find out if you were charging a competitive price?
3. How can being a procrastinator hurt you in business?

CHAPTER 12

USE FINANCIAL STATEMENTS TO STEER YOUR BUSINESS

INCOME, CASH FLOW, AND BALANCE SHEET STATEMENTS

> Money is better than poverty,
> if only for financial reasons.
>
> —Woody Allen

Even the smallest businesses get complicated fast if you aren't tracking your costs and sales. That's why entrepreneurs use three financial statements to steer their businesses: (1) an income statement, (2) a cash flow statement, and (3) a balance sheet. Each of these statements tells you something about your business that you need to know, in order to run it on a day-to-day basis, as well as in the long term.

Please, don't skip this chapter because you think learning to prepare financial statements is going to be complicated or difficult—or worse, because you don't think it is important! My ninth-grade students have learned to prepare them, and you can, too.

THE THREE FINANCIAL STATEMENTS

Income Statement

Entrepreneurs draw up a monthly income statement to track **income** (money earned) and **expenses** (money spent). Monthly income statements are like scorecards that show the financial condition of your business at the end of each month. They show the sales (income) and the costs (expenses) you recorded during the month.

If your sales are greater than your costs, your income statement balance will be positive. That means your business earned a net profit. If your sales are less than your costs, your income statement balance will be negative, meaning your business operated at a loss during that month. That's why the income statement is also called a **profit and loss statement**.

Cash Flow Statement

Have you ever glanced at your bank balance and thought you had plenty of money, but the next day you didn't have any money in there because you had forgotten about some outstanding checks? You have to subtract outstanding checks from your balance to know how much cash you really have available.

For the same reason, you can't guide your business's daily operation using the income statement alone. You also need to prepare a monthly cash flow statement to track the cash going in and out of the business. In fact, you should review your cash flow on a *daily* basis.

See, if a sale is made in June but the customer doesn't pay until August, the income statement will show the sale in June, but the cash flow statement won't show the sale until August, when the cash actually flows into the business. So even when your income statement shows a profit, you may run out of cash and have to shut down because you can't pay your phone bill. The cash flow statement records inflows and outflows of cash *when they occur*.

Balance Sheet

The balance sheet shows a business's assets and liabilities. The balance sheet is typically prepared once a month, and a cumulative balance sheet is prepared once a year (showing all twelve months).

Assets minus liabilities equals the **net worth** of a business. This is also called the **owner's equity**. Monthly income statements track a business's performance over a year's time. The balance sheet is more like a snapshot of the business's condition at the end of the business year.

Read a Classic

Financial Intelligence for Entrepreneurs: What You Really Need to Know About the Numbers by Karen Berman, Joe Knight, and John Case explains financial statements very clearly for new entrepreneurs.

THE INCOME STATEMENT

Because income statements show how a business is performing, they are prepared monthly, quarterly, and yearly.

- **Monthly:** Most small business owners create a monthly income statement.
- **Quarterly:** Most companies also generate an income statement showing income and expenses for the quarter. If you prepare statements monthly, it will be easy to put together quarterly statements.
- **Annually:** Most companies also prepare income statements on an annual basis that show how the company performed in the year. If you do quarterly statements, it will be easier to prepare an annual statement.

Learn the Lingo

Accounting is the system of recording and summarizing financial transactions and analyzing, verifying, and reporting the results that a business chooses to use.

You can choose whether to prepare your annual income statement based on the **calendar year,** which is January 1 through December 31, or based on your business's fiscal year. A **fiscal year** is any twelve-month period you choose to treat as a year for **accounting** purposes, whether it begins in February, July, or in any other month you choose. This is the period you will use when figuring your taxes, too. Once you make this choice, you cannot change it, so make sure to give it some thought. For example, many retail companies choose a fiscal year that starts February 1 and ends January 31 to reflect the holiday season. That way, they can report all the great sales over the holidays, making their business look stronger on its annual financial statements.

The Seven Parts of an Income Statement

An income statement is an entrepreneur's scorecard. If your business is not making a profit, the income statement can tell you what may be causing the loss. You can then take steps to correct the problems before you lose so much money that you have to close the business.

Income statements are made up of the following parts (we'll be using their call letters, A through G, when we place these parts in equations):

A. **Revenue:** How much money the company has received for selling a product.

B. **Total Cost of Goods Sold:** The cost of making one unit multiplied by the number of units sold. *Never disclose your cost of goods sold.* Keep secret how much you are paying to make your product, so you can sell it for a profit.

C. **Contribution Margin:** Sales minus cost of goods sold.

D. **Operating Costs:** Items that must be paid to operate a business, including:

   D1. Fixed Costs. These items include utilities, salaries, advertising, insurance, interest, and rent (referred to as USAIIR).

   D2. Variable Costs.

E. **Profit Before Taxes:** A business's profit before paying taxes but after all other costs have been paid.

F. **Taxes:** Payments required by federal, state, and local governments, based on a business's profit. A business must pay sales, income, and other business taxes.

G. **Net Profit or Loss:** A business's profit or loss after taxes have been paid.

Let's run through an example. Darla Washington is helping to put herself through college with her summertime business. She sells flip-flops on the boardwalk near the beach. She stores her **inventory** in a large locker she rents from a local merchant. Inventory is the amount of merchandise a business has available for sale at a given time. Since Darla lives at her parents' home during the summer, she contributes some of her profit to their utilities.

Darla needs to prepare an income statement for August.

A. **Revenue.** This is the money Darla's Flip-Flops receives from selling its products. Darla sold 240 flip-flops for $20 each. Her revenue is 240 × $20 = $4,800.

B. **Cost of Goods Sold.** Darla buys her flip-flops from a wholesaler for $2 per pair. Since she sold 240 pairs, her COGS is 240 × $2 = $480.

C. **Contribution Margin.** Contribution margin is calculated by subtracting cost of goods sold from revenue. Revenue (A)—COGS (B) = Contribution Margin (C). Darla's contribution margin is $4,800 – $480 = $4,320.

D. **Operating Expenses.** All of Darla's costs in running her business are included in the operating expenses section below. They add up to $650 for August.

E. **Pre-Tax Profit.** Pre-tax profit is calculated by subtracting operating expenses from the contribution margin ($4,320 – $650 = $3,670).

F. **Net Profit (Loss).** The net profit, also called net income, is calculated by subtracting taxes from the pre-tax profit. Taxes in this example are estimated at 15 percent of the pre-tax profit and are rounded off to the nearest dollar ($3,670 × 15 percent = $550.50, rounded to $550).

Income Statement: Darla's Flip-Flops

Month Ended August 31, 2013

Revenue

Gross Sales	**$4,800 (A)**
COST OF GOODS SOLD	
240 flip-flops @ $2 per pair	**$480 (B)**
Contribution Margin	**$4,320 (C)**
OPERATING EXPENSES	
Advertising	**$100**
Insurance	**$200**
Rent	**$150**
Telephone	**$100**
Utilities	**$100**
Total Expenses	**$650 (D)**
Pre-Tax Profit	**$3,670 (E)**
Taxes (15 percent)	**$550 (F)**
NET PROFIT	**$3,120 (G)**

Darla's business earned a net profit of $3,120!

Tech U

You may have heard about hackers who break into a company's computer network and steal financial information and other secrets. **Spyware** lets computer users spy on other users. The spyware gets onto a computer in the same way that a virus does—when the user clicks on a link that causes the computer to download a malicious program.

Another type of spyware is a **screen recorder**. It takes a picture of your screen and could potentially record sensitive information.

Keylogger programs record the letters and numbers (keystrokes) you make on a keyboard. Although you might think you're protected by typing in a password on a website (which is often displayed as asterisks), if a hacker has installed a keylogger program on your computer, they will be able to read what letters or numbers you keyed and could use that information for illegal activities.

Prevent these problems by keeping your computer's antivirus and antispyware software up to date. If you have employees, make sure they do the same for their computers.

BREAK-EVEN ANALYSIS

When income and expenses are equal, the income statement shows no net profit or net loss. The total at the bottom of the income statement is zero. This condition is called the **break-even point**. Many new businesses lose money in the beginning, but a business must eventually begin to break even in order to survive. It is vital for you to know how many units the business must sell during a month to cover costs and break even. **Break-even analysis** allows you to determine this number.

Unit of Sale

Darla has decided to define her unit of sale as one pair of flip-flops. Once you've defined a unit of sale, you can calculate your contribution margin per unit. Contribution margin per unit is the selling price of the unit minus its cost of goods sold. This is the first step toward determining how many units you will have to sell to break even.

Selling Price per Unit − Cost of Goods Sold per Unit
= Contribution Margin per Unit

Let's look at Darla's income statement again, and figure out her contribution margin per unit:

$20 (Selling Price per Unit) − $2 (Cost of Goods Sold per Unit)
= $18 (Contribution Margin per Unit)

Darla's contribution margin per unit is $18.

Calculating Break-Even Units

Because many small business operating costs are fixed, the break-even point is typically calculated by assuming that *all* operating costs are fixed. Using her contribution margin per unit, Darla can calculate how many flip-flops she will need to sell each month to cover her fixed costs—that is the number of **break-even units** she will need to sell each month to break even. Darla uses this formula:

Monthly Fixed Operating Costs ÷ Contribution Margin per Unit
= Break-Even Units

Let's check this out for Darla's business. Look at her income statement to determine her monthly fixed costs. They are $650. We just calculated her contribution margin per unit to be $18.

$650 (Monthly Fixed Operating Costs) ÷ $18 (Contribution Margin per Unit)
= 36 Break-Even Units

Darla has to sell 36 pairs of flip-flops per month to cover her fixed costs and stay in business.

Including Variable Cost in Break-Even Analysis

What if your business has some variable costs? These, remember, are costs that *vary* with the number of sales you make. If you want to calculate break-even units including variable costs, you must first determine your variable cost per unit.

Let's say, for example, that Darla went on vacation in August and offered a friend a commission to run her business in the interim. She pays the friend a commission of $1 per pair of flip-flops sold. This is a variable cost because it will vary depending on how many flip-flops her friend sells.

To figure out how many units the business will have to sell for it to break even, this additional variable cost must be taken into account, using this formula:

Monthly Fixed Costs ÷ (Contribution Margin per Unit – Variable Cost per Unit)
= Break-Even Units

$650 ÷ ($18 – $1) = $650 ÷ $17 = 38 Break-Even Units

This makes sense! If Darla is going to pay her friend a commission, that raises the business's costs, so it will have to sell more flip-flops to break even in August.

Math Moment

Your skateboard-painting business has operating expenses of $3,600 per month. The contribution margin for each skateboard you paint is $12. How many skateboards do you need to paint to reach a break-even point?*

---

*   Answer: 300

INCLUDE DEPRECIATION ON AN INCOME STATEMENT

If you buy expensive, long-lasting assets for your business, such as a computer, you will want to include **depreciation** in your income statement. Depreciation is a portion of the cost of an asset that is subtracted each year until the asset's value reaches zero. It's a method for saving up to replace your asset when it eventually needs to be replaced.

Depreciation reflects the wear and tear on an asset over time. This wear and tear reduces the value of the asset, so it's a cost of doing business. Depreciation is typically shown as a fixed operating cost on the income statement. Darla didn't include depreciation on her income statement because her business doesn't have any assets—such as a computer, a car, or manufacturing machinery—that would have their worth reduced over time by wear and tear.

But let's say you open a restaurant. You buy $3,000 worth of tables and chairs. You know that those tables and chairs will have to be replaced in about five years because they will be worn out. Since 3,000 divided by five years equals $600, if you subtract $600 a year from your income statement and put that money into a bank account, in five years you will have saved $3,000—enough to replace your tables and chairs. That's the point of depreciation—to help you save now so that when it comes time to replace your assets, you will already have the money to do so. Many business owners forget that depreciation is a real yearly cost of using an asset. To forget about depreciation is to grossly overstate your profit.

Lola's Custom Draperies is a more complex business than Darla's Flip-Flops but the income statement follows the same format, and its goal is still the same—to show whether the business is profitable.

Lola's income statement includes depreciation for her four expensive industrial sewing machines, which are designed to handle the heavy brocades and other fabrics she uses. The sewing machines cost $4,000 and she figures she will have to replace them in four years, so she depreciates them at $1,000 per year. She deducts $1,000 ÷12 = $84 per month from her income statement for depreciation.

Income Statement: Lola's Custom Draperies

Month Ended August 31, 2013

Revenue

Gross Sales	**$85,456**
COST OF GOODS SOLD	
Materials	$11,550
Labor	$17,810
Total Cost of Goods Sold	**$29,360**
Contribution Margin	**$56,096**
Operating Costs	
FIXED COSTS	
Factory Rent and Utilities	$8,000
Salaries and Administrative	$12,000
Depreciation	$84
VARIABLE COSTS	
Sales Commissions	$8,000
Total Operating Costs	**$28,084**
Pre-Tax Profit	**$28,012**
Taxes (25 percent)	**$7,003**
NET PROFIT	**$21,009**

Green Tip

Printing out financial statements can use up a lot of ink. Try using the "draft" option on your printer to save ink. You can also install Ecofont, a software that helps your printer conserve up to 20 percent more ink.

ANALYZING YOUR INCOME STATEMENT

Entrepreneurs don't just look at their income statements; they analyze them by dividing sales into each line item. Each item can then be expressed as a **percentage,** or share, of sales.

By expressing each item on the income statement as a percentage of sales, you'll start to see the relationships between the items. A dollar is made up of 100 pennies, so a percentage also helps you express each item as part of a dollar. For example, suppose that 40 cents of every dollar of your sales was spent on cost of goods sold. Your contribution margin per dollar of sales would then be 60 cents (60 percent). Your net profit, after 30 cents spent on operating costs and 10 cents on taxes, would be 20 cents (20 percent). These percentages are referred to as a business's **financial ratios**.

By analyzing your income statement items as percentages of sales, you can see how costs are affecting your net profit.

As you've seen, entrepreneurs use income statements to show how their businesses are performing. The information contained in an income statement may sometimes need to be analyzed by using financial ratios or dramatized in charts and graphs. Two types of analysis based on income statements are **sales-data analysis** and **same-size analysis**.

Sales-Data Analysis

As you saw in the example of Darla's Flip-Flops, you can use monthly income statements to forecast future sales. Combining income statement analysis and a knowledge of the industry (for example, slow periods, new competitors, or other factors that influence sales) will be very helpful in forecasting sales.

Same-Size Analysis

Same-size analysis converts financial information from the income statement into percentages. Same-size analysis makes it clear how each item affects the business's net income (profit). Entrepreneurs review the percentages and look at industry trends in order to make changes to improve their profits.

Simply divide any line item on the income statement by the total sales and then multiply it by 100. This turns the line item into a percentage of sales. In the table below, for example, total sales are $10,000 and net income is 25 percent of sales.

Same-Size Analysis

INCOME STATEMENT	AMOUNT	CALCULATION	% OF SALES
Revenue (Sales)	$10,000	$10,000 ÷ $10,000 × 100	100%
COGS	$4,000	$4,000 ÷ $10,000 × 100	40%
Contribution Margin	$6,000	$6,000 ÷ $10,000 × 100	60%
Expenses	$3,500	$3,500 ÷ $10,000 × 100	35%
Net Income (Profit)	$2,500	$2,500 ÷ $10,000 × 100	25%

Let's say you do some research and learn that the percentage for average cost of goods sold in your industry is 30 percent. But your same-size analysis shows that your cost of goods sold is 40 percent. To be more competitive, look into how you could reduce your cost of goods sold. Could you get a better deal from your wholesaler? Could you find a different wholesaler with better prices?

Same-size analysis lets you easily compare income statements from different months, quarters, or years. Even if the sales are different from month to month or quarter to quarter, a same-size analysis will show you patterns and trends. Look at this example from Darla's Flip-Flops for July and August.

July

INCOME STATEMENT	AMOUNT	% OF SALES
Revenue (Sales)	$50,000	100%
COGS	$19,000	38%
Contribution Margin	$31,000	62%
Expenses	$17,000	34%
Net Income (Profit)	$14,000	28%

August

INCOME STATEMENT	AMOUNT	% OF SALES
Revenue (Sales)	$40,000	100%
COGS	$10,400	26%
Contribution Margin	$29,600	74%
Expenses	$15,200	38%
Net Income (Profit)	$14,400	36%

The same-size analysis shows that sales dropped from $50,000 in July to $40,000 in August. In August, however, the business was able to reduce its cost of goods sold from 38 percent to 26 percent. As a result, the company had an increase in net income over July, despite having a drop in sales. Which month do you think was better for Darla's Flip-Flops?

Math Moment

In a monthly income statement, if the contribution margin is $10,000, the total operating expenses are $4,000, and the taxes are 15 percent, what is the net profit?*

---

*   Answer: $5,100

INCOME STATEMENT RATIOS

Sales-data analysis and same-size analysis will really help you understand how your business is doing over time.

Some other financial ratios are helpful for providing a "snapshot" in the present moment. These ratios provide information you can use to monitor expenses, to compare the performance of the company with competitors in the industry, and to measure profitability.

The two most important financial ratios based on the income statement are **operating ratio** and **return on sales (ROS)**.

Operating Ratio

The **operating ratio** is a very important tool for a business owner because it tells you what percentage of each dollar of revenue is needed to cover expenses.

(Expenses ÷ Sales) x 100 = Operating Ratio (percentage)

If an income statement for Darla's Flip-Flops shows sales of $20,000 and an insurance expense of $1,000, Darla's operating ratio for insurance is 5 percent. Five percent of every dollar she earns in revenue has to go to pay for her business's insurance.

($1,000 ÷ $20,000) × 100 = 5 percent

Use operating ratios to compare your company with other businesses in the industry. If Darla's Flip-Flops is paying $2,000 a month in rent and has sales of $10,000, its operating ratio for rent is 20 percent.

$$(\$2{,}000 \div \$10{,}000) \times 100 = 20 \text{ percent}$$

If 20 percent is higher than the industry average, Darla needs to make a decision: Should she remain in her present location or move to a less expensive one, where the rent would be lower? That depends, in part, on how important her current location is to her sales. If she moves, but her sales drop as a result, a move may not be a good idea.

On the other hand, if she can move to a cheaper location and still keep her sales up, moving could make her business more profitable.

Return on Sales (ROS)

Return on sales (ROS) is a financial ratio calculated by dividing net income by sales and multiplying the result by 100. ROS is an important measure of how profitable a business is, because it shows how much of each dollar of sales the company keeps as profit. ROS is also called profit margin, net margin, net profit ratio, or net profit on sales ratio.

$$(\text{Net Income} \div \text{Sales}) \times 100 = \text{Return on Sales (percentage)}$$

If the income statement for Darla's Flip-Flops shows sales of $30,000 and a net income of $6,000, the ROS percentage for the business is 20 percent.

$$(\$6{,}000 \div \$30{,}000) \times 100 = 20 \text{ percent}$$

A high ROS ratio is usually a good indicator of success for a business. However, the ROS percentage alone doesn't provide a total picture. A business selling high-priced items, such as luxury automobiles, can be very profitable with a 5 percent ROS, while a retailer like Darla's Flip-Flops that sells inexpensive items may need a 25 percent ROS or more. A 5 percent profit on a $100,000 item is much more than a 25 percent profit on a $100 item!

The ROS (Profit Margin) table below shows ROS ranges for various types of products.

ROS (Profit Margin)

ROS	MARGIN RANGE	TYPICAL PRODUCT
Very low	2%–5%	Very high volume *or* very high price
Low	6%–10%	High volume *or* high price
Moderate	11%–20%	Moderate volume *and* moderate price
High	20%–30%	Low volume *or* low price
Very high	30% and up	Very low volume *or* very low price

CREATING WEALTH BY SELLING A PROFITABLE BUSINESS

If your business is successful, your income statements will prove it by showing a net profit. A successful small business can usually be sold for between three and five times its yearly net profit. If your net profit for one year is $10,000, for example, you might be able to sell your business for at least $30,000 (3 x $10,000).

Ultimately, however, a business's value is subjective. You can sell your business for what someone else wants to pay for it—even if you think it is worth more (or less!).

Entrepreneurs can build wealth over time by creating and selling businesses, and then using the money from selling to create or invest in new businesses.

Game Changer

Charles Schwab launched *Investment Indicator* newsletter when he was twenty-seven, and opened his own brokerage firm in 1971 at age thirty-four. As an educated investor himself, Schwab realized there was a group of investors who didn't need someone else to do their research and make their decisions. He began offering discount pricing to investors who were tired of paying hefty commissions to stockbrokers for research the investors were perfectly capable of digging up on their own.

Schwab focused on cutting costs to beat his competition. He cut expensive researchers out of his business and passed those savings to savvy investors, who flocked to Charles Schwab & Company. By 1981, the company's earnings were $5 million.

In 1983, Bank of America bought Charles Schwab & Company for $53 million and left Schwab in place as CEO. Today, Schwab has offices all over the United States and across the world. In 2013, Schwab expanded into online banking—competing with other banks by offering accounts with no ATM fees and no required minimum balances.

Schwab offers stock trading at commissions that are 30 to 40 percent below average. Entrepreneurs create value and jobs, which is why they are considered the engine of our economy.

THE CASH FLOW STATEMENT

An income statement provides a good picture of how well, or poorly, your business is doing. It shows your sales and your expenses. What it does *not* show is the amount of cash you have on hand. For that, you'll come to rely on your **cash flow statement**. **Cash flow** is the money received minus what is spent over a specified period of time.

The cash flow statement records inflows and outflows of cash *when they actually occur*. If a sale is made during the Christmas rush but the customer doesn't pay until March, the income statement will show the sale in December—but the cash flow statement won't show the sale until March, when the business actually receives the cash.

If a business were an automobile, cash would be its gasoline: Without it, the business does not have the necessary fuel to operate.

Let's say your September income statement shows a net income of $3,000, but that's not necessarily the amount of cash you received. If some of your sales were made on credit, you may not get the money from those customers until October, or even later.

A company must have sufficient cash on hand in order to continue operating. If you fail to pay your monthly bills on time, the telephone company may disconnect the phones, for example, or the electricity could be shut off. You must also continue to pay your suppliers, to pay for items you have purchased on credit, and to repay any loans you may have. If you are constantly short of cash, you could lose your business.

Let's take a closer look at cash flow so you can figure out how long your business has to get up and running before it must bring in some cash.

Cash flow is the lifeblood of your business. Run out of cash and your business can't survive.

The Cash Flow Equation

To ensure that you have enough money to operate, you must track your business's cash flow by preparing a cash flow statement every month. The cash flow equation is:

Cash Inflow − Cash Outflow = Net Cash

Here's a cash flow statement for Darla's Flip-Flops for August.

Beginning Cash Balance. Darla started the month with $430 in cash.

Cash Inflow. Darla received $4,400. Darla sells her flip-flops on the boardwalk and accepts only cash payment. If Darla extended credit to her customers, she would show their payments as cash inflow only when the payment was received. If Darla had any investments that increased in value, that would also be shown in this section.

Total Available Cash. The beginning cash balance and the cash inflow for the month show the company's total available cash. In Darla's case, this is $4,830 ($430 + $4,400 = $4,830).

Cash Outflow. This section notes the cash spent on purchases of additional **inventory** of flip-flops ($600). The cash outflow section also includes money Darla spent on operating expenses. The total cash spent in August was $1,575.

Net Cash. The last section shows the net change in cash flow. This tells the entrepreneur whether the business had a positive or negative cash flow that month. Darla's Flip-Flops had a positive net cash flow of $3,255 for the month of August.

Learn the Lingo

Inventory is everything a business has on hand that it could potentially sell, including both merchandise and raw materials.

Cash Flow Statement: Darla's Flip-Flops

Month Ended August 31, 2013

Beginning Cash Balance	**$430**
Cash Inflow	
Sales	**$4,400**
Available Cash	**$4,830**
CASH OUTFLOW	
Cash Purchases of Inventory	**$600**
Insurance Paid	**$200**
Interest Paid	**$300**
Rent Paid	**$200**
Telephone Paid	**$200**
Utilities Paid	**$75**
Total Cash Outflow	**$1,575**
NET CASH	**$3,255**

Ways to Keep Cash Flowing

Here are five ways to avoid being caught without enough cash to pay your bills:

1. **Try to get paid in cash.** When making a sale, ask the customer to use cash rather than credit. You can even offer a small discount for cash sales.

2. **Pay your bills on the due date.** You probably know that it's unwise to pay your bills after the due date has passed—but it also sucks up your cash to pay them too early. Always note the due date on your bills and don't pay them until they are due. Hold on to your cash as long as you can.

3. **Keep track of your cash.** Check your cash balance every single day. Always know how much you have. Keep track of the money your business earns and spends each day. Make sure you receive and keep receipts for every purchase you make. You don't want to be surprised by a lack of cash.

4. **Lease equipment.** When you buy equipment, you'll usually have to put down a large down payment, which reduces your cash on hand. Try to **lease** equipment instead of buying it, unless you would save a lot more money by buying.

5. **Keep as little inventory on hand as possible.** Inventory ties up cash in two ways: the cash you use to purchase the inventory and the cash you spend in storing it. Minimize the amount of inventory you stock (unless it's part of your competitive advantage to offer customers a wide selection). Avoid large purchases of slow-moving inventory.

Cash Flow Is Cyclical

Cash flow is **cyclical** for many businesses, meaning that it varies according to the time of year.

Darla sells flip-flops on the boardwalk in the summertime, and she closes her business in the winter. If you were operating an ice cream stand, your sales during the summer months would be higher than in the winter. If you were selling scarves and gloves, your sales would almost certainly be higher in the cold weather.

Other examples of businesses with cyclical cash flow are flower shops, bridal shops, and college bookstores. Each of these businesses must carefully monitor cash flow in the months of low sales, because they will still have to cover monthly expenses (fixed costs) such as rent, utilities, and insurance. For an example of a cash flow statement, see the chart on the next page.

The Burn Rate

Most new businesses lose money at first. But the question every entrepreneur needs to answer is "How long can I afford to lose money?"

This question is answered by calculating your **burn rate,** the rate at which a company that doesn't yet have a positive cash flow spends cash to cover its overhead costs. This rate is expressed in terms of cash spent per month. A burn rate of $10,000 means that the business is spending $10,000 every month to cover rent and other operating expenses.

Cash on Hand ÷ Burn Rate = Number of Months Before Cash Runs Out

Use the burn rate to calculate how long your company can go without revenue. If your business has $20,000 in cash and its burn rate is $2,000 a month, you can stay "in business" for ten months without making any sales.

$20,000 \div \$2,000 = 10$ months

Next, you'll learn how to use a balance sheet to keep an eye constantly on two ratios—quick and current—that tell you whether your cash on hand is getting too low to cover your debts.

Cash Budget for the Month of _____

	Forecast	Actual	Difference
Cash Inflows			
Cash Sales			
Credit Collections			
Bank Loans			
Other Income			
Total Cash Inflows			
Cash Outflows			
Estimated Variable Expenses			
Insurance			
Salaries			
Advertising			
Interest			
Utilities			
Rent/Mortgage			
Other Fixed Expenses			
_____			
Total Cash Outflows			
Cash Available			

THE BALANCE SHEET: A SNAPSHOT OF THE BUSINESS

A balance sheet provides a clear picture of your business—what it owns and what it owes. The balance sheet has three sections:

1. **Assets.** All items of worth *owned* by the business, such as cash, inventory, furniture, land, machinery, and so on. The balance sheet makes a distinction between two kinds of assets:
   - **Current assets** are assets that can be sold for cash (liquidated) in under a year—furniture or a computer, for example.
   - **Long-term assets** are those that might take more than one year to liquidate—real estate, for example.

2. **Liabilities.** All debts *owed* by the business, such as bank loans, mortgages, lines of credit, and loans from family or friends.
   - **Current liabilities** are those that must be paid within one year.
   - **Long-term liabilities** are those that are paid over a period longer than one year.

3. **Owner's Equity.** Also called capital or net worth, this is the amount that is left over after liabilities are subtracted from assets. Owner's equity is the stated value of the business to the owner.

Preparing a Balance Sheet

Balance sheets are divided into two columns or two sections. All the assets of the business are in the first column (or section) and the liabilities of the business and the owner's equity are included in the second column (or section).

Matt Holden is preparing the annual balance sheet for his business Matt's Merch, which makes hats, T-shirts, and other items for touring rock bands to sell at their shows.

Current Assets. Matt's Merch has $25,000 in cash, and its inventory is worth $100,000. Customers owe the business $20,000 for sales made to them on credit (this is Matt's accounts receivable). Cash, inventory, and accounts receivable are all included in current assets.

Long-Term Assets. Matt's Merch owns a building, which is worth $135,000. The company also owns equipment for printing designs on baseball caps and T-shirts valued at $20,000.

Current Liabilities. Matt's Merch owes $25,000 in short-term bank loans. The company also owes $40,000 to its merchandise suppliers for inventory purchased on credit. This amount is its accounts payable. The company also owes the state $5,000 for sales taxes it collected. These are the company's current (short-term) liabilities.

Long-Term Liabilities. Matt's Merch has a mortgage loan on its building. The company owes the bank $70,000 on the loan, so its mortgage payable is $70,000. This is Matt's only long-term liability.

Owner's Equity. Owner's equity (OE) is calculated by subtracting the total liabilities from the total assets. According to the balance sheet, OE is $160,000. OE is also called "capital."

Assets – Liabilities = Owner's Equity

$300,000 – $140,000 = $160,000

Learn the Lingo

Accounts payable is the amount of money a business owes to its suppliers for purchases made on credit. **Accounts receivable** is the amount of money owed to a business by its customers for credit sales.

Balance Sheet: Matt's Merch

December 31, 2013

ASSETS

Current Assets

Cash	$25,000
Inventory	$100,000
Accounts Receivable	$20,000
Total Current Assets	**$145,000**

LONG-TERM ASSETS

Building	$135,000
Equipment	$20,000
Total Long-Term Assets	**$155,000**
Total Assets	**$300,000**

LIABILITIES AND OWNER'S EQUITY

CURRENT LIABILITIES

Bank Loans	$25,000
Accounts Payable	$40,000
Sales Tax Payable	$5,000
Total Current Liabilities	**$70,000**

LONG-TERM LIABILITIES

Mortgage Payable	$70,000
Total Long-Term Liabilities	**$70,000**
Total Liabilities	**$140,000**
Owner's Equity	**$160,000**
Total Liabilities and Owner's Equity	**$300,000**

($140,000 Total Liabilities + $160,000 Owner's Equity)

Including Depreciation on the Balance Sheet

If an item was purchased with the owner's own money, it was financed with equity.
Equity is listed on the right column of the balance sheet.

Depreciation affects both sides of the balance sheet—it is subtracted from the value of an asset on the left side of the balance sheet and from the value of the owner's equity on the right side.

Say your business, Hometown Restaurant, owns its tables and chairs and has $10,000 in cash, but you took out a $5,000 loan to buy a new stove. The tables and chairs are worth $3,000 and will need to be replaced in five years, so you are deducting $600 yearly for depreciation ($3,000 ÷ 5 = $600). But the $5,000 stove will need to be replaced in ten years, so you need to set aside yearly depreciation of $500 toward a new stove. Your total **depreciation expense** per year is $1,100 ($600 + $500). Depreciation appears on the liabilities side of the balance sheet, because it represents a decrease in the worth of your assets due to wear and tear.

Learn the Lingo

Depreciation expense is the portion of a tangible capital asset that is deemed to have been consumed or expired during a specified period, such as a year, and has thus become an expense for that period.

Hometown Restaurant: Balance Sheet 2014

ASSETS		LIABILITIES	
Tables and Chairs	$3,000	Loan	$5,000
Stove	$5,000	Depreciation	$1,100
Cash	$10,000		
Total Assets	$18,000	Total Liabilities	$6,600
		Owner's Equity	$11,900
		Total Liabilities + OE	$18,000

Liabilities + Owner's Equity = Assets

Notice how assets equals liabilities plus owner's equity on the balance sheet? *On any balance sheet, both sides must show the same total.* If your total on the asset side doesn't match the total on the liability side, you've made a miscalculation.

BALANCE SHEET FINANCIAL ANALYSIS

Entrepreneurs also find it useful to create financial ratios from the data on their balance sheets, which they can use to monitor debt, compare debt with equity, and make sure a business has sufficient cash to pay its debts.

The four balance sheet financial ratios are:

1. Debt Ratio
2. Debt-to-Equity Ratio
3. Quick Ratio
4. Current Ratio

Debt Ratio

If a business is unable to make the payments on its debt, it can be forced into bankruptcy, a legal procedure in which a business sells off its property in order to pay its debts. Basically, if you can't pay your debts, your creditors can take you to court and force you to sell off your assets to raise the money to pay them back.

To avoid bankruptcy, use the **debt ratio** to keep an eye on the money you owe to your creditors. The debt ratio is a business's total debt divided by its total assets.

$$\text{(Total Debts [Liabilities]} \div \text{Total Assets)} \times 100$$
$$= \text{Debt Ratio (percentage)}$$

If Darla's Flip-Flops has $100,000 in total debts (also referred to as its total liabilities) and total assets of $500,000, its debt ratio is 20 percent.

$$(\$100,000 \div \$500,000) \times 100 = 20 \text{ percent}$$

A debt ratio of 20 percent means that Darla's Flip-Flops' debts equal 20 percent of its total assets.

Although it can be a smart strategy to use debt to help finance your business, too much debt will limit your ability to borrow money and can put your business at risk for bankruptcy. Bankers don't like to lend money to businesses with high debt ratios, and a high ratio may also make it difficult for a company to establish credit with suppliers. An ideal debt ratio is determined by the ability of the company to meet its loan payments, and it also depends on what amount of debt is considered acceptable or normal in your industry. So, when starting or operating your business, do some research to find out what the ideal debt ratio is for a company in your industry.

Debt-to-Equity Ratio

The **debt-to-equity ratio** is another ratio entrepreneurs monitor carefully because it indicates how much of the owner's net worth is tied to debt. This is the ratio of the total debts (liabilities) of the business divided by its owner's equity.

(Total Debts [Liabilities] ÷ Owner's Equity) × 100 = Debt-to-Equity Ratio (percentage)

For example, if Darla's Flip-Flops had debts of $100,000 and an owner's equity of $400,000, the debt-to-equity ratio would be 25 percent.

($100,000 ÷ $400,000) × 100 = 25 percent

This means that, for every dollar of debt the business has, it has $4 of equity. What debt/equity ratio is acceptable varies widely depending on your industry.

Quick Ratio

The balance sheet also gives you a snapshot of your business's liquidity. **Liquidity** is the ability to convert assets into cash. You might need to raise some cash to fill a big order, for example, or to take advantage of a great deal from a supplier who is going out of business. Two ratios that help you keep an eye on liquidity are the quick ratio and the current ratio.

The **quick ratio** compares cash to debt, based on the concept that a business should have at least enough money on hand to pay its current debts. The quick ratio is calculated by adding **marketable securities**—investments, such as stocks or bonds, which could be converted to cash quickly—to the cash on hand. If you don't have any investments, just divide your cash on hand by your current debts.

(Cash + Marketable Securities) ÷ Current Liabilities = Quick Ratio

For example, if a company has $50,000 in marketable securities, $150,000 in cash, and $100,000 in current liabilities, its quick ratio is 2 to 1 (which can also be shown as 2:1). Both quick and current ratios are calculated as ratios rather than as percentages.

$$(\$150{,}000 + \$50{,}000) \div \$100{,}000 = 2 \text{ to } 1$$

The quick ratio tells an entrepreneur whether the business has enough cash to cover its current debts. Because a business should be able to pay its debts, the quick ratio should always be greater than 1 to 1.

Current Ratio

The **current ratio** is calculated by dividing your current assets by current liabilities.

Current Assets ÷ Current Liabilities = Current Ratio

For example, if Darla's Flip-Flops has current assets of $250,000 and current liabilities of $100,000, its current ratio is 2.5 to 1.

$$\$250{,}000 \div \$100{,}000 = 2.5 \text{ to } 1$$

Like the quick ratio, the current ratio provides information about the liquidity of the business. The current ratio indicates whether a business would be capable of selling its assets to pay its debts. Most businesses try to maintain a current ratio of 2 to 1.

COMPARATIVE BALANCE SHEETS

A business usually prepares one balance sheet at the beginning of its fiscal year and another at the end . Comparing the beginning balance sheet to the ending one is an excellent way to determine whether the business is succeeding. If the ending balance sheet shows that the owner's equity account has increased, it means that the business has gained value.

Here's a **comparative balance sheet** for Matt's Merch. The balance sheet on the right side was prepared on December 31 of last year. The balance sheet on the left side was prepared December 31 of this year.

Comparative Balance Sheet: Matt's Merch

ASSETS

		December 31, This Year	December 31, Last Year
	CURRENT ASSETS		
	Cash	$20,000	$25,000
	Inventory	$125,000	$100,000
	Accounts Receivable	$25,000	$20,000
Total Current Assets		$170,000	$145,000
	LONG-TERM ASSETS		
	Building	$135,000	$135,000
	Equipment	$25,000	$20,000
	Total Long-Term Assets	$160,000	$155,000
Total Assets		$330,000	$300,000

LIABILITIES AND OWNER'S EQUITY

	CURRENT LIABILITIES		
	Bank Loans	$20,000	$25,000
	Accounts Payable	$30,000	$40,000
	Sales Tax Payable	$2,000	$5,000
	Total Current Liabilities	$52,000	$70,000
	LONG-TERM LIABILITIES		
	Mortgage Payable	$70,000	$70,000
	Total Long-Term Liabilities	$70,000	$70,000
Total Liabilities		$122,000	$140,000
Owner's Equity			
	Matt Holden, Capital	$208,000	$160,000
Total Liabilities and Owner's Equity		$330,000	$300,000

Compare the two balance sheets to see what changed after one year.

CURRENT ASSETS

- **Cash:** Cash has decreased from $25,000 to $20,000. Businesses have cash coming in and going out all the time, so the decrease isn't necessarily bad, as long as there is sufficient cash for daily operations. Remember, a successful entrepreneur prepares and uses cash flow statements to ensure that the business has enough cash on hand.
- **Inventory:** Inventory has risen from $100,000 to $125,000. Matt's Merch has purchased more hats, which it hopes to brand with band logos and sell. Because inventory has value, this asset account has increased.
- **Accounts Receivable:** This asset has increased from $20,000 to $25,000. This means the amount owed by customers to Matt's Merch from sales on credit has increased.

LONG-TERM ASSETS

- **Building:** The Building account has not changed.
- **Equipment:** Matt purchased more equipment for customizing baseball caps and shirts during the year, so Equipment has risen from $20,000 to $25,000.

Total assets for Matt's Merch have risen from $300,000 to $330,000. The company has increased its assets, but does that mean that Matt's Merch has had a successful year? Let's look at liabilities.

CURRENT LIABILITIES

- **Bank Loans:** The amount owed to the banks for the loans taken out by Matt's Merch was reduced from $25,000 to $20,000. Decreasing debt is typically a good business strategy.
- **Accounts Payable:** The amount owed to the various wholesalers and manufacturers Matt's Merch buys its hats from decreased from $40,000 to $30,000. Despite adding inventory during the year, the amount owed to suppliers decreased. This shows that Matt made a deliberate business decision to find suppliers who could offer him better prices.
- **Sales Tax Payable:** Matt's Merch collects sales tax for the state from its customers on every sale. It then makes payments to the state. Matt's

Merch paid some of its taxes, which decreased the amount it owes the state from $5,000 to $2,000.

LONG-TERM LIABILITIES

- **Mortgage Payable:** The amount owed on the mortgage remained the same. This isn't unusual, because mortgages are structured so that payments in the early years of a mortgage are applied to the interest owed on the mortgage, rather than to the principal, which is the amount actually borrowed.
- **Owner's Equity:** Matt's owner's equity for his business, which is its net worth, increased from $160,000 to $208,000. That's good news for Matt, because it means that the business increased in value during that time period.

Despite having less cash at the end of the period, the comparative balance sheet contains very encouraging financial information for Matt's Merch. The company has increased the amount of inventory available for sale, and it is owed more money from credit sales to customers—while at the same time reducing all of its current liabilities. Amounts owed for bank loans, accounts payable, and sales tax payable all have decreased. Remember:

Assets − Liabilities = Owner's Equity

By reducing liabilities, Matt has increased his owner's equity, which is the value of his business. He reduced his liabilities by paying off some of the company's debt. Paying off debt is one of the smartest things a business can do with extra cash.

An Entrepreneur Like You

Lorraine Miller

CACTUS & TROPICALS

www.cactusandtropicals.com

In her early twenties, Lorraine Miller held a secure job as a lab technician, but the lab's owner made belittling comments on a daily basis that made her feel undervalued and disrespected. Lorraine decided that she would rather be her own boss than work for someone who made her feel insignificant, so she quit her job and used $2,000 of her savings to begin selling plants.

Today, the company that Lorraine founded, Cactus & Tropicals, provides indoor and outdoor landscaping for more than five hundred customers in Salt Lake City, Utah, and its retail stores and greenhouses are full of exotic plants and gardening gift baskets.

Lorraine's philosophy has always been that work should be pleasant and fun, not grueling. She believes in treating employees with great respect, as if the company were one big family.

Part of being a member of a company of family members is that self-determination and goal setting are expected from everyone, and at Cactus & Tropicals, employees set goals for their own departments. This includes reviewing the financial statements of the company, and setting financial and other performance goals. Lorraine shares both revenue and cost information with her employees.

As often happens when a company owner is brave enough to share the company's financial statements internally, Lorraine's employees were surprised when they saw how much it really cost to run her business. In fact, they encouraged her to take more personal salary and benefits from the company's profits.

Lorraine argues against the notion that owners do not have time to teach employees to understand, or to share financial statements with them. She says the benefits derived from sharing information far outweigh the cost of taking the time to do so.

Lorraine invested her time in teaching everyone how to read a balance sheet, how to do sales forecasting, how to measure individual and team productivity, and how to earn performance-based bonuses. She gives her employees the opportunity to succeed using their own knowledge, skills, and abilities.

Think Like an Entrepreneur

1. How did Lorraine finance the start-up of her business?
2. Why did Lorraine decide to involve her employees in the financial aspects of her business?
3. What are some risks of teaching employees how to read the company financial statements?

CHAPTER 13

STEP-BY-STEP BOOKKEEPING FOR ENTREPRENEURS

A CLEAR METHOD FOR KEEPING GOOD RECORDS

Most of the important things in the world have been accomplished by people who have kept on trying when there seemed to be no hope at all.

—Dale Carnegie

John D. Rockefeller is number three on the list of the world's twenty-five richest people ever. His net worth was $340 billion when he died in 1937 at ninety-eight.

Rockefeller reportedly kept track of every penny he spent from age sixteen until he passed away. His children said that he never paid a bill without examining it and making sure he understood each item. His biographers learned as much from Rockefeller's accounting books as they did from his letters and correspondence.

A NECESSARY HABIT

Most entrepreneurs don't get as excited about keeping good records as Rockefeller did. For years, I myself have had a hard time paying attention to my own record keeping—so I made a deal with NFTE's financial manager. When I'm late turning in my personal expense accounts to him, I pay him twenty dollars! This motivates me to do it on time. I've found that being up-to-date with my personal financial records gives me a great feeling of organization and self-confidence.

Keeping good records is crucial for any business. Entrepreneurs need to know exactly how much money is coming into and going out of their businesses. In fact, one major reason businesses fail is lack of financial management. Without good records, business owners can't be confident that its income statements, cash flow documents, and balance sheet are accurate. The U.S. Internal Revenue Service (IRS) also insists that you keep accurate records for tax purposes.

If you keep good records, you increase your odds of being a successful entrepreneur. By the time you've finished this chapter, you will have an easy, yet effective, system for keeping your business's financial records straight.

Game Changer

The Federal Deposit Insurance Corporation (FDIC) was created by Congress after many banks went out of business during the stock market crash of 1929. In those days, if your bank failed, you lost any money you had been keeping in it. The stock market crash, the bank failures, and the Great Depression that followed almost destroyed the American economy.

Once the economy recovered, people refused to put their money into the banks because they had lost all faith that the banks were able to protect their savings. In order to restore people's confidence in the banking system and get the economy moving again, the government began insuring bank accounts through the FDIC. Today, even if your bank fails, your money is insured by the FDIC up to $250,000.

ALWAYS KEEP YOUR MONEY IN A BANK

First things first: Always keep your money in a bank. Not under your mattress, and not with your Aunt Sally. In a bank. Your money is much safer in a bank than in your purse or wallet. Money in a bank account is insured by the **Federal Deposit**

Insurance Corporation (FDIC) up to $250,000. The FDIC is an independent agency of the federal government created in 1933 that insures savings, checking, and other types of deposit accounts. This means that even if your bank goes out of business, you still get your money.

As an entrepreneur, you need to set up a separate savings account and checking account for your business. Keeping your personal and your business money separate from the start will make it much easier for you to keep good records and do your taxes.

Having business accounts at a local bank is also important for an entrepreneur because you want to be friends with a banker. Most bank branches have a small business banker on staff. Get to know that person and keep him or her in the loop as you develop your business. Someday, when you apply for a loan for your business, your application will have a better chance of being approved if your banker has gotten to know your character and is enthusiastic about your business.

Tech U

Online banking is convenient, but it also makes it easier for hackers to get into your business accounts and steal money. Small businesses are prime targets for hackers—in fact, 85 percent of data breaches occur at the small business level, according to Visa. Here are some ways to protect your accounts:

1. Always close your browser before and after doing any online banking. Never leave your online banking window open and then navigate to another website.

2. Scan your accounts every day for transactions that look odd. If you see anything strange, contact your bank immediately.

3. Install antivirus and security software and always keep them up to date. Even a one-day lapse leaves you wide open for hackers and viruses.

4. To protect credit card information sent online, websites use a secure sockets layer (SSL) **encryption**. Encryption means that the information is put into a code that only the sender and the receiver can read. To tell if a website uses a SSL, check the address bar first. It should have https:// rather than http:// at the beginning of the address. Another way to tell is by looking at the status bar on the browser. If the status bar is visible, a small, closed lock should appear.

5. Don't check your bank account while using a publicly shared Wi-Fi network.

BANK RECONCILIATION

One of the best ways to maintain good control over cash is to reconcile your business checking account with the bank statement each month. A **bank reconciliation** is the process of verifying that your checkbook balance is in agreement with the ending balance in your checking account statement from the bank.

Here's an example of bank reconciliation:

Assume that the end-of-month balance in your business checkbook is $2,500. Your bank statement, however, shows a balance of $3,180. Follow these steps to reconcile your checkbook with your bank statement:

1. Compare your checkbook activity with the transactions listed in the bank statement to see if there are any outstanding checks. In our example, let's assume checks number 327 and number 330 haven't yet cleared the bank. The total amount of these checks is $1,700.

2. Compare your checkbook with the deposits shown in the bank statement to see if you made any deposits that aren't listed on the bank statement. Let's say you made a deposit on the last day of the month for $1,000. It wasn't recorded by the bank until the next day and isn't shown on the statement.

3. Finally, check to see if the bank statement shows any bank charges or fees. You notice that the bank charged your account $20 to have new business checks printed and sent to you.

Here's how your bank reconciliation would look:

EXPLANATION	CHECKBOOK BALANCE	BANK STATEMENT BALANCE
Balance on October 31	$2,500	$3,180
Less Outstanding Checks		$1,700
Plus Unlisted Deposits		$1,000
Less Bank Service Charges/Fees	$20	
Actual Cash Balance	**$2,480**	**$2,480**

Bank Reconciliation Tips

If your totals don't agree:

1. Look for items on the bank statement that you haven't entered in your checkbook, such as other service charges, interest earned on your account, or ATM withdrawals.

2. Check the amount written on each check against the amounts shown in your checkbook. A common mistake is a transposition error, which happens when you reverse two numbers by mistake. For example, you might have written a check for $73 and accidentally entered $37 as the amount in your checkbook.

USING ACCOUNTANTS AND BOOKKEEPERS

Many entrepreneurs don't keep their own records. They feel their time is better spent managing the business rather than doing record keeping work. This is especially true if the entrepreneur has little or no background in accounting.

Some entrepreneurs pay a part-time accountant or bookkeeper to maintain their books. This, of course, is an additional business expense.

Hiring someone else to keep the records for your business presents another potential problem. If the accountant has the authority to write checks and also does the bank reconciliation, there is the possibility of **embezzlement,** the stealing of money from an employer.

To avoid this, entrepreneurs need to have proper accounting controls in place. **Accounting controls** are checks and balances established so that accounting personnel follow procedures that help to avoid embezzlement and allow the owner to better control the financial operation of the business. Here are some smart controls to implement early on for your business:

1. Require that all checks, purchase orders, and invoices have not only the accountant's signature, but also the owner's signature.

2. Allow only a few trusted employees to make cash deposits, and require these employees to make deposits as soon and as frequently as possible.

3. Store copies of all cash register tapes, receipts, invoices, canceled checks, and any other paper records of cash transactions. Use them to investigate any discrepancies between internal records and bank statements.

Some entrepreneurs pay an auditor to review their books. An **auditor** is an outside accountant who examines a company's financial records and verifies that they have been kept properly. This type of audit is often called an **internal audit**. Don't confuse this with an audit by the Internal Revenue Service, which is done to make sure an individual's or a business's income tax returns are honest.

WHAT IS ACCOUNTING?

Accounting is the system of recording and summarizing business and financial transactions. Accounting helps you keep track of all cash inflows and outflows, and then you use that information to prepare the three financial statements you learned about earlier:

1. Income statement
2. Cash flow statement
3. Balance sheet

Accounting systems can be either manual or computerized, although today most small businesses use accounting software such as QuickBooks or Quicken. Any payment or any income received is a transaction.

You'll want to track:

- All cash inflows (receipts)
- All cash outflows (payments)

To track this information, you'll use **source documents**—the original records of a transaction. Source documents include receipts, canceled checks, invoices, and bank deposit slips. Keeping good records is really very simple, as long as you make sure to do it every business day. If you skip days, or try to keep numbers in your head, it will become difficult to maintain reliable records.

There will be times when you will be too busy to record a credit or debit at the moment it occurs, but if you keep all your source documents, you can catch these later.

All accounting systems use what is called **double-entry accounting**—this just means that every business transaction affects at least two accounts.

Source Document: Purchase Orders

A **purchase order** (often referred to as a PO) is a detailed written record of a business's request for supplies or inventory. When purchasing supplies, write up a purchase order that contains a description of what you are ordering, who it is that you're ordering it from, the price being charged, and who is taking the order. Be sure to date and number the purchase order, and give the supplier the purchase order number when you place the order.

The purchase order system is highly reliable. A purchase order clearly states for the seller what it is that you want to buy, which prevents confusion and helps to make sure your order is fulfilled properly. Another advantage of this system is that it helps you record your business's purchases. Employees who make purchases from suppliers know that they must first prepare a purchase order. They also know that the owner must sign the purchase order before it is sent to the supplier. The PO system helps prevent unauthorized purchases.

Purchase order forms are available in office supply stores or from discount retailers. You can also download purchase order templates and adapt them for your business.

Source Document: Sales Invoices

You use a purchase order when you buy supplies or inventory. But what should you use when you sell goods or services? The bill you give your customer becomes your **sales invoice**—an itemized list of goods or services provided and the amount due. Your invoice copies are records of your business's income.

When you sell your product or service to a customer, always give the customer a bill. You can use phone or tablet apps to mail or text receipts to customers, or go old school and get a receipt/invoice book with two-part carbon-copy receipts/invoices. When you make a sale, give the top copy to the customer as his or her receipt. Keep the second copy as your invoice.

Keep a record of each invoice, organized by either number or customer name. Each invoice that is prepared and sent (or given) to a customer is recorded as a credit entry when the invoice is paid by the customer.

Once you receive the customer's payment, write or stamp "Paid" on the invoice. File all invoices, either by invoice number (in numerical order) or by customer name (in alphabetical order).

As with other receipts and purchase orders, invoice forms are available at many office supply stores and discount retailers. Invoice templates are also available online and can be downloaded and adapted for your business.

Source Document: Receipts

A receipt is a slip of paper with the date and amount of your purchase printed on it. Always get a **receipt** for every purchase you make. Your receipts are records of your business's expenses.

Save your receipts until tax time, when they will be worth money—literally! U.S. tax law allows business owners to deduct many of their expenses from their taxable income. These **deductions** can save you money, but you must keep the receipts to prove that you actually paid for the expenses.

Keeping receipts for every purchase you make will help you get in the habit of tracking your cash flow, which is the amount of cash you actually have on hand, available for use. One measure of your cash flow at any point in time is the cash balance in your accounting journal.

Tech U

Some popular accounting software programs for entrepreneurs are QuickBooks, Sage 50 Accounting, Sage BusinessWorks Accounting, and Mind Your Own Business. You can use them even if you only have a basic understanding of accounting.

The programs all provide simple instructions, and most provide templates. They provide accounts common to most businesses, such as sales revenue and accounts payable.

Most provide examples of how to enter typical business transactions. In some programs you would simply enter a transaction by using the name of the account involved.

The big advantage these programs have over manual accounting is that they can prepare your financial statements automatically.

Accounting software programs are available in a range of prices. Some are free and others can cost hundreds of dollars.

RECORDING TRANSACTIONS

The first step in double-entry accounting is to record transactions. There are two approaches to recording transactions:

Single-Column, Database Approach: This is a simple method. Most computerized systems use it.

Double-Column Approach: This method uses a left-hand (debit) column and a right-hand (credit) column for each account. Most manual accounting systems use a double-column method.

No matter which method you use, all accounting depends on the same basic principle:

Liabilities + Owner's Equity = Assets

You first encountered this equation when you were introduced to the balance sheet. The most important thing to remember about recording transactions is that, just as with a balance sheet, any change on the left side of the equation *must* produce a change on the right side.

Math Moment

The owner of a costume shop pays the supplier $5 for each mask he purchases. In turn, the owner sells the masks for $15 each. In the month of October, the business had mask sales revenue of $2,250. What was the cost of goods sold expense (COGS) for October?*

---

* Answer: $750

Single-Column, Database Approach

Suppose Matt Washington pays $4,000 in cash for a new computer for his business, Matt's Merch. The asset "Cash" would be reduced by $4,000, and the asset "Office Equipment" would be increased by $4,000. Each transaction in this example happened on the left side of the equation, dealing with assets. Therefore, there's no need to make an entry in the liabilities/owner's equity side of the equation.

This transaction can be shown as:

Cash	Office Equipment
– $4,000	+ $4,000

What would happen if, instead of paying cash, Matt's Merch bought the new computer on account? Here, Cash wouldn't be affected. Instead, Office Equipment would go up by $4,000 on the assets side of the equation. And on the other side, liability (Accounts Payable) would also go up by $4,000. The equation would balance.

A single-column accounting database, which is especially suited to computerized systems, shows the equation this way:

Office Equipment =	Accounts Payable
+ $4,000	– $4,000

Double-Column Approach

Manual accounting systems use the double columns of debits and credits. Each account has a left-hand and a right-hand column. The left-hand column is the debit side, and the right-hand column is the credit side.

Here's the key to understanding this approach:

- Increases in assets are recorded on the debit side.
- Increases in liabilities and owner's equity are recorded on the credit side.
- Decreases in assets are recorded on the credit side.
- Decreases in liabilities and owner's equity are recorded on the debit side.

Learn the Lingo

Double-entry bookkeeping ledgers are also called **T-accounts**. It makes sense when you look at them—you can see a capital T on each side of the ledger.

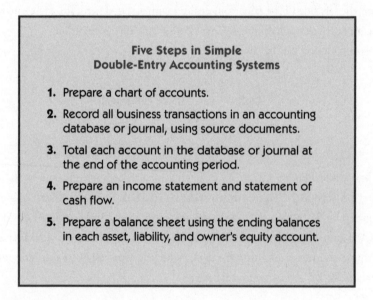

Five Steps in Simple Double-Entry Accounting Systems

1. Prepare a chart of accounts.

2. Record all business transactions in an accounting database or journal, using source documents.

3. Total each account in the database or journal at the end of the accounting period.

4. Prepare an income statement and statement of cash flow.

5. Prepare a balance sheet using the ending balances in each asset, liability, and owner's equity account.

This is a summary of the earlier transaction in which Matt's Merch purchased office equipment for $4,000 cash.

Most transactions can be entered formally in what is called a **general journal,** an accounting record that shows all the transactions of the business. Assets are always entered on the left/Debit side of the accounting journal, so Office Equipment is entered into the Debit column. Since every entry has to be balanced out, the Cash used to buy the Office Equipment goes into the right Credit column.

General Journal

DATE	EXPLANATION	REF.	DEBIT	CREDIT
Aug. 2	Office Equipment		$4,000	
	Cash			$4,000
	Bought new computer			

Rather than using T-accounts, you could make this entry in a general journal, like this:

General Journal

DATE	EXPLANATION	REF.	DEBIT	CREDIT
Aug. 2	Office Equipment		$4,000	
	Accounts Payable			$4,000
	Bought new computer on account			

Again, an asset—office equipment—goes into the debit column. To balance it, you enter a liability, accounts payable, into the credit column. Debits must *always* equal credits when you record a transaction.

USING AN ACCOUNTING WORKSHEET

At first, many entrepreneurs will use a single-column accounting worksheet. After the entrepreneur **posts** each transaction (writes it in the accounting worksheet) in an accounting period (such as a month), she can immediately determine the effect the transaction has on the financial statements. An accounting worksheet is useful primarily in a cash-only accounting system. The only time you will make entries that don't affect Cash is when you remove inventory upon a sale of goods, or when you estimate your tax expense based on the current period's income before taxes. All other worksheet entries will increase Cash when it's collected or decrease Cash when it's paid.

If you aren't familiar with spreadsheet software, search for "Free Excel Spreadsheet Tutorial" on Google or YouTube. Find a tutorial that looks helpful and spend about an hour learning Excel basics. This will allow you to use the accounting worksheet template in a more informed way. It will also help with activities such as preparing budgets, preparing financial statements, and projecting cash flows.

If you keep an accounting worksheet by hand, the entries should be made in pencil so you can erase mistakes. Use a mechanical pencil—it can make very thin lines, allowing you to write more in the limited space available. Write neatly. Since an accounting worksheet has many rows and columns, you can use a long ruler when inputting numbers to ensure that you are placing the numbers on the correct line.

Preferably, however, you will use an Excel spreadsheet or accounting software to record your transactions. Let's explore an example you can use to set up your own accounting system.

Parts of the Accounting Worksheet

Here are the important parts of the accounting worksheet template:

Check or Deposit Number, Date, and To/From Columns: Beginning in cell A11, and running across the first three columns, are the columns for the Cash account.

Chart of Accounts: Cash, Inventory, Capital Equipment, Loans Payable, Income Tax Payable.

Equity: Revenues increase Owner's Equity, and expenses decrease Owner's Equity.

Chart of Accounts (A/C) Code: In column K, beginning in cell K10, the appropriate Chart of Accounts Code is shown for each transaction. The code is taken from the Chart of Accounts. The Chart of Accounts Code is a convenient way of labeling all revenues and expenses. This makes it easier to prepare your income statement.

Explanation for Equity Change: In column L, beginning in cell L10, you can provide an explanation for the change in equity. This serves as a handy reminder of the type of each revenue and expense item.

	A	B	C	D	E	F	G	H	I	J	K	L	M
1	Company Name:			Month/Day/Year:									
2													
3													
4													
5													A= L+E
6			← Total Assets →				= Liabilities		+	E Equity (Net Worth)			
7													
8			← Cash Account →		← Other Assets →								
9	Ck #	Date	To/From	Cash	Inventory	Capital Equipment					A/C Code	Explanation for Equity Change	Pacioli Ck **
10	Balance Sheet Numbers, Beg. of August												
11													
12													
13													
14													
15													
16													
17													
18													
19													
20													
21													
22													
23													
24													
25													
26													
27													
28													
29	Balance Sheet Numbers, End of August												
30													

Transaction Portion of the Accounting Worksheet
The accounting worksheet is organized according to the accounting equation: Assets = Liabilities + Owner's Equity.

Pacioli Check: Column M, beginning with cell M10, is the Pacioli Check column, which ensures that the accounting equation always balances after each transaction. The column is named after the father of modern-day bookkeeping, Luca Pacioli. Pacioli was a Franciscan monk from Sansepolcro, Italy. In 1494 he wrote the first textbook of accounting.

Transaction Portion of the Accounting Worksheet

The accounting worksheet is organized according to the accounting equation you already know:

Liabilities + Owner's Equity = Assets

Entering Transactions

The following example shows you how to use the accounting worksheet for a T-shirt business owned by Jean Waverly called Jean's T-Shirts.

Let's start with Transaction 1. Jean started her business on August 2, 2013, by contributing $2,000 of her personal savings to open a business checking account. When she deposited this money in the business account, she would make the following entry in the accounting worksheet.

Ck #	Date	To/From	Cash	Inventory	Jean Waverly, Capital	Pacioli Ck **
Balance Sheet Numbers, Beg. of August			0	0	0	0
Deposit	8/2/2014	Jean Waverly	2,000		2,000	0

Only the affected accounts are shown.

To get a bit more practice, let's look at Transaction 2. Here, the business purchased two hundred blank T-shirts for $3 each from ACME T-Shirt Supply. The total cost of $600 is subtracted from Cash and added to Inventory (check 101).

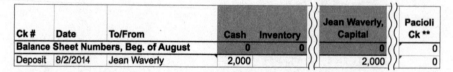

Ck #	Date	To/From	Cash	Inventory	Jean Waverly, Capital	Pacioli Ck **
Balance Sheet Numbers, Beg. of August			0	0	0	0
Deposit	8/2/2014	Jean Waverly	2,000		2,000	0
101	8/2/2014	ACME T-Shirt Supply	-600	600		0

Only the affected accounts are shown.

THE YOUNG ENTREPRENEUR'S GUIDE

Note that Jean's current balance in Cash is $1,400, and her balance in Inventory is $600. You can determine the account balance for *any* account by adding up the numbers from the beginning of the period to the current date.

Using the Accounting Worksheet

Let's start from the beginning for Jean Waverly's business. After she wrote a business plan and studied the market, Jean decided to open a merchandising business selling T-shirts. She began her business on August 2, 2013.

The first thing she did was to prepare a Chart of Accounts for her business and open a business checking account at a local bank. Jean pays the supplier of her T-shirts $3 for each shirt. She sells the shirts for $10 apiece.

The first step in using the accounting worksheet is to enter all the transactions. As an example, here are the business transactions for Jean's T-shirts in August 2013:

August 2   Jean Waverly invested $2,000 from her personal savings account to provide start-up financing for the business. She opened up a business checking account at her local bank.

August 2   The business purchased 200 T-shirts from ACME T-Shirt Supply (200 × $3 = $600). This is check 101.

August 8   The business sold 50 T-shirts at $10 each (50 × $10 = $500). This transaction requires two entries. First, you record the sales revenue. Add $500 to Cash and $500 to Jean Waverly, Capital (as Revenue). Second, you record the Cost of Goods Sold (COGS) expense. The cost per shirt is $3. Thus, the COGS expense is $3 × 50 shirts = $150.

Each sale of inventory requires two entries: one to record the sales revenue and one to record the COGS expense.

August 9   The business paid $100 for advertising flyers (check 102).

August 10   The business paid $500 for a new office machine, a cash register (check 103).

August 11   The business paid its monthly rent of $300 to Ron's Real Estate (check 104).

August 15   The business sold 100 T-shirts at $10 each for the week (100 × $10 each = $1,000). The cost of each T-shirt is $3 apiece. Thus, COGS expense is 100 shirts × $3 = $300.

August 15　The business purchased 400 more T-shirts from ACME T-Shirt Supply (400 × $3 = $1,200) (check 105).

August 16　The business paid its utility bill to Atlantic Electric Company for $225 (check 106).

August 22　The business sold 150 T-shirts for the week (150 × $10 = $1,500). The cost of each T-shirt is still $3. So COGS expense is 150 shirts × $3 = $450.

August 24　The business paid a salary of $125 to a part-time worker, Mary Smith (check 107).

August 25　The business paid its $200 insurance bill for the month to ABC Insurance Company (check 108).

August 26　The business sold 200 T-shirts for the week (200 × $10 = $2,000). The cost of each T-shirt is $3 apiece. So COGS expense is 200 shirts × $3 = $600.

August 31　The business calculated pre-tax net income for the period by adding all revenues and subtracting all expenses. Pre-tax net income is $2,550. At a 15 percent income tax rate, a tax liability, tax expense is calculated to be .15 × $2,550 = $382.50.

Transactions for Jean Waverly's T-Shirts

All the transactions for August have been entered in the accounting worksheet shown in the chart. From the data in this accounting worksheet, do you think that Jean's T-Shirts was profitable in August?

Math Moment

An accounting worksheet showed $30,000 in inventory at the beginning of December. During the month, the business made two additional purchases of inventory—one for $6,000 and the other for $5,000. The COGS expense for the month was $20,000. What is the value of the ending inventory?*

---

*　Answer: $21,000.

Company Name: Jean Waverly's T-Shirts

John Doe
NfFTE Ent 101/01
Mr. Killebrew

Month/Day/Year: 4/8/20—

Total Assets = Liabilities + Equity (Net Worth) E

A= L+E

Cash Account ← Other Assets →

Ck #	Date	To/From	Cash	Inventory	Capital Equipment	Loans Payable	Income Tax Payable	Jean Waverly, Capital	A/C Code	Explanation for Equity Change	Pacioli Ck **
		Balance Sheet Numbers, Beg. of August	0	0	0	0	0	0			0
Deposit	8/2/20—	Jean Waverly	2,000					2,000			0
101	8/2/20—	ACME T-Shirt Supply	-600	600							0
Deposit	8/8/20—	Dep. Cks. from Sales	500	-150				500	R1	Sales Revenue	0
								-150	VE1	COGS Expense	0
102	8/9/20—	Corner Print Shop	-100					-100	FE1	Adv. Expense	0
103	8/10/20—	Otto's Office Machines	-500		500						0
104	8/11/20—	Ron's Real Estate	-300					-300	FE2	Rent Expense	0
Deposit	8/15/20—	Dep. Cks. from Sales	1,000	-300				1,000	R1	Sales Revenue	0
								-300	VE1	COGS Expense	0
105	8/15/20—	ACME T-Shirt Supply	-1,200	1,200							0
106	8/16/20—	Atlantic Electric Co.	-225					-225	FE3	Utilities Expense	0
Deposit	8/22/20—	Dep. Cks. from Sales	1,500	-450				1,500	R1	Sales Revenue	0
								-450	VE1	COGS Expense	0
107	8/24/20—	Mary Smith	-125					-125	FE4	Salary Expense	0
108	8/25/20—	ABC Insurance Co.	-200					-200	FE5	Insurance Expense	0
Deposit	8/26/20—	Dep. Cks. from Sales	2,000	-600				2,000	R1	Sales Revenue	0
								-600	VE1	COGS Expense	0
	8/31/20—						638	-638	VE5	Income Tax Expense	0
		Balance Sheet Numbers, End of August	3,750	300	500	0	638	3,912			0

Transactions for Jean Waverly's T-Shirts

All the transactions for August have been entered in the accounting worksheet.

Predicting. *From the data in this accounting worksheet, do you think that Jean's T-Shirts was profitable in August?*

CREATING FINANCIAL STATEMENTS

After the transactions for a period are entered correctly into the accounting worksheet, you can prepare the balance sheet, income statement, and cash flow statement. It doesn't matter which financial statement you start with.

Blank Accounting Worksheet

The complete worksheet shows an income statement, a beginning and ending balance sheet, a cash flow statement, and an inventory report.

Balance Sheet

First, look at row 29 of Jean Waverly's August transactions and you'll see the ending balances in each of the accounts in the Assets, Liability, and Owner's Equity portions of the balance sheet. Assets are $4,550, Liabilities are $638, and Owner's Equity is $3,912. They are the basis for preparing the balance sheet in the accounting worksheet.

BALANCE SHEET 8/31/2013	
ASSETS	
Cash	$3,750
Inventory	300
Office Machines	500
TOTAL ASSESTS	4,550
LIABILITIES	
Bank Loan	$0
Income Taxes Payable	638
OWNERS EQUITY	
Jean Waverly, Capital, Beg. Bal	$0
Plus: Owner's Personal Investment	2,000
Plus: Net Income	$1,912
TOTAL LIABILITIES & OWNER EQUITY	**$4,550**

Look at the Owner's Equity part of the balance sheet. Compare it to the balance sheet at the beginning of the month. Jean Waverly, Capital had a zero balance on August 1 because the business was just beginning.

On August 2, Jean financed the business by contributing $2,000 of her personal money to the business. Jean's T-Shirts earned a net income of $1,912 during August. So, the August 31 ending balance for Jean Waverly, Capital is $3,912 (August 1 balance $0 + $2,000 equity financing on August 2 + $1,912 net income for August).

As is the case in every balance sheet, the Assets must equal the total of the Liabilities and Owner's Equity. In this balance sheet on August 31, 2013, they do.

Income Statement

For the income statement, begin by looking at cell K10, labeled "A/C Code" (which stands for Chart of Accounts Code). This code allows you to classify revenues, variable costs, and fixed expenses.

Chart of Accounts Codes for Changes in Owner's Equity

 R1 = Revenue Source Number1 (Sales)

VC1 = Cost of Goods Sold (a Variable Expense)

VC2 = Sales Commission (a Variable Expense)

VC3 = Utilities

VC4 = Salary

FC1 = Advertising Expense (Flyers)

FC2 = Rent Expense

FC3 = Utilities Expense

FC4 = Salary Expense

FC5 = Insurance Expense

Using the Account Code, you can add all the accounts for the month to the income statement portion of the accounting worksheet. For example, for your Sales (account R1), add all the R1 transactions:

From August 8, add $500.

From August 15, add $1,000.

From August 22, add $1,500.

From August 26, add $2,000.

Jean Waverly's total sales revenue for the month of August adds up to $5,000. Add that amount to the income statement under Revenue, Sales in cell S3 below.

Here's another example: For Cost of Goods Sold (account VE1), add all VE1 transactions:

From August 8, add $150.

From August 15, add $300.

From August 22, add $450.

From August 26, add $600.

Jean Waverly's total COGS for the month of August is $1,500. Add that amount to the income statement under Cost of Goods Sold in cell S5 below.

Continue in this way for all the accounts with entries in August. Some, such as Office Equipment, will only have one entry (on August 10, when Jean bought a cash register). Others, such as Jean Waverly, Capital, will have multiple entries that you'll need to add up.

Here's the final income statement:

◇	O	P	Q	R	S
1	INCOME STATEMENT				
2	REVENUE				
3	Sales				$5,000
4	COST OF GOODS SOLD				
5	Cost of Goods Sold				-1,500
6	GROSS PROFIT				$3,500
7					
8	OPERATING EXPENSES				
9	Other Variable Expenses (VE)				$0
10	Fixed Expenses (FE):				
11	Advertising Expense				-100
12	Rent Expense				-300
13	Utilities Expense				-225
14	Salary Expense				-125
15	Insurance Expense				-200
16	Total Operating Expenses				-950
17	Pre-Tax Profit				2,550
18	Less: Income-Tax Expense				-638
19	NET PROFIT				$1,912

The net income of $1,912 in the income statement is also reported on the balance sheet as an increase in Owner's Equity.

Cash Flow Statement

In relation to the cash flow statement, there are three basic types of business activities:

1. **Operating Activities:** Day-to-day activities are called operating activities. Most cash changes fall into this category.
2. **Investing Activities:** When a business buys assets that will last more than one year, they are called investing activities. Jean's only investing activity is the purchase of a cash register for $500 on August 10.
3. **Financing Activities:** The third category is financing activities. It consists primarily of debt and equity financing. Jean's only financing activity in October is the $2,000 she personally invested to provide start-up equity financing for her business.

Jean can now prepare the cash flow statement by adding all the changes in the Cash column (Column D) under the appropriate head, as shown here.

STATEMENT OF CASH FLOWS	
Cash from Operating Activities	
Cash Sales	$5,000
Cash Pd for Supplies	-1800
Cash Pd for Advert.	-100
Cash Pd for Rent	-300
Cash Pd for Utilit.	-225
Cash Pd for Salary	-125
Cash Pd for Insur.	-200
Cash from Investing Activities	
Purchase of Equipment	-$500
Cash from Financing Activities	
Jean's Personal Contr.	2000
Change in Cash	$3,750
Add: Beg. Cash	0
Cash Balance, 10/31/13	$3,750

The ending cash balance of $3,750 is the same number as the cash balance reported on the balance sheet.

Tracking Inventory

Every time inventory is purchased, make sure to record the type of inventory, the number of units purchased, and its cost. Every time inventory is sold, make a note of the type of inventory and number of units sold. This is a crucial accounting control to make sure customers or employees aren't stealing merchandise from your business.

Thus, in the accounting worksheet, you see that there should be 100 T-shirts on hand at the end of August. If there are fewer than that, you have a problem. Customers or employees may have stolen T-shirts, or there may be an accounting error.

The inventory of T-shirts has a dollar value. At the end of the month the balance in Inventory is $300 (100 T-shirts × $3).

Now you have a simple system for keeping good records for your business. Use it every day, and you will feel confident and in control of the money going in and out of your business!

An Entrepreneur Like You

Linda Avey and Anne Wojcicki

23ANDME

www.23andme.com

Are you a science geek? You might have a great business opportunity on your hands! Linda Avey and Anne Wojcicki are biologists who founded 23andMe, a company that provides personal DNA testing. The company was named after the number of chromosome pairs in human DNA.

23andMe makes it easy for users to learn about their inherited health traits and genetic links to certain diseases. Just mail the company your saliva sample, and you will receive your results a few weeks later by mail.

When she was starting 23andMe, Anne was married to Google cofounder Sergey Brin, so she turned to "friends and family" financing first. Sergey and Google gave 23andMe $3.9 million in start-up capital, an investment that made sense for Google, whose success is based on searching for data.

At first, 23andMe had to charge more than $1,000 for its genetic testing, to cover the costs, but as the service became more popular, Linda and Anne were able to obtain more financing that helped them bring the price of a personal genetic test down to $299. The price of the tests was still the same for 23andMe to conduct, but Linda and Anne bet that they could grow the company sufficiently with lower prices to make up for the reduction in profit. In 2012, 23andMe raised $50 million in venture capital, almost doubling its existing financing of $52.6 million. The company used this financing to lower the price of a test to $99. They expect this latest price drop to push their customer base from 180,000 to more than 1 million customers.

What's really exciting is that, with that many customers, 23andMe will be sitting on one of the world's largest databases of genetic information. This data could be used by scientists to develop better treatments for diseases such as cancer. 23andMe customers can opt to keep their data private, but so far around 90 percent have been willing to share their information, as long as it is stripped of identifying data.

"By having one million individual users," Anne told *Time* magazine, "you can get to a scale where researchers are running data queries through 23andMe, where drug studies leverage our data, and where individuals can more easily be connected to studies that could benefit them."

Think Like an Entrepreneur

1. What is your opinion of 23andMe's strategy regarding its pricing? What are the pros and cons?
2. What ethical questions does DNA testing for diseases or birth defects raise?
3. Why did investing in 23andMe make sense for Google?

PART 4
PROTECT YOUR BUSINESS

CHAPTER 14

SAFEGUARD YOUR INTELLECTUAL PROPERTY

HOW TO SECURE AND MONETIZE YOUR IDEAS AND CREATIONS

> Americans have been selling this view around the world: that progress comes from perfect protection of intellectual property.
>
> —Lawrence Lessig

Intellectual property (IP) is anything original you create with your intellect that could potentially earn money—from a software program to a song. Books, inventions, and architectural designs are also examples of intellectual property.

Many wonderful careers and businesses have been developed from intellectual property. If you do not obtain legal protection for your intellectual property, however, other people can take it and use it to make money for themselves. This chapter will teach you what you need to know to safeguard your intellectual property and monetize it.

A QUICK REVIEW OF IP PROTECTION

Different kinds of intellectual property require different forms of legal protections. To obtain legal protection for your intellectual property, and prevent anyone else from using it without your permission, you must register it with the appropriate federal government office.

Here are the three main types of IP protection available under U.S. law, and where to register for them:

1. **Copyright: Protects artistic creations.** Artistic creations such as music, drawings, and literature are protected by copyright. **Copyright** is the exclusive right to perform, display, copy, or distribute an artistic work. Copyright applies as soon as a work is created, but you must file a copyright form with the federal government to secure your rights. Once your copyright is granted, no one else can use your creative work—even online—without paying you for permission to use it. If you copyright your book, for example, a blog may not print long excerpts from it without your permission. The symbol © indicates that a work is protected by copyright.

   U.S. Copyright Office: www.copyright.gov.

2. **Patent: Protects inventions.** Inventions are protected by patents. A **patent** is the exclusive right to make, use, or sell a device or process. Many types of creations can be patented, from an improved design for a ketchup bottle, to a variety of tomato used to make the ketchup, to a process for bottling the ketchup. There is no symbol to designate that an invention has been patented, but businesses sometimes use the phrase "patent pending" to indicate that a patent has been filed for a product and is under review by the U.S. Patent and Trademark Office.

   U.S. Patent and Trademark Office: www.uspto.gov.

3. **Trademark: Protects brand symbols and slogans.** A **trademark** protects the logos and slogans a company uses to brand itself. A company uses a trademark so that people will recognize its product instantly, without having to read the company name or even having to think about it. The little bird symbol from Twitter is an example of a logo that most people recognize worldwide.

   A **logo** (short for "logotype") is an identifying symbol for a product or business. The logo is printed on the business's stationery, business cards, and flyers. Some logos appear on the products as well. When a logo has been registered with the United States Patent Office to protect it from being used by others, it is called a trademark.

You may have seen the symbols ® for "registered trademark" and ™ for "trademark" used after certain business logos or slogans. These symbols indicate that that the intellectual property is protected.

U.S. Patent and Trademark Office www.uspto.gov.

Get the Stats

Thomas Jefferson wrote, "Issuing of patents for new discoveries has given a spring to invention beyond my conception." Later, Abraham Lincoln said, "The Patent System added the fuel of interest to the fire of genius." The first patent and copyright law was passed in 1790. The U.S. Patent Office was established in 1836.

INFRINGEMENT

Violating a copyright, trademark, or patent is called **infringement**. A clothing designer who "knocks off" another designer's dress is committing infringement. A filmmaker who puts a band's song in her film without obtaining their permission is also committing infringement.

The legal penalties for copyright infringement are pretty steep! They include:

- Fines from $200 to $150,000 per work. In other words, the clothing designer could be fined for every dress she knocks off.
- Infringer is required to pay all attorney fees and court costs.
- The court can impound the illegal work that was created by the infringement. In other words, the court could prevent the filmmaker's film from being released.
- The infringer could be sent to prison.

In 2012, for example, a man from Seattle who operated two websites that distributed pirated copies of movies, television shows, software, and workout videos was sentenced to forty months in prison for two counts of criminal copyright infringement. The U.S. District Court in Seattle also ordered him to pay a fine of $409,776, which was estimated to be the profit he made from his websites.

Super Success Story

Facebook may be the most popular invention of all time. The social networking site was invented by Harvard computer science and psychology student Mark Zuckerberg and his classmates Eduardo Saverin, Dustin Moskovitz, and Chris Hughes.

Initially, Facebook was a cheesy "hot or not" website called Facemash that let Harvard students look at pictures of other students side by side and decide who was "hot" and who was "not." Zuckerberg got the student ID images he used to populate Facemash by hacking into Harvard's security network.

Facemash, which opened in 2003, lasted only a few days before Harvard shut it down and charged Zuckerberg with breach of security, violating copyrights, and violating individual privacy. He faced expulsion, but eventually all the charges were dropped.

In 2004, Zuckerberg launched a new site, Thefacebook, that enabled Harvard students to put up profiles and network with one another. Six days later, three Harvard seniors, Cameron Winklevoss, Tyler Winklevoss, and Divya Narendra, accused Zuckerberg of stealing their concept for a social network they were going to call HarvardConnection, and developing it into Thefacebook. Winklevoss, Winklevoss, and Narendra sued Zuckerberg, and eventually settled out of court.

Zuckerberg, meanwhile, saw the potential for Thefacebook to grow beyond Harvard. He, Saverin, Moskovitz, and Hughes got to work on developing the business and attracted Sean Parker, founder of Napster, as an investor. In 2004, Parker became the president of the newly named Facebook.

Facebook grew exponentially; as of 2013 more than one billion people around the world were Facebook members. Facebook profits have made Zuckerberg the world's youngest multi-billionaire, with an estimated wealth of more than $13 billion in 2013 at only twenty-nine years old.

It's extraordinary that Zuckerberg has been able to remain CEO of the company he started in his dorm room despite its phenomenal growth, and he was able to do so because he did a lot of things right. Take these lessons to heart for your business:

1. **Your business must have a powerful vision.** Zuckerberg had a vision from the start. In a letter to his shareholders, Zuckerberg wrote, "Facebook was not originally created to be a company. It was built to accomplish a social mission—to make the world more open and connected." In a *Forbes* interview in May 2012, he added, "Building a mission and building a business go hand in hand."

2. **Move fast and break things.** In his shareholder letter, Zuckerberg also laid out this principle that has become a popular slogan at Facebook. He said, "Moving fast

enables us to build more things and learn faster. However, as most companies grow, they slow down too much because they're more afraid of making mistakes than they are of losing opportunities by moving too slowly. The idea is that if you never break anything, you're probably not moving fast enough."

3. **Build a great team.** Zuckerberg has estimated that he spends 25 percent of his time recruiting the best people he can find to work at Facebook. Early on, he recruited Google executive Sheryl Sandberg and put her in charge of building the Facebook business, so he could focus on what he loves best—developing the Facebook platform.

In 2012, Zuckerberg donated $100 million dollars to the Newark, New Jersey, public school system. With Warren Buffett and Bill Gates, he's a signer of the Giving Pledge, promising to donate at least half his wealth to charity in his lifetime.

FAIR USE AND PUBLIC DOMAIN

What about quoting from a book in a newspaper or a college paper? As long as the quote is used with proper attribution crediting the author and the original publication in which it appeared, that usage is considered **fair use** and is legal.

Fair use provides for the limited quotation of a copyrighted work without permission from or payment to the copyright holder.

In addition, copyrights and patents expire over time. When the copyright or patent has expired on a work of art or an invention, they are considered to have passed into the **public domain**. At that point, anyone can use them without having to obtain permission from the creator. The patents on jet engines have expired, for example, and now any person or company can use that technology. Shakespeare's plays and Beethoven's symphonies are examples of creative works that are in the public domain.

When Do Copyrights and Patents Expire?

As a general rule, copyright protection lasts for the life of the creator plus an additional 70 years. For an anonymous work, a pseudonymous work, or a work made for hire, the copyright lasts for 95 years from the year of its first publication or a term of 120 years from the year of its creation, whichever expires first.

Patents have maintenance fees that must be paid to prevent expiration. If maintenance fees are paid on time, the term that a patent lasts is:

- Twenty years from the filing date for patent applications filed on or after June 8, 1995.
- Either seventeen years from the patent issue date or twenty years from the filing date for patent applications filed before June 8, 1995.

ELECTRONIC RIGHTS: HAMMERED BY FILE SHARING

Did you know that any article you read online is protected by copyright? This **electronic right** makes it illegal for you to copy even one sentence from it and put it in your college paper, for example, without giving the author proper attribution.

Traditionally, the creators of IP are considered to be entitled to credit, as well as payment, when their works are enjoyed or used by others. The Internet has turned this concept into a much more complex, much more difficult-to-enforce situation than it used to be. Today, a song can be shared among millions of listeners online without the composer's permission. A hacker from China can break into an American corporation's network and steal trade secrets. Books can be scanned and turned into e-books sold worldwide without the author receiving any royalties on sales.

CREATIVE COMMONS

In 2001, attorney Lawrence Lessig cofounded **Creative Commons (CC),** a nonprofit devoted to expanding the range of creative works available for others to legally use and share. The company created free copyright licenses called **Creative Commons licenses** that enable creators of intellectual property to release it with a variety of different rights.

Let's say you write, record, and release a song, and you would love for your fans to create videos for it. In order for them to do so, you have to give them the rights to use the song. But you don't necessarily want them to be able to profit from your song.

You could release the song under a Creative Commons "Attribution Share Alike" license. This license does not change your copyright—you are still the owner of the song. But this license lets your fans know they can use the song in their own creative work (such as making a video) as long as they provide attribution (let people know you wrote it) and "share alike"—meaning they must allow other people to share and use whatever they create from your music.

The six licenses currently available from Creative Commons are:

1. Attribution (CC BY)
2. Attribution Share Alike (CC BY-SA)
3. Attribution No Derivatives (CC BY-ND)
4. Attribution Non-Commercial (CC BY-NC)
5. Attribution Non-Commercial Share Alike (CC BY-NC-SA)
6. Attribution Non-Commercial No Derivatives (CC BY-NC-ND)

To explore them in detail, visit http://creativecommons.org/licenses.

These licenses give creators of intellectual property greater freedom to choose exactly how their works are shared and attributed. Creative Commons estimates "very conservatively" that there are more than four hundred million CC licenses in operation. Photo-sharing application Flickr has reported it hosts more than two hundred million Creative Commons–licensed photos.

Learn the Lingo

Creative Commons is part of the **copyleft** movement to increase and enrich the content available for use in the public domain. Copyleft is a play on the word "copyright" that describes using copyright law to remove, rather than add, restrictions on intellectual property so it can be more freely shared and adapted.

OPEN SOURCE

You've probably downloaded free software and heard of **open source** software. Open source software is made available by a software developer not only for people to use and share, but also for them to modify, try in new operating systems, and even sometimes market for themselves.

Why would a company do this? Software developers who support open source believe that by allowing others to modify the source code, the application will become more useful and contain fewer errors in the long run.

The Standish Group reported in 2012 that adoption of open source software models saves consumers about $60 billion per year. Today, many companies release free versions of their software to entice consumers to try the software and, hopefully, purchase paid versions that have more features. Sometimes free software has an expiration date of, say, thirty days, after which the consumer must purchase it to continue using it.

THE PATENTS PROCESS

Let's get back to patents for a minute. You may have a great idea for an invention, but a patent cannot be obtained on a mere idea or suggestion.

You don't need to obtain a patent unless you:

- invent a product that you intend to market yourself or sell (or license) to a manufacturer, and
- believe that someone else could successfully sell the product by copying your invention.

On average, a patent takes about two years to obtain. First, a patent search has to be undertaken to make certain that the idea is not infringing on, or violating, someone else's patent. Next, you must fully develop your invention and be able to show that it works consistently before you can seek patent protection. You will need to prepare detailed drawings showing exactly how it works.

A patent application must include the following:

1. An in-depth description of the invention.
2. A drawing of the invention, where necessary.
3. A completed "Declaration for Utility or Design Patent Application."
4. A notarized statement from the inventor to the effect that he or she is the original inventor of the subject of the application.
5. The filing fee ($380 or more).

Obtaining a patent is a complex legal process. Before starting it, see a registered patent attorney. Ask yourself the following questions:

- Does my invention solve a big enough problem—that is, a problem faced by many people?
- Can I locate these people easily?
- Is there competition? Is someone else selling a similar product? How is mine better? Different?

**Don't go to the trouble and expense of applying for a patent unless
your invention is unique and you intend to sell it.**

Game Changer

The Sandbagger, a machine that fills sandbags, was invented in 1993 by Stacey Kanzler after she was surprised to see news footage of soldiers hand-filling sandbags during heavy flooding in the Midwest that year. Within two weeks, Kanzler's prototype was being tested by the National Guard. Today, her company is worth more than $2 million. While she's thrilled with her success, Kanzler is even happier that her invention helps save lives and property.

Step One: Build a Model

When you've invented an idea for a product, make a model of it. This model can be rough. Use cheap materials such as paper, wood, paint, cloth, or plaster of paris. You may go through many models.

Conduct some market research by showing the model to friends, acquaintances, and storekeepers. Collect ideas and suggestions, and incorporate them into your model. Don't be afraid to experiment.

Step Two: Build a Prototype

If you are serious about turning your invention into a business, you will need a **prototype** to show investors and buyers. A prototype is an exact model of the product, made by the manufacturing process that would be used to actually produce your invention for sale.

Building a prototype can be an expensive step. Prototypes typically cost much more than the final production cost of a product once it is in production. Once a product is set up for manufacturing, the costs drop because the manufacturing process has been streamlined and benefits from **economies of scale**. These are cost reductions made possible by spreading costs over a larger volume. Manufacturing one thousand units of a product typically costs less per piece than manufacturing one unit.

To find a manufacturer to build your prototype, visit ThomasNet (www .thomasnet.com).

Try It!

My friend Sylvia Stein has invented several products, including the Nose, an eyeglass holder. When I asked her how she jump-starts her imagination, she said she tries to complete this sentence: I wish someone would make a _____ that _____.

Another way to start thinking like an inventor is to imagine solutions to problems in your neighborhood or community, or in the world. Write or sketch your solutions, pretending that anything is possible.

Read a Classic

The Independent Inventor's Handbook: The Best Advice from Idea to Payoff by Louis Foreman and Jill Welytok explains everything a potential inventor needs to know and the tools he or she needs to use to take a raw concept and turn it into reality.

INVENTIONS AND PUBLIC DOMAIN

If an invention is put into use by the inventor for more than one year without obtaining a patent, the invention is considered in the public domain, and a patent will no longer be granted. Failure to obtain a patent promptly, therefore, can prevent an inventor from profiting from his or her invention.

An unfortunate example involved Lewis Temple, an African American who lived in New Bedford, Massachusetts, and invented the toggle harpoon in the early 1800s. This harpoon greatly increased the efficiency of whaling at a time when whale oil was extremely valuable for lighting lamps and making candles.

To test his invention, Temple gave prototypes to several New Bedford ship captains. In those days, whaling voyages took about two years. By the time the ships returned and reported the harpoon's great success, Temple's invention had become public domain. Temple was never able to profit from his invention and died in poverty.

MINORITY INVENTORS

Like Temple, many early African American inventors made important contributions to American business, yet failed to profit from them. Nobody knows how many inventions were thought up by slaves before the Civil War, for example, because credit for them was taken by their masters. There were probably quite a few, because ideas for making a job easier or completing it faster often come to those who have to do the actual work.

In 1895, an African American congressman, George Washington Murray, read into the *Congressional Record* a list of ninety-two patents that had been issued to

Americans of color. Murray wanted the general public to know that African Americans had made important contributions to the industrial revolution. Murray himself received eight patents for farm machinery improvements.

Early African American Inventors

After the Civil War, many African Americans went to work for the railroads. Some received patents for inventions to make the trains run more smoothly. In 1872, for example, Elijah McCoy invented a device for the self-oiling of railroad locomotives. This invention saved a great deal of time and money. Before it was available, the train's foreman had to get out of the cab and oil the parts by hand so they would not wear out prematurely.

McCoy was inspired to invent this device because he had often been assigned to do this tiresome job. The railroad was the only reliable form of long-distance transportation at the time, so McCoy's invention was very important. When Elijah McCoy died in 1929, he was both financially secure and respected by the engineering community.

Another African American's invention revolutionized the shoe industry. Jan E. Matzeliger received a patent for his automatic shoe-stitching machine, called a "lasting" machine, in 1883. His machine could stitch seven hundred pairs of shoes a day, instead of the few pairs a day that could be sewn by hand. This invention greatly reduced the average price of a pair of shoes.

Few people know that an African American named Lewis H. Latimer invented a more stable, longer-lasting lightbulb filament that made the practical application of Edison's electric lightbulb possible. Latimer worked closely with Edison and installed the first city electric light systems in New York, Philadelphia, London, and Montreal.

Dr. George Washington Carver is one black inventor who was internationally known during his lifetime. Born at the end of the Civil War, Carver completely transformed farming in the South by developing ways to use the peanut (peanut butter being only the most famous), the sweet potato, and the soybean. His efforts went a long way toward reducing the South's dependency on cotton as its only exportable cash crop. Although Dr. Carver did not become rich from his work, he did receive honor and fame.

Modern African American Inventors

There are many contemporary African American inventors, including:
- Lonnie G. Johnson, a former senior systems engineer at the NASA Jet

Propulsion Laboratory, is best known for his silliest invention—the Super Soaker squirt gun.

- Janet Emerson Bashen founded Bashen Corporation in 1994 at her dining room table with very little capital and one client. In 2006, she made history as the first African American female to hold a patent for a software invention—LinkLine, which helps companies track equal employment opportunity (EEO) claims and complaints.

- Dr. Patricia Bath invented the Laserphaco Probe, a surgical tool that uses a laser to vaporize cataracts. The Harlem-born doctor has dedicated her life to treating and preventing blindness in African Americans.

Early Women Inventors

Like the stories of early African American inventors, the stories of women inventors are finally coming to light as interest in women's history has increased. Nuclear fission, solar heating, bras, drip coffee, the ice cream cone, the Barbie doll, dishwashers, rolling pins, windshield wipers, medical syringes—these are just some products invented by women.

Many early women inventors created new products to help them where they spent most of their time—in the home—cooking, cleaning, and sewing. Mary Kies became the first woman patentee in 1809. She invented a process for weaving straw with silk or cotton thread. Her idea was instrumental in boosting New England's hat-making industry. When the War of 1812 cut off supplies of hats from Europe, New England hatmakers used the Kies process to take over the hat market.

As women began to work outside of the home, they invented helpful office products. Bette Graham invented Liquid Paper, or correction fluid, which made it possible to repair a typing mistake instead of having to type an entire page over.

Women Inventors Today

As women have moved into traditionally male-dominated fields, such as medicine and science, their inventions in these areas have been increasing:

- In 1991, Gertrude Elion became the first woman inducted into the Inventors' Hall of Fame. During the thirty-nine years she worked for Burroughs Wellcome, a drug company, Elion patented forty-five medical compounds. She shared the 1988 Nobel Prize for medicine with George H. Hitchings. They invented a compound that prevents recipient patients' immune systems from rejecting transplanted organs.

- In Togo, West Africa, mothers carry their babies around with them all day in a fabric harness. Ann Moore developed this concept into a pouchlike child carrier that is comfortable and washable. Moore began selling the Snugli in 1979. By 1984, annual sales were $6 million— and rising. Moore used her Snugli technology to develop the Airlift—a padded portable oxygen tank carrier for patients who need a steady supply of oxygen.

- Actar 911, the mannequin used to teach cardiopulmonary resuscitation (CPR) techniques, was invented by Dianne Croteau and her partners, Richard Brault and Jonathan Vinden, in 1989.

- Ann Tsukamoto is the co-patentee of a process to isolate the human stem cell, whose patent was awarded in 1991. Stem cells are located in bone marrow and serve as the foundation for the growth of red and white blood cells. Understanding how stem cells grow and how they might be artificially reproduced is vital to cancer research.

Inventions by Other Minority Groups

As they establish themselves in this country, Asian, Hispanic, and other American minorities are inventing important new products and processes.

Dr. Eloy Rodriguez, for example, has developed some important drugs from tropical and desert plants. His formulas are being tested against viruses and cancer. He was drawn to these discoveries by noting that monkeys and other primates eat certain plants when they are sick. Dr. Rodriguez has established a new biology field called "zoopharmacognosy"—the study of self-medication by animals.

Another recent medical breakthrough by a Hispanic American is the invention, by Dr. Lydia Villa-Komaroff and her team of researchers, of the process of harvesting insulin from bacterial cells.

An Entrepreneur Like You

Aden Shank
CHEER LAUNCHER

http://cheerlauncher.com

While sitting in the top row of the bleachers, hungry from skipping lunch, Aden Shank hoped to catch one of the candy-filled rolls being thrown into the crowd by cheerleaders.

"Unfortunately, I realized that unless one of the cheerleaders was on steroids, the candy would never get past the first couple of rows," Aden recalls.

Later, when the mother of one of Aden's friends overheard his plans to repair a broken tennis ball air cannon, she joked that he would do better to make a candy shooter for the cheerleaders instead. Aden took her seriously, and after a year spent refining his prototype, Aden began producing his Cheer Launcher.

The Cheer Launcher works like a giant slingshot, with a crossbow that sends colorfully decorated toilet paper rolls stuffed with candy flying into the stands at high school games. As far as Aden knows, there is nothing else like it on the market. But if the idea came easily, the execution proved more challenging.

"I've always wanted to be an architect or inventor or engineer. I probably spent time with a few too many Legos," says Aden. "I always had all these ideas, but no idea how I could take them and make them and sell them. I thought you had the ideas and they were instantly put in stores, magically."

Aden, who has struggled with dyslexia and other learning challenges, took an entrepreneurship class that gave him new confidence in his abilities. "Before, I was making stuff nobody was interested in, random inventions just for me, but all around me, people were saying 'Don't give up.' I thought, 'Well, nothing I make works and nobody cares, so why bother?' But when I finally got something working, I realized what they meant. I discovered that it doesn't matter how many times you fail; you need to keep on trying."

Aden, whose own sports include barefoot water skiing and tae kwon do (he's a second-degree black belt), hopes to give back to the cheerleaders who inspired him by donating scholarships or subsidizing uniforms for those who cannot pay for them. Of being an entrepreneur, Aden says, "This is what I have always wanted to be. I now have the confidence to do it. Entrepreneurship has been an amazingly positive opportunity for me!"

Think Like an Entrepreneur

1. Let Aden's story inspire you: Quickly jot down ten invention ideas, the more improbable the better.
2. Visit Aden's website and check out his marketing. What marketing techniques does Aden use that you would use on your own website? What do you think he's doing right?
3. What challenges do you face in school or in your social life? How do you think entrepreneurship could help you with them?

CHAPTER 15

INSURANCE FOR ENTREPRENEURS

HOW TO PROTECT YOUR BUSINESS, YOUR EMPLOYEES, AND YOURSELF

The only place where success comes
before work is in the dictionary.

—Vidal Sassoon

Insurance is a contract that you can buy to protect yourself from losses. The insurance company agrees, in exchange for monthly payments from you called **premiums,** to cover, for example, losses of inventory that your business might suffer from a fire.

In this chapter we'll explore the types of insurance that a small business needs to carry. Don't think you can't afford insurance. You can't afford *not* to have insurance. It's a smart, affordable way to protect this amazing business you are creating.

"Hope for the best, but prepare for the worst." An entrepreneur doesn't get far without both high hopes and realistic expectations. Insurance must be a part of your business, so that your hopes can take wing.

MANAGING RISK

Starting a business requires that you take on **speculative risk,** which is risk that holds the possibility of either gain or loss. When an ice cream manufacturer offers a new flavor, for example, it is taking a speculative risk. The new flavor could be a bestseller, or it could be a flop. The company can increase the chances of success by first carrying out market research and taste tests. But it is still taking a speculative risk by introducing a new flavor into the market.

Pure risk, in contrast, is the chance of loss with no chance of gain. Kitchen fires are a pure risk of running a restaurant, for example. Restaurant owners could avoid the risk by serving only cold foods, or reduce the risk of fire by enforcing safety rules for using the stove. Knowing that fire is possible, restaurants keep fire extinguishers on the premises and install sprinklers. They prepare for the worst.

Insurance as Risk Management

There is another option for managing pure risk: **risk transfer,** which means shifting the risk to another party. For business owners, that means purchasing insurance. In this transaction, an insurance company takes on a client's pure risk.

Insurance companies are experts in risk management. They predict the likelihood of a pure risk, such as a kitchen fire, by using the **law of large numbers**. This theory says that if you want to predict how likely an event is to occur, you will get the most accurate answer by looking at the largest number of cases in which it might.

Suppose a grocer wants to know how well the sauerkraut is selling, for example. Over the course of one month, the grocer has 1,500 customers and sells 150 cans of sauerkraut. That averages to one can for every 10 customers. After three months, the customer count is 5,250, who buy 420 cans. The average has dropped to one can for every 12.5 customers. After six months, the totals are 10,400 customers and 1,095 cans of sauerkraut, for an average of one can per every 9.5 customers.

Which average is most accurate? According to the law of large numbers, it's the six-month figure, when the event—the sale of sauerkraut—has had the most chances to occur. Thus, that's the pattern that is most likely to hold true. Each customer represents one chance for occurrence. So if you track sales for a year, the annual average will be more accurate still.

Insurance companies use the same principle. When they insure against a restaurant fire, they don't look at how often fires have occurred at a few restaurants over a few years, but at hundreds of thousands of restaurants over long stretches of time. They can predict how certain factors—such as safety training and keeping fire extinguishers—affect the risk and the extent of the loss.

Using this information, the insurance company creates insurance policies. A **policy** is a written contract between the insurer and the policyholder. The policy details the **coverage,** outlines the protection provided, and lists the **premium,** which is the amount of money the person or business that is insured by the policy will pay for coverage.

TYPES OF BUSINESS INSURANCE

If you are starting a business, you should be aware of three types of insurance:

1. Property insurance
2. Liability insurance
3. Workers' compensation

Property Insurance

Property insurance protects your business's possessions in the event of fire, theft, or damage from the weather. A basic property insurance policy could cover your building, its furnishings, and the equipment, supplies, cash, and inventory stored there or offsite. Construction firms and home remodelers often leave equipment at the work site or in clients' homes, for instance. You want to have your equipment covered, even if it's not in your place of business.

Property can be insured for its actual worth, called **cash value**. Experts recommend, however, insuring property for its **replacement cost,** the cost of replacing it at current prices, which are usually higher. Property insurance also covers electronic data and software lost to physical damage or computer malfunction.

Vehicles owned by or used for business are insured under a separate commercial auto policy. These policies provide additional coverage for damage and injury caused to, or by, the vehicle or driver. Personal auto policies don't apply to commercial uses.

Learn the Lingo

A natural disaster such as a hurricane or tornado is classified as a **catastrophic risk,** which is an unpredictable event that causes severe loss to many people at the same time. It is typically not covered by basic property insurance.

In regions where a particular disaster is likely, catastrophic risk coverage can be extremely expensive. Flood insurance for a restaurant on a river, for example, would be expensive. Business owners have to assess the costs and risks of not purchasing catastrophic risk insurance against the possibility of being wiped out by a natural disaster.

Another useful insurance policy is **business interruption insurance**. This covers losses if a business can't operate due to a covered event, such as a storm or fire. The insurer uses company records to determine what the business would have earned during the shutdown, and covers ongoing operating expenses that must be paid while the business is closed, such as utility bills. It does not cover pay to employees, however. If employees are laid off while the business isn't operating, they can apply to their state governments to collect payments from unemployment insurance.

Liability Insurance

Of all the risks entrepreneurs face, the chance that their inexperience or negligence could hurt someone physically or financially is one of the scariest. **Liability insurance** eases some of those concerns by providing protection when a business's action, or lack of action, injures another party. As with property insurance, different policies cover different risks. Types of liability insurance policies include:

1. **General Liability:** Covers expenses related to injuries sustained on the business premises. It also covers injuries or damage due to employee carelessness at work. Suppose a lumberyard worker is using a hoist to load planks into a customer's truck. The worker misjudges the truck's position and drops the load on its roof. General liability insurance will pay for repairs to the roof. If the truck is the customer's business vehicle, the insurance may also pay for lost income while the truck is unusable. If one of the planks falls on the customer's foot, the policy will pay the customer's medical expenses.

2. **Product Liability:** Protects a business from losses caused by a product it produced or developed. This coverage is particularly important to manufacturers and food producers and processors. In 2010, parents from Billings, Montana, sued Johnson & Johnson after their child died from taking contaminated Children's Tylenol. If the parents win the suit or accept a settlement from Johnson & Johnson, that money

will be paid out of the company's product liability insurance policy.

3. **Professional Liability:** This policy differs from product liability in that it covers harm done by a business's actions or failure to act, not its products. A well-known example is malpractice insurance, taken out by medical professionals. Another example is errors and omissions (E&O) insurance—which would pay for stolen property if a self-storage business failed to hire enough security or used inferior locks, for example.

4. **Identity Theft Insurance:** This protects a business against damage done by the theft of sensitive information. It's recommended for companies that store a great deal of data electronically, which increases the opportunities for theft.

5. **Employment Practices Liability Insurance:** This insurance covers claims against a company by employees charging it with discrimination and other illegal and unfair treatment.

Workers' Compensation

Workers' compensation insurance covers losses to employees due to job-related injury or illness. It is "no-fault" insurance, meaning it pays regardless of who is responsible for the injury or illness.

"Workers' comp," as it is sometimes called, pays employees' medical bills and reimburses them for lost wages. It pays for physical therapy or job training if the injury makes returning to the old job impossible. In case of death, the insurance covers funeral expenses and survivors' benefits to a spouse and dependents.

Requirements for employers to carry workers' compensation insurance vary from state to state. In some states, very small businesses—those with five or fewer employees, for example—are exempt. Other states require it for every business, even if you just have one part-time employee. Business owners may even be required to carry workers' compensation for seasonal or contract workers.

Tech U

To estimate how much your insurance needs are going to cost, go online. Most insurance companies offer free online quotes. Just enter "insurance quotes" into your search engine.

CHOOSING AN AGENT

Choosing an insurance agent is like hiring an important employee. You want someone who has experience and is familiar with your type of business. Check with trade or professional associations. They sometimes have agreements with certain insurers to provide coverage that targets group members' needs. Antiques dealers can get insurance through the Antiques and Collectibles National Association, for instance.

You can also ask for recommendations from other businesspeople in your field. They might recommend both exclusive and independent agents. Exclusive agents work for a single insurance company. They can usually get lower premiums by offering a package called a "business owner's policy (BOP)." Of course, their choices are limited to the policies their company sells.

An independent agent represents several insurers and can offer a wider range of policies, but may not be able to get you exclusive deals.

Game Changer

Numerous entrepreneurs have cited "a positive attitude" as a key to their success ever since Napoleon Hill coined the phrase in his inspirational books.

A man who knew the meaning of "the power of positive thinking" was W. Clement Stone. He turned a positive attitude into a $500 million fortune by building one of the largest insurance companies in America, Combined Insurance Company.

When he was sixteen, Stone began selling insurance policies to help his mother pay the bills. His first assignment was a large office building. He was so afraid to even enter the building that, to get up his courage, he made up optimistic phrases such as "When there's nothing to lose and much to gain by trying, try." Once inside the building, he actually *ran* from office to office trying to sell his policies before his fear of rejection could overwhelm him.

Stone discovered that people responded to his positive attitude by buying insurance policies. While still in high school, Stone was selling forty insurance policies a day. He revolutionized the sales profession with the idea that a positive attitude could help anyone sell better.

CHOOSING POLICIES

The best insurance package is the one that most closely fits your needs. Some standard policies can be modified by adding riders. A **rider** is an amendment to an insurance policy that changes the benefits or conditions of coverage. The owner of a storage company might need a rider to cover antiques, paintings, or other items with a high value.

You'll also have to decide how high a **deductible** you can afford. The deductible is the amount of damages or other expenses that you agree to pay for on your own, before the insurance company pays. The higher the deductible you can afford, the lower your premium will be.

Some occupations have complete insurance packages designed just for them. Livestock producers, for example, need farm and ranch insurance that covers such risks as vehicle collision with animals, or milk loss from contamination or spoilage. Vendors at fairs and organizers of sports tournaments purchase short-term insurance policies tailored to their unique situations.

Tech U

Smartphone apps enable you to take your insurance company with you wherever you go. You can use your insurance company's app to review your insurance policy for auto, home, life, and business coverage, and file a claim directly from your phone.

Reduce Pure Risk for Your Business

Keeping buildings, supplies, and merchandise safe is a good place to start reducing pure business risk. Good lighting, inside and out, discourages crime. Spotlights protect vulnerable areas, such as parking lots, back doors, stairwells, and loading or receiving bays. Locks and alarm systems protect employees and valuable equipment.

Screen and hire your employees carefully and then give them a code of ethics to work by. Train your employees well. The better they understand their own and others' jobs, the better they can recognize signs of theft or fraud.

Teach them effective legal ways to act when they suspect stealing by coworkers or customers. False accusations of customers or attempts to stop a theft in progress can lead to lawsuits, injury, and ill will that can cost much more than the price of the merchandise.

Safeguard Information

Identity theft is on the rise, and if sensitive information you collect from your customers gets into the wrong hands, the consequences can be just as devastating as having a showroom ransacked. Yet many business owners use information and telecommunication technology without guarding against the risks of using them.

Owners and employees alike should know how to use encryption software when sending electronic files. Web pages that register clients' personal and financial information need the same protection. Disks and other data storage units should be guarded like any other tangible property.

Green Tip

You can save electricity—and money!—by turning off your computer when not using it. Shut off your monitor if you aren't going to use it for more than twenty minutes, and shut down the computer if you plan on being away for more than two hours. You can save an average of $90 per year on your electric bill.

Promote Health and Safety

Keeping your employees safe and healthy is a sound financial practice. Maintaining a safe workplace is your legal and ethical responsibility. Every workplace should be equipped with first-aid and emergency supplies. Many workplaces now have defibrillators—devices that restore a normal heartbeat in someone who is having a heart attack. Companies should also practice fire drills and other emergency response routines.

Safety practices that prevent crime also prevent injuries. Many businesses require at least two people to work at night. Bank deposits are made at irregular times, with the money carried in a variety of unobtrusive containers. Some employers sponsor anger management and communication classes to help keep arguments between employees from escalating into violence.

Ergonomics is the study of designing environments to fit the people who use them. An assessment shows whether lighting, workstations, use of storage space, and scheduling of tasks help maintain physical and emotional health. Some insurance companies offer wellness consultations to help business owners develop health and fitness programs.

Milan Alexander
EXCLUSIVE CUTS BARBER SERVICE

"My dad's really big on managing your own money and especially going out there and trying to survive for yourself," says Milan Alexander. "When I was ten, I had a lawn care service, and when I was eleven, I had a car wash service. My parents' friends would come over and I would wash their cars."

When Milan was fifteen, he began developing a new skill. "My friend was cutting hair and I noticed how he was making a lot of money with this," Milan explained. He was looking for a way to help pay for college, and barbering seemed like the perfect solution.

Using an old pair of clippers, Milan practiced on his little cousins and other family members. When he turned sixteen, he bought a professional set. It took Milan two years to become an expert. "If you're not practicing every day, it's very hard," he notes.

Pleasing the Customer: Honesty Is the Best Policy

At first, Milan tried to please all his customers, even when he wasn't sure what he was doing. When a client asked Milan to cut his hair in an unfamiliar style, Milan said yes, even though he didn't know how to do it. Although the client was satisfied, Milan wasn't. "I knew that I didn't perform to the best of my ability on that haircut," says Milan. He decided not to charge the client, who was very appreciative and became a repeat customer.

Milan learned that he needs to be honest with his customers at all times. "You should let people know that you are inexperienced in a certain area and be truthful to them. After that situation, I was very experienced in that haircut because I kept practicing."

Soon Milan started a new business: Exclusive Cuts Barber Service, a mobile haircutting business. Milan will cut his clients' hair at their homes or offices at whatever time is convenient for them. "My competitive advantage is that I come to you," says Milan, "and that I'm open beyond local barbershop hours." Milan will go to his clients late at night, or whenever they have time for a haircut.

Pricing His Services

Milan has raised his prices in the three years he's been in business. He currently charges $10 and up, depending on the type of cut and how long it takes. Because he travels to his clients, his expenses include car maintenance, such as oil changes and gas, and supplies that he needs for the job, including hair spray and razor blades.

He gains new customers mainly through word of mouth and bringing along a poster board showing most of the styles he does. Milan does approximately thirty cuts a month, with fifteen regular biweekly customers. With school and a part-time job as well, it's plenty for him. "I'm not trying to cut the whole of the Chicago area," he says.

A graduate of the Chicago High School for Agricultural Science, Milan is studying agricultural business at the University of Illinois and plans on owning his own barbershop one day. As Milan says, "With the economy now, you want to have multiple incomes."

Think Like an Entrepreneur

1. Milan started earning money at an early age. How did that experience help in becoming an entrepreneur?

2. Milan regretted not telling a customer he was inexperienced with a certain type of haircut. He didn't charge the customer for the cut, even though the customer was satisfied. How would you have acted in that situation?

3. Is Milan's idea of having multiple methods of earning an income a good one? If you were to take this approach, what do you think your sources of income might be?

CHAPTER 16

TAXES AND GOVERNMENT REGULATIONS

WHAT YOU NEED TO KNOW

The best thing we could do on taxes
for all Americans is to simplify
the individual tax code.

—Barack Obama

A **tax** is the percentage of your profit or income that you are required by law to pay to your federal, state, and local governments. These governments use the revenue they receive from collecting taxes to pay for schools, the military, police and fire departments, and many other public services.

The federal government is financed primarily by personal and corporate income taxes. States typically raise money from **sales taxes** on goods (not services). Most states also levy an income tax. City and other local governments are supported primarily by property taxes.

WHY DO WE PAY TAXES?

Oliver Wendell Holmes, Jr., a Supreme Court justice in the early 1900s, said, "I like to pay taxes. With them I buy civilization." Few people can claim they like paying taxes, yet taxation is so important to the nation that it was authorized in the U.S. Constitution.

Article I of the Constitution states, "The Congress shall have Power To lay and collect Taxes, Duties, Imposts and Excises, to pay the Debts and provide for the common Defence and general Welfare of the United States."

Taxes may not "buy civilization," but they do pay for the government and the services it provides.

PUBLIC SERVICES SUPPORTED WITH TAXES

Tax dollars support a country's **infrastructure,** which is the system of organizations, structures, and services that a society needs to function and be productive. Roads and bridges are part of the infrastructure. Workers who lay the roads and repair the bridges are hired through government contracts. City buses, commuter rail services, and Amtrak (the national rail passenger carrier) are given subsidies by the government to keep fares low and encourage ridership.

Learn the Lingo

A **subsidy** is financial aid from the government that supports an industry or public service. The federal government, for example, provides farm subsidies, also known as agricultural subsidies, to help farmers with the costs of running their businesses.

Your tax dollars also help pay for the system of water treatment plants and pipelines that provide clean running water for your home. Government agencies such as the Centers for Disease Control and Prevention and the National Weather Service are supported by tax revenue, also.

Taxes support the entire military, as well as state and local police, firefighters, and other first responders. Your education, too, is at least partly funded by the government. Public schools depend on taxes for teacher salaries, maintenance, and other expenses. Later you may get a government loan or grant to help pay for college, where you may take part in research or other programs that receive government money.

Other public resources supported by taxes include your local library, museums, parks, and recreation areas. You might swim at a community pool, skate in a local skate park, or hike in a protected nature reserve.

Taxes also fund the work of the U.S. Treasury, which prints our money and works with the Federal Reserve Bank to regulate the money supply. The Internal Revenue Service is the government agency charged with collecting taxes and enforcing tax laws. It, too, is supported by your tax dollars.

Social Programs

The Great Depression in the 1930s was a near-collapse of the U.S. banking system and economy that put many Americans in dire financial circumstances. In response, Democratic president Franklin Delano Roosevelt's administration hammered out a "safety net" of government-funded social programs that came to be known as the New Deal.

Some New Deal programs, such as Social Security, are still with us today. The Social Security program's full name—Old-Age, Survivors, and Disability Insurance Program—gives a clue to its scope. Social Security provides benefits for retired workers, dependents of deceased workers, and workers who have disabilities and their dependents. Every American who works pays taxes into this program and becomes eligible in his or her sixties to receive payments from it to help with retirement.

In 1965, Congress used the original Social Security Act passed under Roosevelt to create Medicare, a federal program that provides health insurance to Americans age sixty-five and older, regardless of income or medical history.

Social services like these currently account for almost half of all federal government spending. Some programs are carried out by state or regional offices with funds from a federal agency. Others are supported by matching funds at each level of government.

Department of Defense

The U.S. Department of Defense (DOD) is another prime recipient of tax money. Supporting the U.S. Army, Navy, Marines, and the rest of the armed forces takes about 20 percent of the federal budget.

For their money, taxpayers get more than national security. The armed services also provide education and career training, and assist in humanitarian operations and rescue missions.

The National Guard and the Coast Guard aid in disaster relief, drug enforcement, rescue operations, and environmental protection. Military research benefits civilians, too. To care for wounded service personnel, the DOD has funded medical research, from surgeon training to developing artificial limbs. The Global Positioning System (GPS) that helps drivers find their way in traffic uses DOD satellites. And think how many businesses owe their existence to the Internet, which was created in the 1960s by the Department of Defense.

Business Development

Some tax money returns to business as resources for growth and development. The U.S. Small Business Administration (SBA) is a federal agency that provides information, advice, government contracts, and loan guarantees for small businesses. It seeks to encourage entrepreneurship among underserved business owners, such as women, teens, military veterans, Native Americans, and other minority groups.

Cities and states subsidize entrepreneurs, too, by creating enterprise zones. An **enterprise zone** is a geographic area in which businesses receive economic incentives to encourage development there. Entrepreneurs might be awarded grants to improve a property, or tax credits for hiring employees.

Businesses also benefit indirectly from government programs. Good roads make ground transportation more efficient. Sports arenas, museums, and tourist attractions bring customers to area merchants. Telecommunication networks use satellites built by the space agency NASA.

THE FEDERAL INCOME TAX

The federal income tax is progressive. This means that as your income rises, so does the percentage of your income that you pay in taxes. The idea behind a progressive tax is that poorer people use more of their income to pay for basics such as food and shelter, so they should pay a lower percentage of their income in tax.

The progressive system is based on marginal tax rates—these are tax rates applied to what's happening at the "margins," or ends, of someone's income, not on the total income. Simply put, your income is divided into tax brackets, and each bracket has a different tax rate applied to it. As your income increases, your marginal tax rate also increases, but only on the portion of your income that has moved into a higher tax bracket.

Sandy is a college student who has a small business as a freelance makeup artist that earned her an income of $8,500 this year after expenses. That income puts Sandy in the 10 percent tax bracket. Her income tax will be .10 × $8,500 = $850.

Let's say next year Sandy's business takes off and she earns $10,000 income from it. That puts her in the 15 percent income bracket. Here's the important point: She does *not* pay 15 percent on her entire income. Sandy pays that 15 percent tax rate only on the income that pushed her into the next tax bracket. That amount ($10,000—$8,700) is $1,300.

Sandy will pay 10 percent tax on her first $8,700 in income, and 15 percent on the remaining $1,300. Let's calculate her income tax:

What is 10 percent of $8,700? .10 × $8,700 = $870.

What is 15 percent of $1,300? .15 × $1,300 = $195.

Sandy's total income tax will be $870 + $195 = $1,065.

U.S. Tax Brackets for a Single Individual

10 percent on taxable income from $0 to $8,700

15 percent on taxable income over $8,700 to $35,350

25 percent on taxable income over $35,350 to $85,650

28 percent on taxable income over $85,650 to $178,650

33 percent on taxable income over $178,650 to $388,350

EVALUATING TAXES

People do not agree on who should pay taxes and what government programs and services taxes should support. As a taxpayer, you have the right to ask these questions:

- Where are my tax dollars going?
- Are my tax dollars supporting services that will benefit me and my community?
- Am I paying taxes to support services that could be better supplied by private industry than by the government?
- Are the tax rates fair?

Taxpayers demand answers to these questions from the politicians who represent them in city councils, state legislatures, and the U.S. Congress. One of the most important jobs politicians do each year is plan and pass government budgets and then determine how much to tax citizens to finance those budgets.

ARGUMENTS FOR LOWER TAXES AND FOR SIMPLIFYING THE TAX CODE

Many Americans believe taxes are too high, government spending is too high, and tax rates are unfair. They are putting pressure on politicians to respond to these concerns.

Many business owners argue that the tax laws are so complicated and the rates are so high that people are afraid to start new businesses. The U.S. tax code is more than thirty-eight thousand pages long. The tax code also changes all the time, making it difficult for small business owners to handle their taxes without the expensive aid of accountants.

This is one of my pet peeves, too. I believe the complexity of the tax code, combined with high tax rates, discourages low- to middle-income people from starting new businesses. Or it encourages them to start businesses but keeps them underground.

I have testified before the National Commission on Economic Growth and Tax Reform on this subject. I told the commission that both the complexity of the tax code and the high rates of taxation do more to prevent people from rising out of poverty through entrepreneurship than almost anything else.

Some business owners argue that many of the services that various levels of government provide—such as the U.S. Postal Service, or garbage collection—could be supplied more efficiently by private industry. This would lower taxes. Business owners also argue that the government should make the tax code easier to understand and should make it easier for would-be entrepreneurs to license their businesses and pay their taxes.

WHAT ARE YOUR TAX OBLIGATIONS AS AN ENTREPRENEUR?

You must file federal and state tax returns whether your business is making a profit or not. A **tax return** is a form you fill out in order to calculate your income and determine whether you owe taxes on your income. "Filing" means to turn a tax return in to the state or federal government.

Tax returns have to include different forms depending on what kind of job you have and whether you own a business. If you own a business, you will fill out forms showing whether the business made a profit or a loss. Once your business begins making a profit, you are required by law to pay taxes on those profits.

Green Tip

Save paper and time by filing your tax returns electronically. Since the IRS made e-filing available, it has processed nearly eight hundred million returns electronically. You can also pay your taxes and receive tax refunds electronically. Save those trees!

Filling out a tax return is often the last thing a struggling new business owner wants to think about. But neglecting to file your tax return and pay your taxes are crimes that can cost you your business—and damage your credit report and your reputation.

David opened a small café near a college when he was twenty-two. He didn't set up his accounting system or apply for a tax ID number right away. He figured he'd have more time to do it once he got the business off the ground.

Unfortunately, after his business had been open a few months, his state's Department of Revenue (DOR) did a spot check and found that he was not collecting the required meals tax. The DOR closed his business and obtained a **lien** on his personal assets. This meant the DOR could seize personal assets like David's car and sell them to pay his tax bill.

Learn the Lingo

A lien is a right granted by a court to a creditor to take the property of a debtor as security or payment for a debt. It comes from the French word *lien,* which means "link" or "tie."

Self-Employment Tax (Schedule SE)

When you work for an employer, the employer pays 7.65 percent of your income into your Social Security fund. The federal government takes another 7.65 percent out of your earnings, as your contribution to your own Social Security fund. Between your contributions and those of your employer, your Social Security fund receives 15.3 percent of your income each year.

When you retire, or if you become disabled and can no longer work, these contributions enable you to receive a Social Security or disability payment each month.

If you are self-employed, however, there is no employer to make Social Security contributions for you. You must make up the difference by paying self-employment tax. If you have net income from self-employment of more than $400 a year, you are required to pay 15.3 percent of your business income to Social Security as self-employment tax.

Whether your business makes a profit or not, if your small business earns more than $400 a year, you will have to pay **self-employment tax** on your business income. The tax form used to file self-employment tax is called Schedule SE.

Self-employment covers the Social Security tax obligation for those who are self-employed. If you work for somebody else, Social Security tax is automatically deducted from your paycheck. When you work for yourself, however, you are required to make those deductions yourself from your income and pay them as self-employment tax.

When you are self-employed, you are required to pay your federal income taxes quarterly. This helps prevent you from building up a huge tax bill that you can't afford.

Profit or Loss from Business (Schedule C)

In addition to self-employment tax, you are also required to file a Schedule C form showing the profit or loss for your business. If you made a profit, you will have to pay income tax on your business profit.

The business owner is responsible for calculating and sending in these payments—not once a year, as an employee does, but throughout the year, in the form of estimated taxes.

Entrepreneurs predict what they will owe in income and payroll taxes and send in tax payments every quarter (every three months) in April, June, September, and January. Many business owners estimate conservatively, sending in the smallest amount necessary, to keep more money available for their businesses. They can also skip a payment if they believe they have no liability for that period. They need to be cautious, though, or they may be penalized for underpaying.

Payroll Tax

If you have employees for your business, you are required by law to withhold certain amounts from their wages or salaries as payroll tax, and pay it to the appropriate government entities.

Federal penalties for tax code violations with respect to wage taxes are especially harsh. The government may "sweep" your company bank accounts (take any available funds), assess significant fines, and secure your personal assets. You might be tempted to use taxes you are withholding to pay some bills, or even "forget" to pay them, but those would be bad choices that could seriously harm your business.

As you learned earlier, retirement and disability insurance is one of the biggest items in the federal government's budget. The government pays for these by using payroll taxes, also referred to as FICA. **FICA** stands for the Federal Insurance Contributions Act, the law that requires employers and employees to share the cost of the federal government's insurance and retirement program through deductions from wages and income.

Although both employers and workers contribute to the tax, the employer is responsible for calculating and sending the payments to the IRS. FICA tax is composed of two separate deductions: a larger one for Social Security and a smaller one for Medicare. They are figured as a percentage of the employee's wages or salary and withheld from each paycheck. The employer's own contribution equals the contribution of the employee.

Most states also require employers to deduct state income taxes from an employee's paycheck. This amount is sent to the state government.

Here's an example of how to calculate the FICA if you are an employee making $20,000 a year, with a Social Security amount of 6.2 percent and a Medicare amount of 1.45 percent.

Employee's Gross Salary	**$20,000**
Social Security ($20,000 × .062)	**$1,240**
Medicare ($20,000 × .0145)	**$290**
Employee's Net Salary	**$18,470**

As an employee, your gross salary is always reduced by your Social Security and Medicare payments.

As an employee, you paid $1,530 in taxes. Your employer will deduct this from your paycheck in each pay period and send it to the government. Your employer will also pay an *additional* $1,530 in taxes to the government to match the amount you paid.

Federal Unemployment Tax

FICA taxes fund Social Security and Medicare. **FUTA** tax funds unemployment insurance. FUTA stands for Federal Unemployment Tax Act. This tax is also a percentage of employee wages; however, unlike FICA taxes, the FUTA tax is paid solely by the employer. Also, it's paid only on the first few thousand dollars an employee earns each year.

The FUTA fund is run jointly by the federal and state governments. Depending on individual state law, employers may or may not be required to make payments to the state, as well. If they are, the tax is divided, with the state's portion applied as a credit toward the federal government's share. Payments are typically sent in quarterly.

Corporate, partnership, and individual income tax and self-employment tax returns must be filed with the IRS by specific dates each year. The IRS form used for individual tax returns is called the 1040. Individual tax returns must be postmarked by April 15. If you file late, you may be forced to pay penalties and interest.

If you are only reporting income from a job, not your own business, you can use Form 1040EZ to file your income tax return. It is the simplest tax form to complete. To qualify for Form 1040EZ, you must:

- Be single and younger than age sixty-five.
- Have only one dependent (yourself) or be claimed as a dependent by your parents.
- Earn less than $50,000 gross income.
- Earn less than $400 in interest income.

Tech U

Get help at tax time from the IRS website at www.irs.gov. It provides free forms, instructions, and access to IRS agents who can advise you over the phone or online.

Sales and Excise Taxes

If you sell products or services to the public, most states will require you to charge your customers sales tax, and then turn over the collected money monthly or quarterly to the state. Apply to your state's department of taxation for the necessary forms.

In New York State, for example, entrepreneurs use the New York State and Local Quarterly Sales and Use tax return to report quarterly sales tax. Most states—California, for example—charge tax only on products and not services. Some other states, including Florida and Illinois, charge tax on some services. Alaska is one of the few states that do not have a sales tax.

The sales tax is a percentage of the cost of the item sold and is included in the amount paid. In New York City, for example, the sales tax is 8.25 percent. Tax on a $10.00 item is $0.83, so the total paid by the consumer is $10.83.

Lawmakers decide which goods and services are taxed, and at what rate. Business owners who sell these items decide who pays the tax. They either absorb the entire amount themselves or pass some or all of it on to the customer.

Even figuring the tax on a single product can be complicated. In some states, food products are tax-free. However, a bakery owner might have to collect a tax on a birthday cake based on candles, decorations, and other inedible elements if they make up over half of the cake's retail value.

Additionally, certain items are subject to excise taxes. An **excise tax** is a tax on a specific product or commercial activity. Federal, state, and local governments often impose excise taxes to control consumption or raise money for a project. A city may have a tax on restaurant sales to pay for a civic center, for instance. Excise taxes on large commercial trucks, diesel fuel, and truck tires help pay for highway maintenance. Taxes on alcohol help fund state programs to treat alcoholism.

TAXES ON ONLINE SALES

Laws on taxing goods sold via the Internet are still evolving. Generally, these sales have been exempt from sales tax, but in 2012 the U.S. Senate approved the Marketplace Fairness Act, which would have let states require online merchants to collect sales tax.

When the bill was sent to the House of Representatives, however, House Judiciary Committee chairman Bob Goodlatte said his committee would not take up the act, effectively killing the bill's chances in the House. Goodlatte argued that states should be allowed to reach their own agreements and that the federal government shouldn't get involved.

Amazon founder and CEO Jeff Bezos has explained why he opposes requiring online businesses such as Amazon to collect state and local taxes on their interstate sales. "We're not actually benefiting from any services that those states provide locally," Bezos said at an Amazon shareholders meeting, "so it's not fair that we should be obligated to be their tax collection agent."

Property Tax

Entrepreneurs who own the land or building where their business operates are also subject to an annual commercial property tax. The tax rate for commercial property is set by the local government. Each government sets rates according to its own formula. In some areas, taxes are based on both the property's actual and potential value. Values rise in areas where home buyers are building and the infrastructure is being improved, for example.

In addition, some states assess a tax on personal property used in business, including furniture, fixtures, supplies used for daily operations, and inventory held for sale.

Business tax returns are due on different dates, depending on the legal structure of the business.

Sole Proprietorship: Since a sole proprietorship is considered an extension of the person running the business, its tax return is due on the same date as the person's tax return—April 15. The sole proprietor files a 1040 and also a Schedule C form, which shows the profit/loss for the business.

Partnership: A partnership return is filed on Form 1065, due on March 15. The taxes are due on April 15, when the individual partners file K-1 forms showing their share of the partnership income.

LLC: A single-member LLC is taxed like a sole proprietorship, using Schedule C to calculate net income, so the tax returns are due and taxes are payable on April 15. Multiple-member LLCs are taxed as partnerships, so the March 15 partnership due date applies.

Corporation: A corporation that is not a Subchapter S must file its returns and pay any taxes due on the 15th day of the third month after the end of the company's fiscal (financial) year. So, a corporation with a year-end date of December 31 must file and pay taxes by March 15; a corporation with a year-end date of September 30 must file and pay taxes by December 15.

Subchapter S Corporation: The members of a Subchapter S corporation report their earnings on individual income tax returns, so they are due April 15.

As soon as your business starts earning income, you may want to seek the services of an accountant to help you properly prepare your taxes. Remember, in addition to federal taxes, businesses are subject to state and local taxes.

Tech U

Tax preparation software programs such as TurboTax and H&R Block at Home include versions for small business. Working through these programs is a good way to learn how to file taxes for your business. If you do prepare your own tax returns on a computer, it is still a good idea to have a tax professional review them.

Another advantage of using tax preparation software is that if you use Quicken or bookkeeping software, you can usually transfer data easily from your books directly to the tax preparation software.

PREVENTING AND DEALING WITH AUDITS

You and your tax preparer will have an easier time filing your tax return if you have been keeping accurate records throughout the year. You will have to determine your net income. If you have kept accurate and timely accounting records, this should not be difficult.

Mistakes on your tax return, or just the luck of the draw, could cause the IRS to audit you. The IRS will send an agent to your business to examine your ledgers and receipts and invoices to make sure your taxes were filed correctly. An audit can be a time-consuming and stressful process. This is another excellent reason to keep good records and file all invoices and receipts, whether or not you use an accountant for tax preparation.

Do not confuse accounting with taxation. Your accounting software generates financial records, but you will still need tax preparation assistance, and/or tax software, to prepare your returns. Some accounting software will allow you to export your financial information into your tax program.

One of the best business investments you can make is to hire a top-notch small business tax accountant or attorney as a consultant. An accountant will be familiar with changes to the tax code and can offer valuable advice. Accountants often will not charge for questions asked throughout the year, if they have been hired to prepare your annual tax return. Maximize the amount of professional advice and you will minimize the chances of problems with the IRS.

Get the Stat

In 2012, the IRS collected $1.175 trillion in individual income tax.

THE IRS CAN HELP

The tax code is very complex. The IRS offers booklets and telephone service to help answer questions. Help with the Form 1040 is available from 1-800-424-1040. You can also go to the IRS office in your town and meet with an IRS agent, who will guide you through the forms for free.

Be sure to obtain new forms and booklets each year. Rules, rates, and forms change from one year to the next.

To tap into the Internal Revenue Service's massive and very helpful website, visit www.irs.ustreas.gov. There are even tax tips for small business owners. When in doubt, call the IRS or visit an accountant or tax preparation office, such as H&R Block. Always fully comply with the IRS by keeping good records, and by filing your return and paying your taxes on time. Audits are nerve-racking and time-consuming.

Learn the Lingo

Trying to avoid paying taxes through illegal or deceptive means is called **tax evasion** and is a federal crime. It's punishable by fine, seizure of property, or even imprisonment.

TAX-SAVING STRATEGIES

Unlike tax evasion, which is illegal, **tax avoidance** is the use of legal strategies to reduce one's tax liability. Tax avoidance strategies include tax deductions and tax credits.

Taking Deductions

A **deduction** is an expense you are allowed to deduct from gross income when filing your tax return. Deductions reduce your income, and that reduces your tax burden.

Expenses that are considered "ordinary and necessary" for operating a business are typically tax deductible. Utilities and rent, for example, are common business expenses. Others include:

- **Employees' Compensation:** Employers can deduct the wages and benefits they pay for their employees.
- **Costs of Goods Sold:** A producer or wholesaler can deduct the cost of raw materials, labor, and storage of items sold.
- **Travel:** Reasonable deductions for transportation, meals, and lodging related to business are all permitted.
- **Vehicle Use:** This includes cost of maintenance, repairs, and mileage for business vehicles, and for personal vehicles when used for business purposes.
- **Taxes:** Business taxes, including consumption and property taxes, are themselves tax deductible.
- **Insurance:** Premiums for certain business insurances can be deducted. This includes, for example, special insurance for employees who work in clients' homes.
- **Depreciation:** Depreciation is a tax deduction that allows business owners to recover the cost of property used in the business. Any property that is used for over one year and loses value through wear or because it becomes outdated can be depreciated. A computer can be depreciated, for example.

In addition, new entrepreneurs can deduct start-up costs for up to five years after opening their businesses. That includes money spent on market research and scouting locations. Sole proprietors who aren't covered by an employer's insurance plan can deduct 100 percent of the premiums of private insurance. If you use part of your home to carry out any or all of your business activities, you can deduct a percentage of utilities and certain home maintenance costs.

Entrepreneurs who understand how deductions work can time purchases and collection of receipts to their advantage. Suppose your business is having a very profitable year and you expect a large tax liability. You could lighten the load by increasing the number of deductions. You might buy a needed copier this year rather than next, or put more money in a retirement plan. You could also reduce income by asking customers who owe money late in the year to delay payments until January of the next year.

Using Tax Credits

A **tax credit** is a dollar-for-dollar reduction in taxes owed. Whereas a deduction lowers taxable income, a credit lowers the tax itself.

Tax credits can be taken for a variety of business activities, from using green energy sources to donating goods to a charitable group, or hiring those who are reentering society after serving time in prison. A small business may take a credit for making the workplace accessible to disabled workers, as required by the Americans with Disabilities Act.

Tax credits tend to be less permanent than deductions. Standard deductions may remain the same from year to year. Credits are subject to phasing out, depending on how popular they are with taxpayers or how valuable they are to an industry.

AN OVERVIEW OF GOVERNMENT REGULATION

Not only does the government regulate taxation of business, it also passes laws that affect how you do business.

Just as people disagree on how much the government should tax individuals and businesses, and how much the government should spend, they also disagree on government regulations. Some people believe any government regulation of business hinders the effectiveness of the free market. Other people believe government regulation is necessary to protect consumers and employees.

Whatever your opinion, you need to be aware of government regulations that affect your business and stay on top of them, as they can change frequently.

Learn the Lingo

Red tape is slang for excessive bureaucratic regulations, and is sometimes applied to government regulation of small business. In sixteenth-century Spain, red tape was used to bind certain important government documents. This practice was adopted by other European governments, and spread to the United States during the Civil War, when red tape was used to bind veterans' records.

Occupational Safety and Health Administration (OSHA)

OSHA is the federal agency responsible for setting and enforcing standards of safety in the workplace. OSHA sets general standards that employers are expected to adjust to their own situations.

For example, OSHA regulations require that businesses:

- Provide needed tools and equipment in good working order, and the training to use them safely.
- Supply appropriate safety gear and garments.
- Document serious work-related illnesses, injuries, or accidents, their causes, and the number of workdays missed.
- Display posters telling employees of their right to work in a safe, healthful environment and to report possible violations.
- Give workers access to records related to illness, injuries, or possible exposure to harmful substances in the workplace.

OSHA enforces its rules through workplace inspections. An inspection may be part of routine oversight or triggered by a complaint. Minor violations might bring only a warning. Serious offenses can result in thousands of dollars in fines, with follow-up inspections to ensure the problems have been corrected.

Employers have certain rights that go along with their responsibilities. They can contest inspectors' reports or ask to be exempted from certain standards. OSHA has a nonretaliation policy, which states that employers who ask about health or safety policies are neither more nor less likely to be inspected for violations.

Equal Employment Opportunity Commission (EEOC)

In 1840, President Martin Van Buren made a sweeping proclamation that, without any reduction in their current pay, federal employees could be made to work no more than ten hours a day. The proclamation was progressive for its time.

The concept of fair treatment has grown considerably since then. The Equal Employment Opportunity Commission (EEOC) enforces laws that promote fair treatment in the workplace, such as the following:

- **Fair Labor Standards Act:** A federal law that guarantees most hourly workers a minimum hourly wage, a maximum number of hours worked, and extra pay for working overtime. Some states have a minimum wage that is higher than the national level and add requirements for lunch and rest breaks, pay periods, and severance pay. **Severance pay** is money given to employees when they are terminated for reasons other than performance.
- **Family Medical Leave Act:** Gives parents up to twelve weeks of unpaid leave a year after the birth or adoption of a child or the

placement of a foster child. In cases of serious illness, they can take the same amount of time to care for a spouse, child, or parent—or themselves.

- **Civil Rights Act of 1964; Age Discrimination in Employment Act of 1967:** These outlaw discrimination based on age, gender, religion, race or ethnicity, or national origin. The Civil Rights Act also forbids employers from making hiring decisions based on the assumption that married candidates are more responsible than unmarried ones, and from passing over an individual from a minority group for promotion. The Age Discrimination in Employment Act makes it illegal to ask a potential employee's age during a job interview. Job ads that imply that older workers are not qualified for a position also violate this law.

- **Americans with Disabilities Act (ADA) of 1990:** Requires employers to provide reasonable accommodations to make the workplace and job duties more accessible for qualified workers with disabilities. The ADA also prevents employers from asking during a job interview how a candidate became disabled. They can't make taking a medical exam a condition of being hired unless it's required of all employees.

GOVERNMENT REGULATIONS THAT AFFECT HOW YOU TREAT CUSTOMERS

Treating customers fairly is not only good business sense—it's the law. As a business owner, you are bound by laws regulating how you sell your goods or services, whether the customer is an international corporation or an individual consumer. Let's take a look at these laws and the government agencies that enforce them.

Product Labels

- **Fair Packaging and Labeling Act of 1966:** This law requires that all product packaging identify the item, its manufacturer, and the quantity enclosed, either in weight or number. Other requirements vary depending on the product. Most packaged foods require an ingredients list and nutrition facts. Any health-related claims must meet the definition set by the U.S. Food and Drug Administration (FDA) and the U.S. Department of Agriculture (USDA).

The label must warn if the product contains, or may have had contact with, foods that are major allergens (allergy-causing ingredients). Products that contain hazardous substances, from laundry detergent to pesticides, must be labeled with safety-related information. Manufacturers must describe the dangers associated with the product, its proper use and precautions, and first-aid or emergency treatment if it's misused or mishandled on the product's label.

- **Food, Drug, and Cosmetic Act of 1938:** Forbids any false or deceptive labeling. A product is also considered mislabeled if it leaves out essential information.

Get the Stats

Thinking of starting a business based on your grandma's gooseberry jam recipe? Stop by the FDA's website at www.fda.gov and download its Food Labeling Guide to learn what you'll be required to put on your jar labels.

Product Safety

The FDA and the USDA are also concerned with food and drug safety. They forbid the sale of adulterated products—those containing harmful substances, processed in ways that may be harmful to health, or modified to mask poor quality. Some cases of adulteration that you may have heard of are meats or vegetables contaminated with *E. coli* bacteria and pet foods containing the poisonous chemical melamine.

The task of regulating most other products falls mainly to the U.S. Consumer Product Safety Commission (CPSC), which sets standards for about fifteen thousand consumer goods. CPSC requires, for example, that infants' toys have no small parts that could pose a choking hazard. Fabrics must be flame resistant. Packaging for drugs must be child resistant.

If a manufacturer learns that one of its products does not meet these standards, whether by design or from some defect or flaw, it should issue a recall. A **recall** is a notice for customers to return a product that poses a risk of injury or illness.

Recalls are not required by law, but businesses that learn of problems and don't act to correct them face serious consequences. The CPSC may ban the item from the market and the business can be held liable for the harm it causes.

Fair Competition

A free market needs competition, and certain government regulations seek to promote competition and encourage fairness among competing businesses.

The Federal Trade Commission (FTC) enforces detailed truth-in-advertising laws that cover promotion in all of its forms, including endorsements, testimonials, sales, and special pricing.

The FTC requires ads to be:

- **Truthful and Nondeceptive:** An ad must not mislead customers on any significant point that would affect their buying decisions.

- **Supported by Evidence:** Business must have proof of any stated or implied claims. Health claims must be backed by scientific research. Letters from "satisfied customers" must be made available to confirm that the writers actually exist.

- **Fair:** An ad must not lead customers to "substantial injury," by not mentioning possible dangers, conditions or requirements, or unwanted outcomes that customers could not have foreseen. Customers must be told about any added fees that increase the advertised price, for example.

The FTC also enforces laws to prevent anti-competitive practices. These practices include:

- **Price Fixing:** An agreement among companies to establish the price of goods or services or the terms of business deals. By fixing the prices, the companies are agreeing to not compete, which keeps prices artificially high for consumers. It would be against the law for all the growers at a farmers market, for example, to agree to charge the same price for their produce, or to give the same discount to restaurant buyers.

- **Price Discrimination:** Charging buyers different prices for the same product. This is illegal only when used intentionally, to favor one customer over another. It would not be illegal to charge different prices to buyers in different parts of the state to stay competitive with the market in each area.

- **Monopoly:** A situation that develops when a single supplier becomes a market's only provider of a certain product. This is sometimes called "cornering the market." If a business is able to squash competition and become the monopoly supplier of a product or service, it can raise the price as high as it wants.

To combat monopolies and similar schemes, the FTC uses **antitrust laws,** which forbid anticompetitive mergers and business practices. A trust is a business that uses a legal technicality to evade laws against monopolies. The oldest antitrust law is the Sherman Antitrust Act of 1890, which outlaws "every contract, combination, or conspiracy in restraint of trade or commerce." The Clayton Antitrust Act of 1914 and several later laws have reinforced those restrictions.

Although antitrust laws are not used often, the penalties can be severe. Fines start at a million dollars for an individual, with prison sentences up to ten years.

LICENSES AND PERMITS

A **license** is a legal document issued by a state or local government that allows a business to provide a regulated product or service. Licenses give consumers assurance that a business—such as a beauty salon or a dentist's office—meets standards of professionalism and reliability.

Certain highly regulated industries require national (federal) licenses. These include broadcasting, investment consulting, and meats preparation.

Licensing usually requires some type of certification, either from the state or a professional group. Some states require athletic trainers to be accredited by the Board of Certification for the Athletic Trainer, for example. To become a licensed building contractor, you may need to pass a state exam testing your knowledge of engineering, electrical systems, and carpentry.

A **permit** is a legal document that allows a business to take a specific action. As a home builder, you might need several permits for a house: one for putting in a driveway, perhaps, and another to close street lanes in the construction area. Permits are generally issued by local governments.

ZONING LAWS

A **zoning law**, or **ordinance**, is designed to help ensure that businesses are good neighbors in the community. Some laws determine the areas where a business can locate and the activities it can carry out there. A sheep farm would be located in an agricultural zone. A textile factory that turns the wool into fabric would have to be located in an industrial zone.

A shop that sells the fabric would be sited in a commercial zone. A seamstress who makes clothing from the fabric for individual clients might run the business from home, in a residential zone. Other laws relate to a property's physical appearance, including the building's size, the number of parking spaces, and the type of signage allowed.

A recent trend in city planning is the creation of "walkable" cities, which places small businesses within walking distance of private homes. The goal is to strengthen the residents' sense of community, reduce the need and impact of motor traffic, and encourage people to exercise.

ENVIRONMENTAL PROTECTION

Business owners must also be aware of laws designed to reduce the harmful impact their businesses may have on the environment. Many of these regulations are set by the U.S. Environmental Protection Agency (EPA). These cover a wide range of business activities in almost every field. Some major federal laws you should be aware of include:

- **Clean Air Act of 1963:** Limits the types and amounts of chemicals businesses are permitted to release into the atmosphere. The owner of a road-construction firm, for example, has to avoid causing traffic delays that raise pollutants over the legal level. Farmers must be careful about how they burn crop stubble in their fields in order to meet clean air requirements.
- **Clean Water Act of 1972:** Requires a business to get a permit to discharge wastewater (water left over from almost any human activity, including washing hands). Receiving permission depends on the amount of water released and the substances it contains. The Clean Water Act does not directly address groundwater contamination. Groundwater protection provisions are included in the Safe Drinking Water Act, Resource Conservation and Recovery Act, and the Superfund act.
- **Endangered Species Act of 1973 (ESA):** Designed to protect species of plants, animals, birds, insects, and fish that are in danger of dying

out due to human activity, as well as the ecosystems upon which they depend, the ESA is administered by two federal agencies, the U.S. Fish and Wildlife Service (FWS) and the National Oceanic and Atmospheric Administration (NOAA), which includes the National Marine Fisheries Service, or NMFS. A builder who wants to develop land near a wildlife preserve, for example, may need to submit plans proving that the development will not adversely affect endangered species in the area.

HELP FOR SMALL BUSINESSES

Do you feel overwhelmed after reading all this? Don't worry; regulating agencies provide helpful guidelines and, in many cases, they offer exceptions for small businesses. Businesses with fewer than ten employees are not required to document minor workplace accidents, for example. Businesses with fewer than fifteen workers are exempt from some provisions of the Americans with Disabilities Act. Food sellers with less than $50,000 a year in sales don't need to include all nutrition information on labels.

In addition, regulations can work to your advantage. There are some nice tax credits available for businesses that follow sustainable practices that help them meet EPA standards. Other tax credits offset some of the expenses of complying with the Americans with Disabilities Act.

Regulating agencies sometimes look to small businesses to assist them in developing rules and guidelines. OSHA, for example, has set up Small Business Advisory Review Panels to hear business owners' input on developing safety standards.

The Equal Employment Opportunity Commission recognizes that small businesses are often the best setting for disabled workers, especially those looking for their first jobs. The agency can suggest affordable ways you can make your workplace accessible for disabled employees.

Finally, remember that it is your right as a citizen to vote for or against government spending programs, government regulation, and laws that affect your taxes. Register to vote and exercise that right—for the future of your business!

An Entrepreneur Like You

Warren Brown

CAKELOVE

www.cakelove.com

How does a lawyer with a master's degree in public health from George Washington University become a cake magnate?

Warren Brown was a twenty-eight-year-old attorney when he made a New Year's resolution to learn how to bake. He fell in love with baking and left his law practice to open his first CakeLove bakery in Washington, D.C., seventeen months later.

Today, Warren owns six CakeLove bakeries in the D.C. area. CakeLove pound cakes, brownies, scones, and cookies are available via the Internet for delivery nationwide (http://www.cakelove.com).

Warren's first cookbook, *CakeLove,* arrived on bookstore shelves in the spring of 2008, and his second book, *United Cakes of America,* highlights his favorite recipes from every state. To top it off, he hosted the Food Network's hit show *Sugar Rush.*

Such rapid change demanded a lot of hard work, passion, determination, and cash flow management. When Warren stepped away from his full-time job and into full-time entrepreneurship, he began with $10,000 of personal resources, including his credit card. But in order to open his first storefront, Warren needed $125,000. Fortunately, he was able to secure a commercial loan from his community bank. Commercial lenders at larger, mainstream financial institutions were not convinced that a self-taught baker who had abandoned a promising legal career was a particularly good credit risk, but his smaller community bank, City First Bank, gave him the loan.

Warren maintained 100 percent ownership of CakeLove through the acquisition of start-up capital, and he continues as the sole owner after significant growth. Because CakeLove was new and had little positive cash flow, Warren could not finance the second location with the cash flow of the first. So, he turned again to City First Bank.

Between September 2007 and July 2008, CakeLove opened three additional retail bakeries. Each successive expansion created a need for additional cash. Warren managed to avoid selling shares of the company by leveraging resources and partnering with community lenders like City First.

Growth in the number of retail bakery storefronts has taken the business to new heights. Warren continues to serve as the primary manager of cash flow and human resources for his organization. Inventory theft has not been a significant issue because of the store layouts and procedures, but CakeLove has established cash-handling policies (cash-counting systems) to prevent pilferage from the cash drawers.

Because CakeLove sells baked goods and other perishable items, spoilage and unsold product can become significant contributors to cash flow problems. Warren and his team have instituted a waste-tracking system and have been able to keep a "pretty good eye on the way inventory is moving."

Warren notes that fad diets have been more of a detriment to the business than expansion or an abysmal economy. CakeLove experienced its most significant cash squeeze at the height of popularity for the low-carb Atkins Diet. During times of reduced cash inflow, Warren and his team looked to cut costs, particularly by monitoring labor costs more closely than usual.

When Warren opened his first CakeLove bakery, he had three employees, including himself. By 2013, he had six bakeries and more than one hundred employees. This means meeting the cash flow requirements of a payroll and associated expenses for the six locations, including supporting numerous families.

Warren Brown has the following advice for aspiring entrepreneurs: "Do the homework. Know the industry you want to enter cold, so that you absolutely know how to make or do whatever it is that you want to make or do. Don't rush in. See it well and don't be afraid to get messy and to keep an open mind. There is always a way to improve. Know the product very well and have good confidence in what you are selling. People will always have unsolicited advice for you. If you don't have that confidence, you will get little chinks in your armor that can make your business less enjoyable and even miserable. Confidence is critical."

Warren's recipe for growth has produced sweet rewards.

Think Like an Entrepreneur

1. How has Warren Brown been able to finance the growth of his company?
2. What methods has CakeLove used to manage cash flow? What others might it adopt?
3. What types of cash flow management issues would you expect CakeLove to encounter if it continues to grow at a rate of three bakeries per year or more?
4. How do Warren Brown's recommendations to aspiring entrepreneurs pertain to cash flow?

PART 5
GROW YOUR BUSINESS

CHAPTER 17

MANAGING YOUR BUSINESS

STAYING ORGANIZED, ON TRACK, AND PROFITABLE

Management is all about managing
in the short term, while developing
the plans for the long term.

—Jack Welch

reating a business is one thing, but running it is another. **Management** is the skillful use and coordination of all of a business's resources—money, facilities, equipment, technologies, employees, and materials. Once your business is up and running, you need to manage it well to keep it on track and profitable.

If you earn enough profit, you can hire managers to help you run the business you have created. That frees up your time to create more new businesses!

FOUR MANAGEMENT FUNCTIONS

There are four basic functions involved with managing a business:

1. Planning
2. Organizing

3. Directing
4. Controlling

Let's take a quick look at each function, and then explore some different types of business management.

Management Function Number 1: Planning

Planning includes setting goals, deciding when and how to accomplish them, and determining how best to accomplish them.

Here are three management plans every business should put in place:

- **Strategic Plan:** Lays out a broad course of action to achieve a long-term goal three to five years in the future.
- **Tactical Plan:** Outlines specific major steps for carrying out the strategic plan. Tactical plans typically cover a time period of less than a year and include target dates for accomplishing goals.
- **Operational Plan:** Details the everyday activities the business will execute to achieve the goals of the tactical plan (and thus, ultimately, the strategic plan). Operational plans are short-range, covering days, weeks, or, at most, months.

Management Function Number 2: Organizing

Organizing is the act of arranging and coordinating resources and tasks to achieve specific goals. Organizing creates structure and helps maximize profit.

Organization charts outline the chains of command within a business and the

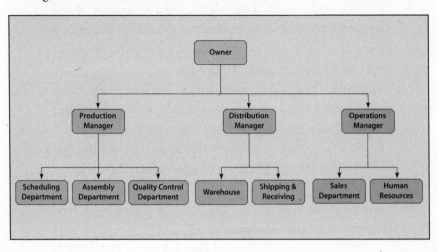

working relationships between different groups of people. Physical resources must also be organized. These include raw materials, machinery and other equipment, and inventory.

Management Function Number 3: Directing

Directing is leading, influencing, and motivating employees to work together to achieve the goals set out in the strategic, tactical, and operational plans.

To be an effective director, you must have good **interpersonal skills,** such as communicating clearly, listening well, and having a positive attitude.

Smart leaders use their interpersonal skills to build teams. Employees willingly follow a leader because they have confidence in that person and share the leader's vision for the future.

Some common leadership styles include:

- **Authoritarian:** The leader tells employees what needs to be done and how to do it, without seeking their advice. Steve Jobs of Apple was a famously authoritarian leader, but be cautious about how you use this style, as it can turn people off and create a lot of resentment. It is useful in some situations, though. New employees might need to be directed in an authoritarian manner, for instance, because they lack the information and experience needed to make important decisions. A leader may also use the authoritarian style when something needs to be done quickly and without discussion (as in an emergency).

- **Democratic:** This type of leader seeks input from employees about what tasks need to be done and how to do them, yet ultimately makes the final decisions. This style is appropriate when employees are experienced and knowledgeable about their jobs. Their input may be valuable to the leader, but the leader, as the manager, bears final responsibility for the success of their tasks.

- **Delegating:** The delegating leader assigns tasks to employees but gives them the freedom to decide how to do them. A leader who delegates responsibilities to trusted employees is able to tackle other matters. This can be a very effective time-management tool, if you train your employees well enough so that they can handle the responsibilities you give them.

In reality, good leaders choose and adjust their leadership styles depending on what's most effective for each situation.

Try It!

IBM has instituted "Think Fridays"—a block of time during which all meetings, emails, phone calls, and instant messaging stop. This time is set aside for problem solving and idea building and for IBM employees to work uninterrupted on new projects.

Intel has introduced a similar concept called Zero Email Fridays, and at 3M engineers are encouraged to devote 15 percent of their time to thinking up innovations.

Try turning your devices off and setting aside time to think, write, and doodle. It might be just what you need to become more creative and innovative.

Management Function Number 4: Controlling

Controlling involves monitoring the quality of what your business puts out. Businesses use **quality control programs,** for example, to ensure that products or services meet specific quality standards. A clothing manufacturer might set a quality control standard for the number of straight seams sewn in a garment, for example.

Enlist your employees in your quality control efforts and actively listen to what they have to say. Often, the employees know best when it comes to finding a solution for a problem that a business is having.

A **quality circle** is a group of employees who suggest ways to improve the quality of the goods or services they produce. Although quality circles are most often associated with manufacturing businesses, they can benefit any type of business.

Super Success Story

After Japan lost World War II, its economy was a mess. Its factories had been destroyed in bombings, including the two nuclear bombs dropped by the United States that completely flattened the important Japanese cities Hiroshima and Nagasaki.

Prior to the war, Japan had exported a lot of cheaply made goods. The words "Made in Japan" stamped on a product had come to mean "cheap," and probably not well made. Nonetheless, this had been a good trade strategy. The world bought Japan's products, and its economy had benefited from its many exports.

After the war, however, Japan needed creative thinking to rebuild its economy. Dr. W. Edwards Deming was a statistician who went to Japan to help with its first census after World War II. While he was there, Deming shared his theory that quality, not price, was the key to profit. His message was simple, but counterintuitive to most Japanese (and American!) businesspeople at the time, who had been taught to keep prices as low as possible in order to profit. Deming argued that by focusing on improving quality, companies will gain market share and profit.

Japanese businesses such as Toyota, Fuji, and Sony applied Deming's concept and became very successful. The quality of their cars, stereos, and other products was far superior to that of their global competitors, and the demand for Japanese products soared.

Read a Classic

Read *Dr. Deming: The American Who Taught the Japanese About Quality* by Rafael Aguayo for the fascinating story of Edward Deming's trip to war-torn Japan and how he helped the country rebuild.

OPERATIONS MANAGEMENT

Operations management is the management of the everyday **operations** that keep a business running.

PRODUCTION MANAGEMENT

One type of operations management is **production management,** which is management of the production of goods and services. Production management's goal is to use materials and resources efficiently to produce the desired quantity and quality of goods and services, while meeting cost and schedule requirements.

In small companies, the business owner typically oversees production management.

Production management focuses on three issues:

1. Scheduling
2. Productivity
3. Quality

Scheduling

Scheduling—meeting deadlines and goals—is a key management activity. Here are some helpful tools:

1.   **Gantt Chart:** A Gantt chart is a bar chart that shows scheduled goals for a list of tasks and the length of time each task will require to complete. A Gantt chart also shows the progress made at achieving each task. A diamond shape is used to indicate a milestone—a significant point of progress. Bars and diamonds are outlined on a proposed schedule and then darkened as tasks are completed.

This Gantt chart shows the schedule for opening a retail book store. Week 3 has just ended.

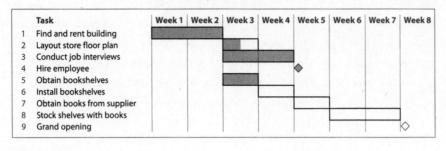

Gantt Chart
A Gantt chart shows the schedule of goals for a list of tasks.

2.   **PERT Chart:** A Program Evaluation and Review Technique, or PERT, chart is a scheduling diagram that shows tasks as a sequence of steps, and illustrates how the steps are dependent on one another.
     PERT charts are useful because they show which tasks must be completed before others can be started. A basic PERT chart uses circles to represent completed tasks. Arrows between the circles illustrate the order in which tasks should be completed.

The illustrated PERT chart covers the same nine tasks that were included in the Gantt chart. The PERT chart makes it obvious that the building should be rented (task 1) before any other tasks take place. Store layout (task 2), job interviews (task 3), and obtaining bookshelves (task 5) can proceed at the same time. They are not dependent on one another. However, hiring an employee (task 4) should be completed before the bookshelves are stocked with books (task 8), so the employee can help with the stocking.

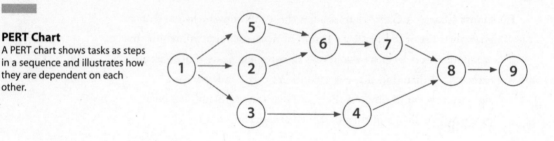

PERT Chart
A PERT chart shows tasks as steps in a sequence and illustrates how they are dependent on each other.

Productivity

Productivity is a measure of business output compared to business input. An example of productivity is the number of items produced per employee or the number of customers served per day. Productivity is a ratio of one numerical value to another numerical value. It can be measured in time intervals (hours, days, or weeks) or labor increments (employee, department, or division). The most common measures of productivity for a small business are: output per employee, output per unit of time, and output per dollar of cost.

BUSINESS POLICIES

Operations management includes establishing business policies. A **policy** is a procedure or set of guidelines that specifies exactly how something should be accomplished or handled.

A small business needs to establish policies involving hours of operation, handling returns and rework requests, delivering products, and extending credit to customers.

Hours of Operation

What hours will your business be open? What days? To answer these questions, think about your target customer. What days and hours does he or she need you to be open?

You may also be bound by local laws that prohibit different kinds of businesses from operating at certain hours or on certain days. In some states, for example, liquor stores must be closed on Sundays.

Return and Exchange Policy

What are you going to do if a customer wants to return your product? Or complains about the service you provided?

Whatever you decide, you need to establish—and display!—a clear and consistent return policy at your business. It's a good idea to post a sign on the wall behind your cash register, print the return policy on receipts, and make it clear on the company website.

Delivery Policy

A delivery policy should specify the amount of time between order placement and order shipment—twenty-four hours, for example. The policy should cover situations in which an order cannot be filled within the specified time, such as when items are out of stock. In addition, some policies include notifying customers by email when orders are shipped, providing a link so the customer can track the shipment online.

A delivery policy should also make clear any conditions or restrictions imposed by the seller. Some businesses will not ship outside of the country, for example, or will not deliver to post office boxes.

If you sell your products online, your order-taking program or fulfillment center should give you an option to specify your delivery policy. That way when customers place an order, they will see it clearly stated.

Customer Service Policy

It costs more to gain a new customer than it does to keep an existing one. Your customer service policy should ensure that people have only good experiences when dealing with your company.

Post your customer service policy where your employees can see it. Make sure they—and you!—follow it every day.

Include these five elements in your customer service policy and you will ensure that your customers come back.

1. **Courtesy:** All customers should be treated politely, even if they are angry and not behaving in a courteous manner themselves.
2. **Respect:** Show respect to customers by dressing appropriately, behaving politely in the workplace, and safeguarding any personal and financial information your customers share with you.
3. **Prompt Attention:** Customers do not like to be kept waiting, either on the phone or in person.
4. **Knowledgeable Employees:** Customers want correct answers when they ask questions. Make sure your employees are knowledgeable

about the company's business so they can answer questions and handle requests properly.

5. **Credibility:** Be consistent and trustworthy, and keep your promises. A business with good credibility builds customer loyalty and enjoys repeat business.

Learn the Lingo

A **warranty** is a written policy from a seller promising that goods or services meet certain standards. It describes the conditions under which particular problems will be taken care of by the seller at no cost to the buyer. A warranty is legally binding, so if you want to offer one for your product, have an attorney help you write it.

Credit Policy

Credit is the ability to obtain goods or services before payment, based on trust that payment will be made in the future. To buy on credit means to buy now and pay later.

A person or business that grants credit is called a **creditor**. Creditors set particular conditions, called **credit terms,** when they grant credit. These terms typically state the time limit when the debt must be paid and any interest charges that will apply.

If you are going to extend credit to your customers, you must have a clear, written credit policy that explains exactly under what conditions credit may be extended, and what it will cost the customer to use it. Since credit is an important part of doing business, let's explore it in more detail.

TYPES OF CREDIT

Although there are many types of credit, two types are of particular interest to business owners.

1. **Trade Credit:** When one business gives another business time to pay for purchased goods or services, this is called a **trade credit**. Trade credit is a useful tool for managing cash flow. Business owners take advantage of trade credit to postpone payment of their expenses.

   Consider a retail store that buys merchandise by using trade credit from a wholesaler that allows the store thirty days to pay for the merchandise. Ideally, the retail store sells enough of the merchandise within the thirty-day period to pay the debt on time. In other words, the cash inflow is sufficient to pay the debt.

Suppose, however, that the store has poor sales and does not earn enough cash in thirty days to pay the wholesaler. This situation is known informally as a credit squeeze. The store will have to dip into cash reserves to pay the debt. A business that consistently can't pay its debts to its suppliers will lose its trade credit and can even be taken to court and forced to sell its assets to pay its debts.

2. **Consumer Credit:** When a business gives its customers time to pay for purchased goods or services, this is called **consumer credit**. Businesses offer consumer credit to generate sales. A furniture store might allow consumers up to a year interest-free to pay for purchases, for example.

Learn the Lingo

A **credit bureau** is a business that collects and maintains **credit history** records and sells the information under certain circumstances. Businesses can access credit records to help them determine if a credit applicant is likely to repay a future debt.

THE THREE CS

Businesses rely on "the three Cs"—character, capacity, and capital—when deciding whether to extend credit to a consumer.

1. **Character:** The financial trustworthiness of the customer. A customer's past credit history is considered essential here. Someone who has made credit payments on time and in full in the past is likely to do so again.
2. **Capacity:** The customer's current income. People with good, steady income are more likely to pay their bills.
3. **Capital:** The customer's total financial assets. Someone who owns financial assets—a house, a business, corporate stock, a savings account—is typically more likely to pay bills on time than an individual who has few or no assets.

PROCUREMENT MANAGEMENT

Procurement is another word for **purchasing** materials, products, and services for business purposes.

All businesses buy products for their own use—for example, office supplies, raw materials, or other items needed for everyday operations. Wholesale and retail businesses also purchase merchandise to sell.

Large companies typically have an entire department that manages procurement. Individuals who have purchasing responsibilities are called buyers, or purchasing managers. In small companies, the business owner is likely to do all the purchasing.

The goal of procurement management is to buy goods and services of the right quality from the right vendors, in the right amounts at the right time, at the right cost and on the best possible credit terms. Managing purchasing is extremely important, because every purchase has a cost, and costs directly affect the profitability of a business.

Green procurement is purchasing goods and services that are environmentally beneficial in some way, such as recycled-content printer paper or a cleaning service that uses all-natural products.

Timing Purchases

Your sales forecasts and inventory data will help you schedule the best times to order merchandise for your business. You can set up orders for items that are used or sold at a relatively constant rate at regular time intervals. This is called **periodic reordering**. Other items may be reordered at irregular time intervals. This is called **nonperiodic reordering**.

Some businesses make purchasing decisions based on seasonal factors. Retail stores, for example, may time their purchases to have certain types of merchandise on hand for cold weather, hot weather, or holiday shopping.

Choosing the Right Vendors

Sourcing is choosing the best vendors to supply your business with goods or services. When comparing vendors take a look at:

- Price
- Quality

- Lead time
- Location
- Delivery and shipping options
- Reliability
- Customer service

You can find potential vendors at **trade shows** and conferences and by using the Internet, business directories, trade journals, and industry publications. As a small business owner, it will be to your benefit to develop close working relationships with a small number of vendors. Once they get to know and trust you, they will be more willing to extend you credit and give you good deals.

Getting the Right Price

Small businesses can and should negotiate with vendors to get discounts. A vendor might give a quantity discount to a small business that commits to placing a certain number of orders over a long time period, for example.

A **quantity discount** is a discount given to buyers for purchasing a large quantity of a product or service from a vendor. Generally, the larger the order, the larger the quantity discount. A **trade discount** is a discount given to resellers who are in the same trade, industry, or distribution chain as a vendor. Trade discounts often vary with the quantity purchased. In other words, a trade discount may also be a quantity discount.

Getting the Right Credit Terms

Businesses that sell to the general public typically demand payment at the time of purchase. Business-to-business purchases are often handled differently. Many vendors allow established business customers extra time to pay for purchases—typically thirty, forty-five, or sixty days. If the buyer pays after that time, the vendor may charge extra fees or refuse to give trade credit to the buyer in the future.

Learn the Lingo

The trade credit term "Net 30" means payment is due within thirty days of purchase. Another trade credit term is "Net EOM." EOM is an abbreviation for "end of month," meaning payment is due at the end of the month.

Vendors who allow trade credit often provide a small discount to the buyer if full payment is made early and in cash. A **cash discount** is a discount given to buyers who pay for purchases in cash, either at the time of purchase or within a set time period after purchase. A cash discount typically ranges from 1 to 3 percent of the total due.

For example, the term "2/10 Net 30" means full payment is due within thirty days but a 2 percent discount is given if the bill is paid within the first ten days of that period. If the amount due is $1,000, a 2 percent discount totals $20. The buyer can pay $980 to satisfy this debt as long as payment is made within the first ten days. The following table gives examples and definitions of some common trade credit terms.

TRADE CREDIT TERMS

Term	Meaning
Net 10	Payment is due within ten days.
1/10 Net 30	Payment is due within 30 days. A 1 percent discount is given for full payment within the first ten days.
2% EOM	A 2 percent discount is given for full payment before the end of the month.
3% EOM 10	A 3 percent discount is given for full payment before the tenth day after the end of the month (that is, the tenth day of the following month).
1% prox 10	A 1 percent discount is given for full payment before the tenth day of the following month. The abbreviation "prox" is short for "proximo," which means "in the next month."

Receiving and Following Up on Purchases

When you receive a shipment from a vendor, double-check the shipment to make sure that all items ordered are there. Discuss any problems, such as delivery delays or incorrect shipments, with your vendor as soon as possible.

Check the bill carefully, also, to make sure it matches what was ordered and that payment terms are those agreed upon before the purchase.

Learn the Lingo

Purchase Order: Document issued by a buyer to a vendor that lists the items to be purchased, their quantities, prices, and other relevant information, such as delivery or payment terms. Once a vendor accepts a purchase order, it becomes a binding agreement between the two parties to complete the purchase.

Invoice: Document issued by a vendor to a buyer on fulfillment of a purchase order. An invoice typically lists the items purchased, their quantities, prices, and other information, such as shipment dates and payment terms. Vendors issue a receipt after each invoice is paid.

Packing Slip: List of all items in a shipment. Purchasing managers should verify that invoices, receipts, and packing slips are accurate, and match the original purchase orders.

Tech U

You can conduct a lot of your purchasing online. This is called **e-procurement**. Many vendors provide e-procurement systems that allow buyers to access product information and specifications, fill out purchase orders, and make purchases online.

Delivery Terms

Large products and large-shipment orders are called **freight,** because they are transported by large trucks, trains, or ships.

Manufacturing and wholesaling businesses use specialized terms to describe their freight-delivery options. One of these terms is "free on board." **Free on board** is a delivery term that is followed by a word or group of words that identify a physical location at which the ownership responsibility for the shipment switches from the seller to the buyer. Free on board may be abbreviated as F.O.B., FOB, fob, or f.o.b.

A wholesaler in Chicago, for example, may use the delivery term "FOB Chicago." This means that as soon as the goods are loaded onto a transport vehicle in Chicago, they become the responsibility of the buyer. The buyer takes responsibility for the shipping costs and bears responsibility for the goods while they are in transport. If they become damaged or lost during transport, the buyer will be responsible for filing an insurance claim.

The more general term "FOB origin" is also used. This indicates that responsibility for the shipment switches to the buyer as soon as the goods are loaded on a transport vehicle at their point of origin. Likewise, the delivery term "FOB destination" means that responsibility for the goods switches from seller to buyer when the goods reach their destination. If the goods become damaged or lost during transport, the seller will be responsible for filing an insurance claim.

INVENTORY MANAGEMENT

Inventory management is concerned with the physical condition of inventory and the amount of space it takes up. The quantity of merchandise is called the **inventory level,** and the monetary value of the merchandise is its **inventory value**.

The goal of inventory management can be summed up in one simple phrase: not too little and not too much. Too little inventory can be disastrous for a business. A **stock-out** occurs when an item in inventory is completely gone. A stock-out leads to lost sales and can cause disappointed customers to go elsewhere to shop. You might be able to place emergency orders with vendors when stock-outs appear likely, but you'll probably pay much higher prices than usual to get rush service and delivery.

On the other hand, inventory costs money—you have to buy it and pay for a place to store it. Your goal is to maintain inventory at a level that satisfies customer demand yet minimizes your costs.

Green Tip

Heard of lean thinking? It's the "green" idea that businesses should try to reduce their use of resources, reduce the waste they produce, and even reduce storage space and transportation. It's an idea that fits well with inventory management. Lean thinking recognizes that there is no positive side to waste and that reducing energy usage and emissions can have a positive impact on your cash flow.

Calculating Inventory Level for a Start-Up

Wise entrepreneurs conduct market research, analyze their competition, and develop a marketing plan and pricing strategy before they go into business. By the time you've done all that, you'll have a pretty good idea of how much inventory you need on hand when you open for business.

Calculating Inventory Level for an Ongoing Business

If you keep good business records, you'll begin to get a good feel for your inventory needs. As you collect sales and cost data and get familiar with vendor lead times, you'll be able to use this data to predict how inventory levels are going to decrease over time and decide when to reorder merchandise.

Businesses typically choose to maintain a certain minimum inventory level called **safety stock**. This is the minimum amount of inventory kept to protect against a stock-out due to unusually high demand or unusually long lead times on delivery.

Game Changer

If you don't have enough inventory, customers will buy from your competitors or production will stop because of missing parts. If you have too much, the inventory might become out-of-date while still on the shelves—and never sell at all.

Walmart is so successful because it has come up with an innovative approach to inventory management. Walmart developed a system called Retail Link that uses bar codes to track products and then sends information to product suppliers about how much of an item—such as a certain brand of cat food—has sold.

The product suppliers use this information to keep Walmart shelves stocked at 98.5 percent at all times. This way, inventory is managed not by the store but by the companies who want their products on its shelves.

As a result, Walmart is rarely short on inventory. If a supplier falls behind on restocking, the retail giant simply gives another supplier an opportunity.

Calculating Inventory Investment

Imagine a company invests $1,200 per year in inventory. It may buy its entire inventory at once or spread the purchases out over the course of the year.

Each purchase represents an **inventory investment**. The average inventory investment for the year is calculated by dividing the total investment for that year by the number of inventory purchases.

**Total Investment ÷ Number of Investment Purchases =
Average Annual Inventory Investment**

If the company makes ten inventory purchases in a year, for example, the average inventory investment is $120.

$1,200 ÷ 10 = $120

Inventory Turnover

Inventory turnover is the number of times during a given time period (typically one year) that inventory is completely sold out (and therefore completely replaced).

In reality, inventory will almost never be completely sold out, but inventory turnover is a useful tool for inventory planning. A low inventory turnover indicates that inventory is selling slowly. A high inventory turnover indicates that inventory is selling quickly. Selling quickly is good, as long as it is not causing stock-outs, because stock-outs drive customers away and hurt future sales.

To calculate inventory turnover, divide the cost of the inventory sold during a time period by the average inventory investment during that same period.

Cost of the Inventory ÷ Average Inventory Investment
= Inventory Turnover

If a business paid $1,000 for inventory it sold in one year and the average inventory investment was $250, the inventory turnover is 4.

$1,000 ÷ $250 = 4

Math Moment

A business owner has a current inventory turnover rate of 4 and wants to achieve the same rate next year. The sales forecast for next year is $2,000, with $1,600 expected to be spent on inventory. What will his average inventory investment be next year?*

---

* Answer: $400.

Controlling Inventory Level

Inventory shrinkage is any loss of inventory that occurs between the time the inventory is purchased and the time it is sold or otherwise removed from the shelves. Inventory levels shrink for a variety of reasons. Items may become damaged during handling or storage and have to be discarded. A business can also lose inventory to **pilferage**—stealing by employees. Retail businesses may also lose inventory to shoplifting.

An **inventory system** helps you count and track your inventory so you can catch problems like pilfering. Small businesses often just physically count their inventory items. This is known as a **visual inventory system**. Even companies using electronic inventory systems rely on occasional visual inventory counts to reconcile recorded inventory levels with actual inventory levels.

Tech U

Technology is making it easier for businesses to track inventory—from their phones. Lowes Home Improvement purchased forty-two thousand iPhones for its store managers, with apps that allow managers to track inventory without leaving a customer's side.

An Entrepreneur Like You

Connor Alstrom
@FLYING

http://caflying.com

Connor Alstrom's dad, a sheriff, was swapping stories with a friend when he mentioned having once used a remote control (RC) helicopter to "defuse a situation." At that moment, Connor came up with his business idea: equipping RC helicopters with cameras for aerial photography.

Connor had been selling RC vehicles at HobbyTown USA, specializing in helicopters, the most difficult ones to master. At seventeen, he realized he had a unique set of skills to offer that could develop into an exciting business. With a GoPro camera mounted to a remote control helicopter, Connor Alstrom shoots aerial footage from up to two hundred feet high. He shoots everything from farms to real estate to weddings.

"My business allows a larger scope of people to utilize aerial photographs to promote their businesses," says Connor. "It allows farmers to have an aerial view of their fields, but it also allows law enforcement agencies to get an aerial view of high-intensity situations." Of the many possible uses for @Flying, Connor says, "The most practical sustainable business application is probably agriculture, for farmers to see exactly where they need to water more or replant their crops, or to see where their cattle are grazing."

For now, Connor equips each helicopter with a video camera, but if his business takes off, he anticipates adding a separate camera on a live feed back on the ground. The high school senior also plans to volunteer his helicopters for search-and-rescue missions, which would allow search crews to spend less time away from their families, while increasing the chances that a missing person could be spotted.

Connor says that becoming an entrepreneur inspired him to study business in college and adds, "Entrepreneurship has improved my public speaking skills tenfold. But the most important thing I learned is the power of friendships in the business world. That's what makes it run. It's like the saying: It's not about what you know, but who you know. It really reinforced that."

Think Like an Entrepreneur

1. What unique hobbies, skills, or knowledge have you developed growing up that you could turn into a business?
2. Connor has come up with a new way to help farmers manage their farms. Brainstorm some innovative ways to help manage a business in your community.
3. Do you agree with Connor's statement about the importance of friendship in the business world? What kind of friends do you have? Do they inspire and support you or do they sometimes bring you down? How could you expand your circle of friends?

CHAPTER 18

IS IT TIME TO HIRE?

RECRUIT GREAT EMPLOYEES, MOTIVATE THEM, AND HANDLE THE PAPERWORK

*Do not hire a man who does your work for money,
but him who does it for the love of it.*

—Henry David Thoreau, author, poet, and philosopher

Successful entrepreneurs add value to scarce resources. A jewelry designer buys sterling silver wire and unpolished amethyst stones for $120, for example, and crafts them into a necklace she is able to sell for $250. She has created something that is worth more to consumers than the resources (the silver wire and the stones) are worth on their own. This creative act defines the magic of entrepreneurship.

It's easy to think of precious gemstones as a scarce resource, but there's another scarce resource entrepreneurs work with all the time—human resources, also known as people! Hiring the right person will add value to your business, but the wrong person will diminish its value. Bringing new people into a company can change everything from your business's culture to its profitability. Hiring (and firing) employees are some of the most important business decisions you will make.

IS IT TIME TO HIRE?

As a new business owner, you will take on lots of roles, such as store manager, bookkeeper, and salesperson. The entrepreneur who keeps trying to do it all will burn out, though. You can't grow your business if you remain your only employee.

But *when* is it time for a new business to hire its first employee? That depends on two factors:

1. Is the business bringing in enough profit to hire an employee?
2. Will the employee bring in enough additional profit to the business to justify continuing to pay him or her?

Successful entrepreneurs tend to be creative individuals who can become really bored with the everyday details of running a business. Wise entrepreneurs recognize this about themselves—and hire honest, smart, hardworking people to help them run their businesses.

Ask yourself:

- Can I afford employees?
- Can I share control?
- Am I willing to delegate authority or responsibility to someone else?
- Do I have the people skills required to manage employees?
- Do I feel comfortable leading and being in charge?

Game Changer

Madame C. J. Walker was born Sarah Breedlove in Louisiana in 1867. Her parents died when Sarah was a child, and she was reared in poverty by her married sister. Nonetheless, in her forties Walker became the first self-made American female millionaire and one of the first African American millionaires.

Breedlove worked for many years in the cotton fields and as a laundress before inventing and marketing her hair-care products for African American women. At first, Madame Walker (her married name) sold her shampoos and hair-growth merchandise door-to-door by herself. Her business breakthrough came when she decided to organize and train other African American women to be her sales agents.

Walker organized her agents into clubs that promoted social and charitable causes in their communities. She offered cash prizes to the clubs that accomplished the most.

She also encouraged her agents to open beauty salons and other businesses. At her business's peak, it had more than two thousand agents selling its products.

Not only did Madame Walker's methods foreshadow the emphasis we see today on socially responsible entrepreneurship, but she also created a rich legacy of black female entrepreneurial leadership.

ADVANTAGES OF HIRING EMPLOYEES

The most obvious advantage of hiring employees is having others to share the work. This choice is easier if an employee's job duplicates the entrepreneur's own. If your one-person limousine service is overwhelmed with calls, it's pretty easy to train a friend who's a good driver to mimic what you do. If your gourmet pizza business can't keep up with demand, hire another pizza maker.

Bear in mind, though, that employees from diverse backgrounds can bring fresh insights to your business. New ideas emerge when people with different backgrounds and personalities work together.

Employees can also supply skills and qualities the entrepreneur lacks. A brilliant-yet-nerdy coder may not have the super-outgoing personality needed to *sell* the apps and software she creates. Hiring a good salesperson will leave this entrepreneur free to invent more products.

An employee can also be a valuable second-in-command when a business owner is called away from work. Sally runs a garden shop from her rural home. Previously, taking a day off meant closing the shop and losing sales. Now she puts her two assistants in charge, and the receipts for that one day are typically enough to cover their wages for the entire week. Knowing the shop is in trusted hands helps Sally enjoy her time off and return to the business rested and recharged.

WHAT KIND OF EMPLOYEES DO YOU NEED?

To determine what kind of employees your business needs, go back to your SWOT analysis and look at the weak areas. Think about how you could find employees to strengthen those areas.

Some entrepreneurs leave the daily management of their businesses to employees so they can focus on the more challenging, rewarding aspects of their work. Hiring an assistant to schedule appointments and take care of day-to-day tasks, for example, gives the business owner more time to research the market for a new service, tinker with improving a product design, or pitch the company to potential investors.

Some entrepreneurs are in demand for unique talents and need employees to help bring them to fruition. A music producer may hire people to operate studio equipment and record a song, but it's the producer's artistic and commercial insight that makes the music a hit.

Finally, many entrepreneurs take satisfaction in hiring entrepreneurially minded people. These employees may someday go on to become entrepreneurs themselves.

EMPLOYEES MEAN PAPERWORK!

Hiring employees means added expenses, paperwork, and legal requirements. The responsibilities of becoming a boss include lots of paperwork, paying employees' wages, paying taxes on those wages, and buying insurance.

Employee Tax Forms

Before you can hire anyone, you must send in Form SS-4 (Application for Employer Identification Number) to the IRS to obtain an employer identification number (EIN).

Once you hire an employee, you will need to fill out a form declaring that the employee has presented documents (photo ID, Social Security card, and so forth) proving his or her identity and that he or she can legally work in the United States. To deduct taxes from the worker's wages, you will file Forms W-2 (Wage and Tax Statement) and W-4 (Employee's Withholding Allowance Certificate) with the IRS.

In addition, you will be required to keep records of the employee's hours worked, wages paid, and taxes withheld. If the worker is injured on the job or files a complaint, the government requires that this, too, be documented.

Once you decide to hire someone, you will also have to complete an I-9 (Employment Eligibility Verification), and tax and payroll forms. The I-9 form must be completed on the first day of hire, to ensure that the employee is legally authorized to work in the United States. For more information, visit the IRS website, specifically http://www.irs.gov/Businesses/Small-Businesses-&-Self-Employed/Businesses-with-Employees.

Learn the Lingo

Most employers ask job applicants to fill out a form and submit a résumé, which is a written summary of work experience, education, and skills.

Workplace Rules and Policies

Hiring employees may mean establishing more detailed workplace rules and policies. If you have a large number of employees, you may need to develop an **employee handbook**. These guidelines must be carefully written to be reasonable, understandable, and enforceable. They must align with federal and state laws regarding fair treatment, employee rights, and workplace safety. In fact, it's a good idea to get your employee handbook reviewed by a lawyer before you start using it.

Most handbooks include a welcome statement that briefly describes the company's history, mission statement, and goals, and cover the following:

- Orientation: Includes forms to fill out with tax and ID information.
- Terms: Defines full- and part-time employment; explains how to clock in; rules for daily breaks, scheduling, and so forth.
- Benefits: Spells out vacation, insurance, and retirement benefits.
- Conduct and discipline policies: Explains grounds for dismissal and rules that must be followed (about sexual harassment or alcohol or drug use, for example).

As the boss, you will also be responsible for fostering good relationships among your employees. Conflicts among them must be addressed before they slow the workflow and sour the workplace atmosphere. If an employee is involved in illegal conduct or unfair treatment, the employer can be held responsible.

LABOR LAW AND HUMAN RESOURCES COMPLIANCE

Federal and state laws govern hiring, treatment, and firing of employees. Laws forbid companies from not hiring or promoting on the basis of age or race, for example. Please memorize this fact: *It is illegal for you to ask potential employees how old they are, whether they are married and/or have children, or where they are from, during the interview process.*

Some laws concerning employees include:

- **Equal Pay Act of 1963:** Requires employers to pay men and women the same amount for substantially equal work.

- **Fair Labor Standards Act:** Requires that employees receive at least the federally mandated minimum wage. It also prohibits hiring anyone under the age of sixteen full-time. Minimum-wage information must be posted visibly in your store or place of business.

- **Title VII of the Civil Rights Act of 1964:** Prohibits discrimination against applicants and employees on the basis of race, color, religion, sex, or national origin, including membership in a Native American tribe. It also prohibits harassment based on any protected characteristics, such as those listed here, and prohibits employer retaliation against those who assert their rights under the act. This act is enforced by the U.S. Equal Employment Opportunity Commission.

- **Age Discrimination in Employment Act (ADEA):** Prohibits discrimination against and harassment of employees aged forty or older. Employers may not retaliate against those who assert their rights under the act. This act is also enforced by the EEOC.

- **Americans with Disabilities Act (ADA):** Prohibits employers from discriminating against a person who has a disability, or who is perceived to have a disability, in any aspect of employment. It also prohibits refusal to hire or discrimination against someone related to or associated with a disability. The ADA prohibits harassment and retaliation in the cases above. This act is enforced by the EEOC and the U.S. Department of Justice.

- **Immigration Reform and Control Act of 1986 (IRCA):** Prohibits employers from discriminating against applicants or employees on the basis of their citizenship or national origin. In addition, it affirms that it is illegal for employers to knowingly hire or retain in employment individuals who are not authorized to work in the United States.

Try It!

Research the antidiscrimination laws in your state. What forms of discrimination do they prohibit? When were they enacted? To which organizations (type and size) do they apply?

ORGANIZATIONAL STRUCTURES

A business's **organizational structure** is its system for dividing work, authority, and responsibility within the company. When you hire employees, you will need to develop an organizational structure that suits the business. Let's explore some traditional organizational structures.

Line Organization

The simplest structure is **line organization,** a direct chain of command through levels of personnel who are directly involved in a business's main occupation. Take Jerry's independent bookstore, Books-4-U. Jerry opened it with two employees, Mitchell and Susan. All three were responsible for waiting on customers, ordering books, taking deliveries, and stocking the shelves. The basic structure when the store opened was a line organization, with both Mitchell and Susan reporting to Jerry.

Line Organization

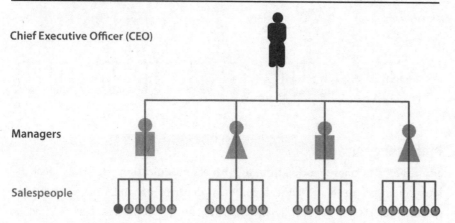

Chief Executive Officer (CEO)

Managers

Salespeople

Line-and-Staff Organization

A business's organization often changes as the business grows or the market changes, and may do better with **line-and-staff organization**. In this type of structure, staff members advise, assist, or support the work of line personnel.

Five years later, Books-4-U has moved to a larger space and grown considerably. Jerry has hired five salespeople to work in the store. These employees became part of the line. As the business grew, Mitchell and Susan took on more specialized tasks. Mitchell became the sales manager, with all salespeople reporting to him. Susan is now the marketing manager. She looks for ways to publicize the store and analyzes trends in publishing and book buying.

Susan is now no longer part of the line, because she doesn't take part in the business's revenue-producing work—she no longer sells books. Instead, she works on marketing, and is considered staff. The final authority to make decisions remains with Jerry.

Line-and-Staff Organization

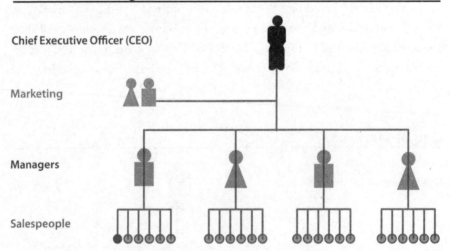

Chief Executive Officer (CEO)

Marketing

Managers

Salespeople

Project Organization

Sometimes a business benefits from the **project organization** structure, which allows employees to float around to different departments and work as teams on specific projects. At Veggies, a vegetarian restaurant, the owner, Tim, wanted to develop a line of healthy frozen meals. He asked the executive chef and the marketing manager to work with an outside dietician on this project. Tim also participated and took on the responsibility of working to finance the initiative through loans and investors.

Once the project is completed, the project organization structure can be dissolved, or maintained for another project.

Trends in Organizational Structures

The traditional organizational structures described above don't always fit today's rapidly changing global economy. Electronic communication has created a virtual workplace, enabling project members from anywhere in the world to meet in videoconferences.

To stay competitive, entrepreneurs are finding that flexibility is more important than strictly defined roles and responsibilities. These are giving way to interdepartmental teams and networks that can be put together as the need arises. Business is no longer contained by physical boundaries, making loose, project-oriented organizational structures increasingly common.

Darren Novak owns a small chemical analysis lab in Nevada. Darren was contacted by a fertilizer manufacturer in Texas. The fertilizer company was concerned when its chemists found unusually high amounts of pollutants in the water discharged as a result of the manufacturing process.

By videoconferencing with other experts the company had assembled, Darren was able to track down a flaw in the sampling method, which had led to incorrect results. Now the fertilizer manufacturer uses Darren's company to randomly double-check its own chemists' findings.

START SMALL

Here are some ways to begin bringing employees into your business without taking on the risk of hiring full-time employees:

- Hire part-time employees. Part-time employees require less paperwork and don't typically receive benefits like health insurance.
- Use consultants and independent contractors. These are people you contract with to work for you. Since your business is buying services from them, not hiring them, you don't have to pay payroll taxes or provide benefits.
- Bring in partners. Partners share the risks and rewards of the venture

and will co-own the business with you. They will have the incentive to work diligently for the company's success.

- Hire experts to accomplish specific tasks on a contractual or hourly basis. You could hire a professional accountant to work one day per month to review your record keeping, for example.

RECRUITING EMPLOYEES

To **recruit** means to find and hire qualified candidates for a job. Recruiting is an investment: The thought and preparation you put into recruiting your employees will be reflected in the quality of the workers you hire. In small businesses, particularly, the impact of a single hiring decision can be felt throughout the company.

Experts calculate that replacing an employee can cost three or four times that person's salary in lost productivity, customer loyalty, company morale, downtime without a replacement, hiring a replacement, training the new employee, and so forth. Choosing employees wisely is critical to a small business.

Start creating a list of potential employees before you even need to hire someone. Take note of people you meet whose talents or work ethic you admire. Include customers or even the employees of your competition.

When Mimi was recruiting a sales representative for her organic pet foods business, she offered the job to the assistant manager of a pet store that carried her products. Mimi knew he was knowledgeable about animal nutrition and experienced at selling.

If you are growing rapidly and are ready to look for a skilled, educated workforce, here are some great ways to recruit employees:

- **Colleges and University Placement Offices:** College counselors keep up with the area job scene, using input from employers to help students prepare for the local market. They often coordinate with professors to send students to companies to work as unpaid interns, to gain experience and credit for coursework. You can usually post job openings and read student résumés on a college website at no charge.
- **On-Campus Recruiting:** Established companies from all industries visit college campuses every year to meet and scout students who are about to graduate. Contact the career service offices of colleges and

universities near you to learn how you can participate in their job fairs and networking events.

- **Executive or Retained Searches:** When companies need to hire a senior executive, they engage in an executive search. These top job openings are often not advertised, and the process is frequently managed by a search firm. Executive search firms perform a full range of recruitment, screening, interviewing, and reference services for a fee. They will work with you to develop a detailed job profile and position description, create a profile of the ideal candidate, and help you find and interview the best possible candidates.

- **Trade Associations:** Check trade association websites and publications for online job banks and other leads. Linda Joseph is a member of the American Saddle Makers Association. When she wanted to hire a skilled leather worker, she phoned a master saddle maker who was listed on the group's website.

- **Help Wanted Websites:** Sometimes it is useful to advertise your job on LinkedIn or "help wanted" sites such as Monster.com. Try to write the most specific online job description that you can—that will help weed out responses from people who are not right for your company.

- **Department of Labor or Commerce:** Your state's labor department also offers job-placement services.

Read a Classic

Lean In: Women, Work, and the Will to Lead by Facebook chief operating officer Sheryl Sandberg is a fascinating bestseller that examines how women can achieve their full potential in business and move into executive roles.

WRITING A JOB DESCRIPTION

You can't fill a position until you can tell applicants what it entails. That's the purpose of writing a **job description,** which is an explanation of a position's purpose, tasks, and responsibilities and the qualifications needed to perform it.

To attract qualified applicants, a job description should list specific skills, activities, and qualifications and rank their importance.

A description for an assistant might read "Answers phones, schedules appointments, and maintains office equipment. Must have experience with database and Internet research; familiarity with accounting software preferred."

Include all required training or credentials. For instance, a child-care provider may need training in CPR and other emergency procedures.

The job description should also describe prospects for advancement and more responsibilities. If you hope the assistant hired today eventually will advance to become your office manager, you might want to also list the skills and qualities you are looking for in an office manager and mention that you hope the position will develop into that.

Be sure to ask applicants to submit a résumé with references, as well. **References** are people the job applicant has worked for previously, or who are familiar with the applicant's skills and work ethic. Before hiring anyone, call their references and ask questions about the applicant's skills, performance, and character.

DETERMINING COMPENSATION

Compensation is the money plus **benefits** that an employee receives in exchange for working. Benefits include health and dental insurance, life insurance, paid holidays, vacation and sick time, and retirement savings plans. Additional benefits may include tuition reimbursement, discounts on auto insurance, and other "perks." Full-time employees expect an array of paid benefits as part of their compensation package.

Here are six forms of compensation:

1. **Wages:** Payment per hour worked or piece of work completed.
2. **Salary:** A weekly, bimonthly, or monthly payment.
3. **Commission:** Payment based on a percentage of sales achieved.
4. **Benefits:** Some benefits, such as family and medical leave, are required by law. Others have become standard, including health insurance, paid vacation, sick days, and investment plans for retirement saving.
5. **Bonuses:** Payments on top of wages or salaries for outstanding work or for meeting specified goals.
6. **Stock Options:** Giving employers stock in your company as part of their compensation package gives them added incentive to help make the company successful, because that are part owners of it.

New entrepreneurs often worry that they can't match the compensation packages offered by larger, established firms. But compensation isn't the only benefit of working for a business. Employees are also attracted by location, scheduling flexibility, on-site day care, the company's culture, and possibilities for advancement.

SCREENING JOB CANDIDATES

To screen potential employees, have them fill out a job application form and submit a résumé, with references. Ask the candidates to provide at least three references from previous employers, or other people (college professors, for example) who could tell you about their character and work performance. You can find job application forms online and tailor them to your business.

What can applications and résumés tell you about a job seeker? Look for good spelling, correct grammar, and attention to detail. You'll also want to see the skills and experience that you need for your business.

Keep an eye out for "red flags," such as an applicant whose résumé shows that she has changed jobs frequently, or has not worked for long periods of time. If someone has gaps in his résumé, don't automatically discount him. Ask, instead, what he has been doing while unemployed. Some people are very productive while unemployed—they volunteer, network, or go back to school. They may have developed skills and contacts that would be valuable to your company.

If you see some résumés you like, check the references that the applicants have provided on their job applications. Definitely call all references provided and listen to what they have to say about your potential employee. Create a few questions that are pertinent to the job being filled and the related career paths. Include questions about how the candidate and his/her reference know each other.

One smart question to ask is: "Would you rehire this person?" Another is "Why is this person no longer working for you?"

INTERVIEWING YOUR CANDIDATES

Contact the most promising applicants for interviews. Make a list of questions you plan to ask. Focus on relevant information that expands on the facts given in the application or résumé. Remember, you cannot legally ask questions about age, race, sexual orientation, marital status, religion, or other personal matters.

Try to put candidates at ease during the interview. Give them time to answer questions and explain statements or information in their résumés.

At the same time, notice how they handle stress or difficult questions. Ask challenging questions, such as "What do you see as your biggest weakness?" A response such as "Sometimes I talk without thinking, so I'm working at listening better" shows not only honesty but also problem-solving skills and the ability to evaluate oneself.

Here are some more good inquiries you can use to get a job applicant to open up:

- How did you get interested in this line of work?
- What achievements are you most proud of?
- What would you like to learn from this job?
- What are your career goals for the next five years?
- Tell me how you solved a problem at work.
- Describe a situation where you resolved a customer complaint.

A face-to-face interview also gives you a chance to assess a potential employee's personality. An employee should be enjoyable to work with and have traits that fit the culture at your company. At the same time, though, don't be too judgmental if someone doesn't dress or act just like you. Diverse styles and points of view can be great assets to your company.

Remember that when you are judging the applicant in the interview the applicant is also judging you as an employer. Encourage the applicant to ask questions, and answer them positively and honestly.

BACKGROUND CHECKS

If you become serious about wanting to hire someone, you should check his or her background for financial problems or criminal activity. You can search public arrest records for free. For more detailed background checks, including credit checks, you will have to pay a fee.

Under the law, employers must have an applicant's consent to check credit history and other information. Applicants must be told if any such information was used to disqualify them from the job.

The nature and extent of a background check (including reference checking) will depend upon the specific position. It is good practice to conduct a basic background check, a criminal background check, and drug testing. The $50 or so investment in a criminal background check could save literally thousands of dollars.

You do not want to be guilty of negligent hiring because you have ignored this precaution.

A small, rural taxi service closed due to bad publicity generated by the arrest of one of its drivers on charges of assaulting an elderly passenger. The driver had a history of assaulting older women, but the company had not bothered to conduct a background check. The company was held liable for putting him in a position in which he had the opportunity to commit another crime, and had to make payments to the victim that forced it to close.

In addition to criminal background checks, you may also want to examine official copies of college transcripts, or a high school diploma, and check previous employment history, such as positions held and dates of employment. If the job requires driving, absolutely check the person's driving record with the Department of Motor Vehicles.

Be certain to comply with all employment laws in carrying out these checks and investigations, and get signed release forms as required. Drug-test authorization and background check release forms are typically provided as part of the employment application package, and should be completed prior to interviewing the candidate.

Learn the Lingo

"Diversity" means variety. When you look around your community, you typically see a variety of people. They may be young or old, tall or short, dark skinned or light skinned. People can be diverse in their religion, their sexual orientation, and their country of origin.

As you move into the working world, you will likely encounter people from all walks of life. Some may be considerably older than you are, some may have disabilities you're not familiar with, and some may be of a race, sexual orientation, or religion different from yours.

In the working world, you will need to let go of stereotypes you may hold that may stand in the way of teamwork and friendly relationships with all of your colleagues. Put aside any preconceived ideas and generalizations about certain groups of people, and recognize that diversity strengthens organizations.

FREELANCERS

As your business grows, you will need help sporadically with things such as financial planning, legal issues, writing, publicity, or accounting. Or you may need to hire someone to build an add-on to your office. In these cases, using freelancers may be your best bet. A freelancer sells his or her services to a company, yet remains independent and self-employed. **Consultants** and **independent contractors** are both types of freelancers.

Learn the Lingo

The word "freelancer" comes from the Middle Ages. It was used to describe soldiers for hire, or mercenaries who fought with long spears called lances and, rather than staying loyal to one country or king, sold their fighting services to the highest bidder.

Consultants

When you are developing your business, you may require the services of a lawyer, an accountant, a writer, a publicist, or other educated professionals. An expert who provides professional services for a fee is called a consultant. If you want to use their services, you will typically do so through a short-term contract that specifies how many hours or what services the consultant will provide, plus deadlines and fees.

In some cases, you may pay a consultant a **retainer,** which is a fee (typically paid monthly) that entitles you to a certain amount of the consultant's time and attention. You might pay your publicist a monthly retainer, for example, to seek publicity for your business and be available for you to call if you have any questions or are contacted by the press.

Choosing an outside expert requires the same type of research as hiring a regular employee. Get recommendations from other business owners, especially those with needs like your own.

Ask candidates for references from other clients. Check for consumer complaints through the Better Business Bureau. Check their credentials through a professional organization or state licensing or regulating agency.

Look for consultants with whom you can establish good long-term relationships. As with a doctor or dentist, you may see them only once or twice a year, but you're entrusting them with a valuable possession: your business's future.

Independent Contractors

An **independent contractor** is a person or business that provides a service to another person or business under terms specified in a contract. Many businesses hire people under independent contracts instead of as employees to avoid paying benefits such as health insurance.

Here's the catch, though: Legally, you cannot treat an independent contractor like an employee. If an employee does not show up for work at the time you have specified, that is fair grounds for dismissal. Independent contractors, in contrast, retain control over their schedule and number of hours worked and may work for other people without your permission. It wouldn't be a good idea to hire an independent contractor to be your store's clerk, for example, since legally you couldn't tell him or her when to be there.

In addition, the IRS requires you to withhold income taxes, pay Social Security and Medicare taxes, and pay unemployment tax on wages or salaries paid to your employees. You do not have to withhold or pay any taxes on payments to independent contractors.

You do, however, have to report to the IRS any payment you make to an independent contractor over a certain amount (currently $600, as of this writing). Before hiring an independent contractor, visit www.IRS.gov and read the section on Small Businesses and Independent Contractors.

A POSITIVE ENVIRONMENT

Google and Microsoft are both companies that threw out the rule books when it came to creating their workplace environments—and found creative, fun ways to motivate their employees to really work hard and love coming to work.

Google has repeatedly topped *Fortune* magazine's Best Places to Work list, with its subsidized massages for employees and a seven-acre sports complex, which includes a roller hockey rink; courts for basketball, bocce, and shuffle ball; and horseshoe pits. The company's perks—free gourmet food, on-site laundry, Wi-Fi commuting shuttles—are legendary in the corporate world. Google monitors its employees' happiness, and when the company's execs noticed that a lot of talented women were leaving, it created a five-month maternity leave plan. After it went into place, Google's attrition rate for new mothers dropped dramatically.

You may not have the money to offer these kinds of perks, but there's plenty you can do to make sure your employees feel happy and fulfilled.

Here are some tips on creating a positive environment that will inspire your personnel to enjoy coming to work and giving their all:

- Give personal recognition for unexpected or little-noticed contributions to the workplace. These can be inexpensive and fun and still get employees psyched about doing their best. Try a Good Egg award, for example—a plastic egg filled with something useful, such as a restaurant gift certificate, for an employee who handled a difficult customer well or brought in some new business.

- Provide a safe and productive workspace. Work is more enjoyable when the physical environment is designed for efficiency and safety. Employees should have ready access to needed tools, such as insulated gloves or graphic arts software.

- Give clear goals and direction. Employees need to feel confident that they're doing their jobs well. Giving employees reasonable yet challenging goals and deadlines will help them decide where to direct their efforts. Providing the opportunity for frequent, informal feedback helps employees feel confident.

- Encourage lifelong learning. Let your employees know you believe in their potential by encouraging them to learn. Keep a library at the office from which they can borrow books anytime, and pay for them to take classes related to their jobs. Encourage them to take free online classes from MOOCs (massive online open courses) such as Coursera to bolster their knowledge in various fields.

- Encourage volunteering. AT&T encourages its employees to volunteer—on company time! The AT&T Foundation helps extend the reach of AT&T employees' community involvement efforts by matching employee contributions to educational and cultural organizations and by providing grants to recognize employee volunteer efforts in communities located in all areas of the country. How could you encourage your employees to volunteer? They will not only build contacts and goodwill for your business that will bring in new customers, but they'll also feel good about themselves and about working for you.

- Have fun! This could mean something as simple as having a pizza party at the end of work on a Friday or providing tickets to a local event. Showing that you value your employees in such a way will increase their loyalty and enthusiasm and will build a sense of community and shared values in the workplace.

Training and Development

Here are some ways to encourage your employees to engage in lifelong learning. Doing so benefits you, too, as your employees bring new skills and ideas to your business.

- **Classes.** You may be able to get group rates for your employees. Encourage them to try online courses, which are convenient and affordable. It's a good idea to meet with each employee and discuss his or her career goals, and brainstorm together what types of classes and training would help him or her reach them.

- **Workshops.** In a workshop, a small group of people gather to learn through discussion, demonstration, and practice. You can bring in experts to hold workshops for your employees. A workshop may be a single session lasting a few hours or several sessions on related topics spread out over a few days.

- **Seminars.** Both you and your employees can attend seminars, which are small groups that get together to hear experts from a field share information. Seminars encourage networking and discussion.

- **Conferences and Expos.** A conference or an expo (short for "exposition") can be a "one-stop shopping" learning experience. These events, which usually run several days, may offer classes, workshops, or seminars at one site, along with panel discussions, vendors' booths, and representatives from professional associations. Attending a conference or expo can be costly in terms of travel, lodging, and time taken off from work. Yet the expense can be worth it because you and your employees can learn new techniques and keep up with the latest developments in your industry.

Game Changer

Milton Hershey, founder of the Hershey Chocolate Company, was a progressive-minded entrepreneur who believed in taking care of the people whose work helped build his fortune. He was also a shrewd businessman who understood that people are motivated to work harder when they feel appreciated. In the early 1900s, he developed the town of Hershey, Pennsylvania, as a model community for his employees. It included good housing, quality schools, parks and recreation facilities, and a trolley for transportation.

Most entrepreneurs can't match Hershey's scale of employee appreciation. Yet all entrepreneurs can follow his example of employee motivation. They can recognize employees' value and importance to the business and encourage them to realize their potential.

Performance-Based Rewards

Try motivating your employees with rewards, too! A **performance-based reward** is linked to a specific, achievable goal and is related to the work involved—in other words, the greater the achievement, the greater the reward.

Suppose you own a trucking firm. You could award points for every mile driven without an accident or ticket. The points could be redeemed as a gift card from a business of the driver's choice.

Or imagine you own a home-cleaning service. You might offer a finder's fee to workers who bring in new customers—or if you're hiring, for new employees. When a customer reports a cleaning crew's outstanding service, you could give the crew points that they could exchange for rewards.

Membership in professional groups is another valued reward. A sales associate in Gemma Gottlieb's quilt shop is also the store's Webmaster. When the site recorded its one millionth hit, Gemma bought the associate a year's membership in the American Association of Webmasters, which entitled him to discounts on online Web design courses and other benefits.

Flexible Work Arrangements

When employees are asked what they value most in a job, it isn't always pay or benefits. It's often flexibility. Having more choices about when and how to work helps employees find a time (or place) when they can focus on the job.

Consider offering **flextime,** or flexible work schedules. Some employees might start and finish work one hour earlier or later than others, or alternate between working four days and five days a week. Or employees could split duties through job sharing. **Job sharing** or **work sharing** is an employment arrangement in which two people are retained on a part-time basis to perform a job normally fulfilled by one person working full-time.

You can also let employees **telecommute,** or work from a home. Through telecommuting, a company can profit from the talents of people who otherwise would not be available—people with disabilities, parents of young children, and those who live far from the workplace.

Workplace flexibility isn't an option for all businesses or all employees, of course, but it may be practical for small operations. Telecommuting is a great solution if you can't afford to rent an office large enough for employees, for example. Employees with families, in particular, are often more attracted to workplaces that offer some flextime and telecommuting options. You might get a higher-quality employee than you thought you could afford by offering these kinds of perks.

HOW TO LEGALLY PROMOTE, FIRE, AND LAY OFF EMPLOYEES

Performance Evaluations

A **performance evaluation** is a regular review of an employee's performance on the job, usually given at least annually. Some companies give formal quarterly or semiannual reviews to reinforce good performance and alert employees to improvements they need to make in their work. The review process is handled by the business owner, the employee's supervisor, or a human resources specialist.

It's a good idea to put a performance evaluation in writing (so you have it on file in case you ever have to fire someone for poor performance), and to sit down and discuss evaluations with your employees.

Suppose you notice that your salesperson is just barely reaching his sales quota each month. In discussing the problem, you find that his sales area overlaps that of a well-established competitor. Revising your training to include better education on your products and the competitor's would help your salespeople sway potential customers.

After discussing the performance evaluation, both the reviewer and employee sign the performance evaluation form, proving they've had the discussion. They may write out and sign a list of goals and a plan for improving employee performance and job satisfaction. Some employers also have employees fill out a form that asks what tools, training, or changes in the work environment would help them do the job better.

Promoting Employees

When a higher-level, better-paying job becomes available at your company, promoting an existing employee into it saves resources spent on training someone from the outside. It also motivates your other employees to work harder so they might be

Performance Evaluation Form

Reviewer: _____   Employee: _____

Criteria	Not Applicable	Excellent	Good	Fair	Unsatisfactory	Comments
Meets work quality standards						
Completes assignments reliably						
Shows initiative in problem solving and decision making						
Adapts well to changing circumstances						
Shows willingness and ability to learn new skills						
Arrives on time and prepared to work						
Effectively gets desired results from subordinates						

General comments on employee's performance:

considered for promotion, too. For these reasons, publicizing a job opening within your own company makes sense.

If you think an existing employee would be a good prospect, you might invite him or her to apply for the position. You might see skills and qualities in someone that could be successfully developed in a higher position. On the other hand, people may know themselves and their priorities better than you do. For example, an employee with a young family may not want to accept a promotion to a position that involves a lot of traveling.

Once the job has been filled, make sure other employees understand why they weren't chosen. This will allow them to work toward preparing for the next opening, if they wish.

Firing Employees

Dismissing an employee may be the most difficult thing an entrepreneur ever has to do. Never fire people lightly or while you're angry. It is illegal to fire someone due to personal feelings, and besides, it takes time and money to hire and train a replacement. The decision to fire should be made only after you have calmed down and explored all your options.

Before considering dismissal, tell the employee how he or she is failing to meet your expectations, and how he or she could improve. The conversation might yield a solution. The job's duties may have changed, for example, and the employee might need retraining or other support to adjust. Perhaps those duties could be reassigned, to develop and better use the employee's strengths. The employee might be happier and perform better in a different position at your company.

If you do decide to fire someone, be sure your reasons for doing so are legally justified. Double-check your policy and your employees' handbook—the grounds for dismissal should be clearly stated and enforceable. All discussions and actions should be documented and retained in the employee's file.

Sometimes you hire someone and it just does not work out, even after repeated attempts to fix the problem. If you have to let someone go, you must document the reasons as they occur. You can be sued for wrongful termination, or breach of contract, if an employee believes he/she was fired for no good reason. The rules for termination vary from state to state, so it is essential to know your state's law.

Protect your company from wrongful-termination claims by conducting regular employee performance reviews. Use performance-improvement or -development plans to give the employee an opportunity to fix any aspects of his or her performance that are subpar.

If an employee is violating rules, give notification in writing (and keep a copy for your records). Work on corrections as the problems arise, rather than waiting for a performance review. If performance continues to be unsatisfactory, and you have to let the employee go, you will have documentation that there were ongoing problems with his or her performance.

Laying Off Employees

Sometimes you might have to **lay off** employees, or let them go because you can't afford to pay them or you no longer need their skills.

Make sure employees who are dismissed for economic reasons know that they are being laid off, not fired. Make sure their former coworkers know this as well. The dismissal should be planned to give the employee plenty of time to make the transition and find another job. You can also help by writing a recommendation or using your business and personal connections to help your employee find another job.

If you can do so, offer laid-off employees severance pay as compensation for being let go. Write them good reference letters and make serious efforts to help them find new jobs.

An Entrepreneur Like You

Bruce and Glen Proctor
BRUCEGLEN

http://bruceglen.com

Bruce and Glen Proctor are identical twin brothers who grew up in Washington, D.C. Their drug-addicted father was gone most of the time, often in and out of jail. When he was home he worked construction jobs but their mother had to accompany him on payday to make sure that she had money for rent. She struggled to make ends meet, often borrowing from relatives, and the boys' older sister helped by holding down a job.

Bruce and Glen made up their minds that they didn't want to struggle the way their parents had. In their junior year at Woodrow Wilson High School, the boys enrolled in a NFTE entrepreneurship class and launched their first business, Twin Sports, which sold headbands and hats decorated with team logos. Nearly one-third of the school population bought accessories from Twin Sports!

The brothers earned more than $10,000 in two years from Twin Sports and became confident that they could support themselves and be successful if they continued to work together. They put themselves through two years of college and then got what Glen calls "an amazingly unbelievable opportunity to intern for House of Deréon. Our career in the fashion industry blossomed from that point . . . a series of miracles, to say the least, landed us in positions we hadn't earned but that God had equipped us for! We were underqualified and young but we were hungry, and if you're hungry, you'll eat!"

Glen adds, "It was one of those internships that sort of pounds you into shape. We were so new to it all . . . to NY, the fashion world, being around celebrities. We had a short sit-down with Diddy and he gave us a few words of wisdom. He told his assistant, 'Shut the door,' and then just schooled us for thirty minutes. I'll always remember that! He's a wonderful visionary and businessman!"

Before getting into entrepreneurship, Bruce and Glen were extremely shy. "Having to present our business plan was great for building our confidence," Bruce says, adding, "Once bitten by the entrepreneurship bug, we discovered our passion. Now we have a leaders' spirit and a fighting attitude."

The dynamic duo launched BruceGlen with a line of bejeweled suede and embossed leather bracelets for men and women that were soon seen on celebrities and in fashion magazines. The brothers quickly followed up with stylish iPad and Kindle Fire cases made from exotic skins such as python and crocodile.

Bruce and Glen creatively promote their business and their larger-than-life personalities with the Web series *Lunch Break,* which gives viewers a sneak peak into their exciting lives as up-and-coming designers living in New York City.

Think Like an Entrepreneur

1. Can you think of a business you could start with a sibling or a close friend? Would you make a good team? Why or why not?
2. What, to you, is the most important thing to bear in mind when developing a team?
3. What would your dream internship be? How could you pursue it?

CHAPTER 19

GROWTH STRATEGIES

EXPANDING, FRANCHISING, AND LICENSING

The two most important requirements for major
success are: first, being in the right place at the
right time, and second, doing something about it.

—Ray Kroc

I t's exciting when your business starts to take off—orders are pouring in, lots of
new customers are showing up. But growth, like any business move, must be
carefully considered. Too much growth, too fast can destroy your business if you find
yourself unable to keep up with orders. You can start shedding frustrated customers
and develop a bad reputation.

Growth spurts require rethinking your business plan and outlining steps for
new strategies to handle growth well and encourage it without tanking the business.

There are three basic ways to grow your business: expansion, licensing, or franchising. But first, it's worth noting some of the challenges entrepreneurs face when
trying to grow their businesses.

Learn the Lingo

Internal or **organic growth** is achieved by expanding a business internally—by adding new products or services for sale. External growth is achieved by acquiring other businesses or merging with them.

SIX PRACTICAL CHALLENGES OF GROWING A BUSINESS

Growing a business presents six practical challenges:

1. **Space:** A growing business usually requires more physical space. If the existing building or rooms are not large enough to handle the expansion, you will have to rent, build, or buy additional space.

2. **Business Structure:** You may need to change the organizational structure of your business—from a sole proprietorship to a limited liability company or corporation, for example.

3. **Materials and Equipment:** You may need to purchase more materials, equipment, and office furniture and supplies.

4. **Information Technology (IT):** IT is the use of computer systems, hardware, and software to store and manage information. IT demands for accounting, purchasing, inventory, payroll, and other operations will increase as your business grows.

5. **People and Skills:** A growing business almost always needs more employees, especially at the management level. Existing staff may have to be trained in new skills to make the growth effort successful.

6. **Money:** Growth takes money. Self-financing means obtaining the funds for growth from existing operations—by reinvesting profits into the business. External financing options include **debt capital,** which is money obtained by a business through a loan, and **equity capital,** which is money obtained by a business from an investor in exchange for a share of ownership (equity) in the business.

EXPANSION

Expanding your business involves growing it yourself. You can do this by adding more employees or products/services, or by acquiring (buying) another business and adding *its* employees or products/services to your business. Or you can **merge** with another company. A **merger** is the combination of one or more companies into a single business.

Let's look at three factors you should consider when you're thinking about expanding your business:

1. **Condition of the Business:** Does your business have a solid base of customers? Does it make sales that meet or exceed forecasts and contribute to a satisfactory net profit? If so, you might be ready to expand.

2. **Economic Climate:** How is the economy? Business owners planning to expand must consider economic conditions at the local, national, and perhaps even global levels. Economies tend to follow cycles of upturns and downturns. A downturn is not necessarily a bad time to expand a business. It depends on the business and its markets. If you are selling a product that saves people money, a recession might be the perfect time to expand. If you are selling luxury goods, on the other hand, a recession may not be the best time for you to expand.

3. **Your Life Goals:** Do you really want to take on the extra work and pressure of overseeing an expansion? Or are you happy with where your business is now and the money it is providing? Expanding a business can be very time-consuming. Think through whether the 24/7 challenges of expansion are something you really want to take on at this time in your life before you go for it.

Product Life Cycles

As a business develops, it cycles through a series of stages—introduction, growth, maturity, and decline—called the **product life cycle**. Understanding where your business is on its product life cycle can help you understand how growth fits into the picture.

If you realize that growth is just one phase for your business, you'll understand why you may not want to jump into expansion, even if you've gained lots of customers and your profits are growing.

Stage 1: Introduction. When a product is introduced, a lot of marketing is devoted to making consumers aware of the product. This is typically an expensive phase with high advertising and promotional costs. Profits may be low during this stage.

Stage 2: Growth. Sales and profit increase steadily as the product is embraced by consumers. Competitors may be few at this stage, allowing the business to expand distribution and take advantage of strong demand.

Stage 3: Maturity. During this stage, sales and profits level off and may begin to decline. By now, the product probably faces stiff competition. The business may have to lower prices or enhance the product in some way to give it a new competitive advantage and extend its life.

Stage 4: Decline. During the decline stage, product sales and profits fall steeply and don't recover. The product loses its appeal to consumers. Now that so many cell phones take great pictures, for example, camera sales are on the decline. Technological advances are just one reason products can go into decline.

Product life cycle curves have many variations. Some products are immensely and immediately popular. Their sales rocket upward but then decline quickly. This cycle is common in the fashion and entertainment industries.

Other products endure for long periods. A **perpetual life cycle** is a product life cycle in which a product never undergoes a final decline, because it remains in the maturity stage forever. Basic food products, such as bread and other items in everyday use, are said to have a perpetual life cycle. Individual brands and products within the bread industry can certainly decline, however. Gluten-free bread is gaining in popularity, for example, but will this trend last?

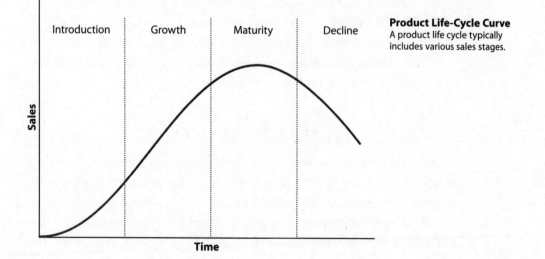

Product Life-Cycle Curve
A product life cycle typically includes various sales stages.

GROWTH THROUGH REPLICATION

There are two other ways to grow your business. Both these growth strategies are called replication strategies because they involve taking what you've created and letting other business owners replicate, or copy, it.

1. **Licensing:** You could rent other businesses a license to use your brand or other intellectual property to sell their own products. Every time a new Disney movie comes out, followed by a slew of dolls and toys of the characters from the film, it's because of licensing. Disney is the licensor, in this case. It doesn't make the dolls and toys; it licenses the rights to use Disney characters in dolls and toys to other companies, who are the licensees. Disney rakes in more than $30 billion in licensing fees per year.

2. **Franchising:** If your business is well organized and has a foolproof operational system, you might be able to franchise it. That is what Roy Kroc did with McDonald's. Today, millions of McDonald's franchises exist worldwide. He created a business operation with specific standards and operating procedures. Every McDonald's you see is a franchise. The owner is called the franchisee, and must follow exact standards and operations specified in the McDonald's **franchise agreement,** a legally binding contract between a franchisor and franchisee that lists the rights and responsibilities of each party. McDonald's, as the franchisor, earns fees and **franchise royalties,** and will also receive an initial **franchise fee**. This is an upfront charge that can range from thousands of dollars to more than a million, and allows the franchisee to join the franchisor's system. The franchisor also gives the franchisee a **franchise operations manual,** which provides detailed instructions about how to operate, staff, and manage a franchise unit.

INS AND OUTS OF LICENSING

Licensing your brand is a way to increase brand recognition and extend your product line, without investing in the costs of entry into additional markets, or investing in the expense of producing new product lines.

If you build a solid brand that people love, you can profitably license it, but you must be wise about the licensees you choose. If Coca-Cola licenses its logo to a

T-shirt maker and the T-shirt maker uses it to create T-shirts with obscene messages, Coca-Cola's reputation would be tarnished, for example.

You also don't want to dilute your brand by licensing to a competitor. Coca-Cola would not license its name to a soft drink manufacturer, for example.

Licensing Agreements

Brand licensing is accomplished through a written licensing agreement between a licensor and a licensee. The licensing agreement grants limited rights to the licensee. The licensor maintains ownership of the brand name and any trademarks or other marks associated with it.

Pros and Cons of Licensing

Successful companies that have worked hard to build a positive brand name or image in the marketplace can benefit greatly from licensing. The two biggest advantages are:

1. **Increased Revenue:** The licensor receives upfront fees, plus royalties.
2. **Brand Enhancement:** Ideally, licensing will increase customer awareness and enhance the brand's reputation.

These advantages will be realized only if the licensor chooses reliable licensees and makes wise decisions about which products to license. Some potential problems with licensing are:

1. **Misbranding:** Choosing the wrong product to brand. There are many famous examples of misbranding, including the failed efforts of the Harley-Davidson motorcycle company to extend its brand name to a cake decorating kit!
2. **Over-Branding:** Occurs when licensors sell a brand name to so many licensees that the original brand concept becomes muddied and unclear to consumers.
3. **Risk to the Brand:** If a company licenses its brand to products or services that disappoint consumers, the company risks losing the good name and image associated with its brand. If a premium luxury company such as Rolls-Royce licenses its name to a line of bicycles, those had better be some very fancy bicycles or Rolls-Royce has just damaged its brand.
4. **Lack of Marketing:** Licensees may mistakenly assume that a well-known brand name will sell their products on its own. As a result, they

may shortchange their advertising campaigns. The licensor should insist on minimum advertising standards and expenses as part of the licensing agreement.

CLONING A BUSINESS: FRANCHISING

As an entrepreneur, you might develop a business that could be reproduced or replicated by other would-be entrepreneurs. If so, you could franchise your business and reap the rewards of all your hard work.

Some entrepreneurs want to start their businesses from the ground up; others are happy to begin with a tested formula. Although there is no guarantee of success, for many, franchising is a great business start-up option.

If you want to buy a franchise in order to get into business, you will have to pay fees and start-up costs. You will also pay the franchisor a percentage of your sales as a franchise royalty.

Below are sample franchise fees, start-up costs, and franchise royalty rates for some popular franchises:

FRANCHISE	FRANCHISE FEE	START-UP COSTS	FEE
McDonald's	$22,000	Various	4%
Arby's	$25,000–$37,500	$550,000–$887,500	4%
GNC	$17,500	$58,700–$137,500	5%
Hardee's	$15,000	$699,900–$1.7 million	4%

Math Moment

You pay a franchise royalty of 5 percent .If your monthly sales for the past three months were $18,500, $20,100, and $27,200, how much did you pay in franchise royalties in total?*

---

*   Answer: $3,290

Super Success Story

In 1965, Fred DeLuca was a seventeen-year-old high school graduate looking for a way to earn money for college when a family friend, Dr. Peter Buck, provided him with $1,000 start-up capital for a sandwich shop.

Pete's Super Submarines has grown into the Subway franchise operation, which has 30,800 franchised units in eighty-nine countries that, together, generate total revenues in excess of $11 billion. The Subway restaurant chain continues to be a privately held company with Fred DeLuca as president. The company is a consistent leader in *Entrepreneur* magazine's annual listing of top franchises.

Subway franchisee candidates receive two weeks of classroom and on-site training and must pass a comprehensive examination before being accepted. With the initial franchise fee of $15,000, the costs of start-up range from $100,000 to $200,000.

The company offers equipment leasing and a franchise fee assistance program for minorities. It also offers loans to existing franchisees for relocation, expansion, and remodeling. Franchisees pay a percentage of weekly sales (approximately 4.5 percent) into an advertising fund and an additional 8 percent royalty on all sales. The company provides national and regional advertising.

The Franchise Boom

Although franchising has been around since the Singer Sewing Machine Company first used it in the 1850s, its popularity has exploded in recent years. Many different kinds of businesses have been franchised, such as fast-food restaurants, auto repair shops, motels, health clubs, and hair salons.

Women and minorities have been especially drawn to franchises as a relatively low-capital way to become entrepreneurs. Recognizing this, Burger King, Pizza Hut, Taco Bell, Kentucky Fried Chicken (KFC), and Baskin-Robbins all offer special financing and other incentives to recruit minority franchise owners. Other franchise programs have focused, with great success, on recruiting women.

Get the Stat!

As of 2013, the number of individual franchises in the United States is over 750,000 and growing. In the United States, franchising accounts for more than $800 billion in annual sales.

Pros of Franchising

The most significant advantage of becoming a franchise owner is the increased probability of success, given that franchise brands have positive track records and instant recognition in most communities. Other advantages include training and financing assistance, purchasing power, advertising and promotional support, and operating guidelines and management assistance.

Tech U

If you are interested in owning a franchise, or perhaps turning your business into a franchise one day, check out these online resources:

- The International Franchise Association: www.franchise.org
- American Association of Franchisees and Dealer: www.aafd.org
- Small Business Administration's Franchise Registry: www.franchiseregistry.com.

Good franchisors provide excellent start-up assistance to new franchisees, as well as ongoing education and support for established ones. In many cases, mandatory training and exams are required before a franchise is even granted to a franchisee. Franchisors may also require you to work at an established franchise to learn the ropes before granting you your own franchise. These requirements are intended to foster franchisee success.

Franchisors may also help you find a great location. In some cases, franchisors provide financing support, in the form of application assistance, agreements with third-party lenders, or direct financing.

INSTANT RECOGNITION

A strong advantage of purchasing a franchise is the instant name and brand recognition that a well-known and reputable franchisor has to offer. A new Starbucks in the neighborhood has the instant recognition that a business called Kiki's Koffee would not.

With a franchise, the name and image are well established and widely understood. You purchase the use of the company's logo, trademark, and advertising, as well as the physical design, layout, and décor that ensure this recognition.

PURCHASING POWER

As a franchisee you will benefit from the purchasing power of the franchisor to get volume discounts from established vendors. Because franchisees are part of a large group of customers for any one vendor, they have more clout with respect to pricing, delivery terms, and product quality.

In addition, the costs of research, prototype creation, and testing are distributed among a far greater number of parties than for a stand-alone business. The cost savings will help offset the franchise fees and royalties you will pay.

ADVERTISING AND PROMOTIONAL SUPPORT

The quality and quantity of advertising support is one of the most valuable aspects of franchising. Franchisors engage advertising and public relations firms to create strong, memorable, and effective national and regional advertising campaigns. They handle the national and regional media purchasing. Franchisors also provide you with templates and promotional materials for local use.

Sometimes franchisees may be required to pay a **cooperative advertising fee,** which goes into a shared advertising fund.

OPERATING GUIDELINES AND ASSISTANCE

Franchisors also provide ongoing operating training; assistance with regulatory compliance, site selection, and development; product research and development; and technology.

Learn the Lingo

You may have seen some interesting twists on franchising lately. One trend is **piggybacking marketing,** a low-cost market entry strategy in which two or more firms represent one another's complementary (but non-competing) products in their respective markets. Another is **co-branding,** which involves two franchises such as Baskin-Robbins and Dunkin' Donuts sharing locations and resources, or two or more businesses marketing a product together, and including all their brand names on a single product or service.

Another is **conversion franchising,** which is the folding of an existing stand-alone business or local chain into a franchise operation. If you happen to be the owner of a gourmet pizza shop, for example, and you're ready to take your business to the next level, you might consider turning it into a Two Boots Pizzeria—a gourmet franchise that has branched out from its New York City home to Nashville, Baltimore, and other locations.

Cons of Franchising

Franchising provides a higher probability of business success, but success is not guaranteed and is not without some cons.

CONSTRAINTS ON CREATIVITY AND FREEDOM

If you want to be an entrepreneur to break away from corporate-style management and supervision, you may not like running a franchise. Franchisees are required to comply with many rules and processes. Products and services may not be altered, added, or dropped without permission. Even pricing, layout, and design of the franchise outlet are typically defined by the franchisor.

Although the formula provided by the franchise guarantees brand recognition, eases the issues of start-up development, and ensures ongoing support, it does remove the creativity and freedom that many entrepreneurs crave. You will have to decide whether the trade-off is right for you.

Try It!

The Small Business Administration has a five-minute questionnaire you can complete at www.sba.gov to help you determine whether franchising might be a good fit for you.

FRANCHISING COSTS

The typical franchisee can expect to pay start-up fees that range from about $3,300 for Jan-Pro to more than a million for a McDonald's outlet. Ongoing costs generally include royalties averaging between 3 and 7 percent of your revenue.

In addition, cooperative advertising fees of 1 to 5 percent (or a flat fee) are due periodically. Some franchisors also require franchisees to spend a minimum amount on local advertising.

Additional start-up costs include the legal costs required for franchise agreement review, and any required plant, property, equipment, inventory, or marketing requirements.

Be wary of franchisors that have a track record of high turnover among franchisees and a reputation for "churning" their franchises for the fees. A quick Internet search will help you weed out such companies.

STANDARDS AND TERMINATION

Franchisors have standards and obligations with which franchisees and prospective franchisees must comply—both initially and long term. Start-up standards may include specific types of experience and skills, as well as net worth and liquidity requirements.

Some of the more established and successful franchisors require less education and experience prior to becoming a franchisee because of their highly developed and effective training programs. For example, Circle K, Jani-King, and Liberty Tax do not require specific industry experience, but do want general business experience.

Home-based franchises have far lower net worth and liquidity requirements than stores or restaurants. Jan-Pro requires you to have a net worth of $1,000 to $14,000. At the other end of the spectrum, Dunkin' Donuts requires you to have a net worth of $1.5 million and liquid assets of $750,000, and requires a potential franchisee to commit to opening a minimum of five stores.

In addition, as a franchise owner, you are expected to meet certain sales targets and comply with ongoing performance standards, and you can lose your franchise if you do not comply. Franchisors may conduct periodic inspections, announced or unannounced, to evaluate compliance and conditions of the unit. Franchisees that stray from the company formula, fail to comply with quality standards, or do not pay their fees are subject to termination and repurchase. Franchisors cannot afford to tarnish their brands with underperforming or noncompliant franchises.

A Word of Caution

Before you decide to either franchise your business or become a franchisee, consult with a franchise attorney and do extensive research. Some eager franchisees have had bad experiences with franchisors who open too many franchises in an area, or fail to hold up their end of the franchise agreement.

Before investing in a franchise, talk to other franchisees of the company you are researching. Ask questions such as: Are you happy with your sales? Are you satisfied with the level of support, training, and advertising provided by the franchisor? Get the answers to all your questions before you agree to become a franchisee.

Visit the International Franchise Association website at www.franchise.org. Find a franchise organization that is unfamiliar to you. Research the following information about the franchisor:

- When did it begin offering franchises?

- How many company-owned units does it have?

- What are its initial financial requirements (start-up fee, net worth, liquid resources)?

- What type of franchisor is it (product or trade name or business format)?

Pros and Cons of Franchising Your Business

If you have created a business that can be replicated, there are two ways to expand geographically: either by opening multiple units that your company owns and operates, or by franchising the business. You'll want to open at least one other company-owned location before attempting to franchise. This helps prove that your business concept and operations are repeatable.

Let's look at some pros and cons of going the franchising route. First, the pros:

1. **Increased Revenue:** The franchisor earns a substantial up-front fee and regular royalty payments from each franchise.

2. **New Locations Without Financial Responsibility:** The franchisee, not the franchisor, takes on the financial responsibilities for loans, leases, and other expenses needed to get a franchise unit up and running.

3. **Franchisee Investment:** Because franchisees invest their own money, they are highly motivated to make their franchise units profitable. This may not be the case for company-hired managers who run company units. Also, company-hired managers may quit at any time. A franchise agreement requires a franchisee to commit to a specific number of years.

4. **Limited Liability:** A franchisor is not directly liable (legally and financially responsible) for the acts of the franchisee's employees, or accidents that take place on franchisee premises.

5. **Builds Brand Awareness:** Franchising builds brand awareness for your products or services.

Potential problems with franchising your business include:

1. **Regulatory and Legal Requirements:** In order to franchise your business, you must comply with substantial government regulations and legal restrictions.

2. **Extensive Preparation:** Preparing a business for franchise and finding and training qualified franchisees is time-consuming.

3. **Substantial Up-Front Investment:** The expenses involved in setting up and developing a franchise have to be paid before a single franchise fee is ever earned.

4. **Time-Consuming:** The franchisor must prepare a thorough and detailed operations manual and provide technical, marketing, and other forms of support throughout the franchise arrangement.

5. **Requires Certain Types of Businesses:** Franchising can be successful only for businesses that are in solid financial condition, easily duplicated, and not dependent on the personal characteristics of their owners. A business owner with a struggling business shouldn't consider franchising. Likewise, a business whose success is due primarily to its owner's personal contacts, charisma, or skills isn't a good candidate for franchising.

An Entrepreneur Like You

Wing Lam, Ed Lee, and Mingo Lee
WAHOO'S FISH TACO
www.wahoos.com

Before it became a successful franchise chain, Wahoo's Fish Taco was a small California restaurant born from three brothers' craving for fish tacos.

Growing up in Brazil and California, Wing Lam, Ed Lee, and Mingo Lee learned a lot about running a business by helping out in their family's Chinese restaurant. After discovering fish tacos while surfing in Mexico, the three brothers combined their love of surfing culture and their restaurant experience into an entrepreneurial venture of their own.

They opened the first Wahoo's Fish Taco in 1988, and decorated it with donations from local surf businesses. The food was a combination of the Brazilian, Mexican, and Asian flavors the brothers loved. The restaurant quickly became popular because of its unique, fresh, and healthy food. Today, there are more than fifty Wahoo's franchise locations in California, Colorado, Texas, and Hawaii.

Wahoo's Comes to Hawaii

Wahoo's first Hawaiian franchise came about in a roundabout way. While working in Los Angeles for the Angels baseball team, Stephanie Pietsch met Wing Lam by chance, and a business friendship developed. Stephanie's brother Mike and sister Noel also liked the Wahoo's franchise concept. Born and raised in Honolulu, all three siblings thought a Wahoo's restaurant would do well in Hawaii's surfing-oriented culture.

The Pietsches invited Wing and his brothers to Hawaii for a surfing trip and asked to be considered as franchisees. Even though the Pietsches' restaurant experience was limited, their knowledge of the local area, and Stephanie's extensive sports-marketing background, gave them an edge. The Pietsches opened their Wahoo's restaurant in 2006.

Wahoo's uses a very hands-on approach with its franchisees. The company provides mandatory training for one month. Close communication continues after that via telephone calls and visits from Wing. Wahoo's open-door policy allows for plenty of give-and-take discussions between franchisor and franchisee. According to Mike Pietsch, "Franchising is a good way to get into business because there are systems already in place." Stephanie adds, "The franchise provides a support system so there's a resource for asking questions, training, and growing the business."

Learning Valuable Lessons

The Pietsch-owned franchise was an immediate success, with customers lining up clear around the restaurant. "The first six months were a blur," Noel recalls. "We were doing better than we ever expected, but at a frantic pace." After only five months, the Honolulu-based franchise became a top franchise for Wahoo's Fish Taco.

Keeping the restaurant staffed with quality employees was very difficult in Hawaii's tight labor market, though. During the first year and a half, almost the entire staff turned over about three times.

"Now," Noel says, "we are rarely hiring because we have a solid team of people who really want to be here and work hard at what they do." Stephanie adds, "We really learned to work on our efficiency. We're setting goals and controlling what we can, be it labor or food costs."

Marketing the Business

The Wahoo's franchise chain targets customers who participate in extreme sports, such as surfing, skateboarding, and snowboarding. A much larger market segment is made up of those who simply want to live vicariously through others who are living a sports lifestyle.

Wahoo's encourages their franchisees to use regional sports and charity events to help market their businesses. The Pietsches' restaurant sponsors many surfing and body-boarding events. Noel remarks, "We support the youth a lot because if we get them eating at Wahoo's, they'll do it the rest of their lives."

To help grow their business, the Pietsch team opened a catering division. To promote it, they take free food samples to the offices of local companies. The Pietsches also came up with the idea, endorsed by Wahoo's, to place a lunch wagon at a local beach. These ideas help generate revenue with lower overhead costs than adding an additional restaurant would require. The initial franchise fee is $35,000 for the first restaurant and $27,500 for each additional one. The ongoing royalty fee is 5 percent of gross sales, paid weekly. Also, each franchisee must allocate 2 percent of gross sales for marketing and advertising. Wahoo's estimates that the cost of building a brand-new restaurant will range between $425,000 and $715,000, depending on store location and size, materials used, and other local factors.

Think Like an Entrepreneur

1. Why did the Pietsches decide to purchase a Wahoo's Fish Taco franchise rather than start a restaurant on their own?
2. Name something the Pietsches could have done better to make their business start-up go more smoothly.
3. What does the Pietsch-owned franchise do on an ongoing basis to maintain and grow success?

PART 6
HARVEST YOUR BUSINESS

CHAPTER 20

EXIT STRATEGIES

SALES, MERGERS, IPOS, AND OTHER WAYS TO HARVEST WEALTH FROM YOUR BUSINESS

Don't let the opinions of the average man sway you.
Dream and he thinks you're crazy. Succeed, and he thinks
you're lucky. Acquire wealth, and he thinks you're greedy.
Pay no attention. He simply doesn't understand.

—Robert G. Allen

As you learned in the previous chapter, there are many ways to grow your business. But what if you want to leave your business, or create a new business? Many entrepreneurs have made their fortunes by starting a small business, selling it, and using the money to create a new business—and then selling that business to raise capital to start another business.

In this chapter, you'll learn about some exit strategies for leaving your business and harvesting as much cash from it as possible that you can use for your next endeavor—whether that is going to school, starting your next business, or supporting a cause that is important to you.

One of the goals of owning a business is to build personal wealth. In fact, business ownership provides a unique opportunity for doing so. Regular profits earned during the lifetime of a business can provide a very good income and a comfortable living for the owner. But when an entrepreneur leaves his or her business, a much more valuable asset is involved—the accumulated and potential worth of the business itself.

WHEN TO HARVEST YOUR BUSINESS

Believe it or not, you need to start thinking about your exit strategies when you write your first business plan! If you plan to show people your business plan in order to interest them in investing in your business, they will want to know what your plan is for **harvesting** the business one day—because that is the day they could make a lot of money.

Ways to harvest your business might include selling it to a private buyer, making an initial public offering (IPO) of your stock on the stock market, or merging with another company. It usually takes at least ten years to build a company of sufficient value to harvest.

Harvesting differs from replication in that, once the business is harvested, the entrepreneur is usually no longer involved. Instead, he or she walks away with a portion of the business's value as cash or stock, or a combination of the two. In the case of a merger, the founding entrepreneur may work in the new business created by the merger—typically only for a specified time period.

Not every business can be harvested. Some are loaded with debt or have not created a product or service of lasting value. The entrepreneur can only leave such a business via **liquidation,** which means to sell all the business's assets for cash.

HOW TO VALUE A BUSINESS

If you are interested in selling your business, first you will have to determine its value. Selling a business can take months or even years. The new owner may insist that the old owner stay for a while after the deal is closed to help smooth the transition process. A business owner must consider these possibilities when selling a business.

The condition of the business and the economy are also important in timing when to sell. The business will be worth more if it's growing and thriving when it goes up for sale. It needs to be operating smoothly and should not be dependent on the owner's extensive day-to-day involvement. Overall economic conditions are also important. A business will probably sell more quickly and for more money when the national and local economies are doing well.

Business valuation is both an art and a science. A business that is profitable and likely to be so in the future can be sold for a sum that represents not only what it is earning today but what it will earn tomorrow. This is called its **net present value**. This is why businesses typically sell for several times their annual net income.

Learn the Lingo

The goal of business valuation is to arrive at a **fair market value,** which, according to the IRS, is "the price at which property would change hands between a willing buyer and willing seller, neither under any compulsion to buy or sell and both having reasonable knowledge of the relevant facts."

There are many ways to estimate the net present value of a business. Value, after all, is subjective, meaning it is subject to an individual's opinion or preferences.

Here are some methods entrepreneurs use to estimate the value of a business:

- **Comparison:** If you are looking to sell your dry-cleaning company, find out what buyers have paid for other dry-cleaning stores in your area.
- **Benchmarks:** In most industries, there are one or two key benchmarks used to help value a business. For gas stations, it might be barrels of gas sold per week; for a dry cleaner, it might be the number of shirts laundered per week.
- **Net Earnings:** Look at a multiple of net earnings. One rule of thumb says a business can sell for around three to five times its annual net earnings. If the business earns $100,000 net profit per year, for example, it could be expected to sell for at least $300,000.

Super Success Story

Stewart Butterfield and Caterina Fake launched Flickr in early 2004 and sold it just over one year later to Yahoo! The sale price was $35 million in cash.

It would appear that the couple harvested their company very quickly, but the story begins several years earlier.

Flickr is an online site that hosts images and videos and is most widely known and used for its photo-sharing capacity. Flickr was actually created by Stewart and Caterina, however, using tools for an online game, Game Neverending, which was never launched.

Fake recognized that the photo-sharing technology was more marketable than the game, and they developed Flickr instead.

The sale to Yahoo! required the couple to remain with the company for three years after the sale. After the three years were up, Caterina founded and became chief product officer at Hunch, an Internet start-up that provided recommendations on a multitude of user-generated topics. She is a board member and investor in Etsy, has written a book about start-ups, and continues blogging on Caterina.net.

In addition, Caterina has invested in 20x200, Small Batch, Flowgram, Maya's Mom, and DailyBooth. Stewart has cofounded Tiny Speck and invested in Flowgram, Etsy, and Rouxbe.

The Science of Valuation

There are three primary methods that buyers and sellers use to value a business: book value, future earnings, and market-based value. In practice, these three methods are often used concurrently, and all provide helpful perspectives on a company's value.

1. **Book Value (Assets − Liabilities = Net Worth).** This is the most common method for computing a company's value. Just subtract its liabilities from its assets. This method doesn't take into account, however, a company's potential to earn money in the future.

2. **Future Earnings.** This method considers not only a company's book value, but also its estimated future earnings. It is most useful for companies that are growing quickly, because in the case of a fast-growing company, past earnings are not accurate reflections of future performance.

3. **Market-Based (Comparable P/E Ratios × Estimated Future Net Earnings = Market-Based Value).** In this approach, the company's estimated future earnings are multiplied by the price/earnings (P/E) ratio of comparable companies with stock trading on the stock market. The P/E ratio is determined by dividing a company's stock price by its earnings per share. This method is effective because of its simplicity, but only works if there are similar companies with which to compare the business.

Despite the sophistication of these three techniques, they are really just estimates. In the end, it will be the entrepreneur's job to use negotiation to get the highest price possible for his or her business.

Tech U

If you want to sell your business, you can list it on www.BizBuySell.com or www.BizQuest .com. These sites send their registered users emails alerting them to businesses for sale.

Goodwill

All the valuation methods described here deal with aspects of a business that can be easily calculated. But one thing can't be calculated: goodwill. **Goodwill** is a catchall term for the intangible positive aspects of a business, such as its good reputation in the community, a great location, talented employees, brand awareness, intellectual property, and excellent relationships with suppliers and customers.

This is where the art side of valuation comes in—because there's no sure way to measure goodwill, yet it can be an important factor in determining the selling price of a business.

CREATING WEALTH BY SELLING A PROFITABLE BUSINESS

As noted above, a successful small business can usually be sold for between three and five times its yearly net profit. If your business's net profit for one year is $10,000, you should be able to get at least $30,000 (3 × $10,000).

If you are in business for three years, however, and increase your net profit each year, your business will be worth even more.

If your company earns $10,000 in year one, $25,000 in year two, and $60,000 in year three, it could be valued at $180,000 by applying the future earnings rule of thumb.

A business with increasing yearly net profit will be considered more valuable than a business with earnings that stay the same each year.

Math Moment

You have received two offers to buy your business, which has a book value of $93,500 and annual earnings of $108,500. Company A has offered to pay $20,000 plus four times the book value. Company B will pay $23,500 plus three times annual earnings. How much is each company offering?*

---

* Answers: $394,000, $349,000

MORE HARVESTING OPTIONS

There other exit strategies besides selling your business. Here are five!

1. **Increase Free Cash Flow:** For the first seven to ten years that you operate your business, you will want to reinvest as much profit into the company as you can, in order to grow. Once the business is well established, and you are ready to exit, you can begin investing only the amount of cash needed to keep the business effective in its current target markets. You can start taking the rest of the cash that the business generates as profit for yourself.

ADVANTAGES

- You retain ownership of the firm with this strategy.
- You do not have to seek a buyer.

DISADVANTAGES

- You will need an accountant to help you time your cash withdrawals so that you don't pay more tax than necessary.
- It can take a long time to execute this exit strategy.

2. **Management Buyout (MBO):** In this strategy, you sell your business to the managers you have hired. They raise the money to buy it from you using their savings and/or you can lend them money to buy it.

ADVANTAGES

- If the business has value, the managers often do want to buy it.
- The entrepreneur has the emotional satisfaction of selling to people he knows and has trained.

DISADVANTAGES

- If the managers need a large loan from you to buy the company, they may owe you money for a long time or never fully repay you.
- If their final payment to you depends on the company's earnings during the last few quarters, the managers may have an incentive to attempt to lower the business's profits.

3. **Employee Stock Ownership Plan (ESOP):** The business establishes an employee stock ownership plan (ESOP), which enables employees to buy stock in the company, typically at a discount (a better price than the stock is selling for on the stock market). When you are ready to exit your business, the ESOP borrows money and uses the cash to buy your stock—essentially buying you out of the company. As the loan is paid off, the stock is added to the employee benefit fund, which employees can sell when they retire.

ADVANTAGES

- The ESOP has some special tax advantages; among them: The company can deduct both the principal and interest payments on the loan, and the dividends paid on any stock held in the ESOP are considered a tax-deductible expense.

DISADVANTAGES

- This is not a good strategy if you do not want the employees to have control of the company. The ESOP must extend to all employees and requires the entrepreneur to show the company's financial records to the employees, as well.

4. **Merger or Acquisition:** Selling your company for **acquisition** to another business or forming a **merger** with another company can be successful exit strategies. In 2012, Facebook bought the photo-sharing app Instagram for $1 billion, and twenty-seven-year-old Instagram founder/CEO Kevin Systrom, who owned 40 percent of the company, made $400 million. As for the other $600 million: $100 million went to cofounder Mike Krieger; $100 million went to the venture capital firm Andreessen Horowitz; $100 went to VC firm Baseline Ventures; $180 million went to VC firm Benchmark Capital; $20 million went to three private individual investors; and the final $100 million was split up by Instagram's twelve remaining employees.

ADVANTAGES

- This strategy can finance growth that the company could not achieve on its own; the entrepreneur can either exit the company at the time of the merger or acquisition, or be part of the growth and exit later.

DISADVANTAGES

- This can be an emotionally draining strategy, with a lot of ups and downs during negotiations; a sale can take over a year to finalize.

5. **Initial public offering (IPO).** "Going public" means you will sell an initial public offering (IPO) of your company's shares in the stock market. It is a complex process that requires choosing an investment banker to develop the IPO, making sales presentations to brokers and investors nationally, and, finally, offering your stock on the market and holding your breath as you watch its price go up—or not.

    Facebook's 2012 IPO, for example, went surprisingly badly. The IPO was the biggest in Internet history, over $104 billion. First, the tech stock exchange NASDAQ, where the sale was being held, suffered a computer malfunction during the first hours of the IPO that led to tens of millions of dollars in trades being wrongly placed. Next, Facebook executives were accused of illegally leaking information about Facebook's earnings to industry insiders before the IPO. Then, following the IPO, Facebook's stock performed poorly, losing over a quarter of its value in less than a month and falling to less than half its IPO value in three months.

    Very few entrepreneurial firms ever complete an IPO but for those that do, it can bring significant financial rewards.

ADVANTAGES

- If your business is hot, this can be a very profitable way to harvest it. The market may place a large premium on your company's value.

DISADVANTAGES

- An IPO is a very exciting but stressful, all-consuming, and very expensive way to harvest a company. It requires a lot of work from the entrepreneur.

MAKING YOUR INVESTORS HAPPY

You are not the only one who will want to profit from exiting your business one day. If you have any investors, they deserve to recoup their investments (and then some!), too. This is why your exit strategy must be spelled out in your business plan.

If you simply claim in your business plan that your business will go public one day, you will probably get a skeptical reaction from potential investors. They understand that you cannot guarantee exactly how they will recoup their investment, but you do need to show them that you understand that for the vast majority of small businesses, going public is a fantasy.

Instead, demonstrate your understanding of exit strategies by thinking through the four possibilities below. Include the one that fits best in your business plan. Which one do you think best describes what you intend to make happen for your business?

1. **Acquisition:** Do you believe you are creating a business that someone would want to buy one day? Your exit strategy could be that you will be focused throughout the creation and operation of your business on making sure it will be valuable for one of your suppliers, or a major competitor, to buy one day. A fair sale price, based on your business's annual net profit, should allow the original investors to realize a good return on their investment.

2. **Earn Out:** To use an earn-out strategy, you will need to include projected cash flow statements in your business plan showing that your business will eventually earn a strong positive cash flow. Your exit strategy will be to use the cash to buy your investors' shares of the business from them at a higher price than they paid for them.

3. **Debt/Equity Exchange:** If your investors will be lending you money, you can offer to eventually trade equity for portions of the debt. This will slowly reduce the interest you will have to pay over time, and will give your investors a share of the business (and its profits!).

4. **Merge:** With a merger, two companies join together to share their strengths. One company might have an extensive customer base, for example, and the other might possess a distribution channel the first company needs. Or perhaps each company is doing well in different geographical areas, and a merger would open up these respective markets to the other's products/services. Regardless, cash will change hands and the original investors can make their shares available for sale to complete the merger.

Your business plan should spell how long you expect it to take before your investors will be able to cash out, and you will need to include research and financial statements to prove that your exit strategy is viable.

Of the thousands of new ventures launched every year in the United States, only a small percentage will ever go public. Yet, many business plans presented to angel investors and venture capitalists cite going public as the primary exit strategy. Be more realistic than that, and potential investors will take you seriously.

EXITING A BUSINESS THAT ISN'T DOING SO WELL

Not all business owners have the luxury of exiting a business that's thriving. In fact, many small businesses limp along or even fail. That's nothing to be ashamed of.

Liquidation

If you want to exit your business and it's not doing well enough to attract any buyers, you can always liquidate it. This means sell the business's tangible assets (furniture, computers, machinery, and so forth) for cash. You can use this cash to pay back your investors and pay off creditors.

Learn the Lingo

Cash is considered **liquid** because you can immediately use it to buy things or pay off debt. Certain investments, such as Treasury bills, are also considered liquid because they can be sold and turned into cash within twenty-four hours. Assets or investments that take longer than twenty-four hours to turn into cash—such as real estate—are considered **illiquid**.

Bankruptcy

Bankruptcy may be the best option if you are really having trouble paying your bills and can no longer keep your business open. Bankruptcy is the legal process by which a person or a business declares its inability or impaired ability to pay its debts.

Bankruptcy secures some breathing room for businesses that are no longer able to pay the bills. The process is meant to ensure fair treatment of creditors as well as the debtor.

A company that enters the bankruptcy process may be forced to liquidate some assets to pay its creditors. The company may also be required to reorganize, which means it will have to come up with a plan to stay in business and do a better job of paying its bills that the bankruptcy court will approve.

Many companies, large and small, have filed for and emerged from bankruptcy.

General Motors, Macy's, and Delta Airlines have all been through bankruptcies and reorganizations, and have emerged as stronger, fitter, more competitive companies.

Bankruptcy does have a very negative effect on your credit rating, so it is truly a last-resort strategy. But sometimes it can be the best way to solve your problems, treat your creditors fairly, and move on to better days.

The Bankruptcy Reform Acts of 1978 and 2005 govern the eight "chapters" under which bankruptcy may be filed. Chapters 7, 11, and 13 generally apply to small businesses, with Chapters 7 and 11 used the most.

CHAPTER 7: LIQUIDATION

This form of bankruptcy requires the business to identify all assets and liabilities, turn the assets over to a trustee (court-appointed or elected by creditors), and allow the trustee to sell them. The funds are used to pay creditors. Once the funds are used, any remaining debts are discharged (no longer owed); and the business is officially dissolved.

It is important to note that debtors cannot avoid the liquidation of assets by transferring ownership to others just ahead of filing for protection. In fact, any transfers of property within the two years prior to filing may be ignored, and the assets can be made a part of the bankruptcy case. Deliberate transfer of assets to avoid debt repayment is a form of fraud, and the entire Chapter 7 bankruptcy petition can be thrown out by the judge if fraud is suspected.

CHAPTER 11: REORGANIZATION

This form of bankruptcy can be a lifeline for a company. Businesses that file for Chapter 11 are allowed to continue to operate under court supervision while they pay off some or all of their debts. Creditors cannot file legal claims against the company while it creates its reorganization plan and schedules debt repayment, or negotiates settlements on the amounts owed.

CHAPTER 13: INDIVIDUAL DEBT REORGANIZATION

This is the consumer version of Chapter 11, and is for individual debtors with secured debts of less than $922,975, or unsecured debts below the sum of $307,675. A sole proprietorship would file for Chapter 13. The repayment plan may include full or partial payment of debts through installments, taking into consideration the debtor's income expectations, and must be approved by a bankruptcy judge. Repayment typically occurs over a three- to five-year period, and can help the filer avoid being forced to sell personal property such as a house or car to pay debt.

THINK: WHAT WOULD YOU DO WITH WEALTH?

If you do gain wealth from exiting your business one day, what will you do with it?

Many entrepreneurs use their wealth to start more businesses. In this way, over time, individuals have built great fortunes. Others use their money to go back to school. Still others become philanthropists and focus on helping others.

The most important lesson entrepreneurship can teach is that you have the power to think for yourself and to create an exciting and fulfilling life. When you use your imagination and skills to grow a small business, you prove to yourself that you can create something real and valuable from an idea.

Whether you become a lifelong entrepreneur, or choose another career entirely, remember that you will always be working for yourself.

Never stop asking yourself:

- What kind of life do I want?
- How can I make my community a better place?
- What makes me happy?
- How can I make others happy?

Use your imagination to grow not only the business of your dreams, but also the life of your dreams. Dare to dream!

An Entrepreneur Like You

Ben Cohen and Jerry Greenfield

BEN & JERRY'S

www.benjerry.com

Ben Cohen and Jerry Greenfield were in their twenties when they started selling homemade ice cream out of a converted gas station in Burlington, Vermont. They were young entrepreneurs who never imagined that their simple little business, Ben & Jerry's, could ever grow into an international brand. Twenty years later, the business had evolved into a multimillion-dollar company with worldwide franchises from Boston to Tokyo to Paris.

This upstart company became famous for putting out offbeat flavors, including Bovinity Divinity, Chubby Hubby, and Cherry Garcia, and for its colorful marketing campaigns. For instance, when Ben & Jerry's decided to hire a new CEO, it held a "Yo, I'm Your CEO!" contest and invited customers to submit application essays for the job. The company holds a yearly "Free Cone Day," giving out over a half million ice cream cones on that day to happy customers.

Investing in the Business . . . and in Philanthropy

From the start, Cohen and Greenfield rejected a profits-only, single-bottom-line approach to managing their business. They chose to invest some of their profits into socially responsible causes and business practices.

They established a policy of contributing 7.5 percent of the company's pre-tax earnings to charity. In 1991, they paid $500,000 to help offset losses suffered by local Vermont milk suppliers during a time of intense price fluctuation in the dairy industry. They also spent many years perfecting their "eco-pint" ice cream container made from unbleached paperboard and nontoxic color dyes.

Unhappy Shareholders

By 2000, Ben & Jerry's was a publicly owned company traded on the NASDAQ and was generating more than $200 million in annual sales with a net income of $3.3 million. But their shareholders were not happy. The stock had climbed to $20 but some shareholders wanted to earn a better return.

A persistent challenge faced by the company was that it did not own its own distribution channels—it had to go through wholesalers to get its pints into grocery stores. Some stockholders wanted to see Ben & Jerry's acquired by a large company that did own distribution channels, to help bring down costs along the distribution chain and improve the price of Ben & Jerry's ice cream in stores.

Takeover

By the end of the year, negotiations were under way between Ben & Jerry's corporate board and Unilever, a $52 billion European-based consumer goods firm. As word spread about the impending sale, grassroots "Save Ben & Jerry's" protest campaigns sprouted all over the United States. Loyal consumers who valued the company's commitment to social responsibility feared that a larger corporate entity would not continue to support causes such as saving the rain forests or employing homeless people.

Ben Cohen and Jerry Greenfield themselves opposed the Unilever sale. Vermont politicians weighed in and broadcast their view that the company should preserve its independence. After all, Ben & Jerry's had created many jobs in Vermont, and the company's policy of buying Vermont-only milk had been a major boon for local farmers. Despite these protests, the company was sold to Unilever in 2000 for $326 million, or $43.60 per share.

How did this happen? According to corporate charter law, company boards are required to put shareholders' interests first. In the case of Ben & Jerry's, Unilever offered to pay more than double the company's stock price, which was $21 per share at the time. The board decided that this was an offer it could not refuse.

An Uncertain Future

Under the terms of the deal, both Ben and Jerry remained employees of the company at annual salaries of $200,000 each. Ben Cohen resigned soon after the sale, however. Since his exit, he has devoted his significant wealth and prominence to social and political causes.

Jerry Greenfield remained at the company as vice chairman of the board and director of mobile promotions. He and Ben Cohen are still friends, and the two ice cream icons actively promote socially responsible business practices. Today, Cohen is "head stamper" at StampStampede.org—a campaign to amend the U.S. Constitution to reduce the influence of money on elections. Greenfield, meanwhile, brings his popular "Evening of Entrepreneurial Spirit, Social Responsibility, and Radical Business Philosophy" event to campuses around the country. In 2012, Social Venture Network honored them at the SVN Hall of Fame Celebration for their work as visionary social entrepreneurs.

A new CEO was hired by Unilever to manage the company's operations. Unilever promised that it would continue Ben & Jerry's commitment to social responsibility, but many were skeptical about this. Several months after Unilever took the helm, Ben Cohen commented to the *New York Times* that "What Ben & Jerry's used to be is one of these smaller 'social values led' businesses. What Ben & Jerry's is in the process of becoming is an entity inside a larger business, trying to infuse those values into that business. We expect that it will be a long and winding road."

As mentioned in chapter 4, however, Unilever actually encouraged Ben & Jerry's to seek B Corporation status, which it achieved in 2012. Today, Ben & Jerry's still stands for progressive values—with some corporate setbacks. The company no longer uses its eco-pint containers, for example, but on the other hand it supports legislation to require the labeling of food products that contain genetically modified organisms (GMOs) and has pledged to make all its products non-GMO by 2014.

Think Like an Entrepreneur

1. Unilever bought Ben & Jerry's for more than double the company's stock price. When Ben & Jerry's was sold, its stock price was $21/share. Unilever purchased the shares at $43.60. Why would Unilever pay that much?

2. When the sale went through, Jerry Greenfield sold his 900,000 shares in the company at $43.60 per share, and Ben Cohen got the same price for his 220,000. How much did Ben & Jerry earn respectively from the sale? When they started their company in 1978, Ben and Jerry each invested $6,000. Calculate the return on investment for each.

3. Go online and conduct research on Ben & Jerry's. Is the company more profitable now under Unilever? Does it still contribute a percentage of its profits to charity? Identify three ways the company has changed since it was sold.

CHAPTER 21

INVEST NOW, LOVE YOUR LIFE LATER

UNDERSTANDING STOCKS, BONDS, AND THE MAGIC OF COMPOUND INTEREST

A goal is a dream with a deadline.

—Napoleon Hill, author of *Think and Grow Rich*

You know that you can work to earn money, but do you realize that your money can work for you? Investing is the use of money to make more money. If you learn to save and invest early in your life, you can create a financially strong future for yourself.

Putting your money to work for you is the essence of investing—and anyone can learn to do it well. Any dollar you aren't using to pay bills is money you can invest. In this chapter you'll learn some basic investing concepts so that you can start using the money you earn as an entrepreneur to build a great life!

THE MIRACLE OF COMPOUNDING

When John D. Rockefeller was a teenager in the mid-1800s, he lent $50 to a farmer. After a year, the farmer paid him back the $50, plus $3.50 in interest. Rockefeller compared that with the $1.12 he had earned hoeing potatoes for an entire week for another farmer, and he decided he'd rather be an investor than a farmer. "From that time on I was determined to make money work for me," Rockefeller wrote in his autobiography, *Random Reminiscences of Men and Events.*

Rockefeller soon discovered that he could make his money grow really fast if he reinvested his returns. This kind of reinvestment is called compounding. Compound interest is the interest you earn on your interest.

If you put $100 in an investment that earns 10 percent, for example, you will have $110 at the end of a year. At that point, you have a choice: You can spend the $10 you earned, or you can reinvest it for another year.

- If you spend the $10, you will have $110 at the end of the first year.
- If you reinvest the $10, you will earn 10 percent on $110. This comes out to $11, so, by the end of the second year, you will have $110 + $11= $121.

If you keep reinvesting your earnings for ten years, your original $100 will grow to $259.37. Without you doing any work at all!

To figure that, use a future value chart like the one on page 398. To calculate how much $1 will grow after a certain amount of time at a certain number of years, look on that chart.

The stock market has historically provided a return to investors of on average 10 percent per year. If you look under "10 percent" and across to 10 years, for example, you will see the number 2.5937. One dollar, therefore, would grow to $2.5937 after being invested for 10 years at 10 percent. If you've invested $100, just multiply $2.5937 by 100 and you will get $259.37.

Future Value of Money

The **future value of money** is the amount to which a given sum will increase over time through investment.

The Future Value of Money chart on the next page shows you how much one invested dollar will be worth over time at a given interest rate. Take a look at the

FUTURE VALUE OF MONEY

Periods (in years)	1%	2%	3%	4%	5%	6%	7%	8%	9%	10%	11%	12%
1	1.0100	1.0200	1.0300	1.0400	1.0500	1.0600	1.0700	1.0800	1.0900	1.1000	1.1100	1.1200
2	1.0201	1.0404	1.0609	1.0816	1.1025	1.1236	1.1449	1.1664	1.1881	1.2100	1.2321	1.2544
3	1.0303	1.0612	1.0927	1.1249	1.1576	1.1910	1.2250	1.2597	1.2950	1.3310	1.3676	1.4049
4	1.0406	1.0824	1.1255	1.1699	1.2155	1.2625	1.3108	1.3605	1.4116	1.4641	1.5181	1.5735
5	1.0510	1.1041	1.1593	1.2167	1.2763	1.3382	1.4026	1.4693	1.5386	1.6105	1.6851	1.7623
6	1.0615	1.1261	1.1941	1.2653	1.3401	1.4185	1.5007	1.5869	1.6771	1.7716	1.8704	1.9738
7	1.0721	1.1487	1.2299	1.3159	1.4071	1.5036	1.6058	1.7138	1.8280	1.9487	2.0762	2.2107
8	1.0829	1.1717	1.2668	1.3686	1.4775	1.5939	1.1782	1.8509	1.9926	2.1436	2.3045	2.4760
9	1.0937	1.1951	1.3048	1.4233	1.5513	1.6895	1.8385	1.9990	2.1719	2.3580	2.5580	2.7731
10	1.1046	1.2190	1.3439	1.4802	1.6209	1.7909	1.9672	2.1589	2.3674	2.5937	2.8394	3.1059
11	1.1157	1.2434	1.3842	1.5395	1.7103	1.8983	2.1049	2.3316	2.5084	2.8531	3.1518	3.4786
12	1.1268	1.2682	1.4258	1.6010	1.7959	2.0122	2.2522	2.5182	2.8127	3.1384	2.4985	3.8960
13	1.1381	1.2936	1.4685	1.6651	1.8057	2.1329	2.4098	2.7196	3.0658	3.4523	3.8833	4.3635
14	1.1495	1.3195	1.5126	1.7317	1.9799	2.2609	2.5785	2.9372	3.3417	3.7975	4.3104	4.8871
15	1.1610	1.3459	1.5580	1.8009	2.0789	2.3966	2.7590	3.1722	3.6425	4.1773	4.7846	5.4736

▲ This chart shows the future value of $1 over a period of years at a specified growth rate.

chart. Can you see that $1 invested for ten years at ten percent will grow to $2.59? (So $100 invested at ten percent for ten years will increase to $259.)

Risk Factors: Time and Liquidity

Two factors affect the risk associated with an investment:

- **Time.** The longer someone has your money, the greater the chance that your investment could somehow be lost. The longer you have to wait for the payback on your investment, the greater the return should be.
- **Liquidity.** As you remember from chapter 12, liquidity refers to the ability to convert assets into cash. You always want to know how liquid your investment is. Can you get your money out in 24 hours? Or do you have to commit your investment for a specified period?

How Compounding Works

Compounding is affected by variables such as:

1. **The Amount You Invest:** The more you invest, the greater the eventual value of your portfolio. Investing an extra $50 per month can

increase your wealth by hundreds of thousands of dollars given enough time.

2. **The Rate of Return You Earn:** You may not think there is a significant difference between a 10 percent and a 12 percent return, but over time there is. Let's say two twenty-year-olds, Max and Sara, each invest $5,000 each year until they reach retirement at age sixty-five. The first earns a 10 percent return, the second 12 percent. In the end, Max will retire with $3.6 million. Sara, on the other hand, will retire with $6.8 million, or nearly twice as much!

The magic of compounding happens only if you reinvest your interest:

- Jason earns 5 percent per year on his investment of $100,000. He spends that 5 percent on meals at gourmet restaurants. What does Jason have after ten years? Love handles and $100,000.

- Moniqua earns 5 percent per year on her investment of $100,000 and puts her interest income in a shoe box. She earned $5,000 per year on her investment for 10 years, so she earned $50,000 total in interest. Add that to her initial $100,000 investment, and Moniqua ended up with $150,000 in ten years.

- Tara also earns 5 percent per year on her investment of $100,000 and she reinvests her interest. Every dollar she invests will become $1.6289 dollars in ten years compounded at 5 percent. In ten years, she'll have $162,890.

I bet you're thinking, "Tara was really smart, but how did you figure out how much money she was going to have after ten years of compounding her interest?"

The Future Value Chart shows you how much one dollar will be worth over a certain time period if it is compounded at a given interest rate. In Tara's case, she let $100,000 compound at 5 percent over ten years. Run your finger down the left side of the chart under "Years" until you find "10." Now move your finger across that row until you're under "5%." Multiply that number by $100,000 and there's your answer.

Learn the Lingo

Compound interest is the money you earn on the interest you made in a previous period. It's interest on your interest. Compound interest enables your money to grow exponentially (a lot!).

TIME IS ON YOUR SIDE

The longer your money compounds, the richer you'll get. Letting time work for you is the key to growing your green. The earlier you start investing, the better off you'll be. In fact, the difference between someone who starts investing at age twenty-two and someone who waits until age twenty-eight is really dramatic, as illustrated here:

- Sirena invests $2,000 a year for six years at 12 percent, starting at age twenty-two. Her total investment after six years is $12,000.
- Jeryl spends her first six years out of college blowing her salary on facials and designer suits. But then she settles down and invests $2,000 a year for the next thirty-five years at 12 percent. Her total investment after thirty-five years is $70,000.

Get this—at age sixty-two, Sirena, who only invested $12,000, has earned $959,793. Jeryl, who invested $70,000, has earned $966,926. Sirena earned nearly as much as Jeryl even though she invested $58,000 less! Why? Because Sirena started early.

What's the moral of the story? All together now, kids: Start early. Let time work for you!

THE 10 PERCENT HABIT

In the likelihood that you're over the age of twenty-two, don't despair. (Between you and me, how many twenty-two-year-olds do you know who are investing in anything but having fun?) If you are in your early twenties, though, I hope you're feeling fired up enough to start investing—if only so you can spend your thirties feeling smug.

There's a great psychological advantage to starting early. It's easier to get into the investing habit when you're unencumbered by kids. You may be sharing an apartment and making a fairly low income, but you don't have to send anyone to college and you're certainly not staring down the barrel of retirement.

Try It!

An easy way to figure out how long it will take an investment to double is to use the **Rule of 72**. Take any fixed annual interest rate, and divide it into 72 (the average human life span nowadays). The result will be the number of years it will take your investment to double. If you expect to earn 6 percent, for example, divide 6 into 72. Your investment will double in twelve years!

Bear in mind that this formula is based on the assumption that the interest rate never changes.

No matter what your age, the sooner you get in the habit of investing 10 percent of every paycheck, the more time your investment plan will have to work. Why 10 percent? It's not a big chunk, but it's not insignificant either. Most people can find ways to cut their spending by 10 percent pretty easily.

THE RULE OF 72

Growth Rate	Years to "Double"
4%	18 Yrs
6%	12 Yrs
8%	9 Yrs
10%	7.2 Yrs
12%	6 Yrs

The government allows you to set up a retirement account called an **IRA (Individual Retirement Account)**. This type of investment is tax free, meaning that you typically won't have to pay taxes on the money in the account until you withdraw it. The goal is to save this money, allowing it to compound, so you'll have money after you retire.

One type of retirement account, the Roth IRA, can be a good choice for a young person because it allows you to make a one-time withdrawal of funds to buy a house. With the Roth, you can save not only for your retirement but for buying a house as well.

The government establishes a maximum amount of money that you are allowed to save in an IRA each year. To encourage people to save, the government has been steadily increasing that figure.

HOW TIME AFFECTS INVESTING

When talking about investing, time is simply how long you can let your investment program work. Time affects your investment decisions in two ways:

- The more time you have, the longer your investment has to compound.
- The more time you have, the more risk you can handle.

The single most important thing you can do for yourself as an investor is to develop a long-term horizon. This will inoculate you against persuasive pitches to buy the latest hot investment and prevent you from selling based on bits of news and rumors. "Just how long is long-term?" you ask. Think ten years or more.

"Risk" is defined as the potential for permanent loss of capital. One of the biggest influences upon the amount of risk involved in any investment is the amount of time you are financially and emotionally able to hold an investment. Let's take a look at how this time and risk relationship works in the stock market.

In the business world, "capital" refers to assets (cash, stocks, bonds, machinery, inventory, and so forth) that generate income. As you've already learned, stock is simply a share of ownership in a corporation. A stockholder owns a piece of a company. When you buy AT&T stock, for example, you become one of many owners of AT&T. This, in turn, entitles you to a share of AT&T's profits (or losses!).

That share is paid to stockholders as a dividend. Just like an interest payment, you can reinvest a dividend or spend it.

Learn the Lingo

Stocks are bought and sold on the stock market. The stock market doesn't exist as a physical place—stocks are traded at various stock exchanges, such as the New York Stock Exchange or the American Stock Exchange. The Dow Jones Industrial Average (DJIA) is an average of thirty well-known companies, such as AT&T and McDonald's, chosen by the editors of the *Wall Street Journal* to represent trends in the stock market.

Over time, the total return for stocks has averaged nearly twice that of risk-free government bonds and three times the inflation rate. Stocks are clearly worth the risk if you can afford to hold them for ten years or longer.

Every investing goal will have a different time frame based upon your personal goals. You might want to buy your first house in five years, for example, in which case your savings would need to be in investments that don't fluctuate significantly. Perhaps you just got married, and, although there might not be a child on the scene for a couple years, you want to begin a twenty-year savings plan for his or her college education. Under these circumstances, your investment choices are much broader.

In general, the less time you have to achieve your goal, the less risk you can take with your principal.

THE THREE BROAD INVESTMENT CLASSES

There are basically three broad classes of investments from which you can choose when you build your portfolio:

1. Stocks
2. Bonds
3. Cash (money market instruments)

Bonds are a form of debt financing. When you buy a bond you are lending money to a company for a specified length of time. In return, the company pays you interest.

Money market instruments are very liquid. This means they can be converted to cash easily and quickly. Because they are not very risky, they pay lower rates of interest than bonds and do not have the potential for growth of stocks.

Examples of money market instruments include:

- Certificates of deposit (CDs)
- Treasury bills

Stocks are riskier investments than money market instruments or bonds, but because they are riskier, they generate higher returns.

YOUR ALL-IMPORTANT EMERGENCY FUND

If you keep selling off your investments to cover your monthly bills or to pay for emergencies, you will never build wealth. Before you start investing, build up your savings. Get three to six months' worth of your expenses (rent, utilities, groceries, and so forth) into your savings account, so that if you lose a job or face an expensive emergency, you won't have to gut your investments. This is your **emergency fund**.

Hospitalizations, funerals, weddings, auto or home repairs, gifts, taxes, and so on, don't show up neatly on a calendar. They occur with little or no advance warning, and if you don't have funds set aside to cover them, you will go into debt. And going into debt can take the fun out of a happy event or make a sad one even sadder.

Your umbrella for those times when life drenches you with unexpected expenses is your emergency fund. This is the single most important thing you can do to secure your financial future, because an emergency fund ensures that you never have to touch your investments. They can keep on growing and compounding.

WHAT ABOUT CREDIT CARDS?

These days, once a person hits eighteen, he or she is inundated with tempting credit card offers. Please remember that a credit card is not free money; it's a loan—usually at a sky-high interest rate. You might be tempted to use credit cards to finance your business, but this is a bad idea. A really bad idea! Here's why:

- Credit card companies charge very high rates of interest and you will soon find yourself trying to pay off a mountain of debt.

- If you fail to make even one credit card payment, your interest rate may be jacked up even higher, and the credit card company may report you as a bad credit risk. This can destroy your chances of ever getting a loan to sustain your business, to buy a house, to go to school, or even to buy a car. Very humiliating!

- There is one excellent use for a credit card, however: Use it to make as many of your purchases as possible—and pay it off in full *every month*. The credit card company will send you, each month, a list of all your purchases. Use the list to keep an eye on your spending and to back up your financial records. The key phrase here, though, is "and pay it off in full *every month*."

   If you know you don't have the discipline to do this, don't get a credit card. Or, apply for an American Express card or another charge card that has to be paid off each month in order to avoid interest charges or fees.

Tech U

When you do start applying for investment accounts, charge cards, and other financial tools, watch out for **phishing**. This is an online scheme that involves defrauding someone with financial information by posing as a legitimate company, such as your bank, for example. Phishing can steal your identity, and your money.

Spammers use **spam bots**—programs that crawl the Internet to collect email addresses. Spam bots can get addresses from web pages, newsgroups, and chat-room conversations. This information can then be used to put together a mailing list.

With phishing, you receive an email that appears to be from a legitimate business, such as your bank, requesting that you verify certain information, such as your Social Security number or bank account number, by clicking on a hyperlink. Never do this! Your bank or any other financial institution will never ask you to give your Social Security number or bank account number via email.

If you do give away this information, it can be used for identity theft—someone can pretend to be you and use your financial information to make purchases.

Phishing emails often appear to be legitimate. They have the look of the institution, including the logo, and the "From" field appears to have the correct name. Hiding the origin of an email message—the information in the "From" field—is called **spoofing**. It's commonly used for spam email and phishing.

RETIREMENT PLANNING

Investing is about putting your money to work—so that one day you won't have to work anymore and can enjoy **retirement**. Upon leaving the workforce or retiring, most people support themselves with savings and with investments that provide income in the form of interest.

If your employer offers a **401(k) plan,** sign up at your first opportunity. A 401(k) is a retirement savings plan funded by employee contributions and (often) matching contributions from the employer. If you invest $1 into your 401(k), for example, your employer will match by also investing $1 into your plan. That's free money—take it!

If you do not have a 401(k) plan, divert some of your paycheck into an Individual Retirement Account or IRA. An IRA is an investment account into which you can place stock and other investments and allow them to grow until retirement without their earnings being taxed. There are tax penalties, however, for withdrawing money from an IRA before the legal retirement age.

Setting up automatic contributions to either one of these retirement vehicles at a young age will help you build wealth painlessly.

Let's say you invest $200 a month beginning at age twenty-five, and you earn 7 percent annually on that money. By the time you turn sixty-five, you will have about $525,000 saved up. If you wait until you're thirty-five to begin saving, assuming the same monthly investment and rate of return, you'll have amassed less than half that amount—about $244,000.

Start investing as soon as you possibly can. Let your youth work for you, and your investments will grow.

START INVESTING WITH MUTUAL FUNDS

Many types of investments are available, but stocks are among the most profitable over the long run. But what if you invest all your money in the stock of a great company—and that company goes bankrupt?

Stocks can be risky unless you can afford to buy a wide variety of stocks from many different high-quality companies. If you put all your money in General Motors stock, for example, and General Motors goes out of business, there goes all your money.

For this reason, many small investors buy shares of **mutual funds,** instead of individual stocks. A mutual fund is a company that pools together money from a large number of investors and invests in a wide variety of stocks, bonds, or other assets. The investors buy shares of the mutual fund, which helps them spread their money across a larger number of investments than they could buy on their own.

Buying shares of a mutual fund provides an investor with excellent **diversification**. Diversification is the spreading of money among many different investments in order to reduce risk. If you put all your money in one investment, and it fails, you lose all your money. If you diversify and put your money in a wide variety of investments, and one fails, you still keep much of your money. Mutual funds invest in a wide range of investments, providing diversification.

The Standard & Poor's 500 Stock Index, which tracks five hundred stocks in the American stock market, has earned an average rate of return of 11 percent since 1957. If you had invested $1,000 in a mutual fund that bought those five hundred stocks forty years ago, you would have $65,000 today—without having lifted a finger.

Read a Classic

If you invest $1 a day in an investment yielding 12 percent, you will have $1 million in fifty years. Your total investment would be only $18,000! Learn more in *Investing from Scratch: A Handbook for the Young Investor* by James Lowell.

Mutual fund companies will be delighted to send you information about investing in their funds. They can even set up programs that automatically deduct $50 or $100 from your savings account every month, so you don't even have to think about it. Here are a few mutual fund companies you can explore online:

- Vanguard Funds: www.vanguard.com
- T. Rowe Price: www.troweprice.com
- Janus Capital Group: www.janus.com

The calls are free, but if you are under the age of eighteen, you will need a parent or guardian to approve any investments you make.

If you get interested in the stock market and want to buy and sell individual stocks, I recommend you do so as a hobby, and still invest most of your money in well-diversified mutual funds.

To explore stock trading, check out E*TRADE (www.etrade.com) and Charles Schwab (www.schwab.com). These "discount brokers" offer lots of free research and trading tools for individual investors, with good discounts on trade commissions and other expenses that go along with stock trading.

Super Success Story

You can evaluate every decision you make by asking one simple question: "If I invest my money (or time) this way, will my return on my investment be satisfying?"

Going to college is an investment that can be analyzed in this way. You spend time and money to get an education because you expect that this investment will increase your ability to make money in the future.

Some young entrepreneurs, however, have decided to skip or postpone college and invest in starting businesses instead. Kenneth Johnson's parents were not happy when he dropped out of Wichita State University, but now that his restaurant delivery business, Dial-A-Waiter, pulls in revenues of over $750,000 a year, they feel better!

Johnson noticed that few of the restaurants in Wichita delivered. He persuaded six Wichita restaurants to let him provide a delivery service for them. Today, he has ten drivers delivering food for forty Wichita restaurants. Johnson charges customers the menu price plus $6 per delivery. He also gets a 30 to 35 percent discount from the restaurants, so he gets to keep the difference between the menu price and the discount price.

Johnson is even developing a franchise—he charges $7,500 to show entrepreneurs in other cities how to start Dial-A-Waiter businesses.

Other entrepreneurs have started successful businesses but still decided to go to college. John Magennis, seventeen, founded Internet Exposer Corporation, an Internet marketing company, when he was only fourteen. Although he earns $65,000 a year, he decided to go to Babson College to major in entrepreneurial studies. Why? "You need to have a minimum amount of certifications and credentials behind you," John told *Forbes*.

SOCIALLY RESPONSIBLE INVESTING

Have you heard of socially responsible investing (SRI), or green investing? Socially responsible investing is any investment strategy that seeks to consider both financial return and social good. Like socially responsible and green business practices, SRI is investing in companies with good track records on the environment, human rights, diversity, and consumer protection.

Get the Stat

Socially responsible investing has really grown in popularity. In 1995, there were only 55 mutual funds that engaged in SRI, with $12 billion in assets. As of this writing, there are 493, with assets of $569 billion.

If this is important to you, seek out mutual funds that invest in socially responsible companies. Currently, around 11 percent of all assets that are professionally managed are designated "socially responsible."

There is even an index now for SRI companies called the iShares MSCI KLD 400 Social Index. Its five-year return has closely followed the S&P 500 index—which tracks the stock market's top 500 companies—coming out just 0.2 percent lower. Turns out SRI investing can be a pretty good deal!

An Entrepreneur Like You

Seth Goldman

HONEST TEA

www.honesttea.com

You have probably seen Honest Tea bottles in your grocery store or deli, but you probably never imagined that this successful business was started by a young entrepreneur!

Seth Goldman likes to say that his business got started because he was thirsty. A natural-born athlete, Seth was always searching for a satisfying drink to quench his thirst after a tough workout. While there were plenty of sports drinks and sodas he could buy, most of them were loaded with sugar, which didn't appeal to him.

Seth, who was studying at Yale's business school at the time, began concocting fruity beverages in his kitchen as a hobby, but he wasn't happy with his creations. One day he decided to call his professor, Barry Nalebuff, to discuss the problem. Barry had just returned from India, where he had been studying the country's tea industry. He told Seth that beverage companies that purchased their raw materials from Indian tea plantations did not use whole tea leaves in their manufacturing. Instead, they took whatever was left over after the quality leaves had been packaged into other products, such as tea bags.

Barry and Seth decided to start a tea company. Barry had already come up with a name for a company that would make beverages using top-of-the-line organic tea leaves. The company would be called Honest Tea. Seth loved the name and what it represented. He hung up the phone and resolved to continue his experiments by brewing tea leaves in his kitchen until he came up with the perfect product.

Today, Honest Tea sells thirty different kinds of bottled iced teas as well as a growing line of bagged and loose teas. By 2007, the company had generated $22.8 million in sales. In February 2008, Coca-Cola bought 40 percent of Honest Tea for

$43 million. With the help of Coca-Cola's improved distribution, Honest Tea's sales rose 215 percent, reaching $71.7 million in 2012.

Honest Tea's Competitive Advantages

Although Barry has retired, Seth continues to work hard as "TeaEO" to define the company around the features that make Honest Tea stand out from the competition. For example, Honest Tea is the only bottled tea company whose products are 100 percent USDA organic certified. When an item is labeled "USDA organic," it confirms that certain pesticides and other toxic chemicals have not been used in growing or producing it. Increasingly, consumers, particularly the health conscious, are seeking out organic goods in the marketplace.

Honest Tea also uses up to two-thirds less sugar in its teas compared with its competitors, such as Snapple and Arizona. This feature appeals to consumers who care about their health and diet, and who are turned off by the sugary taste of most teas on the market.

Socially Responsible Business

The "honest" part of Honest Tea extends beyond using organic ingredients. Seth goes to great lengths to educate customers about the company's ethical and socially responsible business practices. For example, Honest Tea purchases peppermint leaves for its First Nation Peppermint iced tea from a woman-owned herb company on the Crow Indian Reservation in Montana, where the unemployment rate is a staggering 67 percent. By purchasing peppermint leaves from this supplier, Honest Tea is promoting economic activity in a location where many suffer from poverty and joblessness. A percentage of the revenue from the sale of this product is donated to nonprofit organizations that help at-risk Native American youth.

Seth wants customers to know that when they buy Honest Tea, they are also doing something good for the community. As Seth puts it, "A commitment to social responsibility is central to Honest Tea's identity and purpose. The company strives for authenticity, integrity, and purity in our products and in the way we do business."

Staying in the Game

Comparable brands such as Snapple, Lipton, and Arizona iced teas may cost 25 to 50 cents less per bottle but do not offer the same quality and promised health benefits. However, some newer high-end organic tea companies, such as Tazo iced and loose teas, sold at Starbucks and other retail locations, may pose a threat to Honest Tea in the long run. In order to stay in the game, Seth needs to continue to enhance and market the features that make Honest Tea a specialty product.

Think Like an Entrepreneur

1. Brainstorm a list of Honest Tea's competitors. What are the competitive advantages of their products? How can Honest Tea stay competitive?
2. What are some ways you plan to make your business socially responsible? Why?
3. Perform a SWOT analysis of Honest Tea.

PART 7

WRITE A WINNING BUSINESS PLAN

CHAPTER 22

SAMPLE BUSINESS PLAN FROM A SUCCESSFUL YOUNG ENTREPRENEUR

EVA'S EDIBLES

N ow that you've read the first twenty-one chapters of *The Young Entrepreneur's Guide,* you are ready to write a business plan that will help you raise money to start your own small business. This chapter provides a terrific sample business plan that you can use as a model. One of my students wrote it and used it to launch her successful small business.

The next chapter is a blank business plan workbook with worksheets that will take you step-by-step through writing your own business plan. But, before you begin, make sure to read Eva's plan. It'll make it easier for you to understand how to write your own business plan.

EVA'S EDIBLES

Executive Summary

A Personal Chef Service

Company Background

<u>Business Description:</u> Eva's Edibles is a personal chef service that sells packages of five freshly cooked gourmet dinners to business professionals who don't have time to cook for themselves. Eva's Edibles is structured as a limited liability corporation (LLC).

<u>Business Model:</u> Eva's Edibles will prepare homemade dinners for clients. Each dinner will be based on a client's personal preferences. Dinners will be cooked in clients' kitchens, with all cleanup performed by Eva. The dinners will be stored in a client's refrigerator or freezer. Clients can reheat the dinners when convenient. It is estimated that this service will save a client nine to ten hours per week by reducing shopping, meal preparation, and cleanup.

<u>Mission Statement:</u> Eva's Edibles, a personal chef service, will provide busy clients with healthy and delicious dinners that are based on clients' preferences and prepared in their kitchens. Dinners are stored in clients' refrigerators or freezers to be reheated at their convenience.

Contact Information

Eva Tan
614–555–6208
eva@evasedibles.com
Eva's Edibles
303 Olentangy River Rd.
Columbus, OH
43202

Year Founded
2012

Number of Employees
1

Investment Opportunity
$4,073

Annual Operating Costs
$5,844

Annual Sales
$81,900

Annual Profit
$10,180

Return on Sales
12.4 percent

Return on Investment
250 percent

Break-Even Units/Month
7 units

Projected.

Market Opportunity

Opportunity: Columbus, Ohio, has a large population of professionals with substantial amounts of disposable income, but busy schedules that do not afford them time to prepare dinner. On average, these professionals eat out or order in four out of five workdays each week. Eva's Edibles seeks to provide these individuals with a healthy, homemade, and affordable alternative to ordering from area restaurants.

Target Market: Business professionals, couples, and families with an annual household income of more than $50,000. These individuals live hectic lives and rarely cook, but they want healthy and convenient meal options that won't break the bank.

Industry Overview: According to the American Personal and Private Chef Association (APPCA), about 9,000 personal chefs are currently serving some 72,000 clients nationwide. Those numbers are expected to double over the next five years.

Market Research: Of the 301,800 Columbus households having two or more people, 36.7 percent have annual combined incomes of over $50,000. The people in this market have busy lifestyles and want healthy dinners. On average, the target household goes out to dinner or orders in four out of five workdays each week.

Leadership

Eva Tan, CEO: Eva Tan has an associate's degree in business management from Columbus State Community College, and worked as assistant to the director of Campus Dining Services at Ohio State University. She also ran her own event-planning business, Eva's Entertainment Services, for four years. Eva has completed an intensive training course offered by the U.S. Personal Chef Association (USPCA), and has received the federally recognized trademarked designation of certified personal chef (CPC).

EVA'S EDIBLES
Business Plan
A Personal Chef Service

1. OPPORTUNITY RECOGNITION AND BUSINESS STRUCTURE
1.1 Business Opportunity
The personal chef business is a viable opportunity for the Columbus, Ohio, area. Columbus has a large population of professionals, from the business and medical spheres, primarily, which is growing steadily. Individuals from these professions earn $50,000 or more per year, providing them with substantial amounts of disposable income. What these individuals have in terms of income, they lack in terms of time. As a result, they go out to dinner or order in four out of five workdays each week. Eva's Edibles seeks to provide these individuals with a healthy, homemade, and affordable alternative to ordering from area restaurants.

1.2 Type of Business
Eva's Edibles will be a service business preparing healthy dinners that can be easily reheated by clients.

1.3 Type of Business Ownership
Eva's Edibles will be a limited liability company (LLC), wholly owned and operated by Eva Tan. The LLC status will protect Eva Tan's personal assets and will allow the company to enjoy some tax benefits.

1.4 Mission Statement
Eva's Edibles, a personal chef service, will provide busy clients with healthy and delicious dinners that are based on clients' preferences and prepared in their kitchens.

Dinners are stored in clients' refrigerators or freezers to be reheated at their convenience.

1.5 Social Responsibility

Eva's Edibles will use natural, organic, and locally grown ingredients whenever possible. The company's code of ethics directs that the business be as "green" as possible. It will choose vendors that are environmentally and socially responsible.

Eva's Edibles will also provide internships for interested culinary students in the community. In the future, Eva Tan hopes to volunteer at local elementary schools to speak with students about healthy eating and lifestyle choices. After three years, Eva's Edibles plans to contribute 1 percent of yearly net profit to a local food bank.

1.6 Qualifications

Eva Tan has an associate's degree in business management from Columbus State Community College. As assistant to the director of Campus Dining Services at Ohio State University, Eva acquired experience in the management of various types of food-service operations, as well as catering. She also ran her own event-planning business, Eva's Entertainment Services, for four years. Eva has completed an intensive training course offered by the U.S. Personal Chef Association (USPCA), and has received the federally recognized trademarked designation of certified personal chef (CPC).

Eva has many personal characteristics and skills that are valuable in the personal chef business: a passion for cooking, attention to detail, organizational skills, flexibility, creativity, sociability, ability to multitask, high physical energy, and endurance.

2. MARKET RESEARCH
2.1 Market Research

The personal chef business is one of the fastest growing segments in the food-service industry. According to the American Personal and Private Chef Association (APPCA), about 9,000 personal chefs are currently serving some 72,000 clients nationwide. Those numbers are expected to double over the next five years.

Of the 301,800 Columbus households with two or more inhabitants, 36.7 percent have annual combined incomes of more than $50,000. The people in this market have busy lifestyles and want healthy dinners. In general, the target household goes out to dinner or orders in four out of five workdays each week. Eva's Edibles will provide people an opportunity to eat healthily, without compromising a busy and productive lifestyle.

2.2 Target Market

Demographic Information: Professional couples and families, with household incomes of more than $50,000.

Geographic Information: Greater Columbus, Ohio, area.

Psychographic Information: Desires healthy food, often dual-income households living hectic lives, hardworking, would like to spend more time at home without increasing time in the kitchen cooking and cleaning up.

Buying Patterns: Eats out often (four times per week) but would like to reduce the cost of eating out.

2.3 Competitors

Direct Competition: There are currently fifteen personal chefs, or businesses performing some type of personal chef service, in the greater Columbus area. Of these, only seven advertise that they are members of one of the professional personal chef associations. Based on website research, only one direct competitor is federally recognized as a certified personal chef. Only two indicated specifically that they were focused on preparing healthy meals. On average, similar personal chefs in the Columbus area charge between $300 and $500 for their chef services. Groceries are an additional cost. Eva's Edibles will charge $325 per week, including groceries, making its pricing very competitive.

Indirect Competition: Columbus area restaurants, including fast food and takeout establishments, will indirectly compete with Eva's Edibles. The upscale restaurants are generally expensive and will not be an everyday option. The majority of lower-priced, "family-style," and fast food restaurants offer meals much lower in quality and nutrition than the dinners that will be provided by Eva's Edibles.

2.4 Competitive Advantage

Eva's Edibles has three major competitive advantages:

1. It will focus on customer service by allowing clients to choose their menus.
2. It will focus on preparing healthy versions of client favorites and, after consultation with clients, will tailor dinners to meet their special dietary needs.

3. Eva Tan will be one of the few personal chefs in Columbus to have the federally recognized designation of certified personal chef. Eva Tan is an active member of the U.S. Personal Chef Association.

2.5 Business Growth

Short-Term Business Goals: In its first year, Eva's Edibles plans to build a profitable customer base so that by the end of the year it will be cooking in clients' kitchens twenty-two days per month. This will allow the company to reach its revenue goal of $81,900. Additionally, the company expects to pay $1,200 against the initial loan of $2,000 received from Eva Tan's parents.

Long-Term Business Goals: Eva's Edibles anticipates that, after a profitable customer base has been built, the company will develop an intensive growth strategy. Eva's intends to increase its market penetration by leasing or buying a commercial kitchen. This will allow increased storage and allow the company to serve more clients and increase its revenues and profits. Dinners will be delivered to customers.

2.6 Challenges

Short-Term Business Challenges: The biggest challenge facing Eva's Edibles in its early years will be its business model. Cooking dinners at clients' homes will limit the number of clients that the company can serve.

Long-Term Business Challenges: The biggest long-term challenge for the company is space. Eva's Edibles will need to change its business model and lease or buy a commercial kitchen to increase the number of clients. This, in turn, may require additional financing and will require additional employees, particularly those with some degree of cooking skills.

3. PROMOTION AND SALES
3.1 Marketing Plan

Eva's Edibles plans to market exclusively to professionals with an average annual income of $50,000 or more. Based on her research, Eva found that professionals in Columbus live hectic lives and don't have time for grocery shopping, cooking, and cleaning. The marketing plan will highlight the following customer benefits:

1. Less time spent planning and shopping for dinners.

2. Less time spent in the kitchen cooking and cleaning up.

3. The convenience of eating dinner whenever the client wishes.

4. Delicious and healthy dinners tailored to the client's personal choices.

5. Less money spent eating out.

6. More time to spend with friends.

7. Dinner choices that can be tailored for diabetics, vegetarians, and those who need low-cholesterol or low-sodium meals; have allergies to peanuts, shellfish, and other allergens; or are lactose- or gluten-intolerant.

3.2 Promotion

Eva's Edibles will engage in five promotional activities: establishing a website, maintaining a referral listing on the USPCA website, in-store promotions, promotions at local events, and programs for retaining current clients.

1. Company Website: Eva's Edibles will construct its own website, which will provide full information about services and display a selection of dinner menus. The website will offer monthly catering promotions and offer a sign-up list for prospective clients. Sample dinners will be showcased. The website will promote Eva Tan as one of the few personal chefs in the Columbus area who has the federally recognized designation of certified personal chef. It will indicate that Eva Tan is an active member of the U.S. Personal Chef Association.

2. USPCA Referral Website: Eva's Edibles will use a referral listing provided by the USPCA. Because of her membership in the USPCA, Eva Tan can access its referral listing at www.hireachef.com. Eva's Edibles will be able to create and modify its listing, as well as track listing statistics. According to the USPCA, this service "is the most effective, efficient method to put customers and personal chefs in touch with each other." Annually, hireachef.com logs more than five hundred thousand listing views, and ninety-five thousand clicks for more information. These statistics represent more than simple web page hits, which can be deceiving. The hireachef.com system has actual clients reviewing personal chef pages and making contact. Inquiries from potential clients are sent directly to the chef's email account.

3. In-Store Promotions: Eva's Edibles will offer in-store promotions at local cookware shops on a regular basis. One store, the Wire Whisk, has agreed to host an hour-long presentation by Eva Tan every other week, which will be dedicated to healthy eating and feature the company's dinners. At each event, the company will offer a brochure describing its philosophy, and provide sample menus.

4. *Promotions at Local Events:* Eva's Edibles will also participate in local events at shopping malls, cultural fairs, environmental exhibits (Earth Day), and other appropriate venues. It will offer free samples, gift baskets, and discount raffles. Eva's will offer its brochures and sample menus at each of these events as well.

5. *Strategies for Retaining Current Clients:* Eva's Edibles will provide current clients with "extras" for their loyalty, such as free snacks and desserts, after purchasing three Five-Dinner Plans. Another strategy will be to offer current customers a 10 percent discount when they refer her to a potential client.

3.3 Sales Methods

Eva's Edibles will depend heavily on personal selling. This involves contacting past customers of the event-planning business and pursuing business contacts through Ohio State University.

Direct mail pieces and the brochure will have a mail-back card to capture a prospective client's email address and telephone number. Eva Tan will follow up on all mail-back cards personally by email or phone.

Future selling strategies will include asking customers for referrals and recommendations of potential clients. Again, Eva will get in touch with each prospect personally.

Steps a Consumer Follows to Purchase Services

1. Customer will contact Eva by phone or email for a free meal plan consultation.
2. Customer will schedule an appointment for Eva to cook one meal package (five dinners)—customers must be at home during first visit. (Homeowners will not need to be present during subsequent visits if they choose to give Eva a spare key so she can let herself in.)

3.4 Sales Estimates

FACTOR	INFLUENCE ON SALES
MARKET ANALYSIS	Given the large number of target households in the Greater Columbus area (27,690 households), Eva must only sell to less than 0.08 percent of this potential market to meet her sales estimates. Eva believes this is highly feasible.
MAXIMUM CAPACITY	Eva has a maximum capacity of seven units per week (forty-two hours), which means she can serve a maximum of twenty-eight customers per month. As a result, Eva's sales estimates are aligned with her maximum capacity.
BREAK-EVEN UNITS	Eva must sell at least seven units per month to cover her operating expenses. Eva's sales estimates are above her break-even point.
SEASONALITY	Eva's business will not be affected by seasonality because her clients will continue to eat dinner, regardless of the time of year.

Sales Forecast

MONTH	UNITS	REVENUE
January	20	$6,500
February	20	$6,500
March	20	$6,500
April	20	$6,500
May	21	$6,825
June	21	$6,825
July	21	$6,825
August	21	$6,825
September	22	$7,150
October	22	$7,150
November	22	$7,150
December	22	$7,150
Annual Total	**252**	**$81,900**

4. FINANCIAL INFORMATION AND OPERATIONS

4.1 Definition of One Unit

One unit is defined as cooking five dinners for a client in the client's kitchen.

4.2 Variable Costs

Materials

Material Description	Bulk Price	Bulk Quantity	Quantity per Unit	Cost per Unit
Misc. groceries (specific ingredients vary from client to client)	$100	5 dinners	5 dinners	$100
Total Material Costs per Unit				**$100**

Labor

Cost of Labor per Hour	Time (in Hours) to Make One Unit	Total Labor Costs per Unit
$25.00	6 hours	**$150**

EOU

Material Costs	Labor Costs	**TOTAL EOU**
$100	$150	**$250**

4.3 Economics of One Unit

Selling Price per Unit	$325
Variable Costs per Unit Costs of Goods Sold Materials	$100
Labor	$150
Total Cost of Goods Sold	**$250**
Other Variable Costs Commission	$0
Packaging	$0
Other	$4
Total Other Variable Costs	**$4**
Total Variable Costs	**$254**
Contribution Margin per Unit	$71

4.4 Delivery of Service

DESCRIPTION OF STEP	TIME (MINS.)	COST
Consult with potential client to determine what types of meals he or she likes best	15	$0.00
Travel to supermarket to shop for groceries for client's meals	15–30	$1.50
Shop for and purchase groceries	60	$100.00
Travel to client's home	15	$0.50
Organize kitchen and groceries	15	$6.25
Clean and chop vegetables	60	$25.00
Cook client's meal package	240	$100.00
Clean up kitchen	45	$18.75
Return home	30–45	$2.00

4.5 Fixed Expenses for One Month

EXPENSE TYPE	EXPLANATION	MONTHLY COST
Insurance	As a food service business, it is imperative that Eva's Edibles is insured to protect against liability.	$117
Salary	Eva will be paid an hourly wage.	$0
Advertising	Advertising will include direct mailings and postage, as well as marketing collateral and samples to be distributed at in-store promotions and local events.	$146
Interest	Eva's Edibles has a financing strategy that does not include repaying loans with interest.	$0
Depreciation	Eva will depreciate her cooking equipment over a five-year period of time ($1,373 over 60 months).	$23
Utilities	Because Eva cooks in her clients' kitchens, the only utility she will pay will be service for her mobile phone.	$100
Rent	Because Eva cooks in her clients' kitchens, she will not incur costs related to rent.	$0
Other Fixed Expenses	These costs are associated with automobile maintenance and gas to drive to promotional events.	$107
TOTAL FIXED EXPENSES		**$493**

4.6 Income Statement for First Year of Operations

REVENUE			$81,900.00
	Gross Sales	$81,900.00	
	Sales Returns	0.00	
Net Sales			$81,900.00
VARIABLE COSTS			
Costs of Goods Sold			
Materials		25,200.00	
Labor		37,800.00	
Total Cost of Goods Sold		63,000.00	
Other Variable Costs			
	Commission	0.00	
	Packaging	0.00	
	Other	1,008.00	
Total Other Variable Costs			1,008.00
Total Variable Costs			64,008.00
Contribution Margin			$17,892.00
FIXED OPERATING EXPENSES			
	Insurance	1,404.00	
	Salaries	0.00	
	Advertising	1,752.00	
	Interest	0.00	
	Depreciation	276.00	
	Utilities	1,200.00	
	Rent	0.00	
	Other Fixed Expenses	1,284.00	
Total Expenses			$5,916.00
PRE-TAX PROFIT			$11,976.00
Taxes (15 percent)			1,796.40
NET PROFIT			$10,179.60

4.7 Start-Up Investment

ITEM	WHY NEEDED	VENDOR	COST
Victorinox Swiss Army Cutlery Set (8-Piece)	Needed to chop vegetables and meat	Macy's	$618
Anolon Nouvelle Copper Hard Anodized Nonstick 10-Piece Cookware Set	Needed for basic cooking	Amazon.com	450
Misc. Cooking Equipment	Need specialty equipment for preparing gourmet meals	Amazon.com	305
Spices, Oils, etc.	Needed to season food	Whole Foods	100
Wheeled Cart	Needed to transport all cooking supplies and groceries	Globalindustrial.com	269
TOTAL START-UP EXPENDITURES			**$1,742**
Emergency Fund (½ of start-up expenditures)			871
Reserve for Fixed Expenses (covers three months of fixed expenses)			1,479
TOTAL START-UP INVESTMENT			**$4,092**

4.8 Financial Ratios

RETURN ON SALES (ROS)

$$\frac{\text{Annual Net Profit}}{\text{Total Annual Sales}} \rightarrow \frac{\$10,179.60}{\$81,900.00} = \$0.12 \times 100 = 12.4\%$$

RETURN ON INVESTMENT (ROI)

$$\frac{\text{Annual Net Profit}}{\text{Total Start-Up Investment}} \rightarrow \frac{\$10,179.60}{\$4,092.00} = \$2.49 \times 100 = 249\%$$

BREAK-EVEN UNITS (MONTHLY)

$$\frac{\text{Monthly Expenses}}{\text{Contribution Margin per Unit}} \rightarrow \frac{\$493.00}{\$71.00} = 6.94 = 7 \text{ units}$$

4.9 Exit Strategy: Franchising or Acquisition

The market for personal chef services is growing as more women enter the workforce and more families are headed by parents who are both busy professionals. This means Eva's Edibles is a good candidate for franchising in the future. Because Eva's Edibles will develop menus and preparation standards that could be taught to other personal chefs, this business could execute a franchise exit strategy.

Alternatively, it could be sold to another entrepreneur or to a large business that wishes to create a chain of Eva's Edibles.

Either exit strategy—franchising or acquisition—will provide the owner and potential investors with solid returns.

MATH CHEAT SHEET

Start-Up Costs + Emergency Fund (equal to ½ Start-Up Costs) + Reserve for Fixed Costs (3 Months of Fixed Costs) = Start-Up Investment

Start-Up Investment ÷ Net Income per Month = Payback (in Months)

Monthly Debt Payments ÷ Monthly Income × 100 = Bank Debt Ratio

Total Sales ÷ Total Market Size × 100 = Market Share (percentage)

Click-Throughs ÷ Impressions = Click-Through Rate (percentage)

Selling Price per Unit − Cost of Goods Sold per Unit = Gross Profit

Total Revenue − Total Cost of Goods Sold = Total Gross Profit

Gross Profit − Operating Costs = Net Profit

Net Profit ÷ Units Sold = Profit per Unit

Selling Price − Variable Costs = Contribution Margin

Revenue − Cost of Goods Sold = Contribution Margin

Selling Price per Unit − Cost of Goods Sold per Unit = Contribution Margin per Unit

Contribution Margin − Operating Costs = Profit

Monthly Fixed Operating Costs ÷ Contribution Margin per Unit = Break-Even Units

Monthly Fixed Costs ÷ (Contribution Margin per Unit − Variable Cost per Unit) = Break-Even Units

Expenses ÷ Sales × 100 = Operating Ratio (percentage)

Net Income ÷ Sales × 100 = Return on Sales (percentage)

Cash Inflow − Cash Outflow = Net Cash

Cash on Hand ÷ Burn Rate = Number of Months Before Cash Runs Out

Assets − Liabilities = Net Worth (also called Owner's Equity or Capital)

Liabilities + Owner's Equity = Assets

Total Debt (Liabilities) ÷ Total Assets × 100 = Debt Ratio (percentage)

Total Debt (Liabilities) ÷ Owner's Equity × 100 = Debt-to-Equity Ratio (percentage)

(Cash + Marketable Securities) ÷ Current Liabilities = Quick Ratio

Current Assets ÷ Current Liabilities = Current Ratio

(Monthly Income + Operating Expenses) × 100 = Income Exposure

Total Investment ÷ Number of Investment Purchases = Average Annual Inventory Investment

Cost of the Inventory ÷ Average Inventory Investment = Inventory Turnover

Annual Net Profit ÷ Total Start-Up Investment = Return on Investment

GLOSSARY

360° marketing Marketing that communicates with customers from all directions, blending low-tech methods and high-tech methods to reach as many customers in a target market as possible.

401 (k) plan A retirement savings plan funded by employee contributions and (often) matching contributions from the employer.

Accounting System of recording and summarizing business and financial transactions and analyzing, verifying, and reporting the results.

Accounting controls Rules a business requires accounting personnel and staff to follow to help prevent embezzlement and other misuses of company funds.

Accounts payable Amount of money a business owes to its suppliers for purchases made on credit.

Accounts receivable Amount of money owed to a business by its customers for credit sales.

Acquisition Gaining ownership of another business by purchasing a majority of its shares.

Active listening Listening consciously and responding in ways that improve communication.

Advertising Public, promotional message paid for by an identified sponsor or company.

AIDA (attention, interest, desire, and action) Popular communication model used by companies to plan, create, and manage their promotions.

Angels Equity investors who finance start-up ventures in industries in which they are interested.

Antitrust laws Laws that forbid anticompetitive mergers that would lead to monopolies and business practices like price fixing.

Apprenticeship Internship in which a technical or trade skill is taught. See also **Internship**.

Artisan Someone skilled at a traditional manual craft, such as brewing, beekeeping, or woodcarving.

Artisanal   Describes a business based on a traditional craft, such as brewing, furniture making, or sewing; typically focused on quality rather than quantity.

Asset   Cash or any item that can be sold for cash.

Auditor   Accountant who examines a company's financial records and verifies that they have been kept properly.

Background check   The process of investigating a potential employee's criminal and financial records.

Balance sheet   Financial statement that summarizes the assets and liabilities (debts) of a business.

Bank debt ratio   The ratio between a business's monthly debt payments and its monthly income.

Bank reconciliation   Process of verifying that a checkbook balance is in agreement with the ending balance in the checking account statement from the bank.

Bankrupt   Declared by a court to be unable to pay debts or bills. .

Bankruptcy   A legal procedure for selling off the property of a business that cannot pay its debts from its current assets, in order to raise money to pay credits.

Banner ad   Ad that runs along the top or side of a web page.

Barter financing   Trading of items or services between businesses.

Benefit   Reasons customers choose to buy a product; types of compensation employees receive in addition to salary or wages.

Benefit corporation (B corp)   A business legal structure that requires a business to have a mission to benefit society as well as to create profit for shareholders. B Corps undergo annual audits to verify their positive impacts on the environment, the community, their employees, and on society.

Bid   An offer made on an item that is for sale.

Board of advisors   A group of people who agree to share their expertise and advice to help a business develop.

Bond   A debt investment offered by corporations to raise capital. The investor lends the corporation a specified amount of money to be paid back at a later date with interest. Bonds may traded on the bond market.

Bonus   An amount of money, typically tied to performance, that an employee receives (usually annually) in addition to compensation and benefits.

Book value   Most common method for assessing a business's value: total assets minus total liabilities. Also referred to as **net worth** or **owner's equity**.

Bootstrapping   Starting a business without any outside investment, using cost-reducing strategies.

Brand   Marketing strategy designed to establish a business's competitive advantage in the minds of its target customers.

Break-even analysis   Examination of the income statement that identifies the break-even point for a business.

Break-even point   Point at which a business has sold exactly enough units for sales to cover its expenses.

Break-even units   Number of units of sale a business needs to sell to arrive at the break-even point.

Bubble   Speculative trading that drives the price of an item up far beyond its value, which in turns attracts more speculators, further increasing the price.

Bulk   A large number of unpackaged products, as typically ordered from a manufacturer by a wholesaler.

Bundling   Offering several different products or services for one price.

Burn rate   Rate at which a company that doesn't yet have a positive cash flow spends cash to cover its overhead costs; expressed in terms of cash spent per month.

Business   Organization that provides products or services in exchange for money.

Business ethics   Moral principles applied to business issues and actions.

Business incubator   Provides affordable office space, equipment, and supplies to small-business start-ups.

Business interruption insurance   Covers losses in revenue suffered when a business can't operate due to an event specified in the insurance contract.

Business opportunity   Consumer need or want that potentially can be met profitably by a new business.

Business plan   A written statement that describes in detail the goals a new business has set and how it plans to achieve them.

Business-to-business (B2B) company   Company that sells to other companies.

Business-to-consumer (B2C) company   Company that sells to individuals.

C corporation   Any corporation that, under United States federal income tax law, is taxed separately from its owners and provides them with limited liability.

Calculated risk   Risks that are carefully considered before starting a business.

Calendar year   January 1 to December 31.

Call to action   The act of asking a customer to take an action, during a sales call or through an ad or direct mail campaign.

Capital   Wealth in the form of money or assets that can be sold for money.

Capitalism   Economic system based on private ownership of businesses and scarce resources (such as capital), in which business owners and consumers are free to engage in trade; also called "free market system."

Carbon footprint The amount of carbon dioxide emitted due to the consumption of fossil fuels by a particular person or business.

Carbon offset The practice of buying carbon to help offset a person's or business's carbon footprint. Offsets are sold by companies that invest the money in renewable energy producers or resource-conservation projects.

Cash Money in a form that can be spent immediately, such as coins or paper notes. In accounting, cash also includes a business's bank account balance, customer checks, and marketable securities. It may also include the unutilized portion of a line of credit.

Cash discount Discount given to buyers who pay for purchases in cash, either at the time of purchase or within a set time after purchase.

Cash flow Money received minus what is spent over a specified period of time; amount of cash on hand.

Cash flow statement Accounting document that records inflows and outflows of cash when they actually occur.

Cash value The amount equal to the replacement cost of damaged or stolen property minus any depreciation.

Catastrophic risk Risk of an unpredictable event that causes severe loss to many people.

Cause-related marketing Marketing partnership between a business and a nonprofit group for the benefit of both.

Chart of accounts Section of accounting worksheet showing accounts used in a business, including assets, liabilities, owner's equity, income, and expense accounts.

Checking account Bank account against which the account holder can write checks to pay bills or make purchases.

Click-through rate (CTR) A measurement of the success of an online advertisement; the number of times a click is made on the advertisement divided by total impressions (the times an advertisement was served).

Co-branding Two or more businesses marketing a product together, and including all their brand names on a single product or service.

Cold call Sales call to someone the salesperson does not know, without prior notice; also called canvassing.

Collateral Property or assets pledged to a bank to secure a loan.

Command economy   Economic system in which the government controls the production, allocation, and prices of goods and services.

Commerce server   Server that runs commerce-based applications, such as credit card processing and inventory management.

Commission   Amount paid to a salesperson based on the volume of products or services the salesperson sells; typically a percentage of total sales.

Comparative balance sheet   A comparison of a business's current balance sheet with those of previous years so financial trends over time can be identified.

Compensation   Money and benefits that an employee receives in exchange for working.

Competitive advantage   A benefit a business can deliver better than its competition does.

Competitive intelligence   Data a business collects about its competitors.

Competitive matrix   Grid used to compare characteristics of a business with those of its direct competitors.

Compound interest   Interest earned on interest; when an investment earns interest and then that interest is added to the principal, the interest compounds, or grows.

Compromise   An agreement arrived at between two or more parties that involves each party making concessions in order to arrive at the agreement.

Conference call   A meeting that involves three or more parties in different locations speaking to each other over the same phone line.

Confidentiality agreement   Agreement that binds parties to secrecy to protect intellectual property, such as a trade secret or other sensitive information. Also called **nondisclosure agreement (NDA).**

Conflict of interest   Situation in which personal loyalties and professional obligations interfere with each other.

Consultant   Any professional who provides expert, professional services for a fee.

Consumer   A person who purchases goods and services for personal use.

Consumer credit   Credit extended from a business to consumers for the purchase of goods or services.

Contract   Agreement between competent parties in which each party promises to take or avoid a specified action.

Contribution margin   Amount per unit that a product contributes toward a company's profitability, before its fixed expenses are subtracted.

Controlling   Management process that includes setting performance standards, measuring actual performance, comparing actual performance to the standards, and taking corrective action if actual performance does not meet performance standards.

Conversion   The act of converting a customer's interest in a product or service into a sale.

Conversion franchising   The folding of an existing stand-alone business or local chain into a franchise operation

Cooperative   A business legal structure that is owned, controlled, and operated for the mutual benefit of its members, who use its services, buy its goods, or are employed by it.

Cooperative advertising   Sharing of advertising costs by two companies that both have an interest in selling the same product.

Cooperative advertising fee   Fee paid in exchange for participation in cooperative advertising program; often part of franchise agreements.

Copyleft   The use of copyright law to remove, rather than add, restrictions on intellectual property so it can be more freely shared and adapted.

Copyright   Exclusive right to perform, display, copy, or distribute an artistic work.

Corporate social responsibility (CSR)   The concept that a business should behave in ways that balance its focus on profits and growth with the good of society.

Corporation   Legal business structure that considers the business a "person" or "entity" under the law, and grants limited liability to the business owner(s).

Cosigner   A person who signs a loan with another person, pledging to pay the loan if the person taking out the loan fails to pay it back.

Cost-based pricing   Pricing method that sets a product's price based on what it costs the business to provide it.

Cost-benefit analysis   A method for calculating risk that adds up all the expected benefits of an opportunity and then subtracts all the expected costs. If the benefits outweigh the costs, the opportunity may be feasible.

Cost of goods sold (COGS)   The cost required to make one additional unit of a product.

Cost of services sold (COSS)   The cost of serving one additional customer.

Coverage   Protection provided by an insurance policy.

Creative Commons (CC)   A nonprofit devoted to expanding the range of creative works available for others to legally use and share.

Creative Commons licenses   Free copyright licenses that enable creators of intellectual property to choose from a variety of rights to apply to their IP.

Credit   The ability to obtain goods or services before payment, based on trust that payment will be made in the future.

Credit bureau   Business that collects and maintains credit history records and sells or provides the information.

Credit history   Record of a person's or business's credit transactions, including information about whether debts were repaid in accordance with the credit terms set by the creditor.

Credit score   A statistically derived number between 300 and 850 that reflects a person's credit history. The higher the number, the more likely the person is deemed to use credit responsibly.

Credit terms   Conditions, such as interest and due dates, set by creditors when they grant credit.

Credit union   Nonprofit cooperative organization that offers low-interest loans to members.

Creditor   Person or business that grants credit.

Crowdfunding   Financing a business or project by raising small amounts of money from a large number of people, typically via the Internet.

Crowdsourcing   Using the Internet to get feedback and business insights from a large number of customers.

Current assets   Short-term assets that can be converted into cash within one year.

Current liabilities   Short-term debts that must be repaid within one year.

Current ratio   Current assets divided by current liabilities.

Customer financing   Type of financing in which a customer provides either debt or equity financing for your business.

Customer profile   Detailed description of the characteristics of a business's target customer.

Cyclical   Describes something (sales or cash flow, for example) that varies according to the time of year.

Debt capital   Capital (money) obtained by a business to start or expand through borrowing.

Debt/equity exchange   Business exit strategy that involves trading equity for portions of debt that was borrowed to finance a business. This will slowly reduce interest payments, and will give investors shares of the business in exchange for money they lent to the business.

Debt financing   Obtaining money, by borrowing it, to start or expand a business.

Debt ratio   Ratio of a business's total debt divided by its total assets.

Debt-to-equity ratio   Ratio of the total debts (liabilities) of a business divided by its owner's equity.

Deductible   Amount the insured must first pay before the insurance company is required to pay.

Deduction   Item or expense subtracted from gross income on a tax return, in order to reduce one's taxes.

Demand   The quantity of goods and services consumers are willing to buy at a specific price and specific time.

Demand-based pricing   Pricing method that focuses on customer demand—how much customers are willing to pay for a product.

Democratic leadership style   Management style that involves the leader seeking input from employees about what tasks need to be done and how to do them.

Demographics   Objective social and economic facts about people.

Depreciation   Accounting method of spreading the total cost of a piece of equipment over the number of years it will be used—for tax purposes and to save money to replace the equipment when it wears out.

Depreciation expense The portion of a tangible capital asset that is deemed to have been consumed or expired during a specified period, such as a year, and has thus become an expense for that period.

Differentiator   Unique characteristic that distinguishes a business from other businesses.

Direct competitor   Business in your target market that sells a product or service similar to yours.

Direct selling   Describes a company that manufacturers and delivers products, and provides training to entrepreneurs who become sales representatives of the company and use its products to build their own sales prospects and business.

Directing   Management process of leading, influencing, and motivating employees to work together to achieve specific goals.

Distribution chain   Series of steps through which a product flows from manufacturing to wholesalers, retailers, and consumers. The price of the product is typically marked up as it travels along the chain.

Distribution channel   Way in which a product can reach the consumer; series of steps through which products flow into or out of a business. Also referred to as a **distribution chain**.

Diversification   Investment strategy that involves investing in a wide variety of investments as a protection against volatility.

Dividend   A distribution of a portion of a company's earnings to its shareholders. Owning stock entitles a shareholder to receive a share of a company's earnings.

Double-entry bookkeeping   An accounting method that records every transaction as both a credit and a debit.

E-commerce   Buying and selling goods online.

E-procurement   Purchasing conducted online.

Earn out   Business exit strategy that involves using cash to buy your investors' shares back from them at a higher price than they paid for them.

Economics   Social science that studies how people satisfy their demands for goods and services, when the supply of those goods and services is limited.

Economics of one unit   Calculation of the profit (or loss) for each unit of sale made by a business; a method for examining the business's profitability.

Economy   The system used by a society to allocate goods and services among its people. The wealth and resources of a country or region, in terms of the production and consumption of the goods and services it produces. Also called **economic system**.

Economies of scale   Cost advantages that a business obtains from expansion, such as volume discounts.

Electronic right   A copyright extended to the right to use a creative work online.

Embezzlement   The crime of stealing money from an employer.

Emergency fund   Amount of money every business or individual should have in liquid savings to cover expenses for three to six months.

Emoticon   Symbol or combined punctuation marks used to convey an emotion during online communication.

Employee   Person who works in a business owned by someone else.

Employee handbook   A written explanation of guidelines and rules employees of a business are expected to follow.

Employee-owned corporation   A business legal structure created when a company makes its employees owners of the company by issuing stock to them through an **employee stock ownership plan (ESOP)**.

Employee stock ownership plan (ESOP)   Plan set up by a business owner that enables the employees to buy stock in the company, typically at a discount.

Encryption   Coding of data sent via the Internet to keep the information secure.

Enterprise   A organization that sells goods or services, also known as a "business."

Enterprise zone   An impoverished area in which tax breaks and other incentives are offered to encourage businesses to open, invest, and provide jobs to residents.

Entrepreneur   A person who creates and owns a business.

Equilibrium point   Point at which the supply curve and the demand curve intersect. It is the point at which supply and demand are balanced.

Equilibrium price   Price at which supply equals demand.

Equity   A stock or any other security representing an ownership interest in a company.

Equity capital   Money obtained by a business to start or expand from an investor, in exchange for a share of ownership (equity) in the business.

Equity financing   Method of financing a start-up business by selling shares of ownership in the business.

Ergonomics   The applied science of designing equipment environments to maximize the comfort and efficiency of people using them.

Ethical sourcing   The practice of sourcing supplies for a business from vendors who provide safe working conditions and respect workers' rights, social justice, and the environment.

Ethics   Moral principles used to evaluate one's decisions and actions.

Excise tax   Tax on a specific product or commercial activity.

Executive summary   One- or two-page summary of a business plan's highlights and the key selling points of the investment opportunity.

Expense   A cost of doing business.

Expense report   List of expenses incurred while doing business activity (sales, for example). Submitted for payment with receipts proving each expense item.

Exporting   Business activity in which goods and services are sent from one country to another country, and sold to foreign consumers.

External sales   Sales obtained by hiring another company, or an outside individual, to do selling for you.

Facilitated giving   Type of cause-related marketing in which a business makes it easier for customers to contribute to a cause.

Fair Labor Standards Act   Federal law that guarantees most hourly workers a minimum hourly wage, a maximum number of hours worked, and extra pay for working overtime.

Fair market value   The price at which an asset would change hands voluntarily between a buyer and seller who both have all relevant facts about the asset.

Fair trade   Policy encouraged by private organizations with the goal of ensuring that small producers in developing nations earn sufficient profit on their exported goods to improve their working, environmental, and social conditions.

Fair use Doctrine that provides for limited quotation of a copyrighted work without permission from or payment to the copyright holder.

Fax (facsimile) Exact copy of a document sent over a phone line.

Feasibility An estimate of how possible it is to pursue and achieve a goal.

Features What a product does and how it appears to the senses (sight, sound, taste, smell, and touch).

Federal Deposit Insurance Corporation (FDIC) Federal government agency that insures savings, checking, and other bank deposit accounts.

Federal Trade Commission (FTC) U.S. government agency that administers consumer protection laws and regulates certain business practices.

FICA Acronym for Federal Insurance Contributions Act, which requires employers and employees to share costs of the federal government's insurance and retirement programs through deductions from wages and income.

File sharing Practice of sending or "sharing" files between computers logged in to a network; circumvents intellectual property laws by allowing sharers to enjoy IP (films, music, etc.) without having to pay for and store copies on their individual computers.

Financial ratio Relationship between financial data expressed as a fraction or percentage.

Financing Money raised to start or grow a business; may be debt, equity, or gift.

Fiscal year Any 12-month period a business chooses to treat as a year for accounting purposes.

Fixed cost A subcategory of operating costs, which must be paid no matter how few or how many units a business sells.

Flexible purpose corporation (Flex corp) A business legal structure free from the corporate requirement to maximize profit as long as the business is fulfilling at least one "special purpose" defined in its charter that benefits society.

Flextime Flexible work schedule.

Focus group Sampling of people from a specific target market that a company surveys for feedback about a product or service.

Foundation A nonprofit organization that either donates funds and support to other organizations or provides the source of funding for its own charitable works.

Franchise Business arrangement in which an established company sells the right for others to use the company's name and operating plan to sell products or services.

Franchise agreement   Legally binding contract between a franchisor and franchisee that lists the rights and responsibilities of each party.

Franchise fee   Upfront charge that is usually sizable—from many thousands of dollars to more than a million—and allows the franchisee to join the franchisor's system.

Franchise operations manual   Manual produced by a franchisor that gives detailed instructions to a franchisee about how to operate, staff, and manage a franchise unit.

Franchise royalty   Regular, ongoing payment paid by the franchisee to the franchisor; typically a percentage of franchisee sales.

Franchisee   Franchise buyer.

Franchisor   Franchise seller.

Free enterprise system   An economic system in which people are free to own and operate enterprises (businesses). Also called **market economy** and **capitalism**.

Freelancer   Person who sells services to businesses as an **independent contractor,** rather than being hired as an employee.

Free on board   Delivery terms that identify a specified location at which the ownership responsibility for a shipment switches from seller to buyer.

Freight   Large products and large-shipment orders that are transported by large trucks, trains, or ships.

FUTA   Acronym for Federal Unemployment Tax Act, which requires employers to pay into a fund that provides unemployment insurance.

Future earnings   Method of business valuation that considers not only a company's book value, but also its estimated future earnings.

Future value of money   Amount to which a given sum will increase over time through investment.

Gantt chart   Bar chart that shows scheduled goals for a list of tasks, and the progress made toward achieving each task.

General journal   Accounting record that shows all of a business's transactions.

General partnership   Partnership in which all partners have unlimited liability.

Geographics   Market segments based on where consumers live or where businesses are located.

Goodwill   Intangible positive aspects of a business, such as location, employee knowledge and skills, brand awareness, intellectual property, relationships with suppliers and customers, and reputation in the community and the industry.

Green company   Company that adopts sustainable business practices aimed at protecting or improving the environment.

Green procurement   Act of purchasing goods and services that are environmentally beneficial.

Greenwashing   Fraudulent marketing designed to make a company seem more environmentally friendly than it really is.

Gross profit   A business's revenue minus its total cost of goods (or services) sold.

Harvest   To exit a business and gain the value of the business in cash as one leaves.

Human resources   The people, or "personnel," who work in a business.

Illiquid   Describes asset or investment that takes longer than 24 hours to sell and convert into cash, e.g., real estate.

Importing   Business activity in which goods and services are brought into a country from foreign suppliers and sold to domestic consumers.

Income   Money earned.

Income statement   Financial document that summarizes a business's income and expenses over a given time period and shows whether the business made a profit or took a loss. Also called a **profit and loss statement**.

Independent contractor   Person or business that provides a service to a business in exchange for a fee, as specified in a contract.

Information technology (IT)   Study, design, development, implementation, support, and management of computer-based information systems.

Infrastructure   System of physical structures and services, such as roads and bridges, that a society needs to function and be productive.

Infringement   The act of violating a copyright or patent holder's rights.

Initial public offering (IPO)   First sale of shares of stock on the stock market to the general public by a corporation.

In-kind donations   Donations of goods or services, instead of money.

Insolvent   Being unable to pay one's bills or debts.

Insurance   A contract that requires an insurance company to pay compensation for losses from specified events or contingencies.

Intangible   Describes something that has value but does not have a physical presence; cannot be touched.

Intellectual property (IP)   Any work resulting from creativity that could potentially earn money, such as an invention, literary or artistic work, and symbol, name, image, or design.

Interest   Money paid for the use of money, such as interest paid by the borrower on a loan; typically calculated as a percentage of the amount borrowed (the principal).

Internal audit   Audit performed by an accountant hired by a company to check its books.

Internship   Work program that provides practical, on-the-job training in a business setting, often in exchange for college credit. See also **Apprenticeship**.

Interpersonal skills   Skills, such as communication and negotiation, used to interact effectively with other people.

Intrapreneurship   Practice of giving employees opportunities to be creative and entrepreneurial within a company.

Inventory   Everything a business has on hand that it could potentially sell, including both finished products and raw materials.

Inventory investment   Money invested into inventory.

Inventory level   Quantity of merchandise on hand at a business.

Inventory management   Process of keeping track of items for sale, storing them and shipping orders.

Inventory shrinkage   Loss of inventory due to damage or pilferage between the time inventory is purchased and the time it is sold or otherwise removed from the shelves.

Inventory system   Process for counting and tracking inventory.

Inventory turnover   Number of times during a given time period that inventory is completely sold out (and therefore replaced), or the number of times during a given period that the average inventory investment is recouped (earned back). Also called "inventory turns."

Inventory value   Monetary value of merchandise on hand at a business and available for sale.

Invest   To commit time, money, or energy to something in anticipation of a future return (typically financial), with awareness of the potential risk as well.

Investment   Something in which time, money, or energy is invested with expectation of potential return and awareness of potential risk.

Investor   A person who invests time, money, or energy to something in anticipation of a future return (typically financial) and with awareness of risk and potential for loss.

Involuntary exchange   Transaction in which one person or business forces another to give up something.

IRA Individual retirement account, an account into which one can place stock and other investments and allow them to grow until retirement without their earnings being taxed; withdrawals are taxed, however, and there are penalties for withdrawing money from an IRA before the legal retirement age.

Job description Explanation of a position's purpose, tasks, and responsibilities and the qualifications needed to perform it.

Job sharing An employment arrangement in which two people are retained on a part-time basis to perform a job normally fulfilled by one person working full-time. Also called **work sharing**.

Joint venture A business created jointly by two or more businesses that work together on the new business yet still retain their distinct identities.

Just-in-time (JIT) inventory system System in which the goal is to maintain just enough inventory to keep the business operating, with virtually no inventory kept in storage.

Keylogger Short for "keystroke logger"; program that records the letters and numbers (keystrokes) made on a keyboard.

Keystone To double the cost of goods sold of a unit in order to arrive at a selling price.

Keyword A word or phrase that summarizes a web page's content.

Law of demand An economic law which states that (all other factors being equal), as the price of a good or service increases, consumer demand for the good or service will decrease, and vice versa.

Law of large numbers A rule of statistics that says that as the number of samples tested increases, the more likely the test result will be accurate.

Law of supply An economic law which states that (all other factors being equal), as the price of a good or service increases, the quantity of goods or services offered by suppliers increases, and vice versa.

Lay off To dismiss an employee, not for performance reasons, but for business reasons such as lack of work.

Lead time Period between starting an activity and realizing its result—for example, the time between order placement, and receipt of shipment.

Lean start-up A business started with minimal capital and planning and the flexibility to evolve in response to feedback from customers.

Lease Written contract in which an equipment or property owner gives temporary use of that equipment or property to another party.

Leveraged Financed with debt.

Liability The legal obligation of a business owner to use his or her personal money and possessions to pay any debts the business incurs.

Liability insurance Insurance that provides coverage when a business's action or lack of action injures someone.

License Right granted by owner to use intellectual property; legal document issued by the government that allows a business to provide a regulated product or service.

Licensee A person or business who receives a license to market a product or service owned by another person or business.

Licensor A person or business who grants a license to another person or business.

Lien A right to keep a person's or company's property until a debt is paid, or sell it to pay the debt.

Limited liability Liability for business debts that is limited to a fixed sum, or an amount based on a percentage of ownership of the business; protects a business owner from potentially having to sell personal assets to pay business debts.

Limited liability company Legally defined type of business ownership similar to a C corporation but with simpler operating requirements and tax procedures, and greater liability protection for the business owners (who are called members).

Limited partnership Partnership in which at least one partner has limited liability for the debts of the business.

Line organization Direct chain of command through levels of personnel who are directly involved in a business's main occupation.

Line-and-staff organization Expanded version of a line organization, which adds staff members to support employees in the line organization.

Liquid Describes an asset or investment that can be sold for cash within 24 hours, e.g., Treasury bills.

Liquidation Sale of the tangible assets of a closing business for cash.

Liquidity Ease of converting a non-cash asset (such as a business) into cash.

Locavore A person who eats food grown locally and patronizes businesses that source locally.

Logistics Management function that involves handling and organizing materials, equipment, goods, and employees.

Logo A symbol that identifies a business or product/service.

Long-term assets Assets that usually take longer than one year to turn into cash.

Long-term liabilities Debts that usually take longer than one year to repay.

Management Skillful use and coordination of a business's resources—money, facilities, equipment, technologies, materials, employees—in a systematic and effective way to achieve particular goals.

Management buyout (MBO) Exit strategy in which a business owner sells his or her ownership shares to the business's managers.

Manufacturer Business that converts scarce resources into tangible products; also called a manufacturing business.

Markdown price Price created when a retailer reduces the price of an overstocked product in order to encourage sales.

Market Group of potential customers—people or businesses—who are interested in and able to purchase a particular product or service.

Market-based valuation Method of business valuation in which estimated future earnings are multiplied by the price/earnings (P/E) ratio of comparable companies on the stock market.

Market clearing price Price at which supply and demand curves for a product or service cross, which is the price at which all the supply being produced will be bought.

Market economy Economic system in which suppliers are free to produce whatever goods and services they wish and set prices based on what consumers are willing to pay.

Market research Information gathered about a business's potential market.

Market segment A group of consumers or businesses within a particular market that has one or more things in common.

Market share The percentage of a target market that is buying a product or service from a particular business.

Marketable securities Investments, such as stocks or bonds, that can be converted to cash.

Marketing All the forms of communication a business uses to reach its market and convey the competitive advantage of its product or service.

Marketing mix Combination of five marketing elements called the Five P's: people, product, place, price, and promotion.

Marketing plan Detailed plan used by a business to implement its marketing strategies and reach its marketing goals.

Markup Price increase imposed by each link in a distribution chain or channel.

Markup price The new price created when a wholesaler or retailer adds a markup to the price of an item in order to make a profit.

Mass market   A marketing strategy that involves attempting to promote and sell a product or service to the widest market possible.

Media   Communication channels that can be used to reach potential customers, including radio, television, newspapers, magazines, and blogs.

Memo   Short for "memorandum": a brief note (typically under one page) that informs employees about a business-related matter.

Mentor   Person who provides free guidance, tutoring, and advice to help another person achieve his or her goals.

Merge   To combine two or more businesses to create a single new business.

Merger   The combining of two or more businesses to create a single new business.

Message thread   Series of emails that shows every previous message between two or more correspondents.

Microloan   A small loan, typically extended by a nonprofit organization at low interest rates to encourage entrepreneurship.

Milestone   Significant point of progress in a process or timeline.

Mind share   Awareness or popularity a certain product has with consumers.

Minimum viable product (MPV)   Per the lean start-up philosophy, the smallest amount of product a business needs to have on hand to be viable.

Minority enterprise small business investment company (MESBIC)   Private investment firms, chartered by the Small Business Administration, that provide equity and debt financing for new small businesses, often at lower loan interest rates than banks or credit unions.

Mission   A plan that outlines how to achieve your vision; answers the question "How do I achieve what I want to achieve?"

Mission statement   A short summary of the aims and values of a company, organization, or individual.

Mixed economy   Economic system that blends elements of a command economy and a market economy.

Monopoly   Single supplier who is a market's only provider of a certain product.

Mortgage   A bank loan used to buy real estate.

Mutual fund   A company that pools money from investors and invests it in stocks, bonds, or other assets. The investors are purchasing shares of the mutual fund.

Need   Something that people must have to survive, such as water, food, clothing, or shelter.

Negotiation   Process in which two or more parties reach an agreement or solve a problem through discussion and bargaining.

Nepotism   The unethical practice of favoring relatives or friends in business by giving them jobs for which they may not be the best candidate; or other preferential treatment.

Net income   The amount a business earns after expenses.

Net present value   A sum that represents what an investment or a business is worth today that includes an estimation of what it will be worth in the future.

Networking   Meeting new people though current friends and business contacts in order to expand one's network.

Net worth   Total assets minus total liabilities; Also called **book value** or **owner's equity**.

Nondisclosure agreement   Legal document that binds the signers to keep sensitive business information secret; also called **confidentiality agreement**.

Nonperiodic reordering   Ordering items at irregular intervals.

Nonprofit corporation   Legally defined type of business ownership in which the company operates not to provide profit for its shareholders but to serve the good of society.

Notary   A person authorized to witness the signing of documents and certify the signatures as valid.

Occupational Safety and Health Administration (OSHA)   The federal agency responsible for setting and enforcing standards of safety in the workplace.

Open source   Software made available by a software developer for people to use, share, modify, and market.

Operating cost   A cost that must be paid regularly to keep a business operating, such as USAIIR (Utilities, Salaries, Advertising, Interest, Insurance, Rent). Also called "overhead."

Operating ratio   Percentage of each dollar of revenue, or sales, needed to cover expenses.

Operational plan   Detailed plan of the everyday activities that will enable a business to achieve its tactical and ultimately its strategic goals.

Operations   Everyday activities that keep a business running.

Operations management   Management of the everyday activities that keep a business running.

Opportunity cost   The potential benefit that you forfeit when you choose one course of action over another; vital to consider when deciding whether to invest money, time, or energy.

Ordinance   Local law specifying where different types of development of activities can and cannot take place; also called **zoning law**.

Organic growth   Growth achieved by expanding a business internally—by adding new products or services, for example.

Organizational structure   System for dividing work, authority, and responsibility within a company.

Organizing   Management process of arranging and coordinating resources and tasks to achieve specific goals.

Orientation   Process of gradually integrating a new employee into a workplace.

Other people's money (OPM)   Money raised from other people as debt or equity and used to start or grow a business.

Outsourcing   Hiring an outside company or individual to handle part of a business's everyday operations or special projects.

Owner's equity   Value of a business on a specific date if all its assets were sold and its liabilities were paid; total assets minus total liabilities. Also referred to as **net worth** or **book value**.

Pacioli check column   Column in an accounting worksheet that ensures that the accounting equation always balances after each transaction.

Packing slip   List of all items packed in a shipment.

Partnership   Business legal structure in which at least two individuals share management, profit, and liability.

Partnership agreement   Legal document that clearly defines a business partnership, including percentages of ownership, responsibilities, and liabilities.

Patent   A grant made by a government that gives an invention's creator the sole right to make, use, and sell that invention for a set period of time.

Payback   Amount of time, measured in months, that it takes a business to earn enough profit to pay back its start-up investment.

Peer-to-peer network   A network of personal computers, each of which acts as both client and server, so that each can exchange files; used to enable file sharing.

Performance-based reward   Incentive for employees linked to a specific, achievable goal.

Performance evaluation   Review of an employee's performance on the job.

Periodic reordering   Ordering of items at regular time intervals.

Permit   Legal document that permits a business to take a specific action.

Perpetual life cycle   Product life cycle in which a product never undergoes a final decline, because it remains in the maturity stage forever.

Personal selling   Direct (person-to-person) effort made by a company's sales representatives to build customer relationships and sell products or services.

PERT chart   Scheduling diagram showing tasks as a sequence of steps and illustrating how the steps are dependent on each other.

Philanthropy   The act of donating money, time, or other resources to a socially beneficial cause.

Phishing   Scam that involves sending email that appears to be from a legitimate business, such as a bank, and asking the reader to click on a hyperlink to verify personal financial information, such as a Social Security number or bank account number, in order to access an account or steal an identity.

Piggyback marketing Low cost market entry strategy in which two or more firms represent one another's complementary (but non-competing) products in their respective markets.

Pilferage   Stealing of inventory by employees, particularly of small amounts over time.

Piracy   The unauthorized use or reproduction of copyrighted or patented intellectual property.

Pitch letter   Cover letter sent with a press release to introduce it and "pitch" a story to the media.

Planning   Management process of setting goals and determining how best to accomplish them.

Policy   Written contract between an insurer and a policyholder; procedure or set of guidelines specifying exactly how something should be done.

Positioning   Process of creating a strong image for a business and establishing its competitive advantage in the minds of its target customers.

Post   Act of writing a transaction in an accounting ledger.

Premium   Promotional gift that usually has the company's name, address, and telephone number printed on it; amount of money an insurance policyholder pays monthly or annually to maintain coverage.

Press release   Written statement sent to media about an event, such as the launch of a new product, consisting of several paragraphs of factual information.

Price discrimination   The illegal (only when done intentionally) act of charging competing buyers different prices for the same product.

Price fixing   Illegal act of agreeing with a competitor to set prices of goods or services, or the terms of business deals.

Principal   The amount borrowed, or the amount still owed, on a loan—not including interest.

Procurement   Buying materials, products, and services for business purposes.

Product   An article or substance produced for sale (also called "good").

Product development   The period during which businesses develop new products or enhance their existing products.

Product life cycle   Series of stages—introduction, growth, maturity, and decline—that a product may pass through while it is on the market.

Product mix   Combination of products that a business sells.

Production management   Management of the processes that produce goods and services.

Profit   A business's gross profit minus its operating costs.

Profit and loss statement   A financial statement (also called an **income statement**) that tracks a business's sales and expenses.

Profit motive   Incentive that encourages entrepreneurs to take business risks in the hope of making a profit.

Project organization   A form of organizational structure that involves employees from more than one department working together as a team on a specific goal.

Promissory note   A signed, written promise to pay a specific sum to a specified person or to the holder of the promissory note on a specified date.

Promotion   Any method used to make potential customers aware of a business and to influence them to buy it, including advertising and publicity.

Promotional mix   Combination of promotional elements, such as advertising, visual merchandising, public relations, publicity, personal selling, and sales promotions.

Property insurance   Insurance that provides payment to replace a business's physical assets in the event of most events that could damage property, such as fire, theft, and some specified weather damage.

Prospect   Person or company with key characteristics of a business's target market.

Prototype   An exact model of an invention made by the manufacturing process that would be used to make a product sale.

Psychographics   Psychological characteristics of consumers, such as attitudes, opinions, beliefs, interests, personality, lifestyle, political affiliation, and personal preferences.

Public domain   Status of creative work or invention for which the copyright or patent has expired or was never granted; indicates the intellectual property may be used by the public.

Public relations (PR)   Activities aimed at creating goodwill toward a product or company.

Publicity   Any promotion for which a company does not pay, such as a mention in a magazine article; sometimes referred to as "free advertising."

Purchase order   Detailed, written record of a business's request for supplies or inventory, referred to as a P.O.

Purchasing   Buying materials, products, and services for business purposes.

Pure risk   A category of risk for which loss is the only outcome, such as risk of flood or fire.

Quality circle   Group of employees that provides input and suggestions about ways to improve the quality of the goods or services that they produce.

Quality control program   Program used by a business to ensure that its products or services meet specific quality standards.

Quantity discount   Discount given to buyers for purchasing a large quantity of a product or service from a vendor.

Quick ratio   Comparison of cash to debt, based on the concept that a business should have at least enough money on hand to pay its current debts.

Recall   Notice for customers to return a product that has been found to pose a risk of injury or illness.

Receipt   Written proof of a purchase.

Recruit   To find and hire qualified candidates for a job.

Reference   A person who is willing to vouch for another person's skills, qualifications, and character.

Referral   The act of providing contact information for a business to someone who might be interested in the business's products or services.

Repeat business   Customers who return to a business to buy repeatedly.

Replacement cost   Current cost of replacing an asset.

Request for proposal (RFP)   Formal way of asking a company to make a bid for a sale; includes details about what the prospect wants.

Reseller's permit   Permit required by most states for retailers to obtain in order to purchase goods tax-free from wholesalers, and collect sales tax from consumers.

Reserve for fixed expenses   Money that a business should have set aside to cover their fixed expenses for at least three months.

Resource   Money, materials, staff, and other assets that can be used by a business to create and sell products or services.

Résumé   Written summary of one's work experience, education, and skills used to apply for jobs.

Retailer   Business that buys products, usually from wholesalers, to resell in smaller quantities directly to consumers. Also referred to as a retailing business.

Retain, retainer   To pay someone to be available to provide his or her professional services to a person or business.

Retirement   Choosing to leave the workforce and support oneself with savings and investment income.

Return on investment (ROI)   Profit on an investment expressed as a percentage of the total invested.

Return on sales (ROS)   Financial ratio calculated by dividing net profit by sales.

Revenue   Money earned from sales of a product or service.

Rider   Amendment to an insurance policy that changes the benefits or conditions of coverage.

Risk   Possibility of loss.

Risk transfer   The shifting of risk from one party to another.

Rule of 72   Quick way to figure how long it will take to double your money at a given rate of return.

Safety stock   Minimum amount of inventory kept on hand to protect against a stock-out due to unusually high demand or unusually long lead times on delivery.

Salary   Fixed amount of money that an employee is paid on a regular basis, such as weekly, biweekly, bimonthly, or monthly.

Sales account   Customer that buys from a business regularly.

Sales call   Pitching a product or service to a sales lead, prospect, or sales account (established customer) by telephone or in person.

Sales contract   Written agreement regarding a sale that lists items, selling prices and payment terms.

Sales-data analysis   Using sales data to forecast future sales.

Sales force   Employees in a company who are directly involved in the process of selling; another term for salespeople or sales representatives.

Sales forecast   Prediction of the amount of future sales a business expects to achieve over a certain period of time.

Sales forecasting   Predicting future sales based on past sales data or other available information and expected market conditions in the future.

Sales invoice   Itemized list of goods delivered or services rendered and the amount due.

Sales lead   Person or company in your target market who might want to buy a business's product or service.

Sales promotion Short-term buying incentives provided to customers, such as coupons, free samples, or product demonstrations.

Sales quota   Target amount of units that a salesperson is expected to sell per month, quarter, or year.

Sales tax   A tax on retail goods and services that is collected by the retailer and passed on to a state government.

Sales territory   Specified geographical area for which a salesperson is responsible, such as a city, county, state, or region.

Salutation   The greeting that begins an email or letter.

Same-size analysis   Comparison of total revenue or other financial data against that same data converted into percentages of sales.

Savings account   Bank account in which money is deposited and on which the bank pays interest to the depositor.

Scarce resources   Resources that are not unlimited and are used by an entrepreneur to create a product or service to sell. The entrepreneur's goal is to combine scarce resources to create a product or service that is worth more than the scarce resources are worth separately, in order to earn a profit.

Screen recorder   Type of spyware that can take pictures of a computer screen.

Search engine optimization (SEO)   Variety of techniques that improve a web site's ranking with search engines.

Secure sockets layer (SSL)   Security measure that "locks" a website; enables secure credit card processing online.

Seed money   Initial financing to open a business; another term for **start-up capital** or **start-up investment**.

Self-employment tax   The contribution a self-employed person makes to Social Security and Medicare as a percentage of business income. Self-employment tax is due when an individual has net earnings of $400 or more in self-employment income during the tax year.

Self-financing   Obtaining funds to grow a business from existing operations—by reinvesting cash reserves (profits), for example.

Serial entrepreneur   Entrepreneur who starts a series of businesses in his or her lifetime.

Service   Work performed by a person or business for another person or business in exchange for money.

Severance pay   Money given to an employee who is terminated for reasons other than performance.

Share of stock   A percentage of ownership in a company.

Shareholder   Holder of a share of ownership in a company.

Small business   A business with fewer than 100 employees (500 if a manufacturing business).

Small business investment companies (SBICs)   Institutions, partially financed through government grants, that provide equity and debt financing—often at lower interest rates than banks—to small businesses.

Social enterprise   A business with a mission that includes improving society or the environment.

Sole proprietorship   A business owned by a single individual who owns the business, collects all profit from it, and has unlimited liability for its debt.

Source document   Original record (source) of a transaction, such as a receipt, canceled check, invoice, or bank deposit slip.

Sourcing   Choosing appropriate vendors to supply desired business goods or services.

Speculative risk   An exposure to loss that may result in either gain or loss.

Sponsorship   Paying for a community event or service in exchange for advertising.

Spoofing   Hiding the real origin of an email message by faking the information in the "from" field.

Spyware   Software that installs itself on a computer without the owner's permission and covertly gathers information such as passwords and Internet use.

Start-up capital   Another term for **seed money** or **start-up investment**.

Start-up cost   A onetime initial expense of starting a business.

Start-up investment   Onetime sum required to start a business and cover start-up costs. Also called **seed money** or **start-up capital**.

Stock   A share of ownership in a corporation.

Stockholder   An owner of stock in a corporation. Also called **shareholder**.

Stock market   The market created by a collection of different stock exchanges, such as the New York Stock Exchange and NASDAQ, where shares of stock may be listed, bought, and sold.

Stock option   An option given by a company to an employee as a benefit to buy stock in the company at a discount or fixed price.

Stock-out Situation that occurs when demand for an item cannot be satisfied because the item is sold out.

Strategic plan Plan for a broad course of action to achieve a long-term goal, typically three to five years in the future.

Subchapter S corporation A legal business structure for a business with fewer than 100 employees; it offers the limited liability of a corporation yet is taxed like a partnership.

Subsidy Financial aid from the government that helps support an industry or public service.

Supply Quantity of goods and services a business is willing to sell at a specific price and a specific time.

Supply and demand curve Graph that includes both a supply curve and a demand curve. It shows the relationship between prices and the quantities of a product or service that is supplied and demanded.

Supply curve Curve on a graph that shows the quantity of a product or service a supplier is willing to sell across a range of prices over a specific period of time.

Survey The gathering and evaluation of data regarding consumers' preferences for products and services.

Sustainable A business practice that strives to have no negative impact on the environment.

SWOT analysis Business evaluation method named for the four areas it evaluates: Strengths, Weaknesses, Opportunities, and Threats.

T-account A double-entry bookkeeping ledger, so-named for the "T" shape of the accounts on each side of the ledger.

Tactical plan Plan that outlines specific major steps for carrying out the strategic plan.

Target market The group of customers within a business's market who are most likely to buy its product or service.

Tariff Fee, similar to a tax, that importers must pay on the goods they import.

Tax A legally required contribution to government revenue leveled by the government on workers' income, business profits, or the cost of items for sale.

Tax avoidance Using legal strategies to reduce one's tax liability.

Tax credit Dollar-for-dollar reduction in taxes owed.

Tax evasion Trying to avoid paying taxes through illegal or deceptive means.

Tax-exempt To be free from, or not subject to, taxation by regulators or government entities.

Tax return A form used to report income and expenses to a government and to calculate taxes owed.

Telecommute To work from a location other than on-site at a business, using telecommunication technology.

Thought leader An individual or firm recognized as an innovator and authority in a specific field.

Trade business A wholesale or retail business.

Trade credit Credit extended from one business to another for the purchase of goods or services.

Trade discount Discount given to resellers who are in the same trade, industry, or distribution chain as a vendor.

Trademark A symbol, word, or words legally registered, or established by use, as representing a company's brand.

Trade-off An exchange that involves making a choice to give up the benefit of one situation for the benefits of another.

Trade-out Trading a company's products or services for promotion on a radio station.

Trade secret Any information that a business or individual keeps confidential to gain a competitive advantage.

Trade show Convention where related businesses come to promote their products or services.

Transparency Openness and accountability in business decisions and actions.

Triple bottom line "People, planet, and profit"—an evaluation of a business's performance that includes not only profit but also the business's positive impact on the environment and society.

Unit of sale The quantity of its product or service that a business defines as one unit.

Unlimited liability Liability for all the debts of a business, including exposure to potentially being legally forced to use personal money and possessions to pay business debts.

Variable cost Subcategory of operating costs, a variable cost changes or "varies" based on the amount of product or service a business sells.

Vendors Businesses that sell products or services to other businesses.

Venture capital Money invested in a potentially profitable business by a company that specializes in investing in start-ups.

Videoconference   Meeting during which participants in different locations can see and hear each other using monitors, cameras, microphones, and speakers.

Viral marketing   Marketing strategy that uses social media to spread information and opinions about a product or service from person to person.

Vision   "Picture" in your mind of something you want to achieve.

Visual inventory system   System of inventory management that involves physically counting inventory items.

Visual merchandising   Use of artistic displays to attract customers into a store or visually promote products inside a store.

Volume discount   Discount offered to businesses that buy large quantities of a product.

Voluntary exchange   Transaction in which two people or businesses engage in freely.

Wage   Payment to employees per hour worked or piece of work completed.

Want   Product or service that people desire.

Warranty   Written statement from a seller promising that purchased goods or services meet certain standards, and describing conditions under which the seller will cover repairs, replacements, etc.

Web search engine   Program that searches online documents for specified keywords and returns a list of the documents where the keywords were found.

Whistle-blower   One who reports illegal or unethical business conduct to superiors or to the public.

Wholesaler   Business that buys products in large quantities from manufacturers and sells them in smaller batches to retailers. Also referred to as a wholesaling business.

Window of opportunity   Period of time in which you have to act before a business opportunity is lost.

Workers' compensation insurance   Insurance that covers losses to employees due to job-related injury or illness.

Work sharing   The sharing of one full-time job between two part-time employees. Also called **job sharing**.

Zoning law   Local law specifying where development and activities are allowed; also called **ordinance**.

ACKNOWLEDGMENTS

I would like to thank my writing partner Debra DeSalvo, without whose gift for organization and rewriting, this book would never have been possible. I am also grateful to literary agent Jeff Herman, for introducing me to our original editor at Random House, John Mahaney, and his assistants, Eleanor Wickland and Luke Mitchell; to the editor for this edition, Derek Reed, who has helped us take this book to an entirely new level; and to reviewers Jessica Cohen and Kene Turner. I must also thank my long-time writing partner, Tony Towle, who from NFTE's very beginning has helped me organize my thoughts and experiences.

I would like to acknowledge the contributions of NFTE's CEO Amy Rosen; Director of Teacher Support and Development for Chicago Jason Delgatto; Vice President of Learning Rupa Mohan; our dedicated Executive Directors: Terry Bowman, Tricia Granata Eisner, Jennifer Green, Alice Horn, Krista Katsantonis, Laura Maczka, Christine Poorman, Estelle Reyes, Diane Rosenthal, and Sylvia Watts McKinney, and all of NFTE's wonderful supporters and donors, including MasterCard Worldwide; Ernst & Young; Microsoft; the Coleman Foundation; E*TRADE Financial; McKinsey and Company; New York Life; Sam's Club; SAP; the Diana Davis Spencer Foundation; Daddy's House Social Program; the Ladera Foundation, Mary Myers Kauppila, and George Myers; Multinational Scholar Charitable Trust; and Karen Pritzker and Michael Vlock.

I also thank the NFTE Board of Directors for their support and commitment: Patrica Alper, Matthew J. Audette, Peter J. Boni, Ted Dintersmith, Noah Hanft, Landon Hilliard, Mary Myers Kauppila, Michael Kempner, Stephen McDonnell, Victor Oviedo, Maria Pinelli, Anthony Salcito, Leonard A. Schlesinger, Dia Simms, Diana Davis Spencer, David Spreng, Peter B. Walker, and Tucker York.

I would also like to thank the NFTE Board of Overseers for their guidance: Michelle Barmazel, Stephanie Bell-Rose, Stephen Brenninkmeijer, Eddie Brown, Dr. Thomas Byers, Russ Carson, James L. Cash, Ray Chambers, Sean Combs, Kathryn Davis, Mark Ein, Stedman Graham, Michael J. Hennessy, Reid Hoffman, Daymond

John, Moushumi Khan, Elizabeth Koch, Loida Nicolas Lewis, James Lyle, Dr. Richard K. Miller, Wes Moore, Alan Patricof, Jeffrey S. Raikes, Anthony Scaramucci, Jane Siebels, John P. Stack, Professor Howard Stevenson, and John Whitehead.

Finally, I want to thank my mother, Nancy, a wonderful special-education teacher who taught me that one great teacher affects eternity.

INDEX